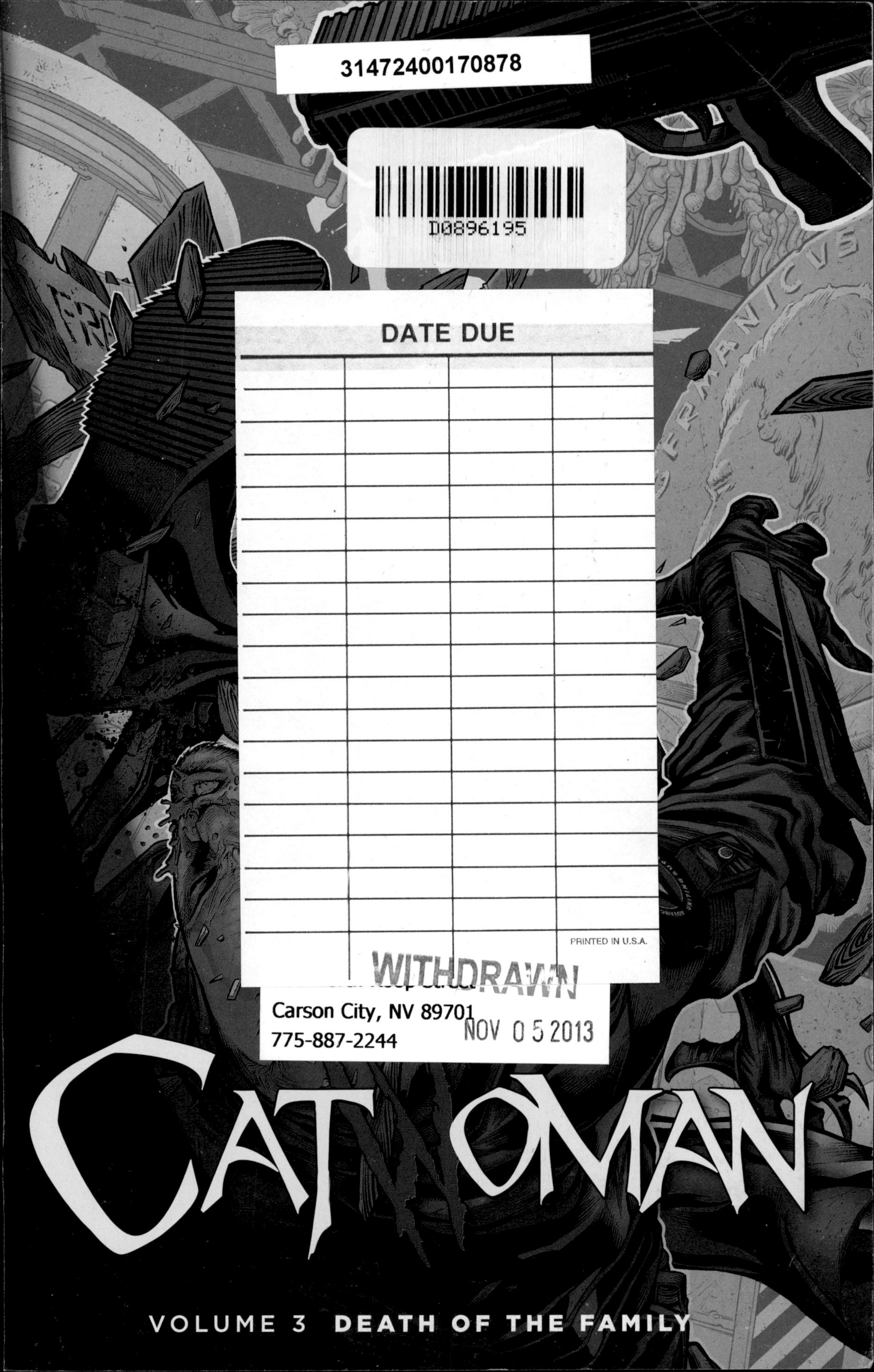
CATWOMAN
VOLUME 3 DEATH OF THE FAMILY

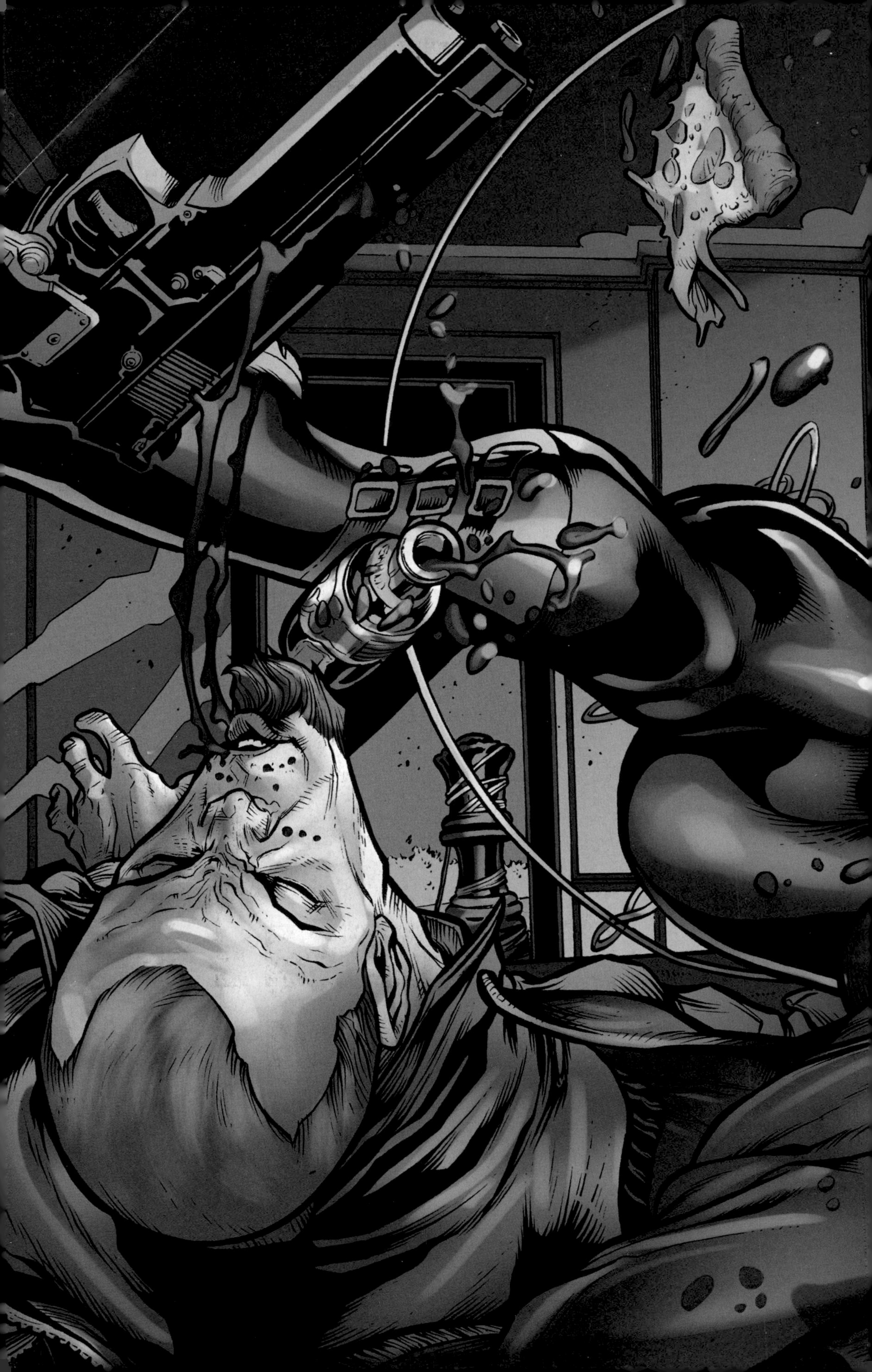

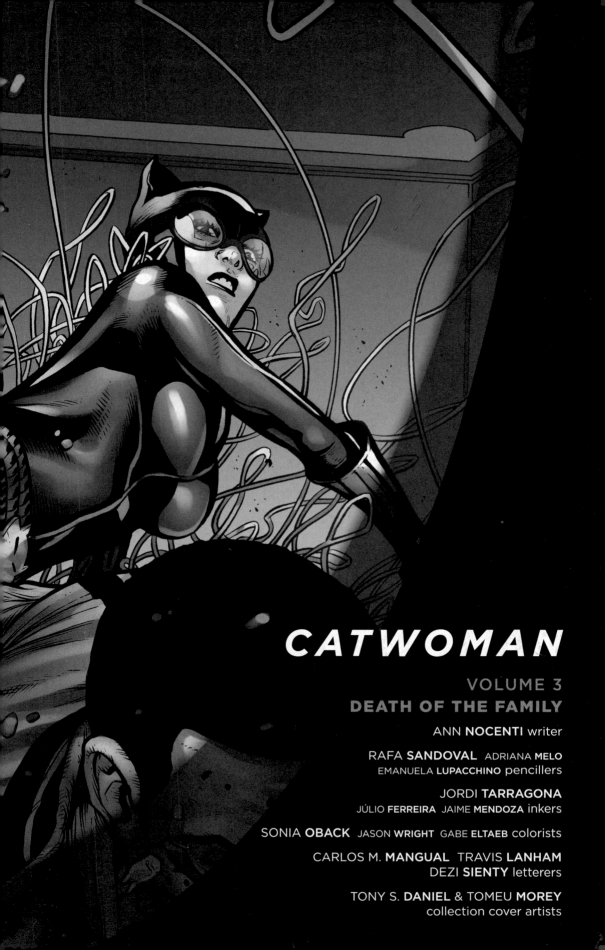

CATWOMAN

VOLUME 3
DEATH OF THE FAMILY

ANN **NOCENTI** writer

RAFA **SANDOVAL**   ADRIANA **MELO**
EMANUELA **LUPACCHINO** pencillers

JORDI **TARRAGONA**
JÚLIO **FERREIRA**   JAIME **MENDOZA** inkers

SONIA **OBACK**   JASON **WRIGHT**   GABE **ELTAEB** colorists

CARLOS M. **MANGUAL**   TRAVIS **LANHAM**
DEZI **SIENTY** letterers

TONY S. **DANIEL** & TOMEU **MOREY**
collection cover artists

RACHEL GLUCKSTERN EDDIE BERGANZA Editors – Original Series
RICKEY PURDIN DARREN SHAN Assistant Editors – Original Series ROBIN WILDMAN Editor
ROBBIN BROSTERMAN Design Director - Books ROBBIE BIEDERMAN Publication Design

BOB HARRAS Senior VP – Editor-in-Chief, DC Comics

DIANE NELSON President DAN DIDIO and JIM LEE Co-Publishers
GEOFF JOHNS Chief Creative Officer
JOHN ROOD Executive VP – Sales, Marketing and Business Development
AMY GENKINS Senior VP – Business and Legal Affairs NAIRI GARDINER Senior VP – Finance
JEFF BOISON VP – Publishing Planning MARK CHIARELLO VP – Art Direction and Design
JOHN CUNNINGHAM VP – Marketing TERRI CUNNINGHAM VP – Editorial Administration
ALISON GILL Senior VP – Manufacturing and Operations HANK KANALZ Senior VP – Vertigo and Integrated Publishing
JAY KOGAN VP – Business and Legal Affairs, Publishing JACK MAHAN VP – Business Affairs, Talent
NICK NAPOLITANO VP – Manufacturing Administration SUE POHJA VP – Book Sales
COURTNEY SIMMONS Senior VP – Publicity BOB WAYNE Senior VP – Sales

CATWOMAN VOLUME 3: DEATH OF THE FAMILY

Certified Chain of Custody
At Least 20% Certified Forest Content
www.sfiprogram.org
SFI-01042
APPLIES TO TEXT STOCK ONLY

Library of Congress Cataloging-in-Publication Data

Nocenti, Ann.
Catwoman. Volume 3, Death of the family / Ann Nocenti, Rafa Sandoval.
pages cm
"Originally published in single magazine form as Catwoman 0, 13-18, Young Romance 1."
ISBN 978-1-4012-4272-5
1. Graphic novels. I. Sandoval, Rafa. II. Title. III. Title: Death of the family.
PN6728.C39N63 2013
741.5'973—dc23
2013020538

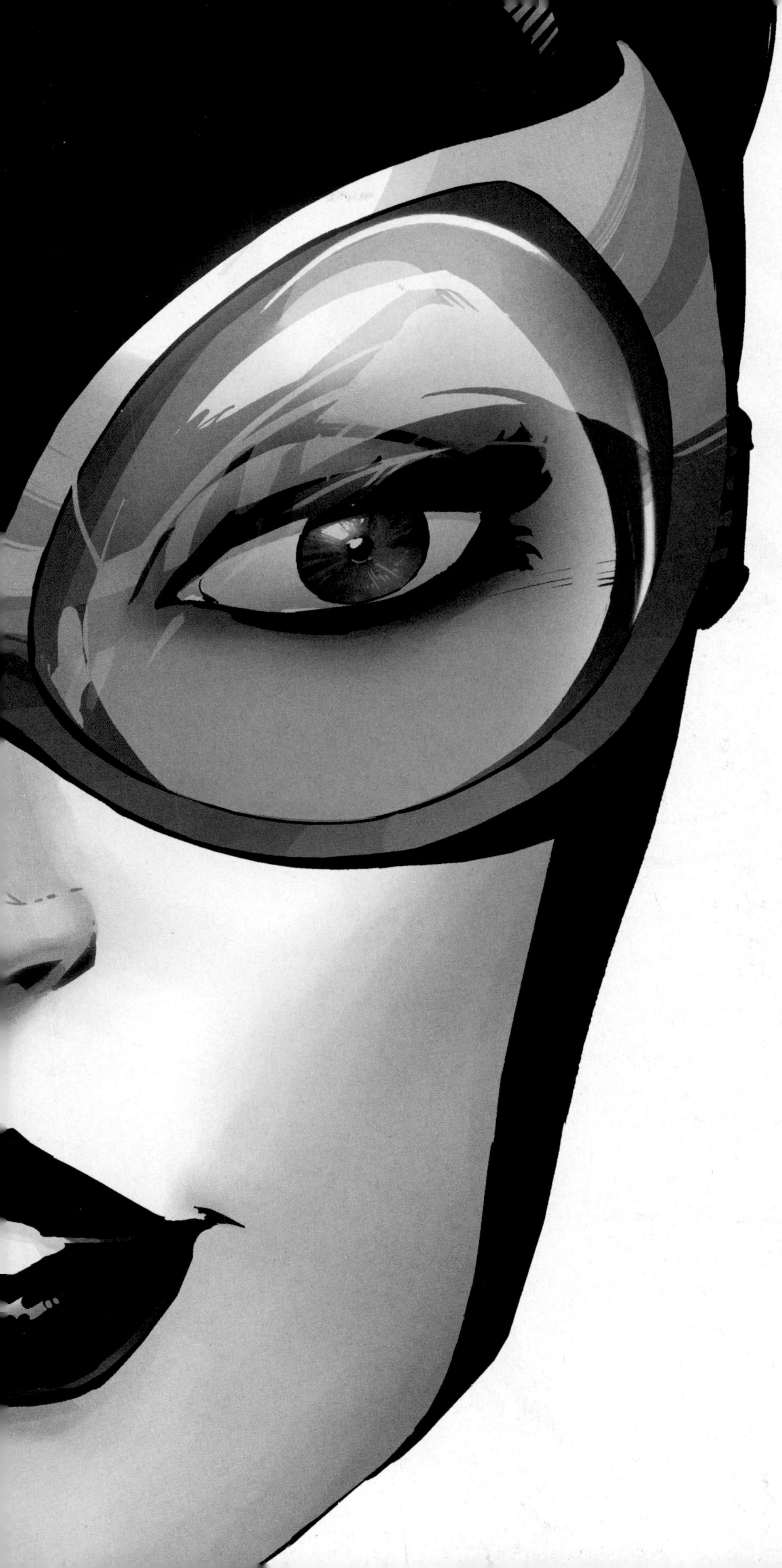

ANN NOCENTI writer RAFA SANDOVAL penciller JORDI TARRAGONA inker cover by GREG CAPULLO

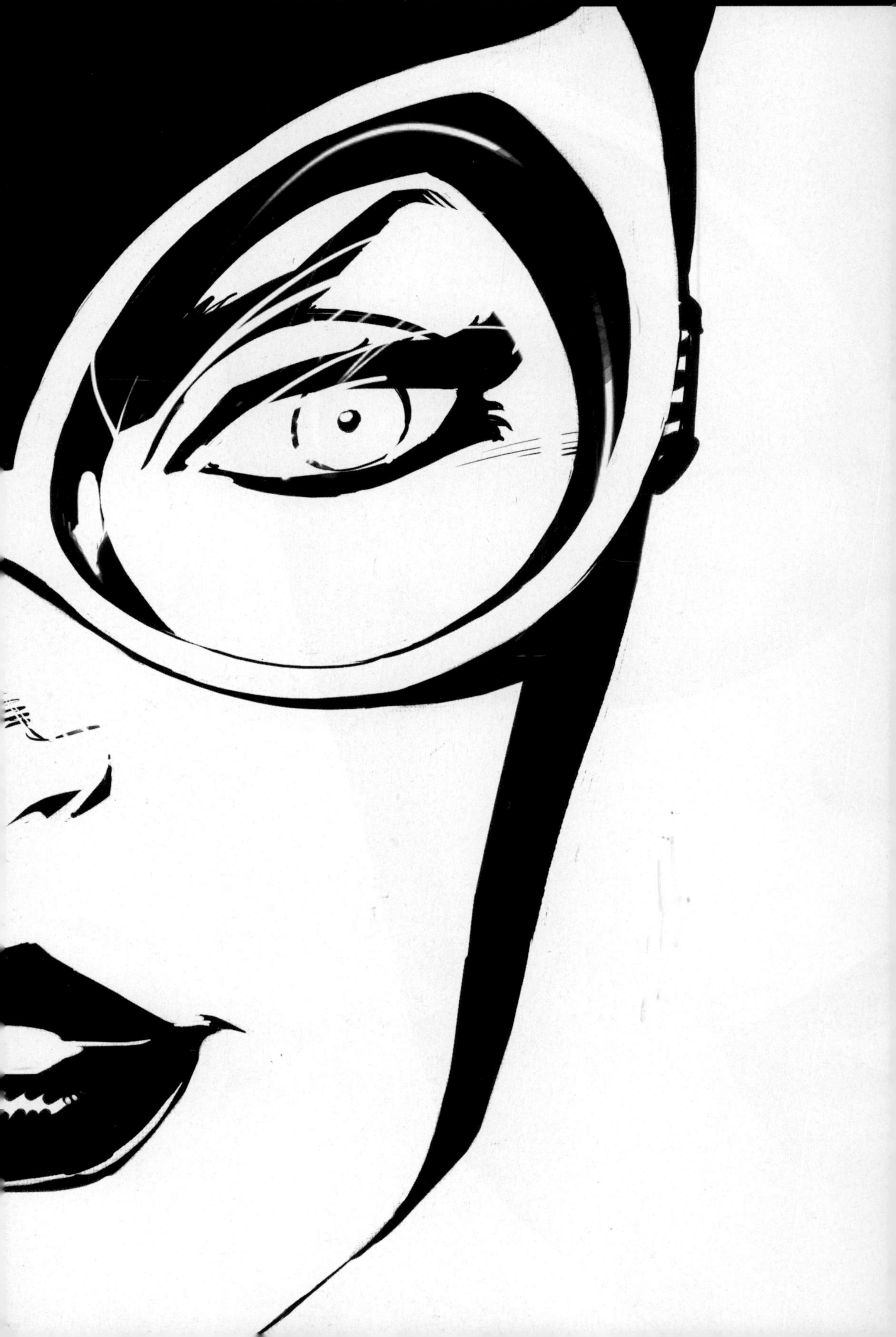

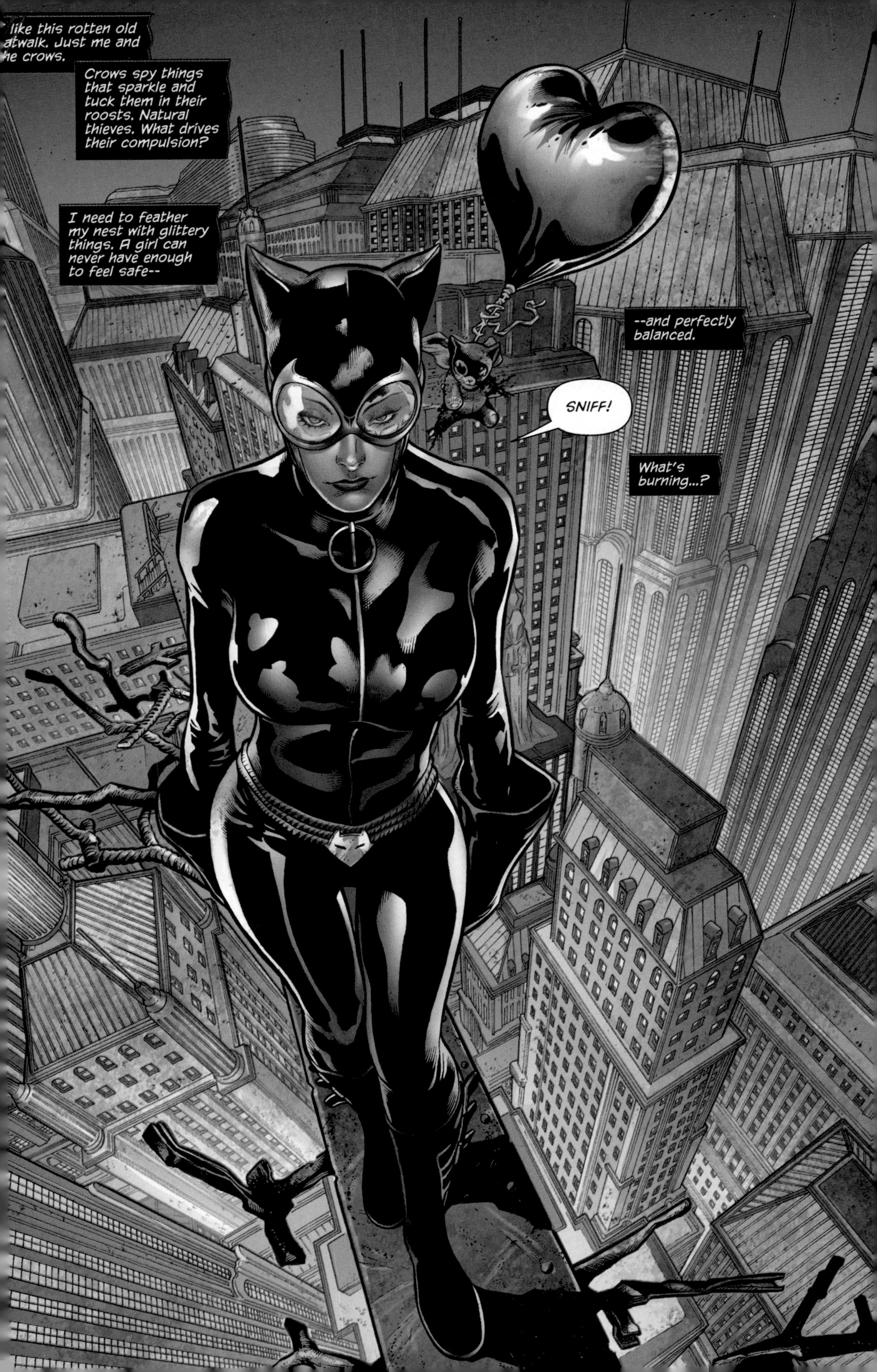

' like this rotten old
atwalk. Just me and
he crows.
Crows spy things that sparkle and tuck them in their roosts. Natural thieves. What drives their compulsion?
I need to feather my nest with glittery things. A girl can never have enough to feel safe--
--and perfectly balanced.
SNIFF!
What's burning...?

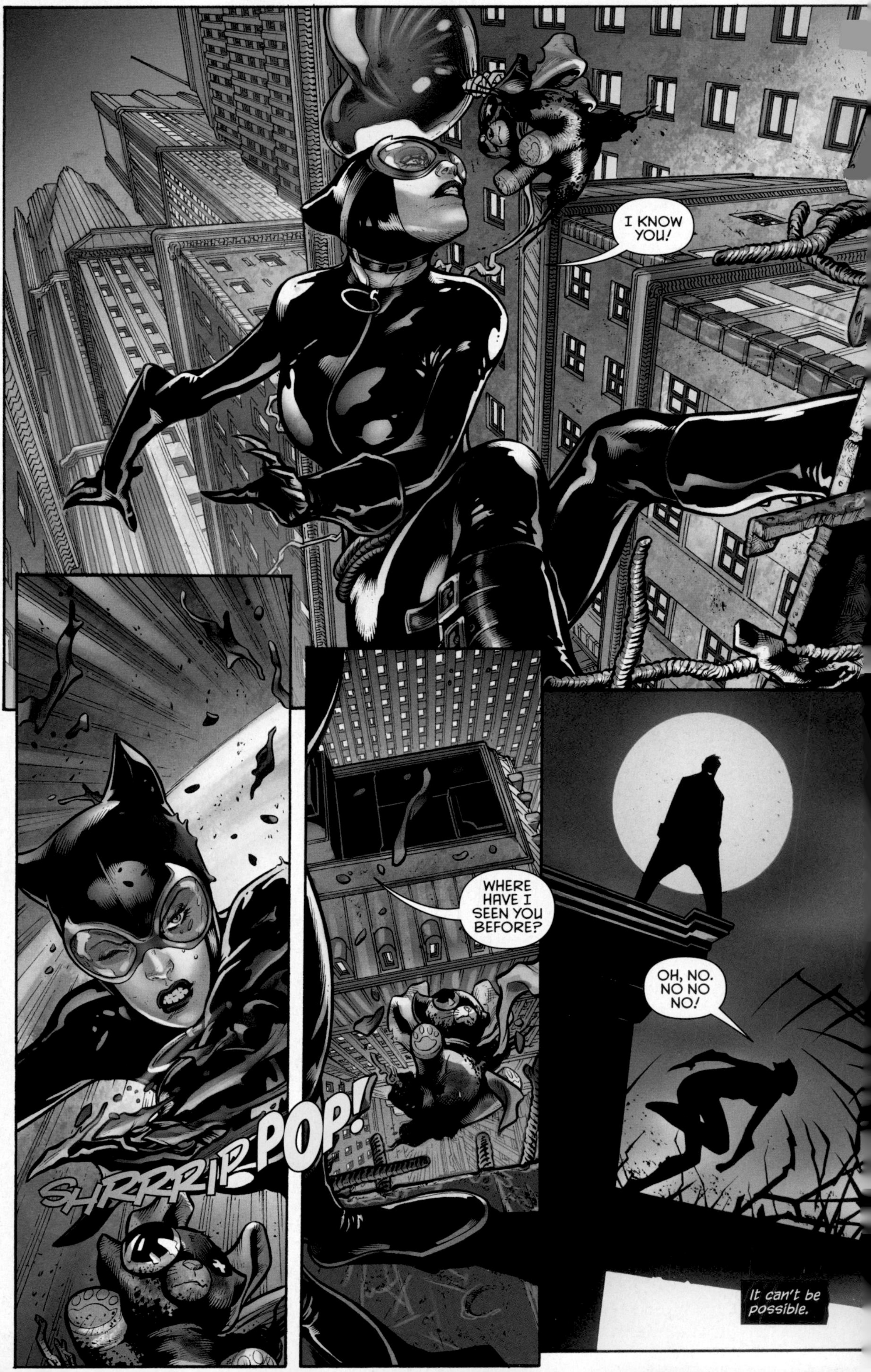
I KNOW YOU!
SHRRRIP
POP!
WHERE HAVE I SEEN YOU BEFORE?
OH, NO. NO NO NO!
It can't be possible.

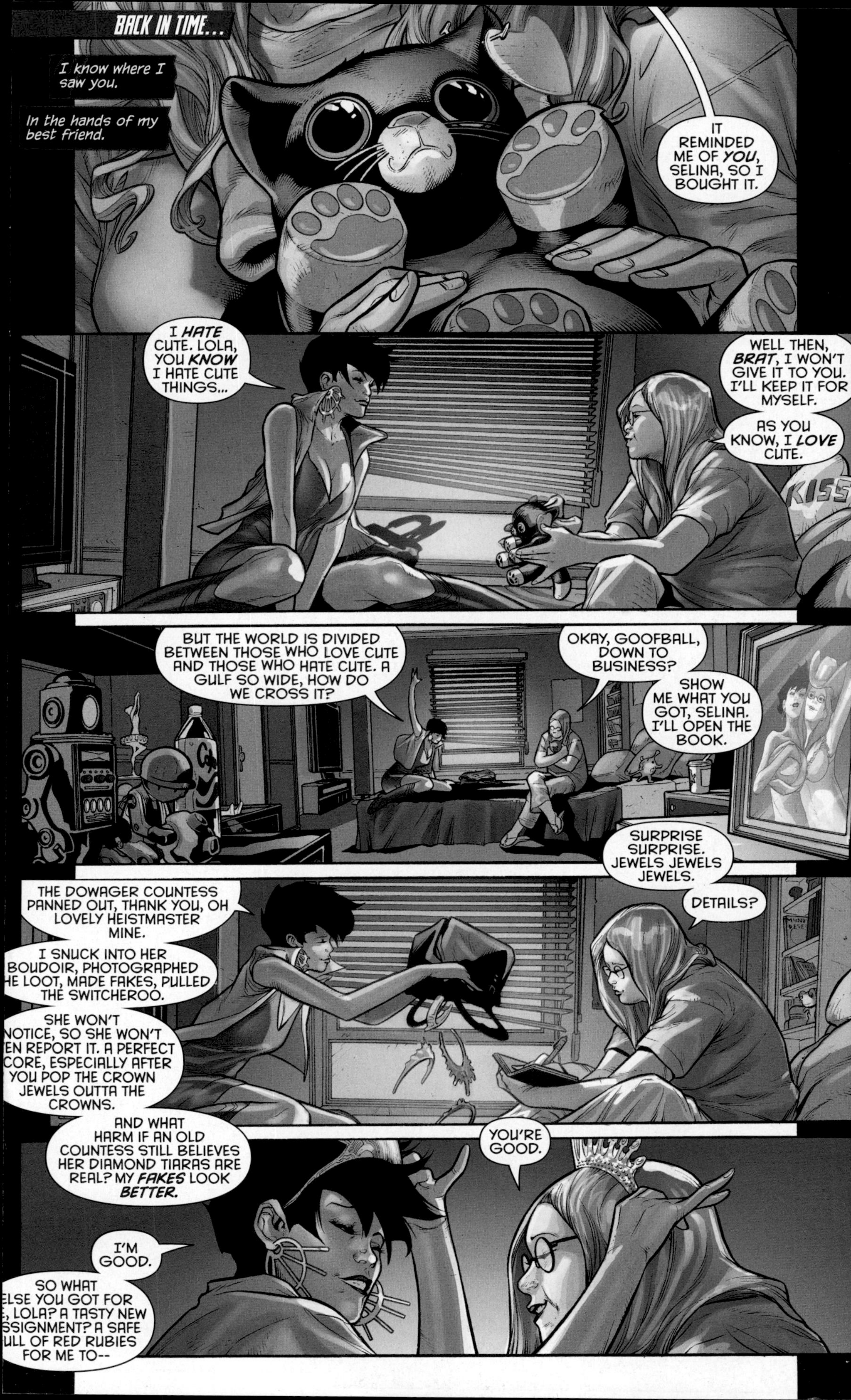
BACK IN TIME...
I know where I saw you.
In the hands of my best friend.
IT REMINDED ME OF YOU, SELINA, SO I BOUGHT IT.
I HATE CUTE. LOLA, YOU KNOW I HATE CUTE THINGS...
WELL THEN, BRAT, I WON'T GIVE IT TO YOU. I'LL KEEP IT FOR MYSELF.
AS YOU KNOW, I LOVE CUTE.
KISS
BUT THE WORLD IS DIVIDED BETWEEN THOSE WHO LOVE CUTE AND THOSE WHO HATE CUTE. A GULF SO WIDE, HOW DO WE CROSS IT?
OKAY, GOOFBALL, DOWN TO BUSINESS?
SHOW ME WHAT YOU GOT, SELINA. I'LL OPEN THE BOOK.
SURPRISE SURPRISE. JEWELS JEWELS JEWELS.
DETAILS?
THE DOWAGER COUNTESS PANNED OUT, THANK YOU, OH LOVELY HEISTMASTER MINE.
I SNUCK INTO HER BOUDOIR, PHOTOGRAPHED HE LOOT, MADE FAKES, PULLED THE SWITCHEROO.
SHE WON'T NOTICE, SO SHE WON'T EN REPORT IT. A PERFECT CORE, ESPECIALLY AFTER YOU POP THE CROWN JEWELS OUTTA THE CROWNS.
AND WHAT HARM IF AN OLD COUNTESS STILL BELIEVES HER DIAMOND TIARAS ARE REAL? MY FAKES LOOK BETTER.
YOU'RE GOOD.
I'M GOOD.
SO WHAT ELSE YOU GOT FOR , LOLA? A TASTY NEW SSIGNMENT? A SAFE ULL OF RED RUBIES FOR ME TO--

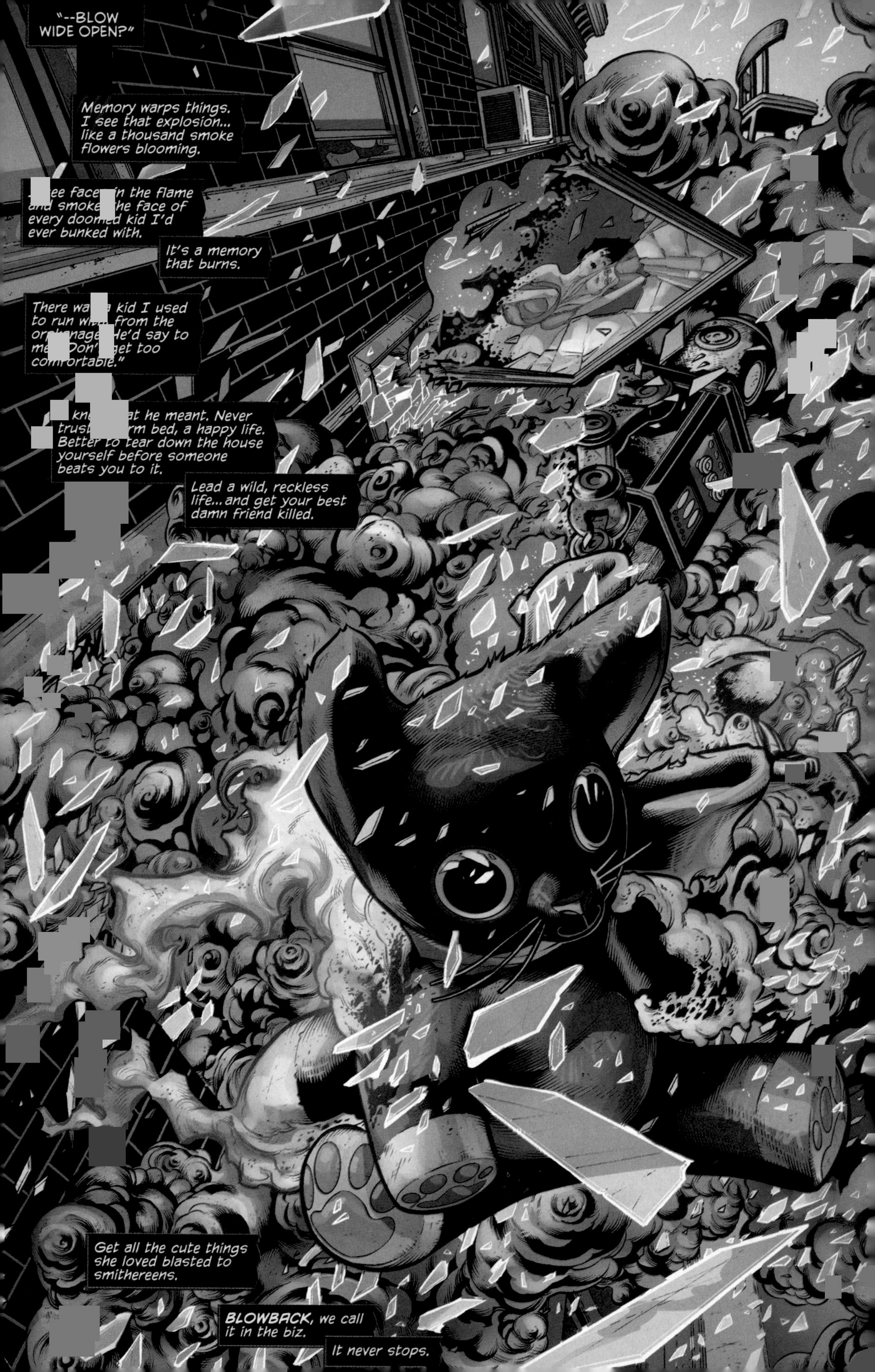

"--BLOW WIDE OPEN?"
Memory warps things. I see that explosion... like a thousand smoke flowers blooming.
ee faces in the flame and smoke the face of every doomed kid I'd ever bunked with.
It's a memory that burns.
There wa kid I used to run wi from the orphanage. He'd say to me, "Don't get too comfortable."
kn at he meant. Never trus rm bed, a happy life. Better to tear down the house yourself before someone beats you to it.
Lead a wild, reckless life...and get your best damn friend killed.
Get all the cute things she loved blasted to smithereens.
BLOWBACK, we call it in the biz.
It never stops.

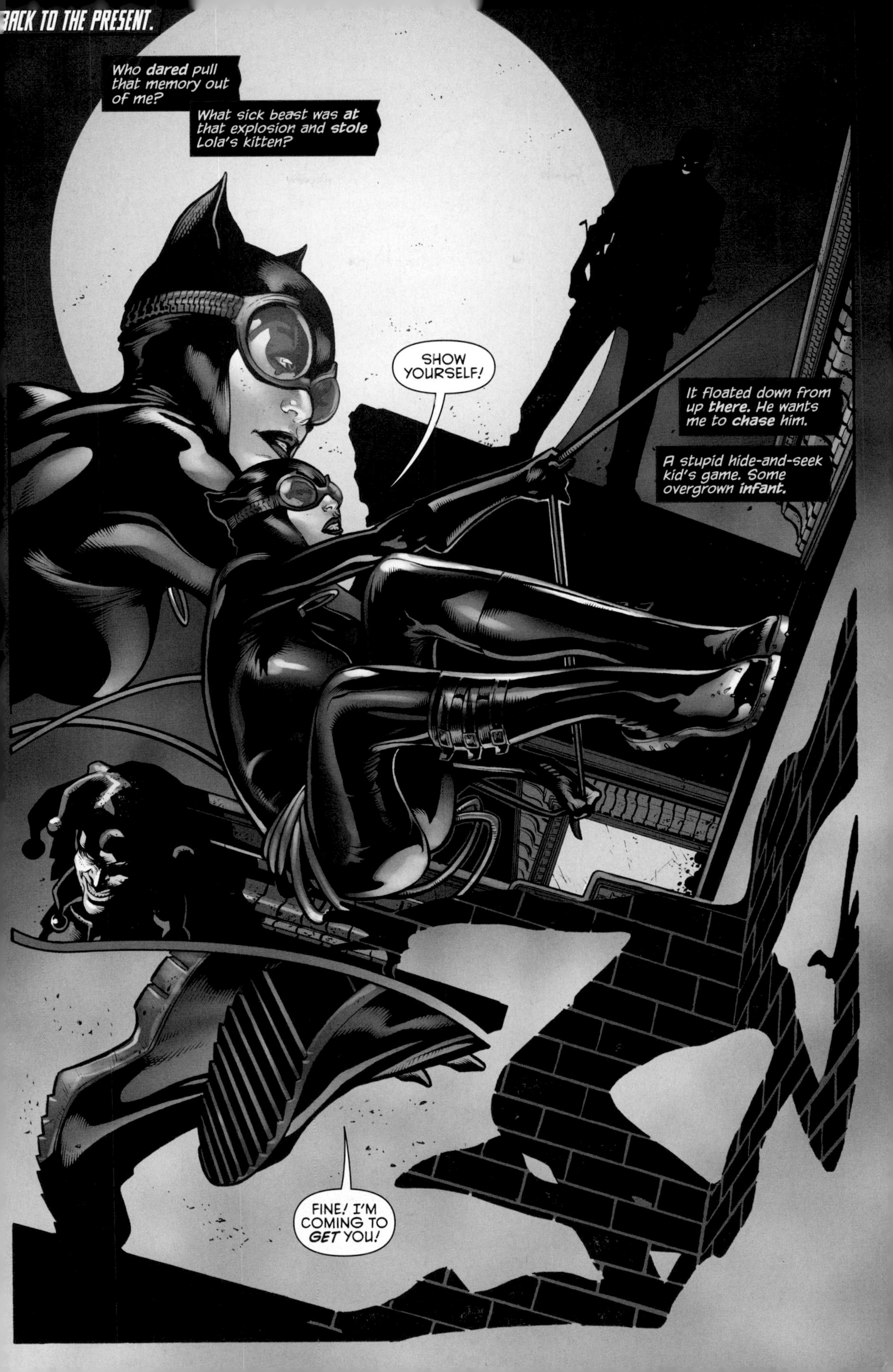
BACK TO THE PRESENT.
Who dared pull that memory out of me?
What sick beast was at that explosion and stole Lola's kitten?
SHOW YOURSELF!
It floated down from up there. He wants me to chase him.
A stupid hide-and-seek kid's game. Some overgrown infant.
FINE! I'M COMING TO GET YOU!

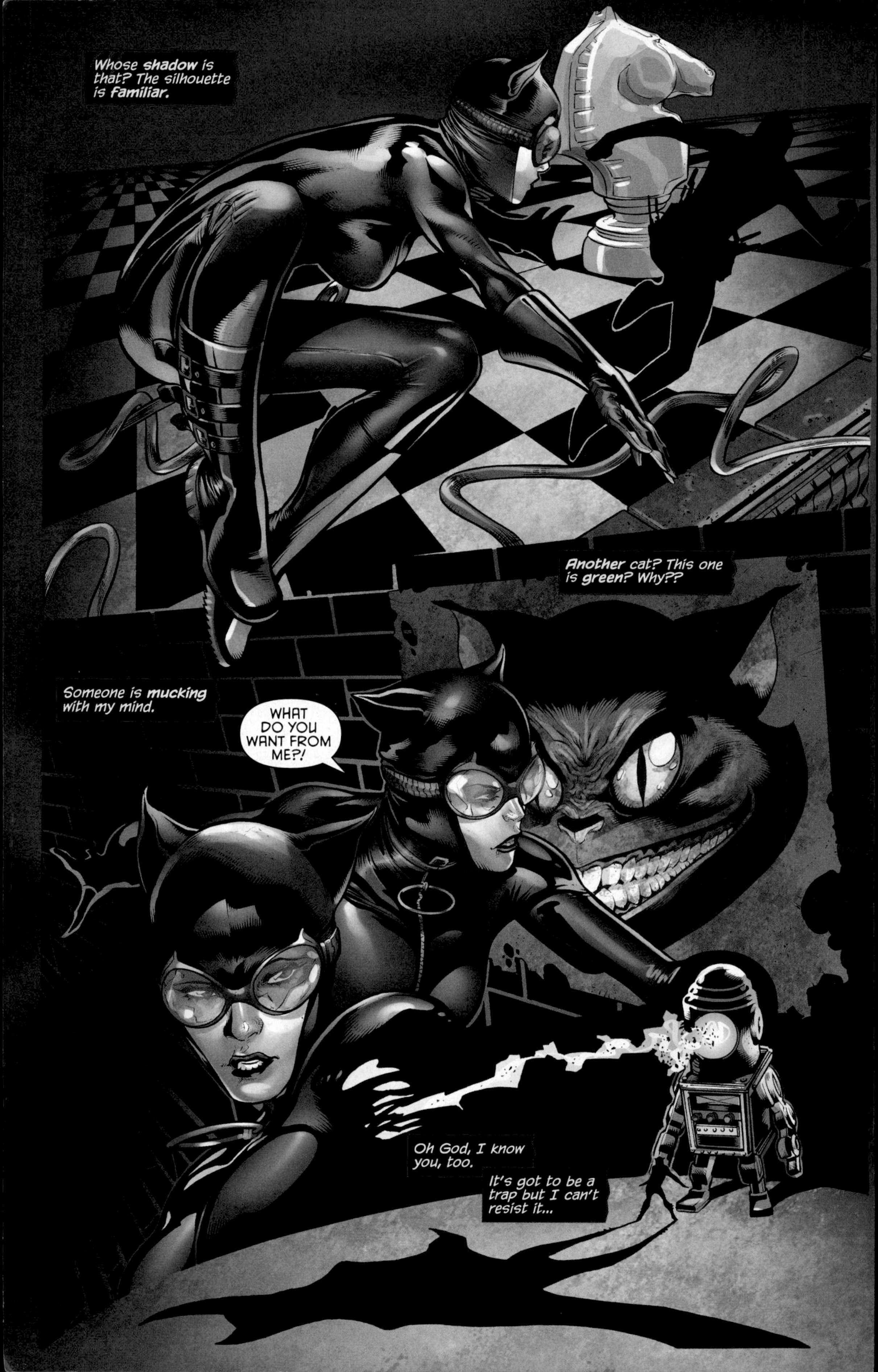
Whose shadow is that? The silhouette is familiar.
Another cat? This one is green? Why??
Someone is mucking with my mind.
WHAT DO YOU WANT FROM ME?!
Oh God, I know you, too.
It's got to be a trap but I can't resist it...

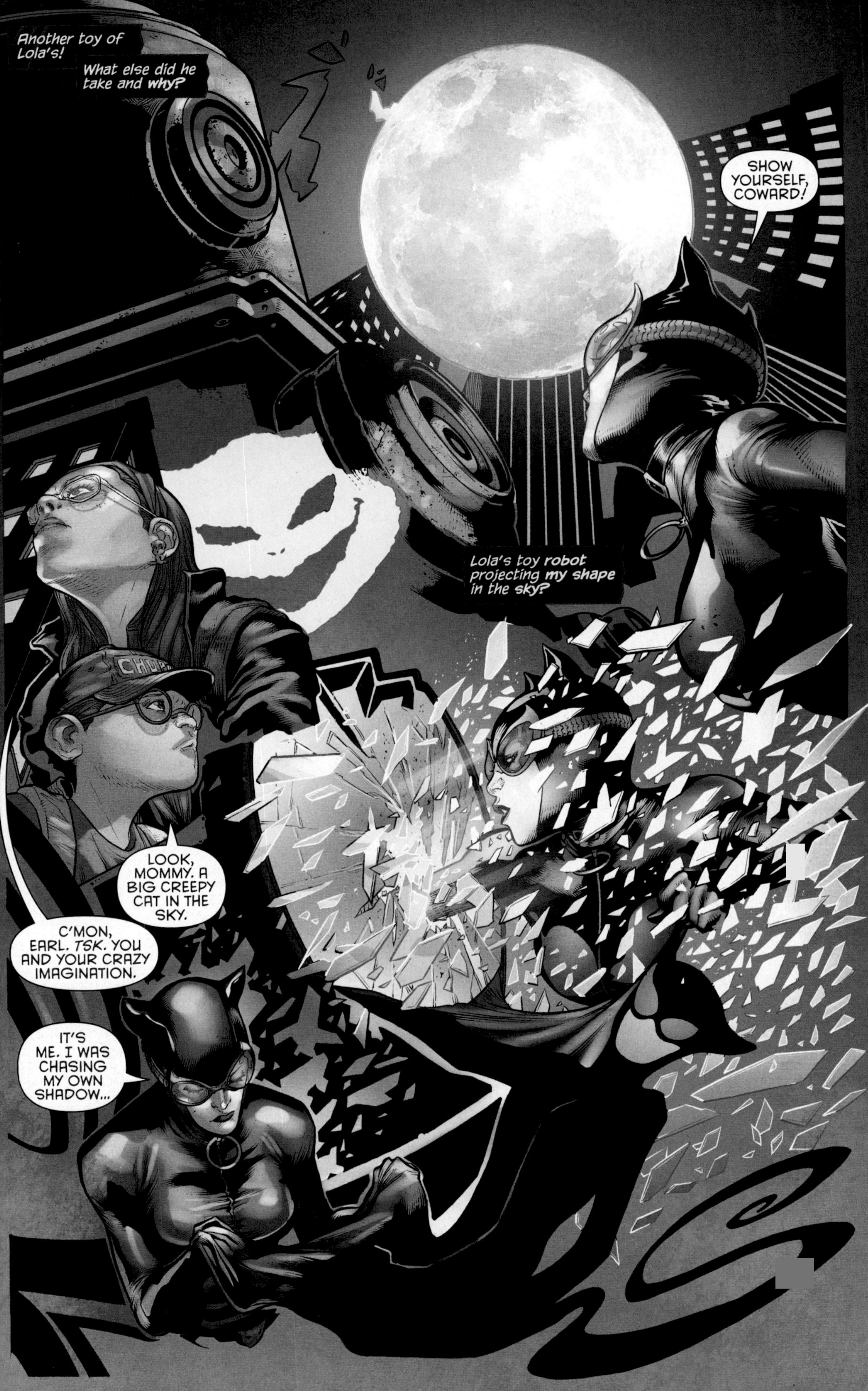
Another toy of Lola's!
What else did he take and why?
SHOW YOURSELF, COWARD!
Lola's toy robot projecting my shape in the sky?
LOOK, MOMMY. A BIG CREEPY CAT IN THE SKY.
C'MON, EARL. TSK. YOU AND YOUR CRAZY IMAGINATION.
IT'S ME. I WAS CHASING MY OWN SHADOW...

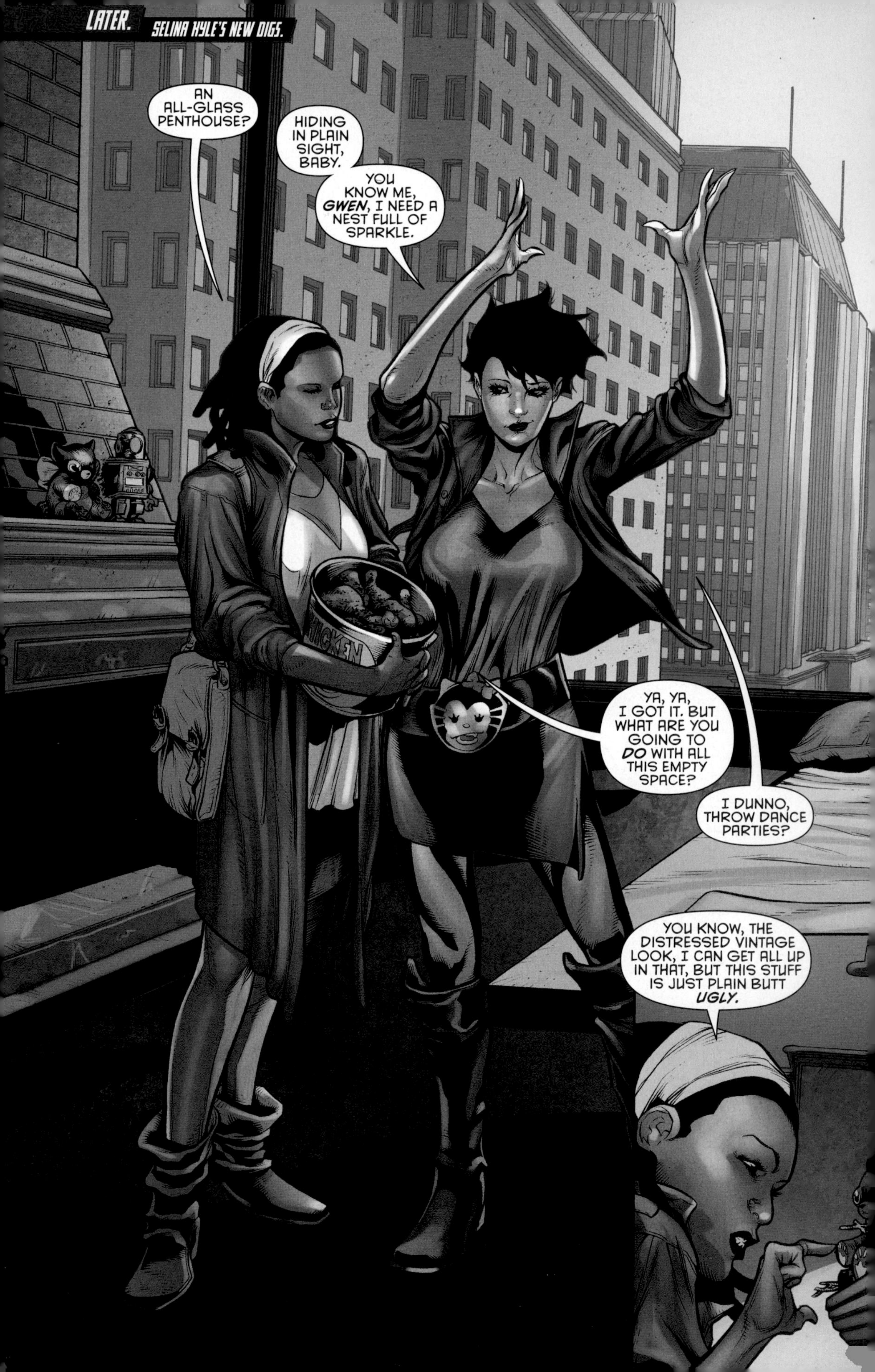
LATER.
SELINA KYLE'S NEW DIGS.
AN ALL-GLASS PENTHOUSE?
HIDING IN PLAIN SIGHT, BABY.
YOU KNOW ME, GWEN, I NEED A NEST FULL OF SPARKLE.
YA, YA, I GOT IT. BUT WHAT ARE YOU GOING TO DO WITH ALL THIS EMPTY SPACE?
I DUNNO, THROW DANCE PARTIES?
YOU KNOW, THE DISTRESSED VINTAGE LOOK, I CAN GET ALL UP IN THAT, BUT THIS STUFF IS JUST PLAIN BUTT UGLY.
CHICKEN

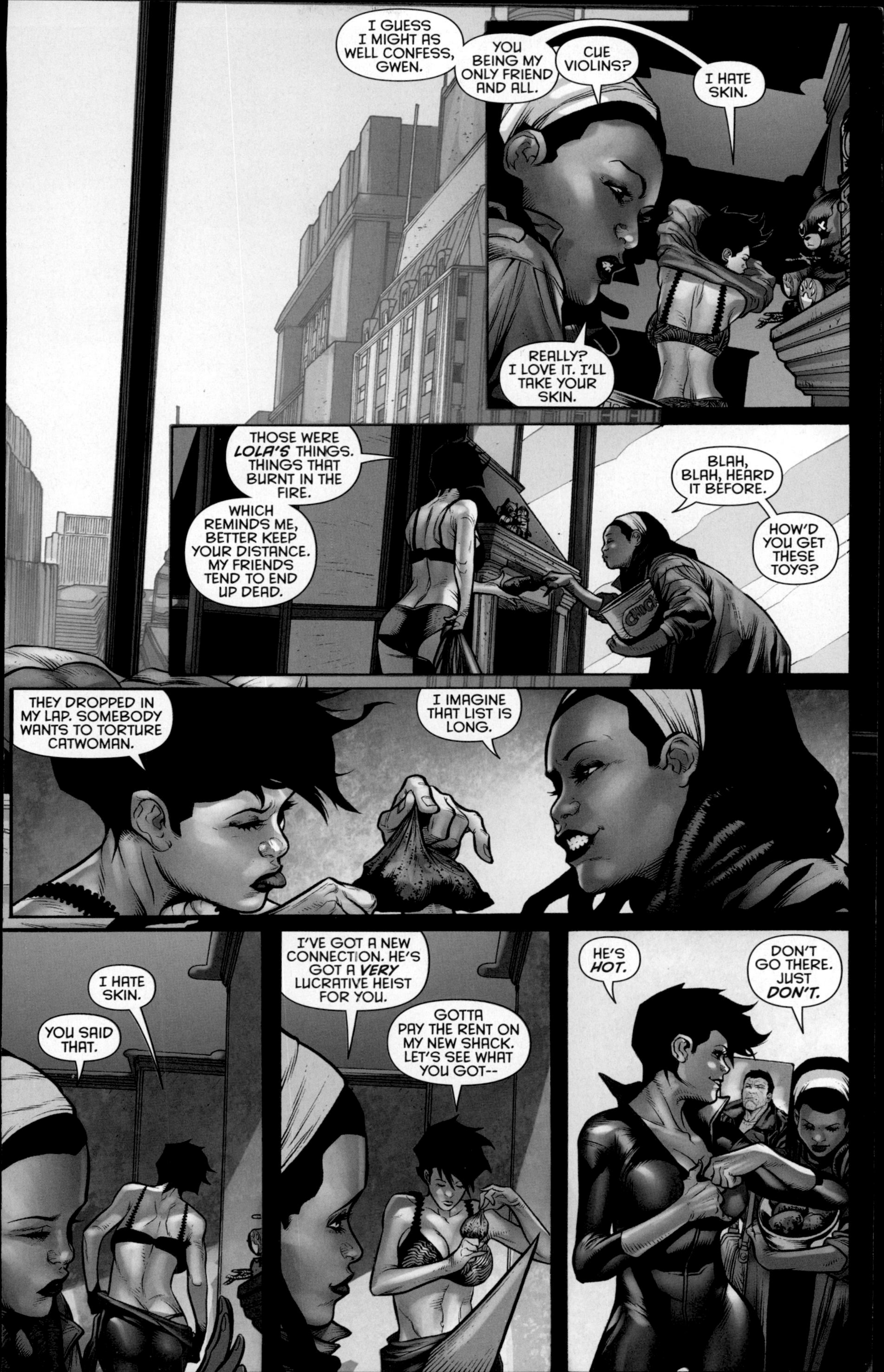
I GUESS I MIGHT AS WELL CONFESS, GWEN.
YOU BEING MY ONLY FRIEND AND ALL.
CUE VIOLINS?
I HATE SKIN.
REALLY? I LOVE IT. I'LL TAKE YOUR SKIN.
THOSE WERE *LOLA'S* THINGS. THINGS THAT BURNT IN THE FIRE.
WHICH REMINDS ME, BETTER KEEP YOUR DISTANCE. MY FRIENDS TEND TO END UP DEAD.
BLAH, BLAH, HEARD IT BEFORE.
HOW'D YOU GET THESE TOYS?
THEY DROPPED IN MY LAP. SOMEBODY WANTS TO TORTURE CATWOMAN.
I IMAGINE THAT LIST IS LONG.
I HATE SKIN.
YOU SAID THAT.
I'VE GOT A NEW CONNECTION. HE'S GOT A *VERY* LUCRATIVE HEIST FOR YOU.
GOTTA PAY THE RENT ON MY NEW SHACK. LET'S SEE WHAT YOU GOT--
HE'S *HOT.*
DON'T GO THERE. JUST *DON'T.*

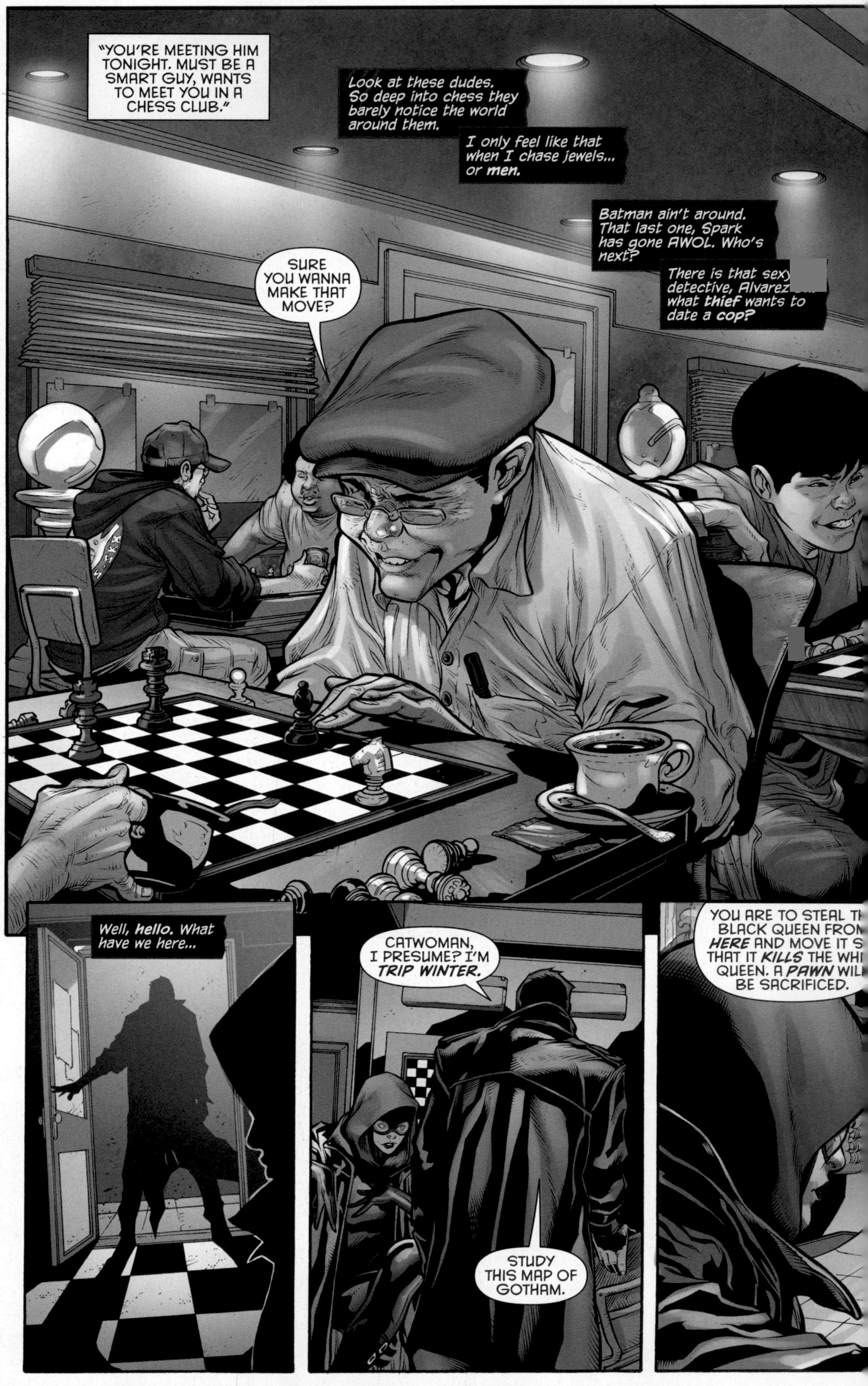

"YOU'RE MEETING HIM TONIGHT. MUST BE A SMART GUY, WANTS TO MEET YOU IN A CHESS CLUB."
Look at these dudes. So deep into chess they barely notice the world around them.
I only feel like that when I chase jewels... or **men.**
Batman ain't around. That last one, Spark has gone AWOL. Who's next?
There is that sexy detective, Alvarez what **thief** wants to date a **cop?**
SURE YOU WANNA MAKE THAT MOVE?
Well, **hello.** What have we here...
CATWOMAN, I PRESUME? I'M ***TRIP WINTER.***
STUDY THIS MAP OF GOTHAM.
YOU ARE TO STEAL T BLACK QUEEN FROM ***HERE*** AND MOVE IT S THAT IT ***KILLS*** THE WHI QUEEN. A ***PAWN*** WIL BE SACRIFICED.

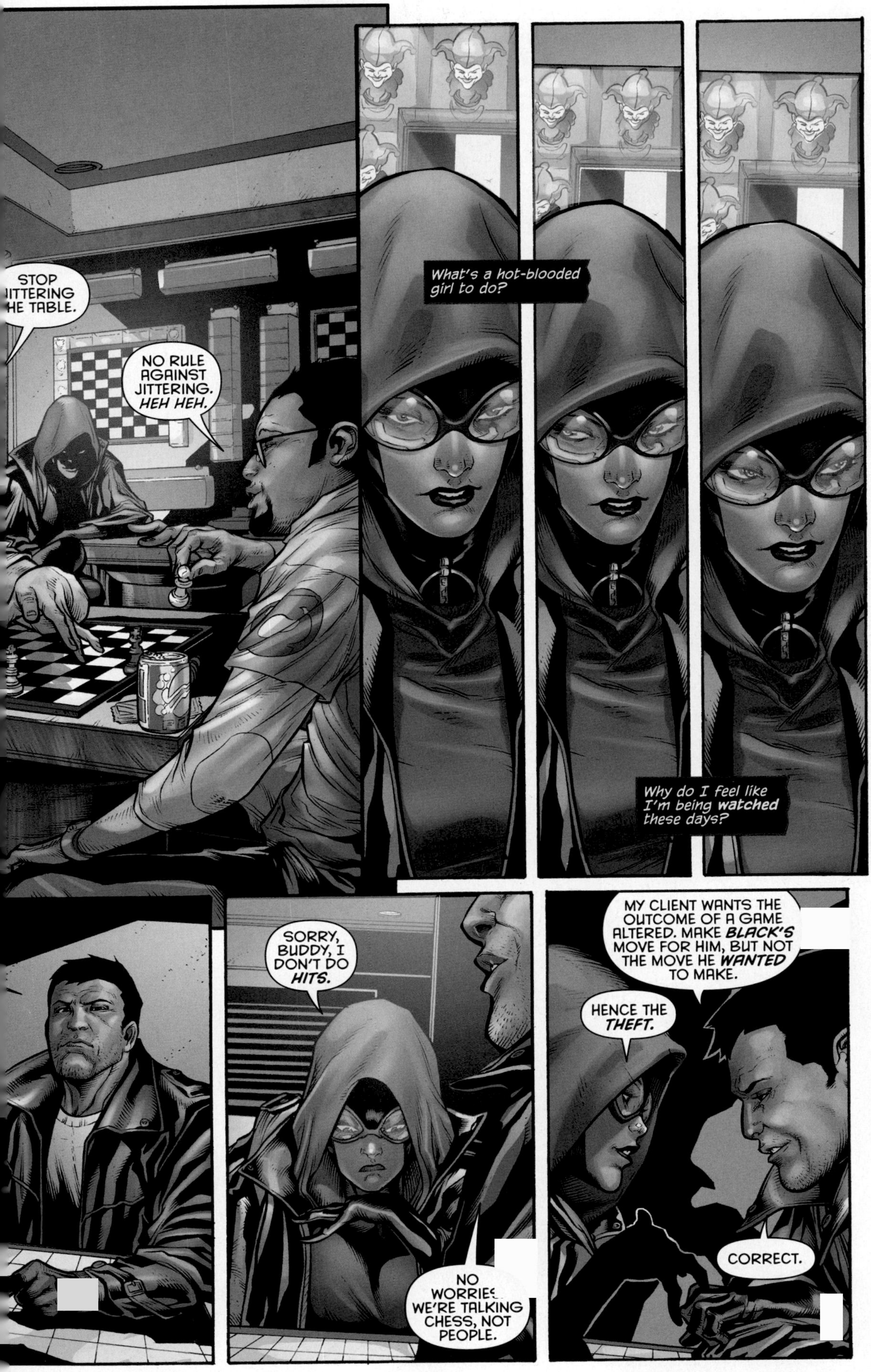

STOP JITTERING THE TABLE.
NO RULE AGAINST JITTERING. HEH HEH.
What's a hot-blooded girl to do?
Why do I feel like I'm being watched these days?
SORRY, BUDDY, I DON'T DO HITS.
NO WORRIES. WE'RE TALKING CHESS, NOT PEOPLE.
MY CLIENT WANTS THE OUTCOME OF A GAME ALTERED. MAKE BLACK'S MOVE FOR HIM, BUT NOT THE MOVE HE WANTED TO MAKE.
HENCE THE THEFT.
CORRECT.

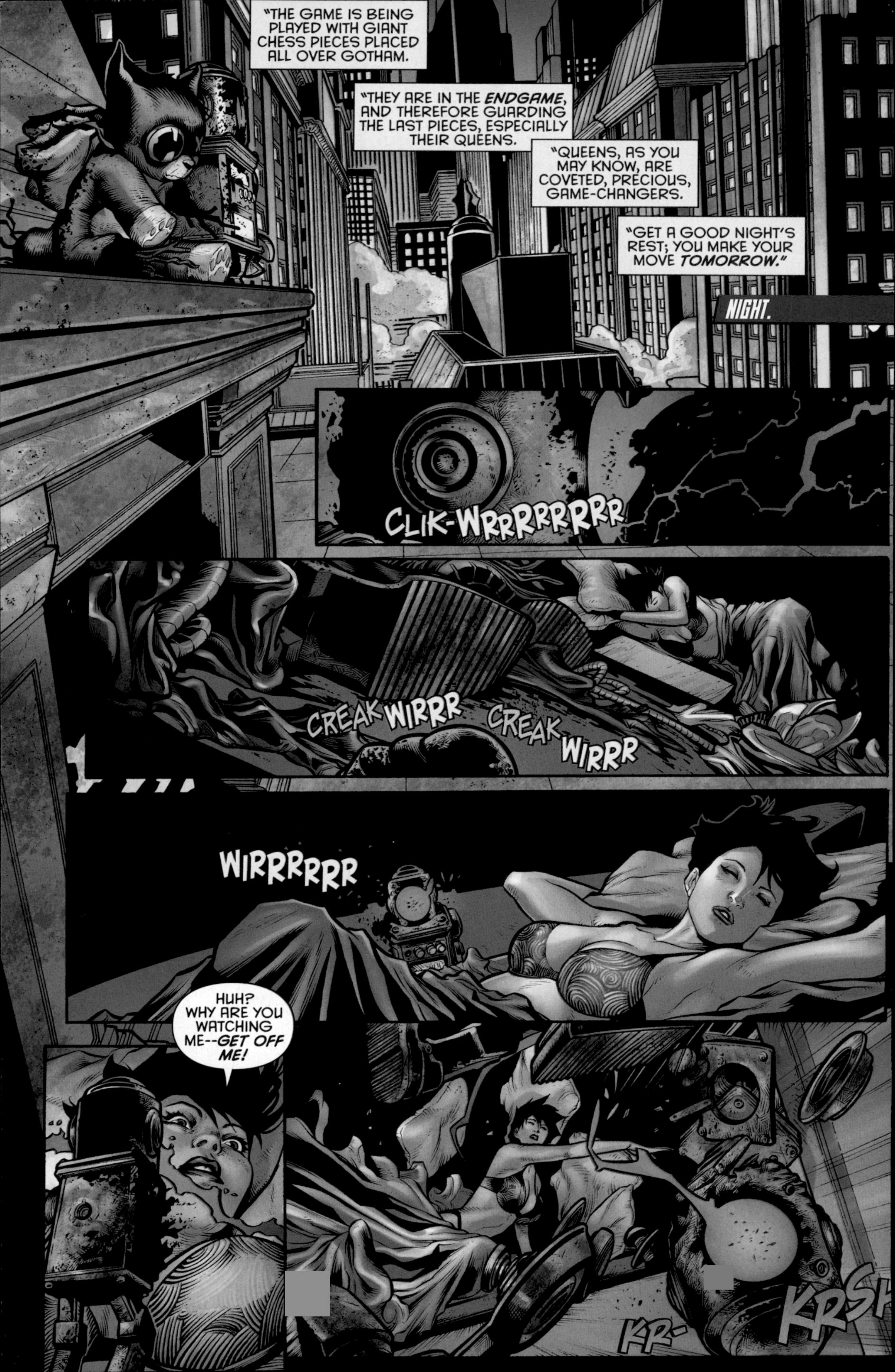

"THE GAME IS BEING PLAYED WITH GIANT CHESS PIECES PLACED ALL OVER GOTHAM.
"THEY ARE IN THE *ENDGAME*, AND THEREFORE GUARDING THE LAST PIECES, ESPECIALLY THEIR QUEENS.
"QUEENS, AS YOU MAY KNOW, ARE COVETED, PRECIOUS, GAME-CHANGERS.
"GET A GOOD NIGHT'S REST; YOU MAKE YOUR MOVE *TOMORROW*."
NIGHT.
CLIK-WRRRRRRRR
CREAK WIRRR
CREAK WIRRR
WIRRRRRR
HUH? WHY ARE YOU WATCHING ME--*GET OFF ME!*
KR-
KRSH

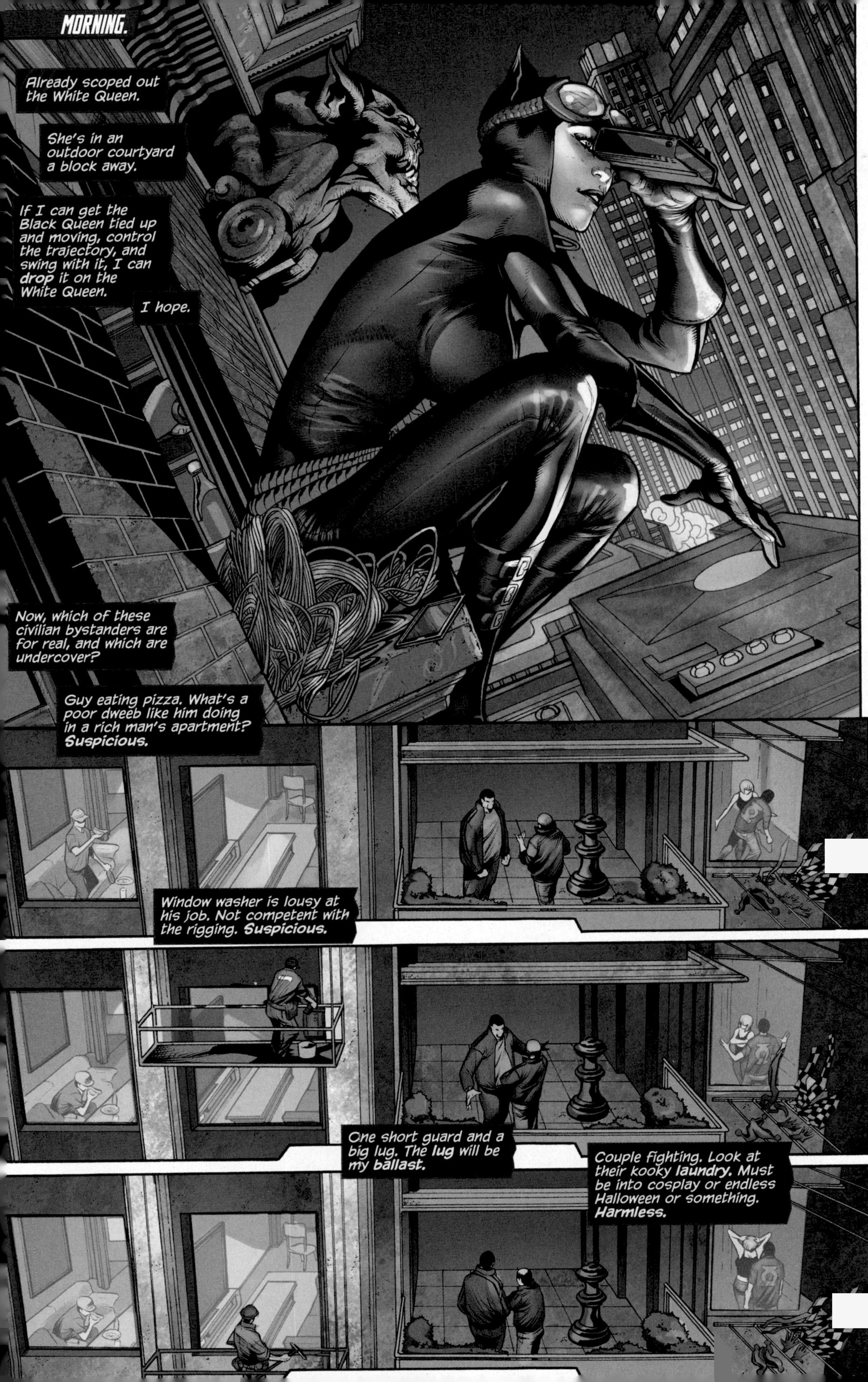
MORNING.
Already scoped out the White Queen.
She's in an outdoor courtyard a block away.
If I can get the Black Queen tied up and moving, control the trajectory, and swing with it, I can drop it on the White Queen.
I hope.
Now, which of these civilian bystanders are for real, and which are undercover?
Guy eating pizza. What's a poor dweeb like him doing in a rich man's apartment? Suspicious.
Window washer is lousy at his job. Not competent with the rigging. Suspicious.
One short guard and a big lug. The lug will be my ballast.
Couple fighting. Look at their kooky laundry. Must be into cosplay or endless Halloween or something. Harmless.

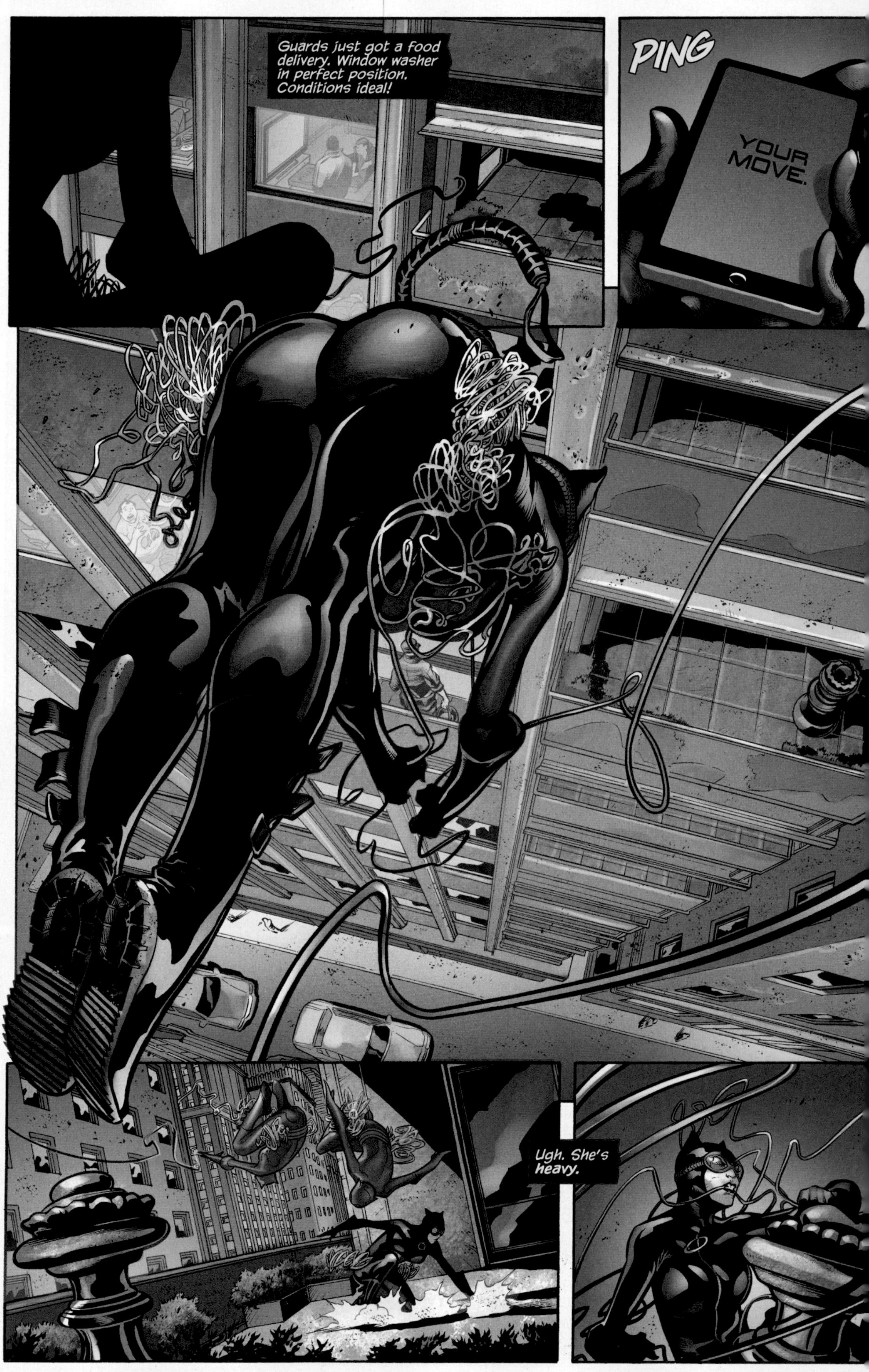
Guards just got a food delivery. Window washer in perfect position. Conditions ideal!
PING
YOUR MOVE.
Ugh. She's heavy.

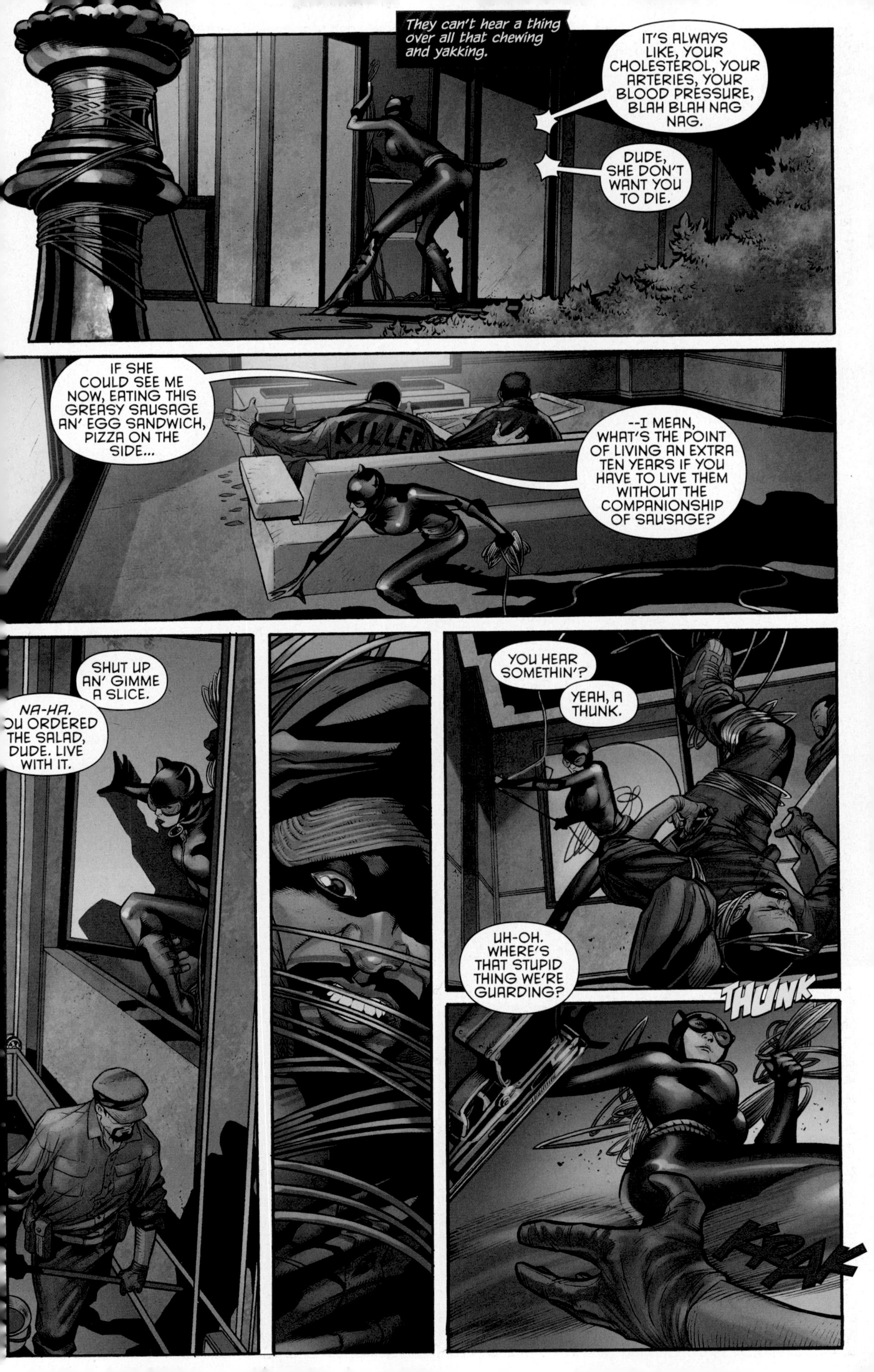
They can't hear a thing over all that chewing and yakking.
IT'S ALWAYS LIKE, YOUR CHOLESTEROL, YOUR ARTERIES, YOUR BLOOD PRESSURE, BLAH BLAH NAG NAG.
DUDE, SHE DON'T WANT YOU TO DIE.
IF SHE COULD SEE ME NOW, EATING THIS GREASY SAUSAGE AN' EGG SANDWICH, PIZZA ON THE SIDE...
--I MEAN, WHAT'S THE POINT OF LIVING AN EXTRA TEN YEARS IF YOU HAVE TO LIVE THEM WITHOUT THE COMPANIONSHIP OF SAUSAGE?
KILLER
SHUT UP AN' GIMME A SLICE.
NA-HA. OU ORDERED THE SALAD, DUDE. LIVE WITH IT.
YOU HEAR SOMETHIN'?
YEAH, A THUNK.
UH-OH. WHERE'S THAT STUPID THING WE'RE GUARDING?
THUNK
KRAK

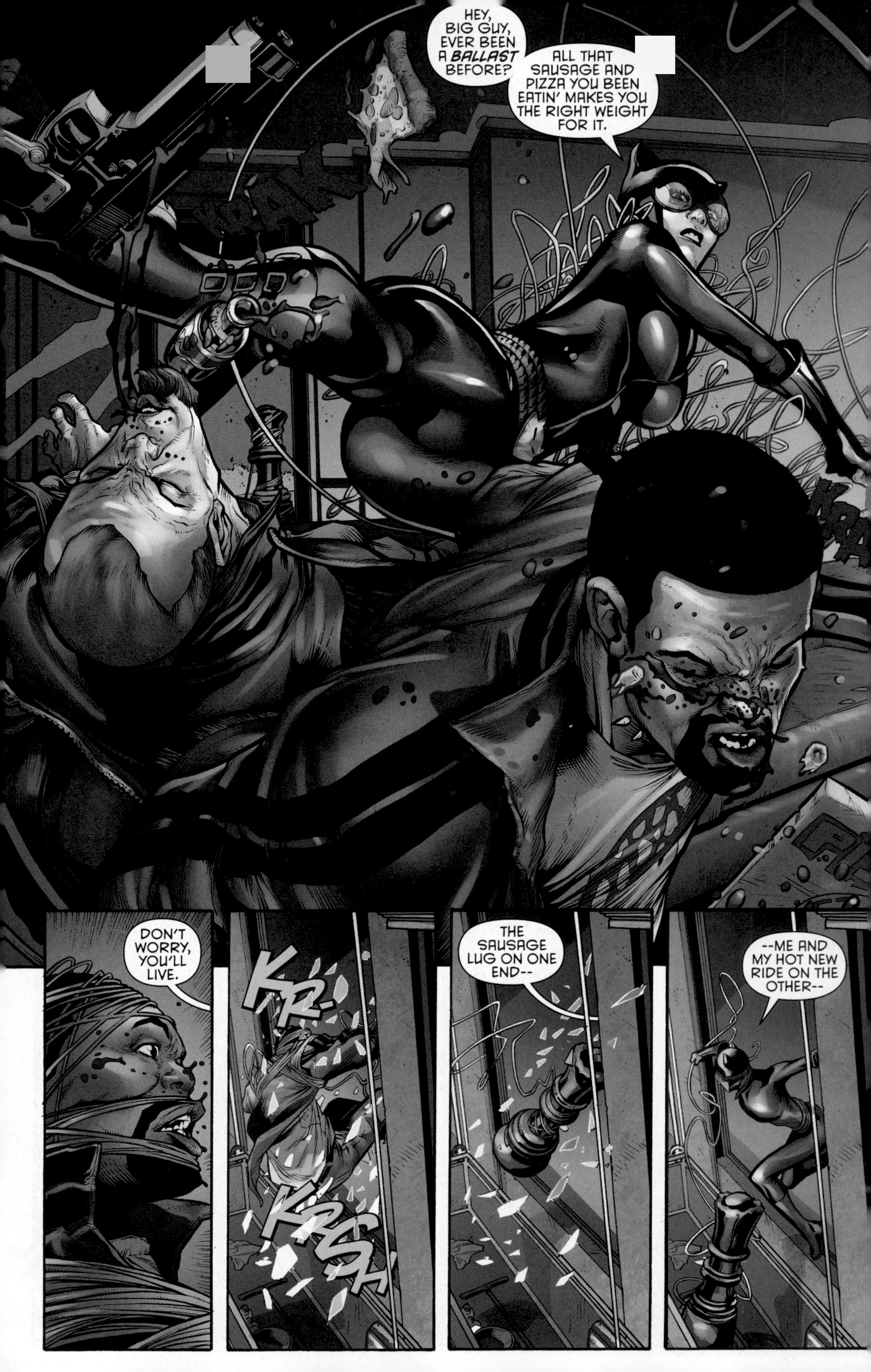
HEY, BIG GUY, EVER BEEN A *BALLAST* BEFORE?
ALL THAT SAUSAGE AND PIZZA YOU BEEN EATIN' MAKES YOU THE RIGHT WEIGHT FOR IT.
KRA
DON'T WORRY, YOU'LL LIVE.
KR-
KRSH
THE SAUSAGE LUG ON ONE END--
--ME AND MY HOT NEW RIDE ON THE OTHER--

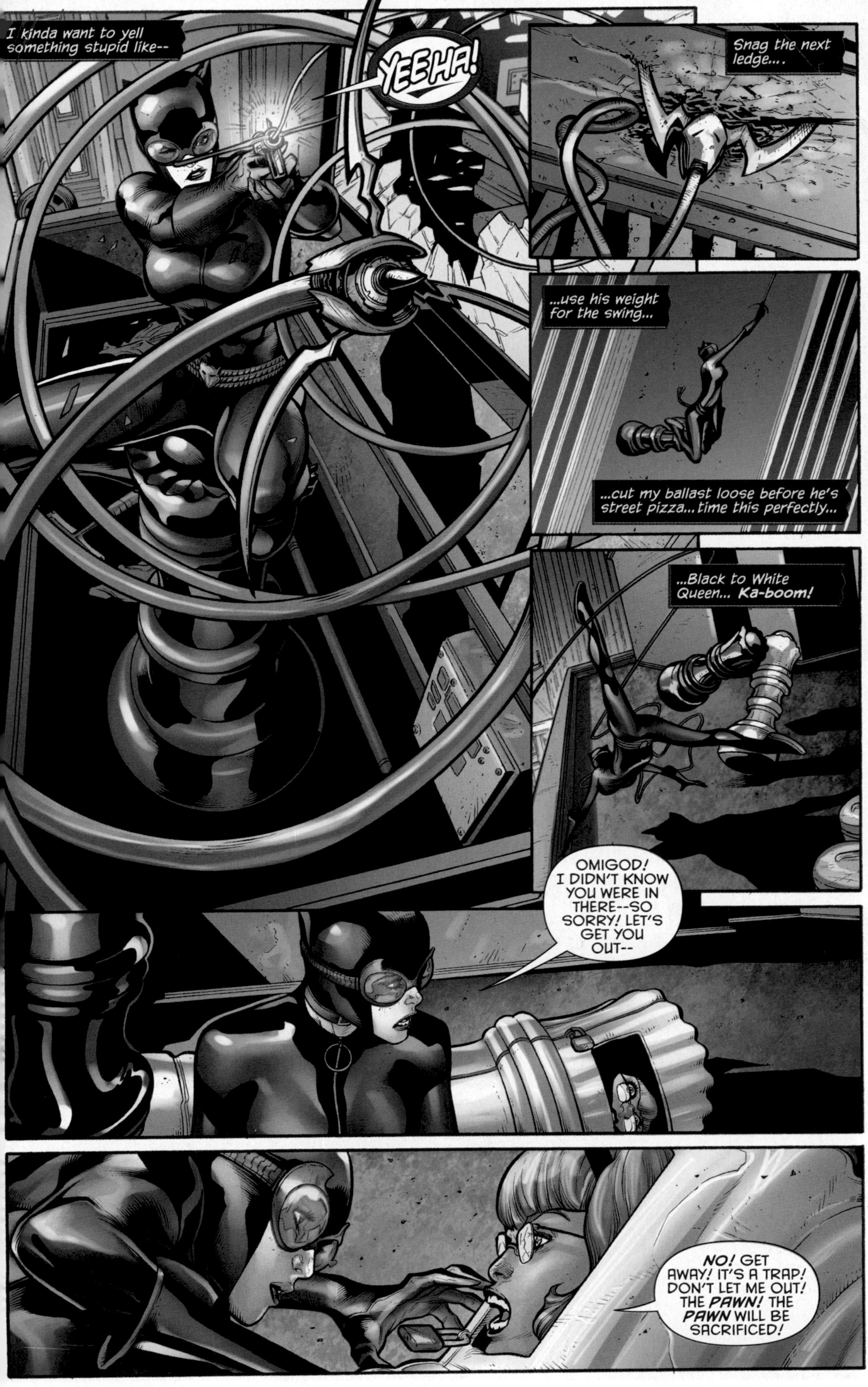
I kinda want to yell something stupid like--
YEEHA!
Snag the next ledge....
...use his weight for the swing...
...cut my ballast loose before he's street pizza... time this perfectly...
...Black to White Queen... Ka-boom!
OMIGOD! I DIDN'T KNOW YOU WERE IN THERE--SO SORRY! LET'S GET YOU OUT--
NO! GET AWAY! IT'S A TRAP! DON'T LET ME OUT! THE PAWN! THE PAWN WILL BE SACRIFICED!

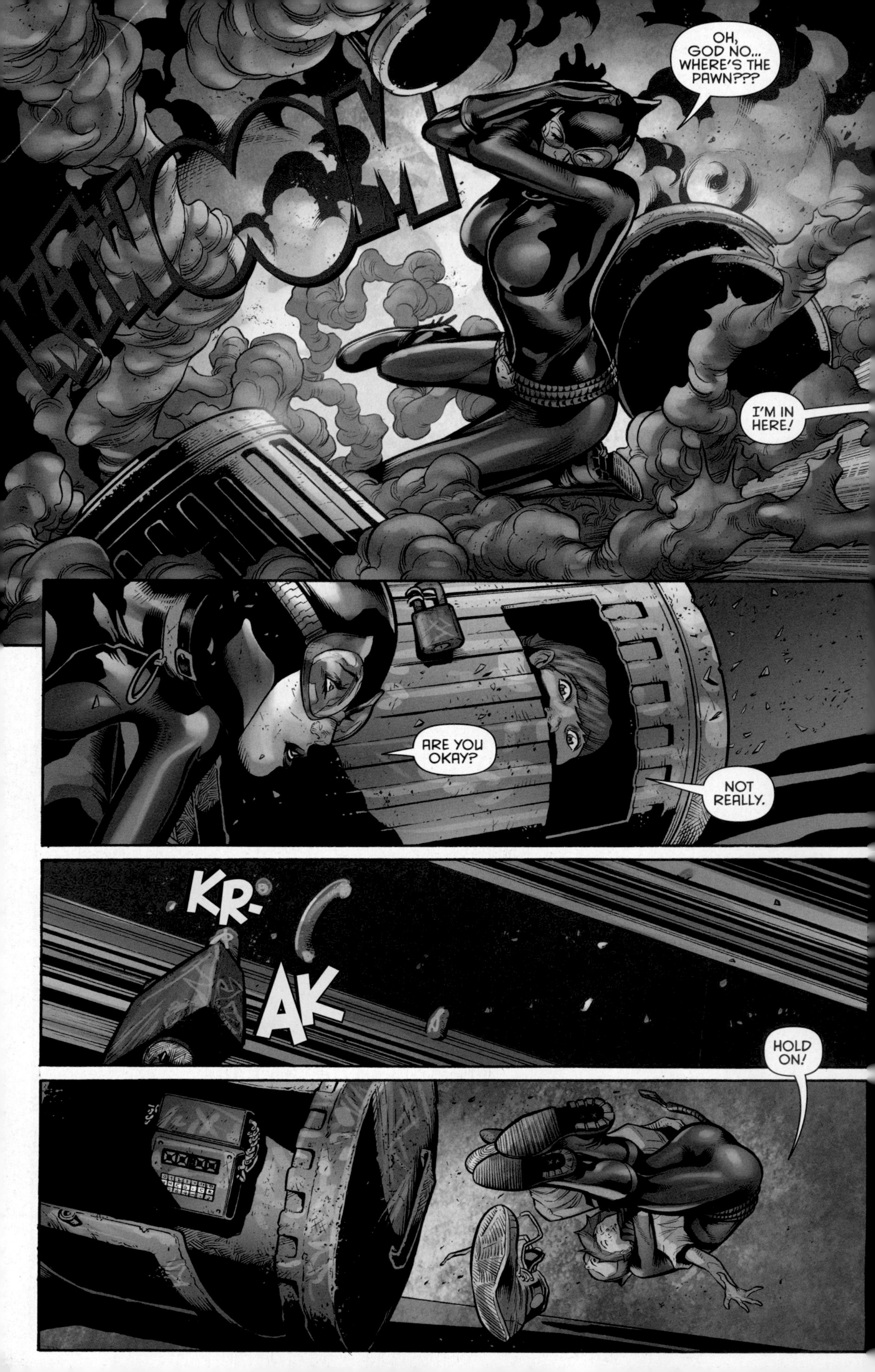
OH, GOD NO... WHERE'S THE PAWN???
I'M IN HERE!
ARE YOU OKAY?
NOT REALLY.
KR-
AK
HOLD ON!

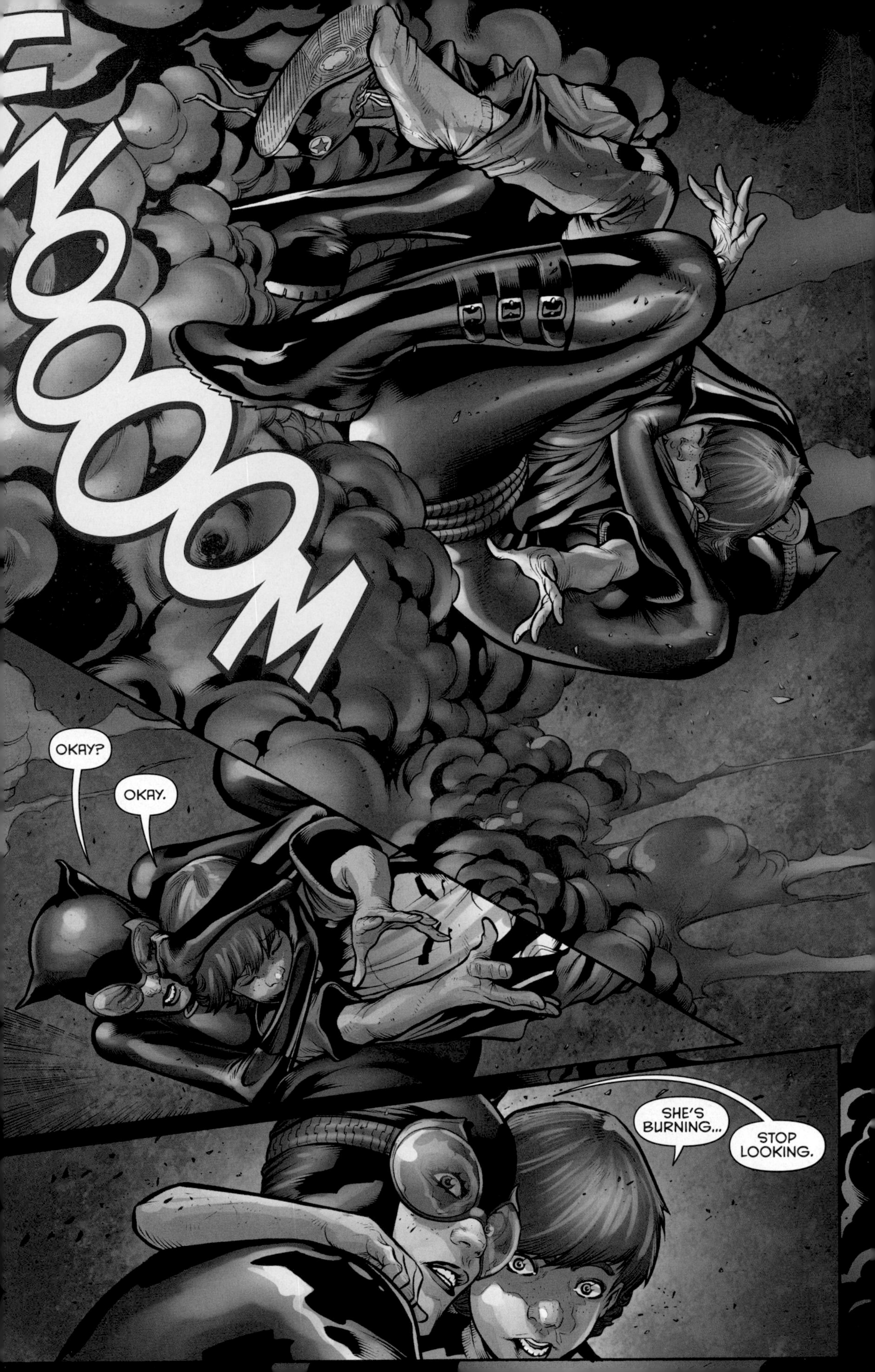
WHOOOOOM
OKAY?
OKAY.
SHE'S BURNING...
STOP LOOKING.

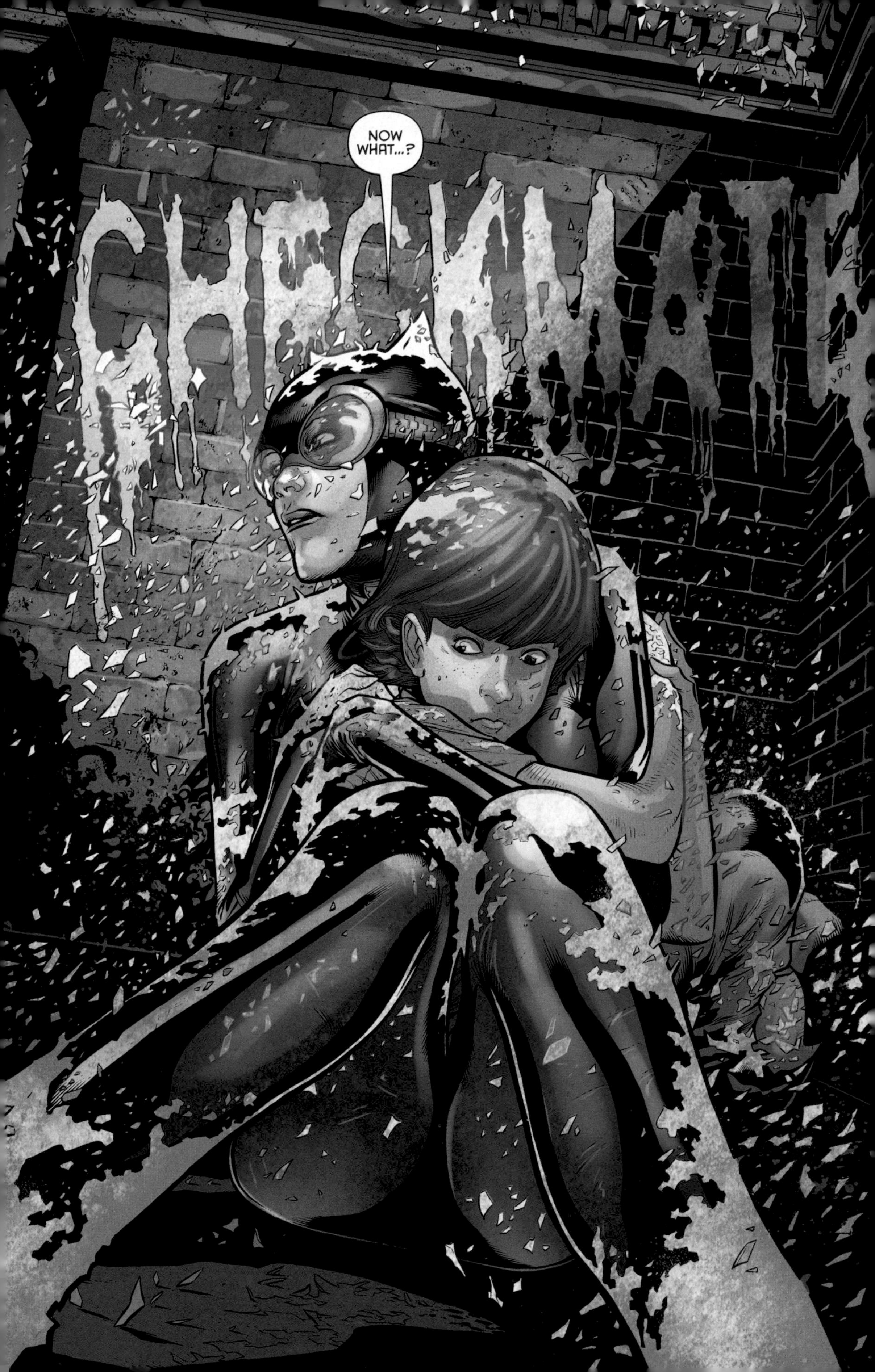
NOW WHAT...?

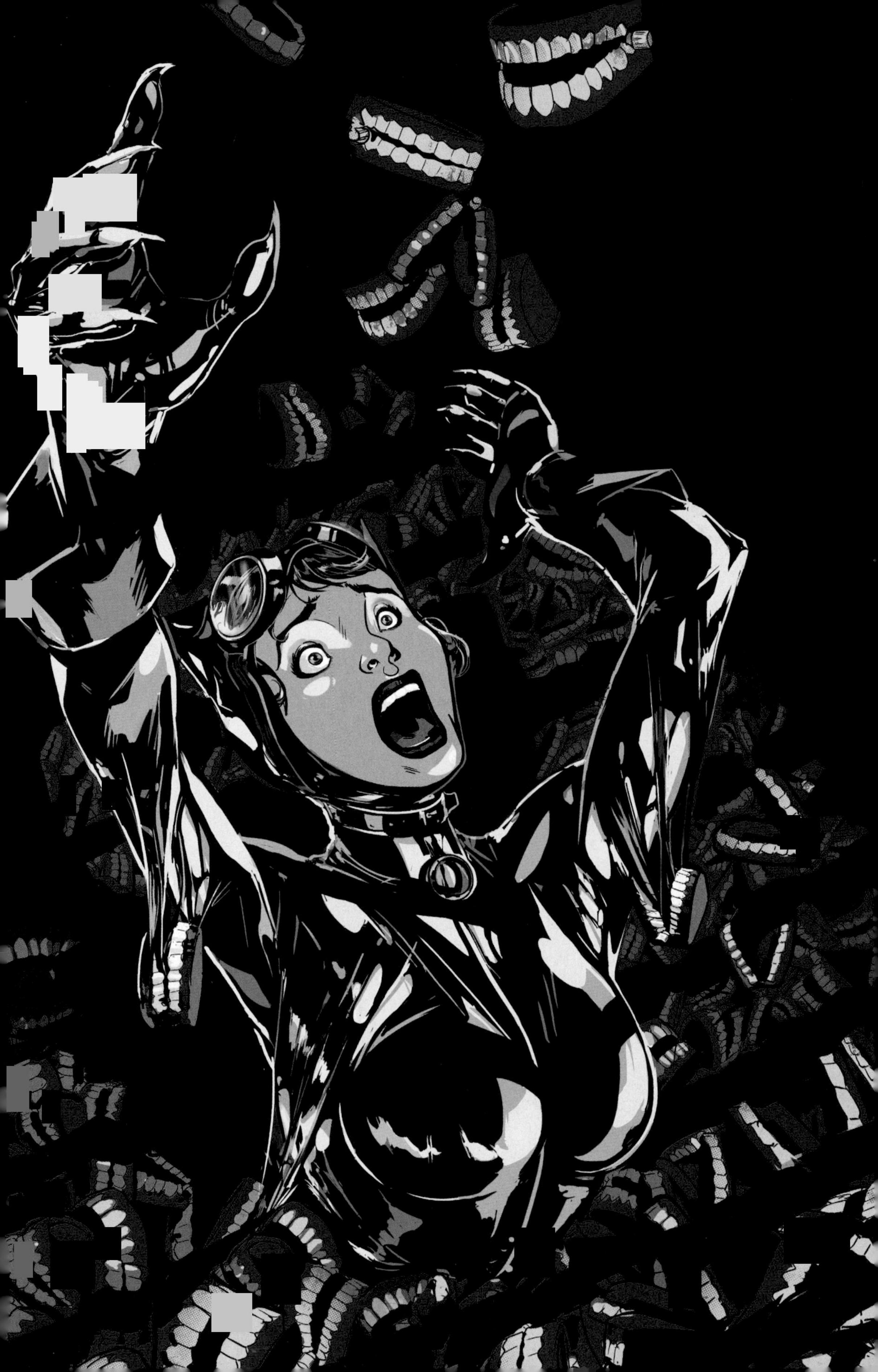

ANN NOCENTI writer RAFA SANDOVAL penciller JORDI TARRAGONA inker cover by TREVOR McCARTHY

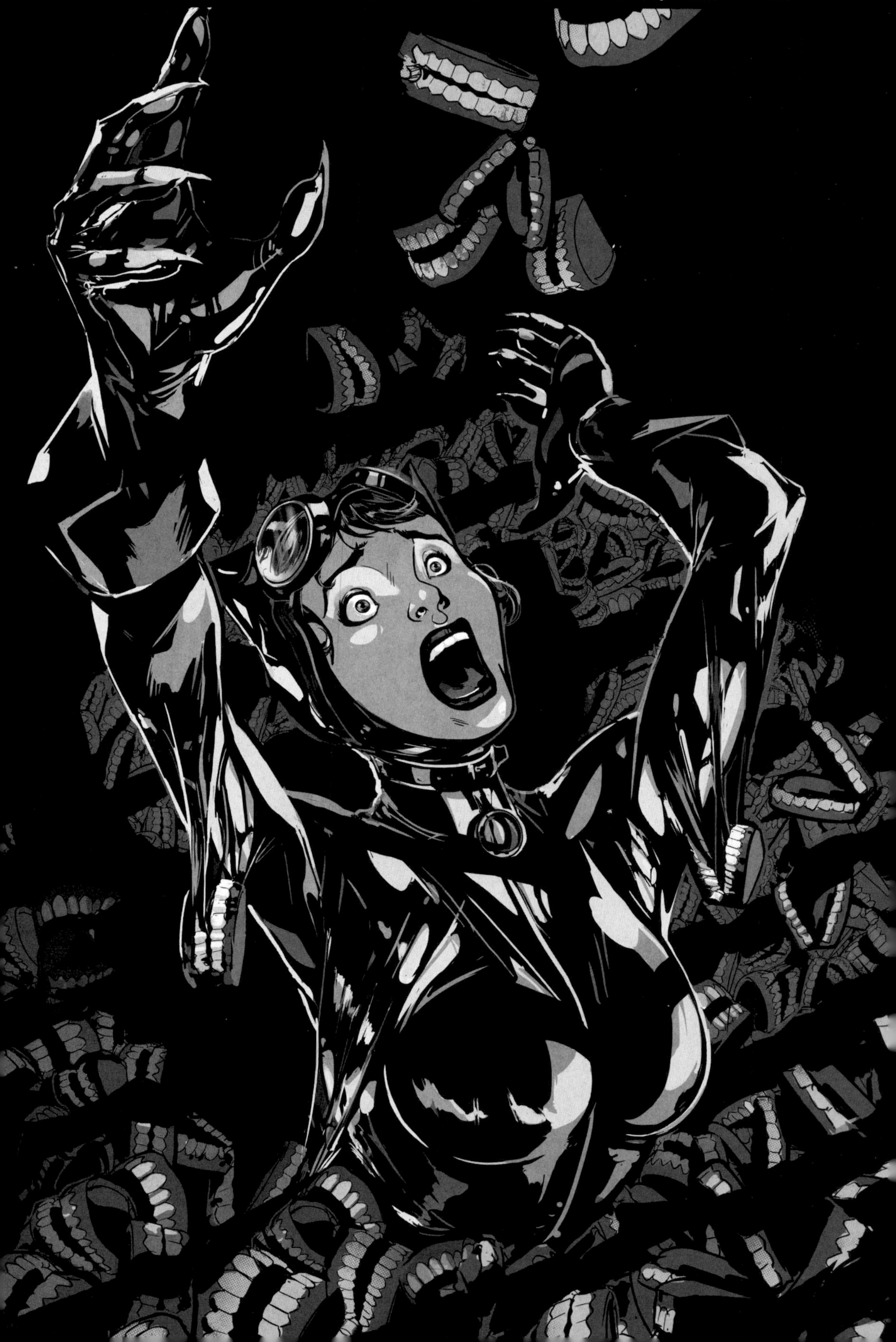

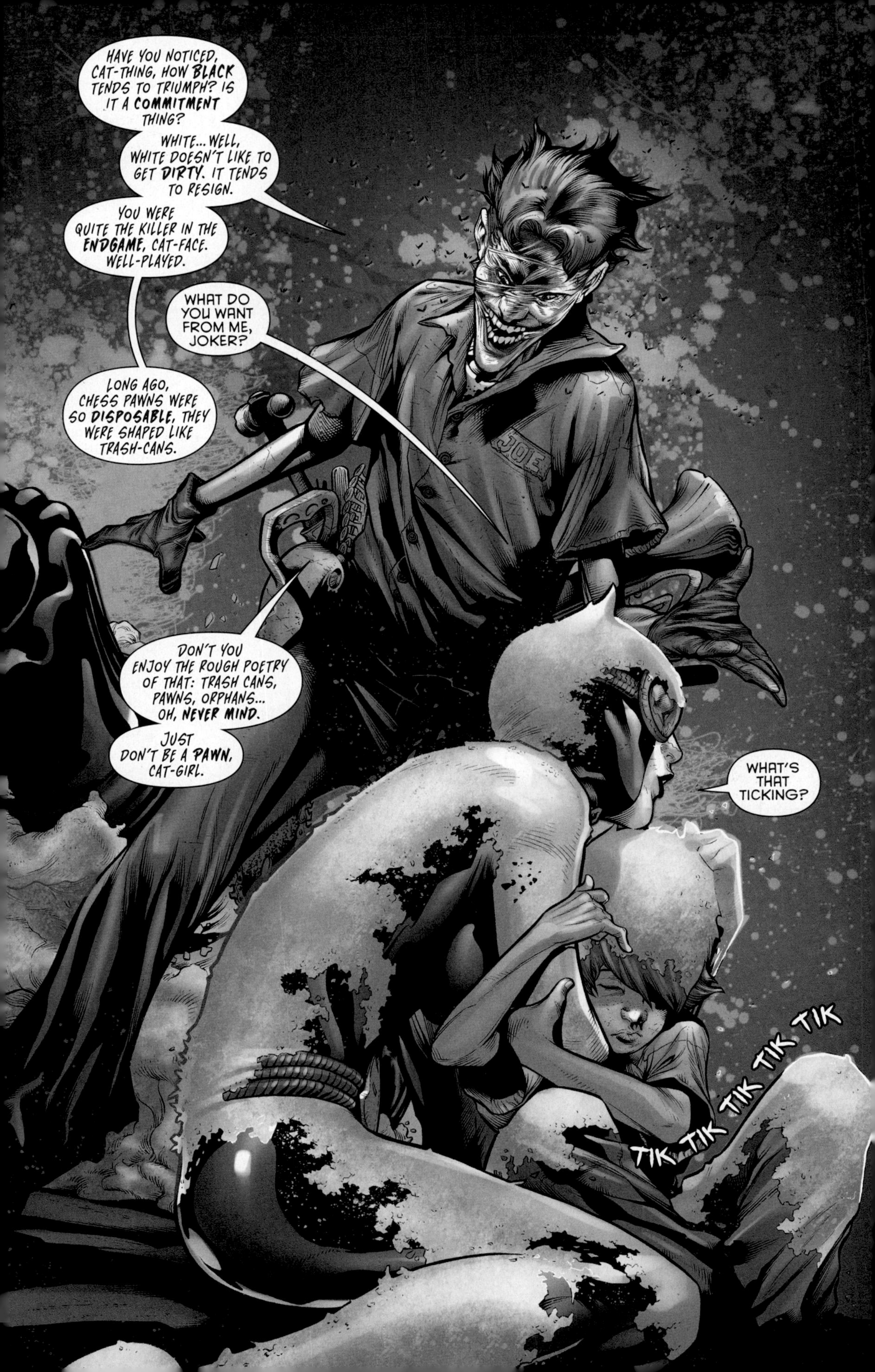
HAVE YOU NOTICED, CAT-THING, HOW BLACK TENDS TO TRIUMPH? IS IT A COMMITMENT THING?
WHITE... WELL, WHITE DOESN'T LIKE TO GET DIRTY. IT TENDS TO RESIGN.
YOU WERE QUITE THE KILLER IN THE ENDGAME, CAT-FACE. WELL-PLAYED.
WHAT DO YOU WANT FROM ME, JOKER?
LONG AGO, CHESS PAWNS WERE SO DISPOSABLE, THEY WERE SHAPED LIKE TRASH-CANS.
DON'T YOU ENJOY THE ROUGH POETRY OF THAT: TRASH CANS, PAWNS, ORPHANS... OH, NEVER MIND.
JUST DON'T BE A PAWN, CAT-GIRL.
WHAT'S THAT TICKING?
TIK TIK TIK TIK TIK

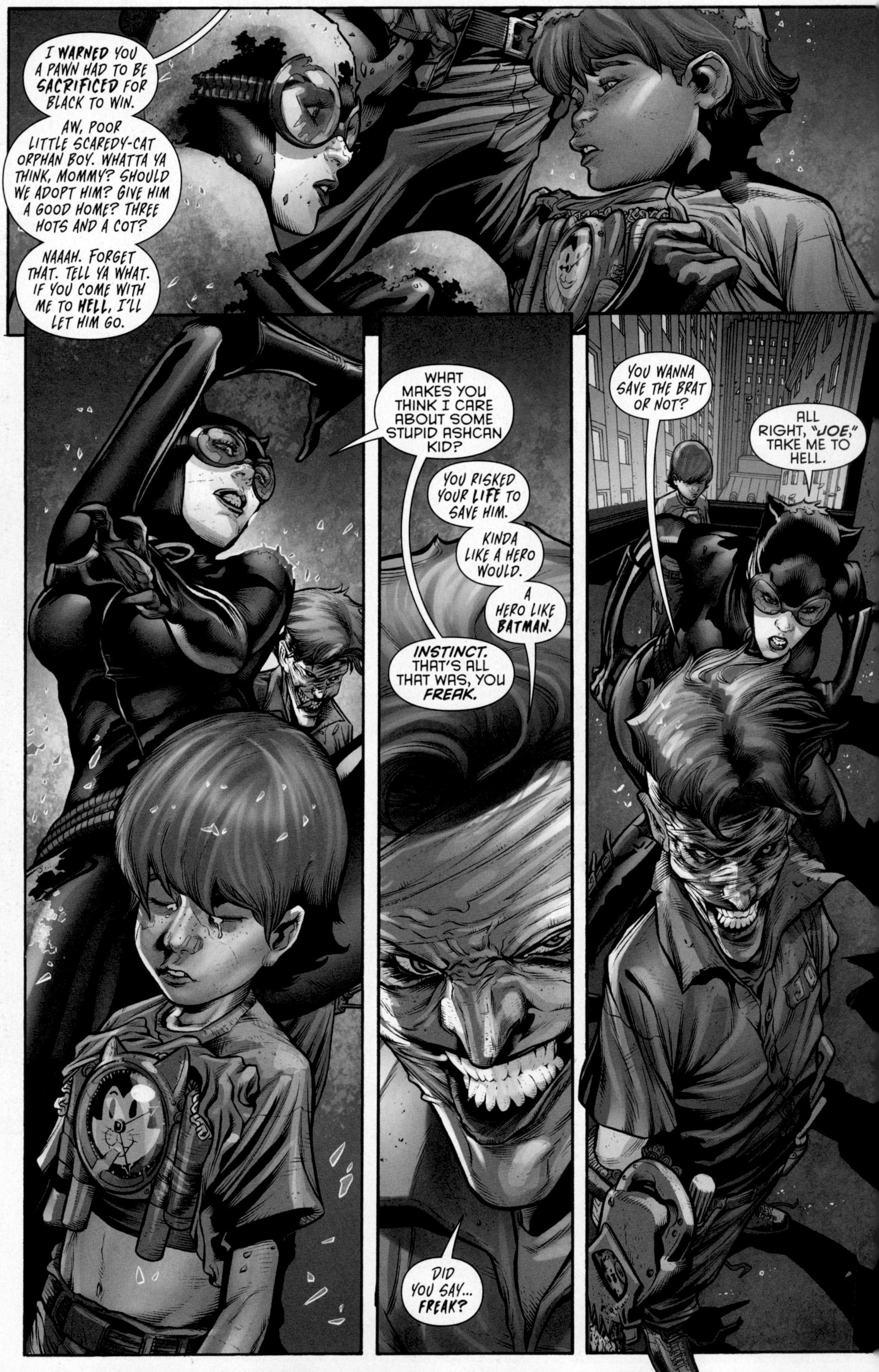
I **WARNED** YOU A PAWN HAD TO BE **SACRIFICED** FOR BLACK TO WIN.
AW, POOR LITTLE SCAREDY-CAT ORPHAN BOY. WHATTA YA THINK, MOMMY? SHOULD WE ADOPT HIM? GIVE HIM A GOOD HOME? THREE HOTS AND A COT?
NAAAH. FORGET THAT. TELL YA WHAT. IF YOU COME WITH ME TO **HELL**, I'LL LET HIM GO.
WHAT MAKES YOU THINK I CARE ABOUT SOME STUPID ASHCAN KID?
YOU RISKED YOUR **LIFE** TO SAVE HIM.
KINDA LIKE A HERO WOULD.
A HERO LIKE **BATMAN**.
INSTINCT. THAT'S ALL THAT WAS, YOU ***FREAK.***
DID YOU SAY... **FREAK?**
YOU WANNA SAVE THE BRAT OR NOT?
ALL RIGHT, "*JOE*," TAKE ME TO HELL.

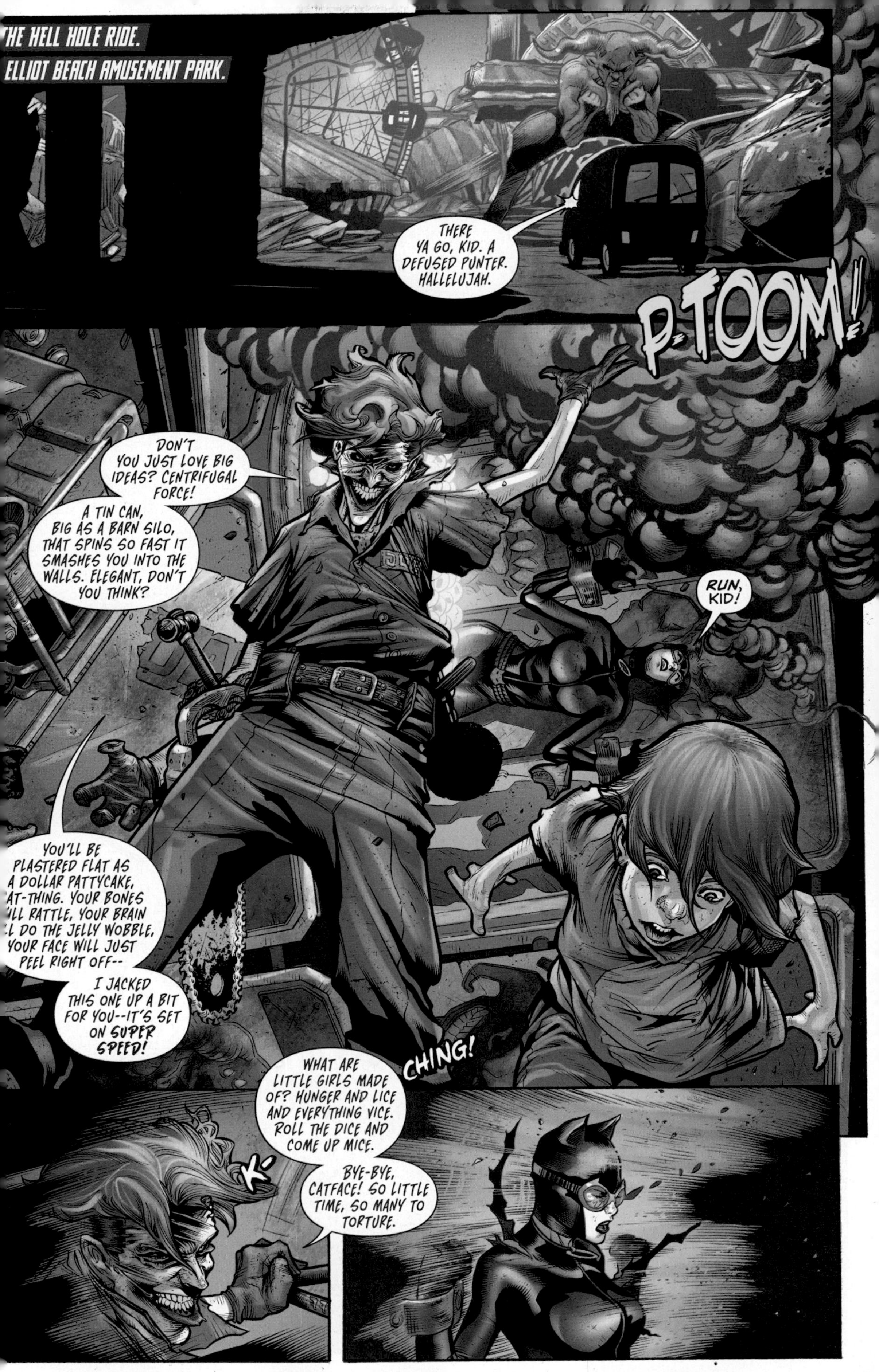
THE HELL HOLE RIDE.
ELLIOT BEACH AMUSEMENT PARK.
THERE YA GO, KID. A DEFUSED PUNTER. HALLELUJAH.
P-TOOM!
DON'T YOU JUST LOVE BIG IDEAS? CENTRIFUGAL FORCE!
A TIN CAN, BIG AS A BARN SILO, THAT SPINS SO FAST IT SMASHES YOU INTO THE WALLS. ELEGANT, DON'T YOU THINK?
RUN, KID!
YOU'LL BE PLASTERED FLAT AS A DOLLAR PATTYCAKE, AT-THING. YOUR BONES ILL RATTLE, YOUR BRAIN L DO THE JELLY WOBBLE, YOUR FACE WILL JUST PEEL RIGHT OFF--
I JACKED THIS ONE UP A BIT FOR YOU--IT'S SET ON SUPER SPEED!
CHING!
WHAT ARE LITTLE GIRLS MADE OF? HUNGER AND LICE AND EVERYTHING VICE. ROLL THE DICE AND COME UP MICE.
BYE-BYE, CATFACE! SO LITTLE TIME, SO MANY TO TORTURE.
K-

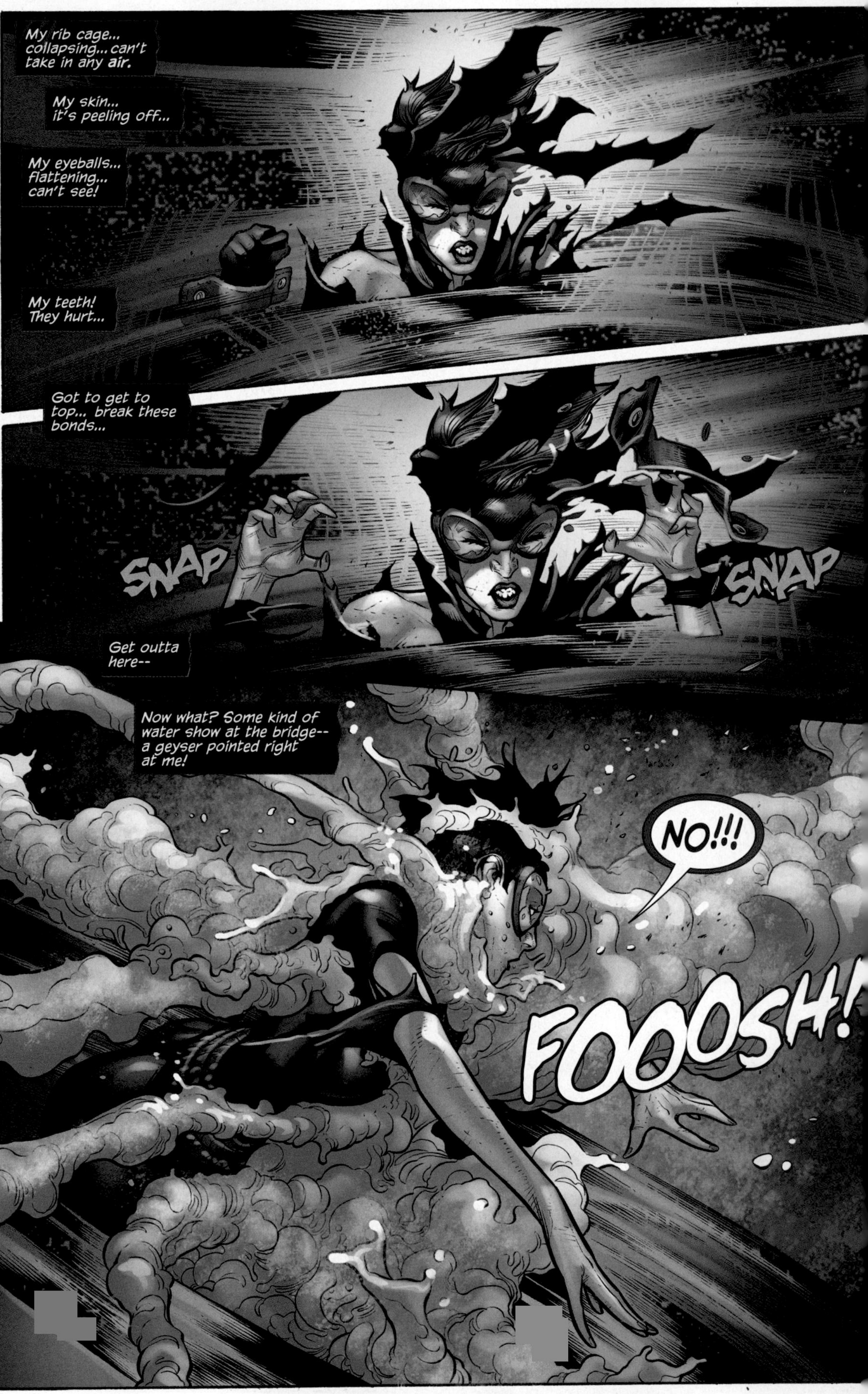
My rib cage... collapsing... can't take in any air.
My skin... it's peeling off...
My eyeballs... flattening... can't see!
My teeth! They hurt...
Got to get to top... break these bonds...
SNAP
SNAP
Get outta here--
Now what? Some kind of water show at the bridge--a geyser pointed right at me!
NO!!!
FOOOSH!

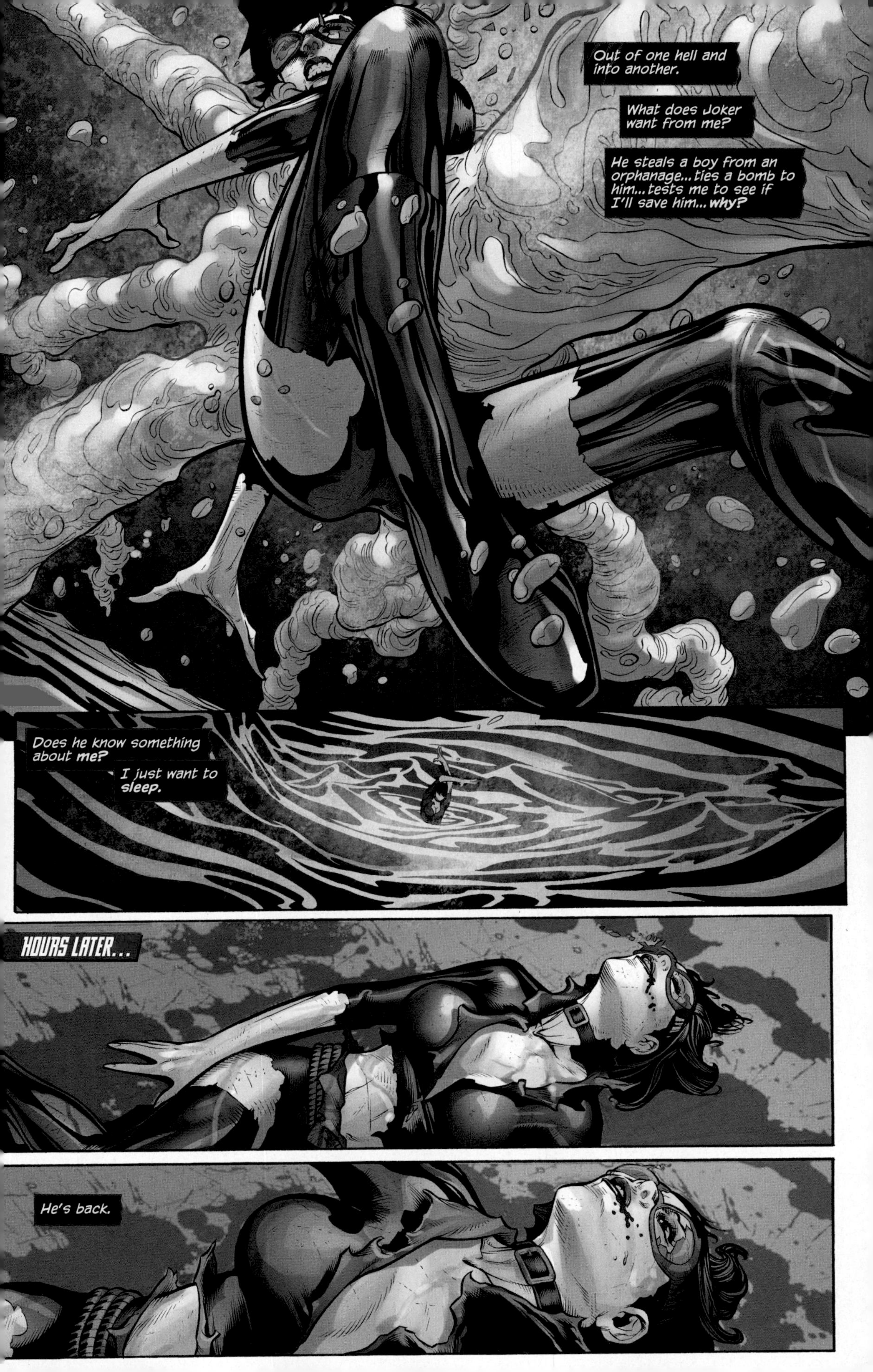

Out of one hell and into another.
What does Joker want from me?
He steals a boy from an orphanage...ties a bomb to him...tests me to see if I'll save him...**why?**
Does he know something about **me?**
I just want to **sleep.**
HOURS LATER...
He's back.

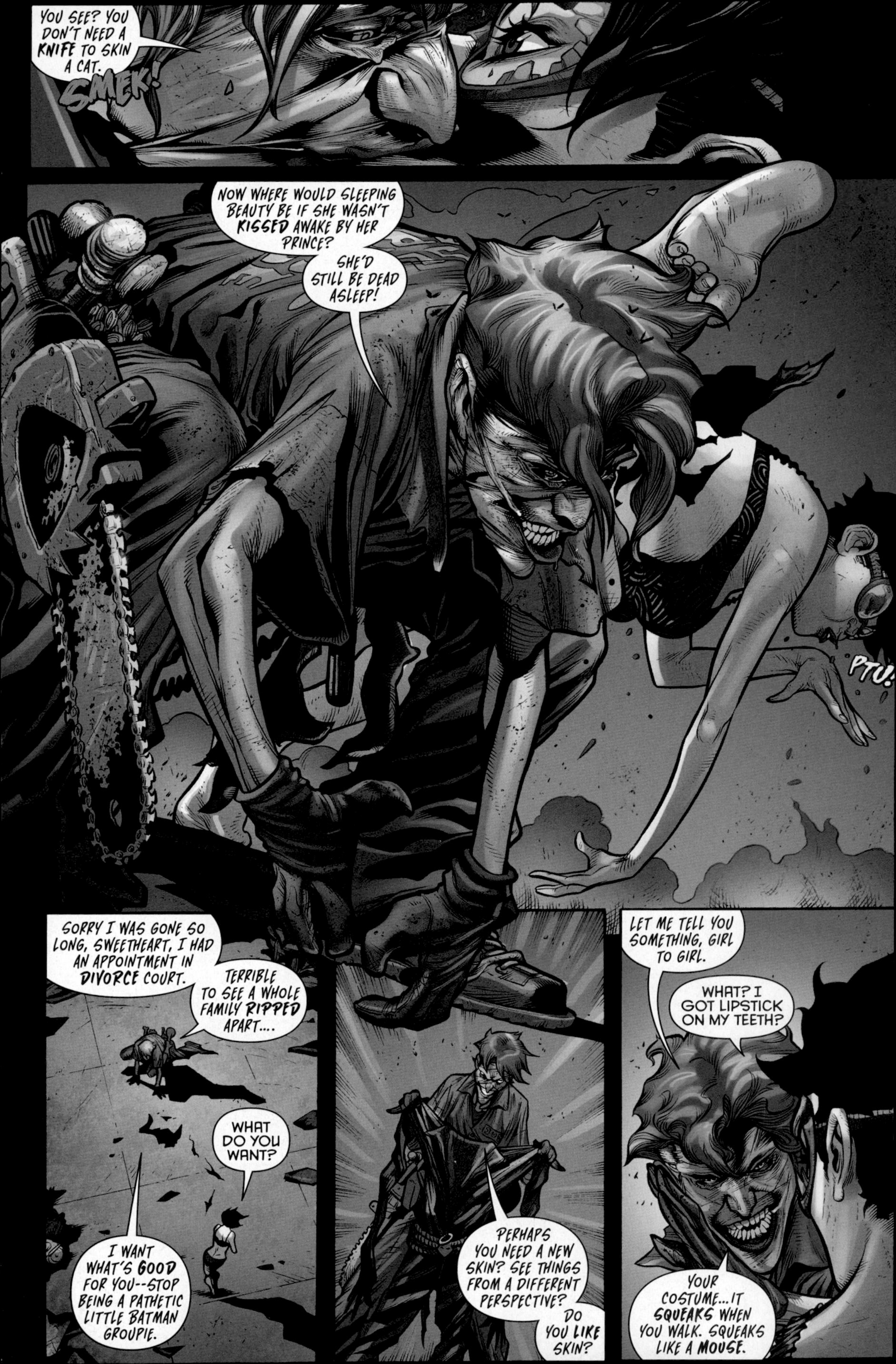

YOU SEE? YOU DON'T NEED A KNIFE TO SKIN A CAT.
SMEK!
NOW WHERE WOULD SLEEPING BEAUTY BE IF SHE WASN'T KISSED AWAKE BY HER PRINCE?
SHE'D STILL BE DEAD ASLEEP!
PTU!
SORRY I WAS GONE SO LONG, SWEETHEART, I HAD AN APPOINTMENT IN DIVORCE COURT.
TERRIBLE TO SEE A WHOLE FAMILY RIPPED APART....
WHAT DO YOU WANT?
I WANT WHAT'S GOOD FOR YOU--STOP BEING A PATHETIC LITTLE BATMAN GROUPIE.
PERHAPS YOU NEED A NEW SKIN? SEE THINGS FROM A DIFFERENT PERSPECTIVE?
DO YOU LIKE SKIN?
LET ME TELL YOU SOMETHING, GIRL TO GIRL.
WHAT? I GOT LIPSTICK ON MY TEETH?
YOUR COSTUME...IT SQUEAKS WHEN YOU WALK. SQUEAKS LIKE A MOUSE.

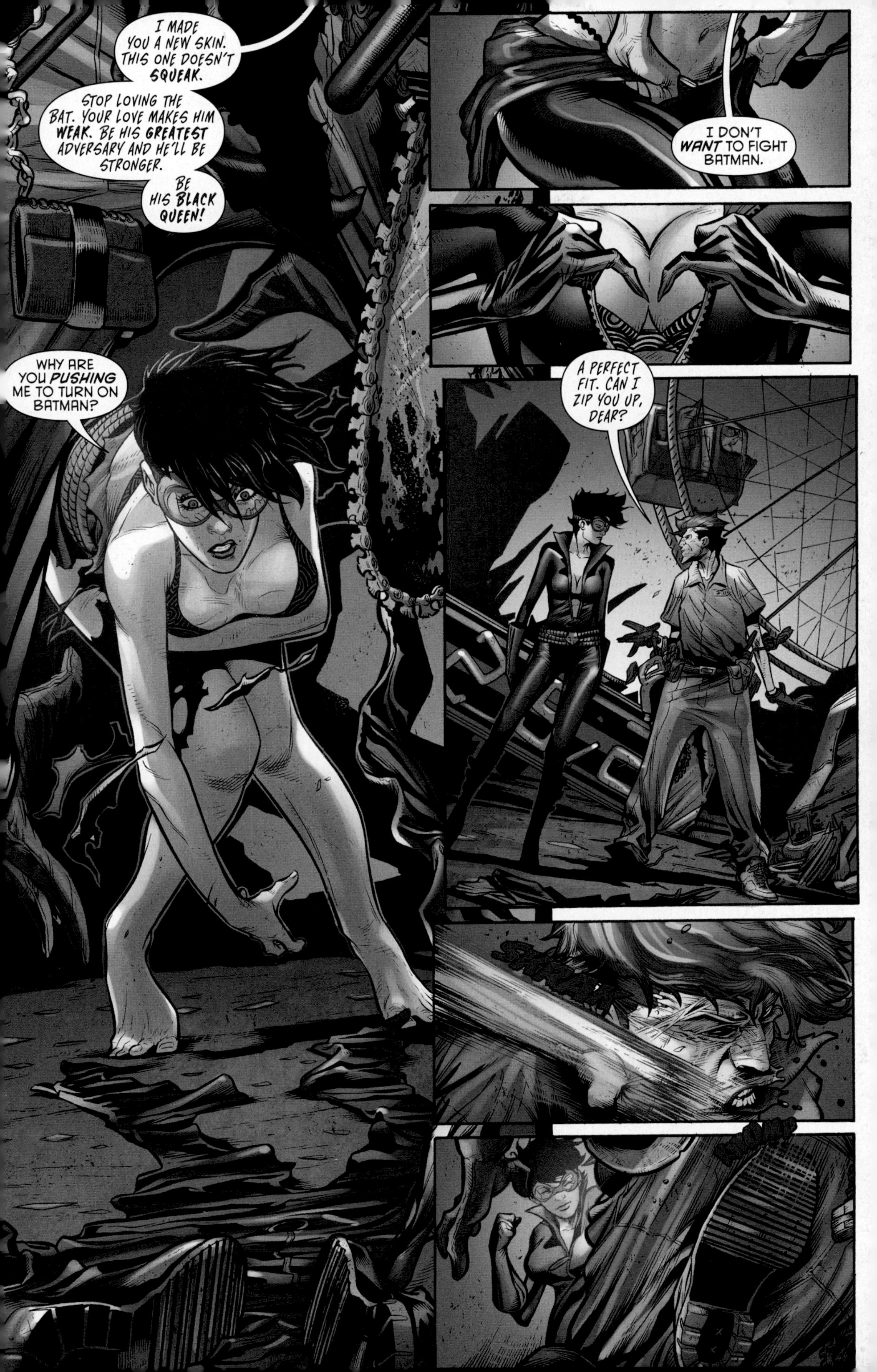

I MADE YOU A NEW SKIN. THIS ONE DOESN'T SQUEAK.
STOP LOVING THE BAT. YOUR LOVE MAKES HIM WEAK. BE HIS GREATEST ADVERSARY AND HE'LL BE STRONGER.
BE HIS BLACK QUEEN!
WHY ARE YOU PUSHING ME TO TURN ON BATMAN?
I DON'T WANT TO FIGHT BATMAN.
A PERFECT FIT. CAN I ZIP YOU UP, DEAR?

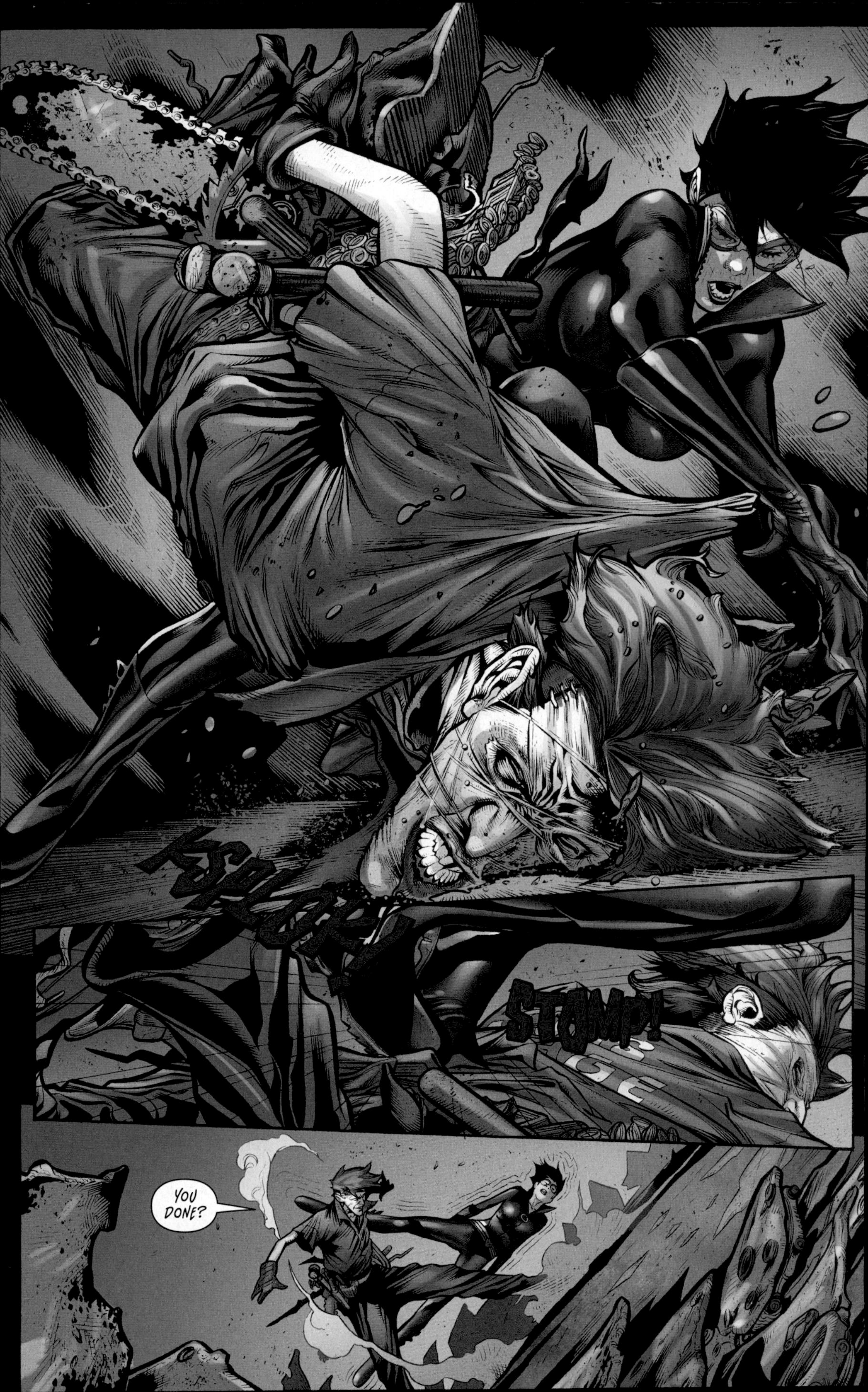
STOMP!
YOU DONE?

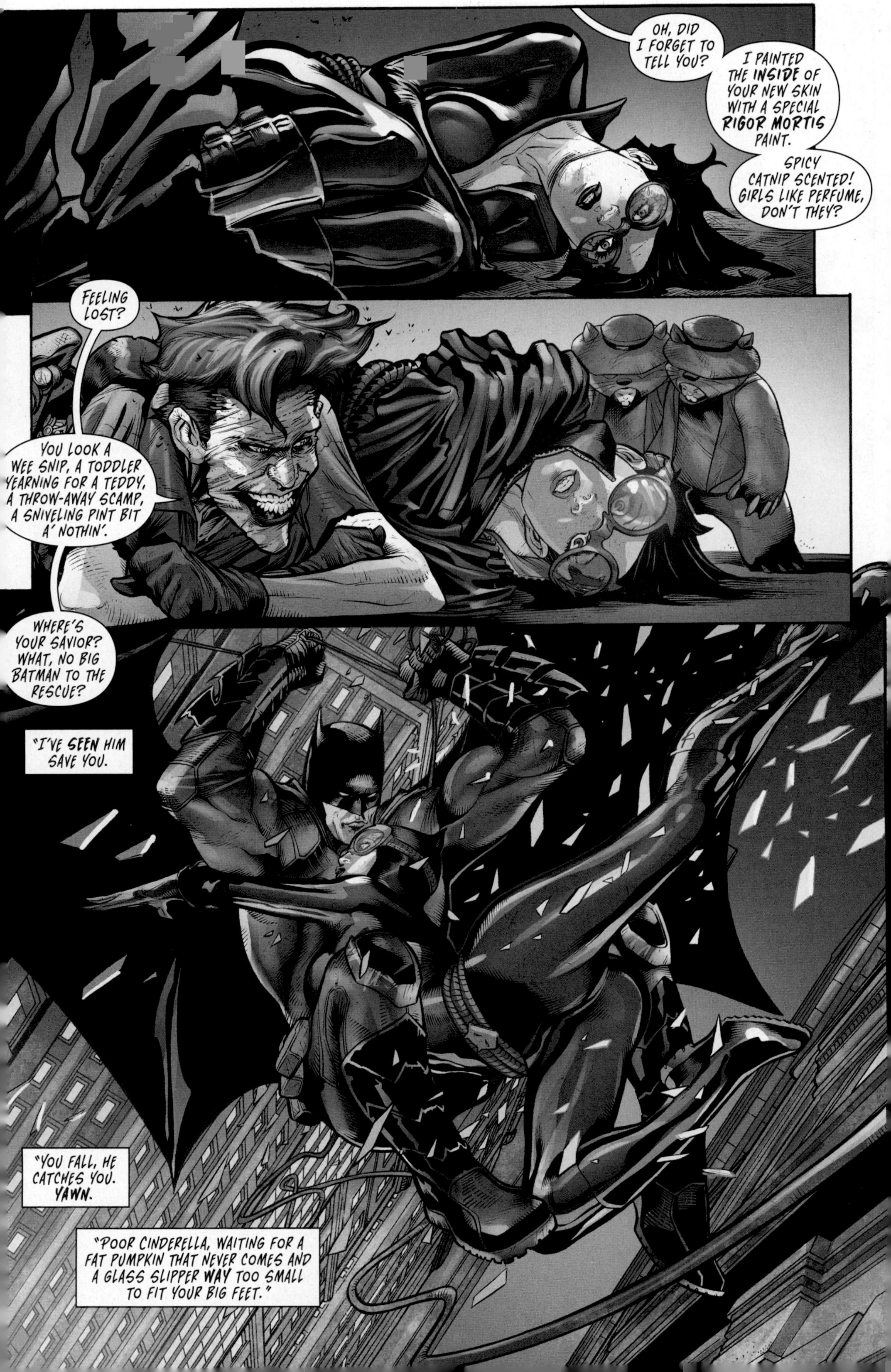
OH, DID I FORGET TO TELL YOU?
I PAINTED THE INSIDE OF YOUR NEW SKIN WITH A SPECIAL RIGOR MORTIS PAINT.
SPICY CATNIP SCENTED! GIRLS LIKE PERFUME, DON'T THEY?
FEELING LOST?
YOU LOOK A WEE SNIP, A TODDLER YEARNING FOR A TEDDY, A THROW-AWAY SCAMP, A SNIVELING PINT BIT A' NOTHIN'.
WHERE'S YOUR SAVIOR? WHAT, NO BIG BATMAN TO THE RESCUE?
"I'VE SEEN HIM SAVE YOU.
"YOU FALL, HE CATCHES YOU. YAWN.
"POOR CINDERELLA, WAITING FOR A FAT PUMPKIN THAT NEVER COMES AND A GLASS SLIPPER WAY TOO SMALL TO FIT YOUR BIG FEET."

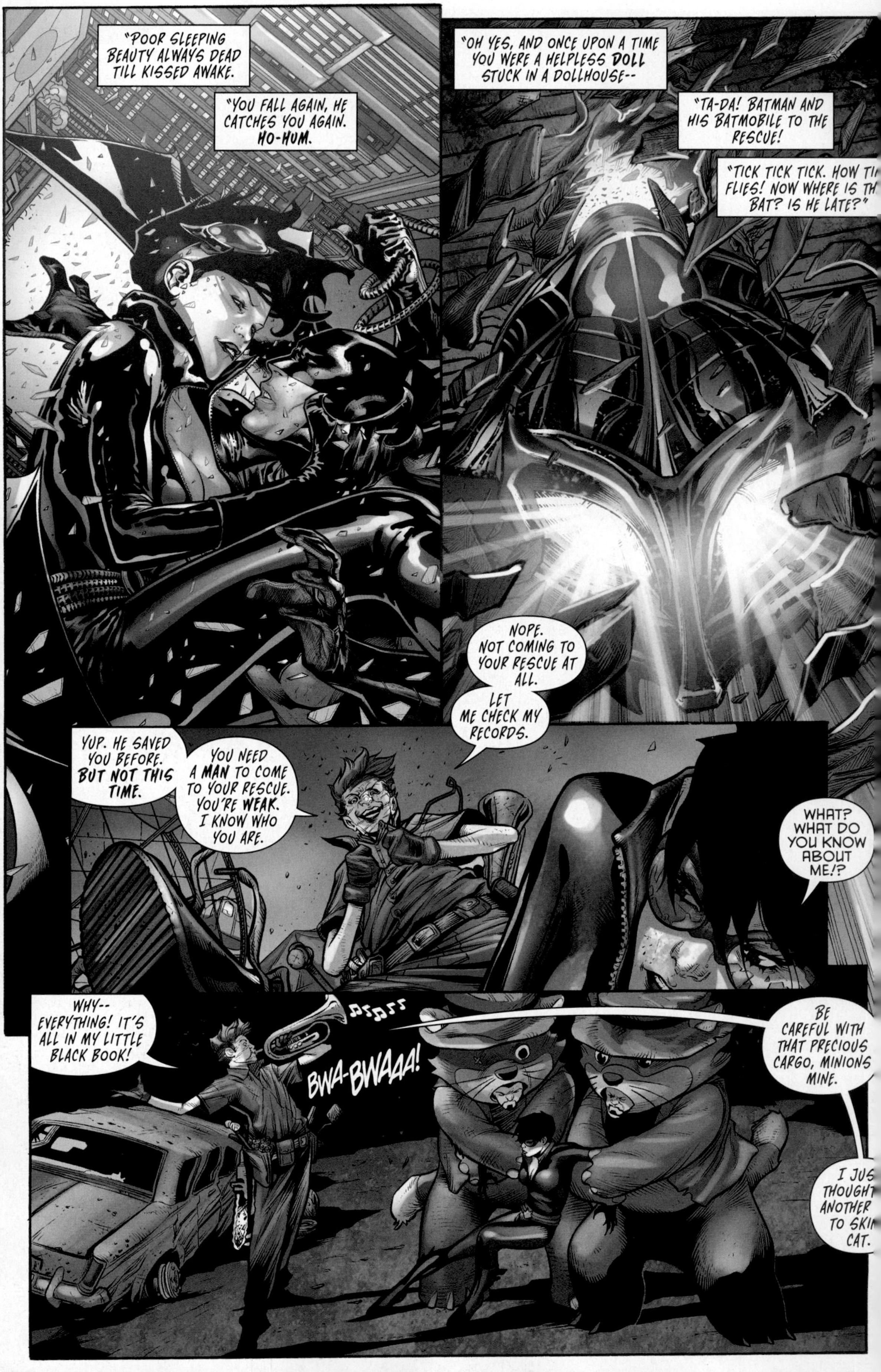

"POOR SLEEPING BEAUTY ALWAYS DEAD TILL KISSED AWAKE.
"YOU FALL AGAIN, HE CATCHES YOU AGAIN. HO-HUM.
"OH YES, AND ONCE UPON A TIME YOU WERE A HELPLESS DOLL STUCK IN A DOLLHOUSE--
"TA-DA! BATMAN AND HIS BATMOBILE TO THE RESCUE!
"TICK TICK TICK. HOW TI FLIES! NOW WHERE IS TH BAT? IS HE LATE?"
NOPE. NOT COMING TO YOUR RESCUE AT ALL.
LET ME CHECK MY RECORDS.
YUP. HE SAVED YOU BEFORE. BUT NOT THIS TIME.
YOU NEED A MAN TO COME TO YOUR RESCUE. YOU'RE WEAK. I KNOW WHO YOU ARE.
WHAT? WHAT DO YOU KNOW ABOUT ME!?
WHY-- EVERYTHING! IT'S ALL IN MY LITTLE BLACK BOOK!
BWA-BWAAA!
BE CAREFUL WITH THAT PRECIOUS CARGO, MINIONS MINE.
I JUS THOUGHT ANOTHER TO SKI CAT.

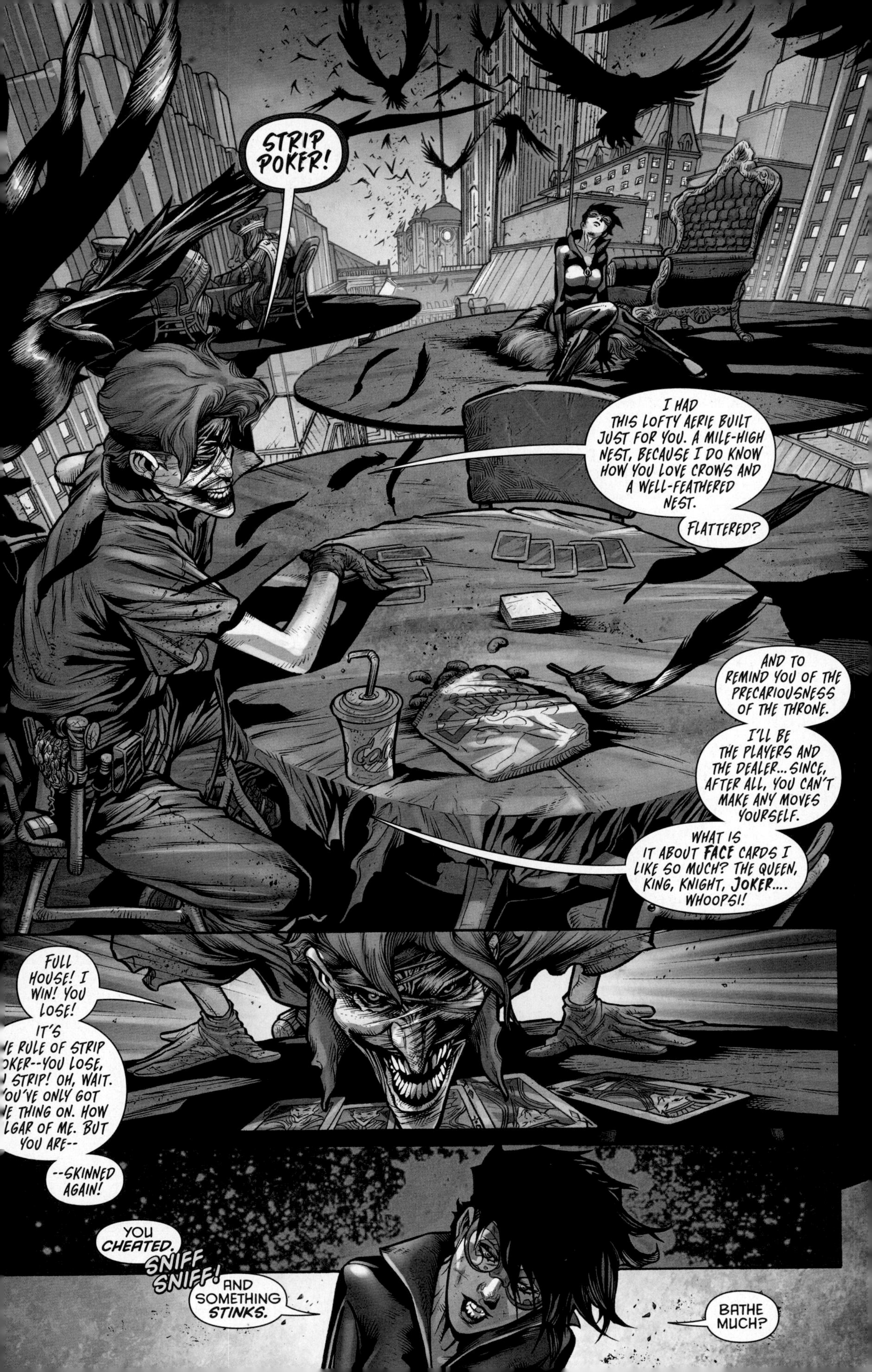
STRIP POKER!
I HAD THIS LOFTY AERIE BUILT JUST FOR YOU. A MILE-HIGH NEST, BECAUSE I DO KNOW HOW YOU LOVE CROWS AND A WELL-FEATHERED NEST.
FLATTERED?
AND TO REMIND YOU OF THE PRECARIOUSNESS OF THE THRONE.
I'LL BE THE PLAYERS AND THE DEALER... SINCE, AFTER ALL, YOU CAN'T MAKE ANY MOVES YOURSELF.
WHAT IS IT ABOUT FACE CARDS I LIKE SO MUCH? THE QUEEN, KING, KNIGHT, JOKER.... WHOOPS!
FULL HOUSE! I WIN! YOU LOSE!
IT'S
E RULE OF STRIP
OKER--YOU LOSE,
STRIP! OH, WAIT.
OU'VE ONLY GOT
E THING ON. HOW
LGAR OF ME. BUT
YOU ARE--
--SKINNED AGAIN!
YOU CHEATED.
SNIFF SNIFF!
AND SOMETHING STINKS.
BATHE MUCH?

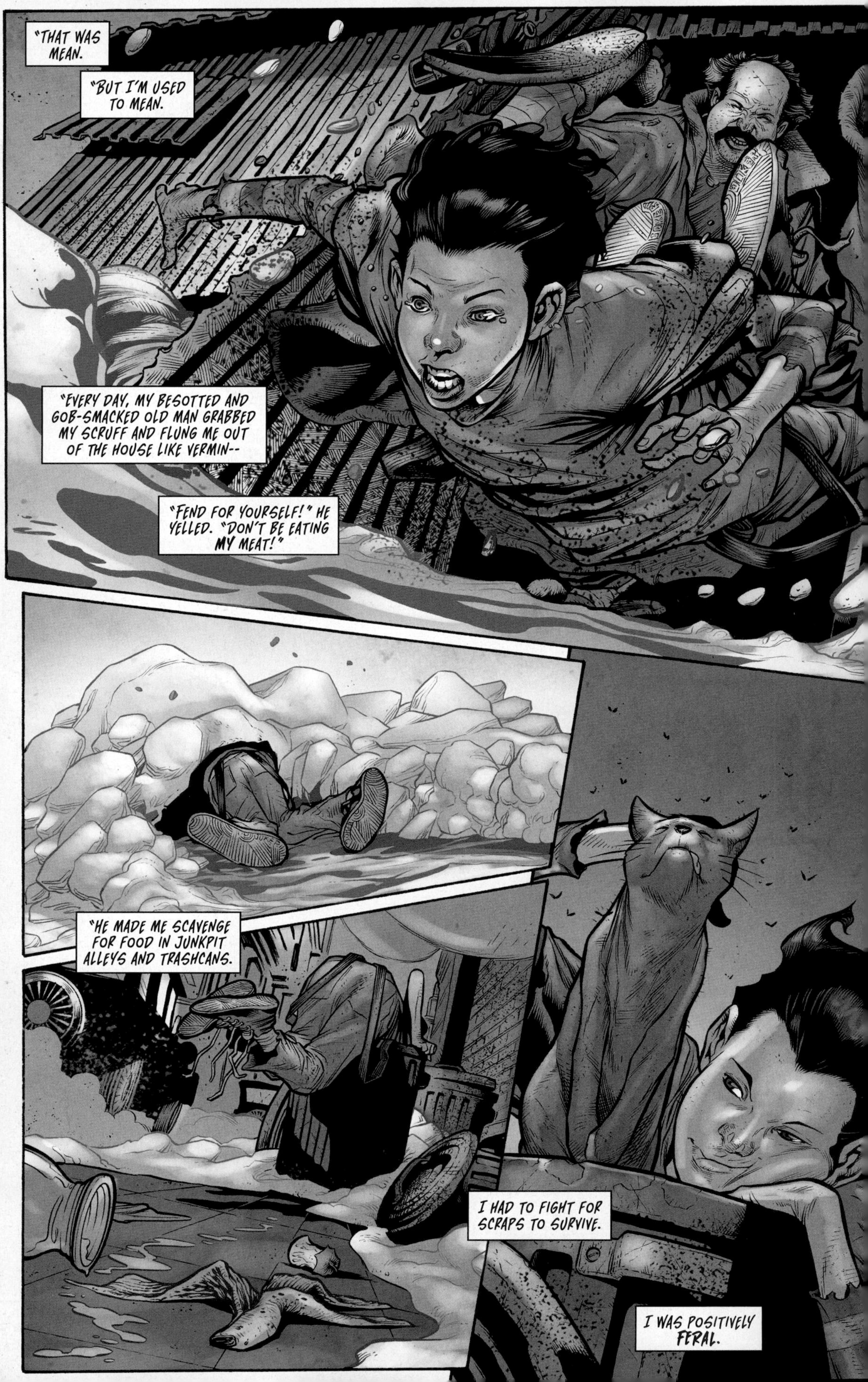
"THAT WAS MEAN.
"BUT I'M USED TO MEAN.
"EVERY DAY, MY BESOTTED AND GOB-SMACKED OLD MAN GRABBED MY SCRUFF AND FLUNG ME OUT OF THE HOUSE LIKE VERMIN--
"FEND FOR YOURSELF!" HE YELLED. "DON'T BE EATING MY MEAT!"
"HE MADE ME SCAVENGE FOR FOOD IN JUNKPIT ALLEYS AND TRASHCANS.
I HAD TO FIGHT FOR SCRAPS TO SURVIVE.
I WAS POSITIVELY FERAL.

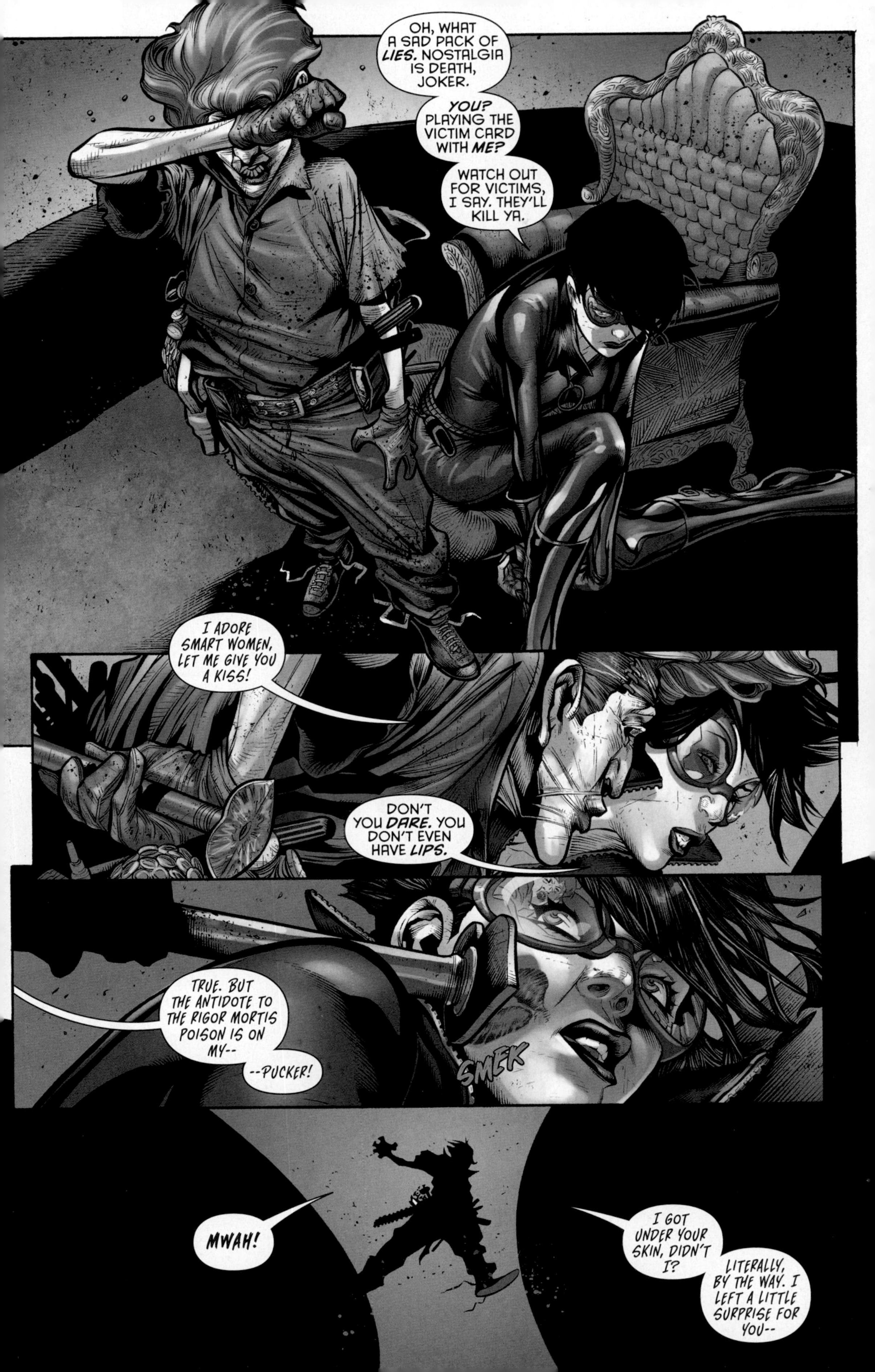

OH, WHAT A SAD PACK OF LIES. NOSTALGIA IS DEATH, JOKER.
YOU? PLAYING THE VICTIM CARD WITH ME?
WATCH OUT FOR VICTIMS, I SAY. THEY'LL KILL YA.
I ADORE SMART WOMEN, LET ME GIVE YOU A KISS!
DON'T YOU DARE. YOU DON'T EVEN HAVE LIPS.
TRUE. BUT THE ANTIDOTE TO THE RIGOR MORTIS POISON IS ON MY--
--PUCKER!
SMEK
MWAH!
I GOT UNDER YOUR SKIN, DIDN'T I?
LITERALLY, BY THE WAY. I LEFT A LITTLE SURPRISE FOR YOU--

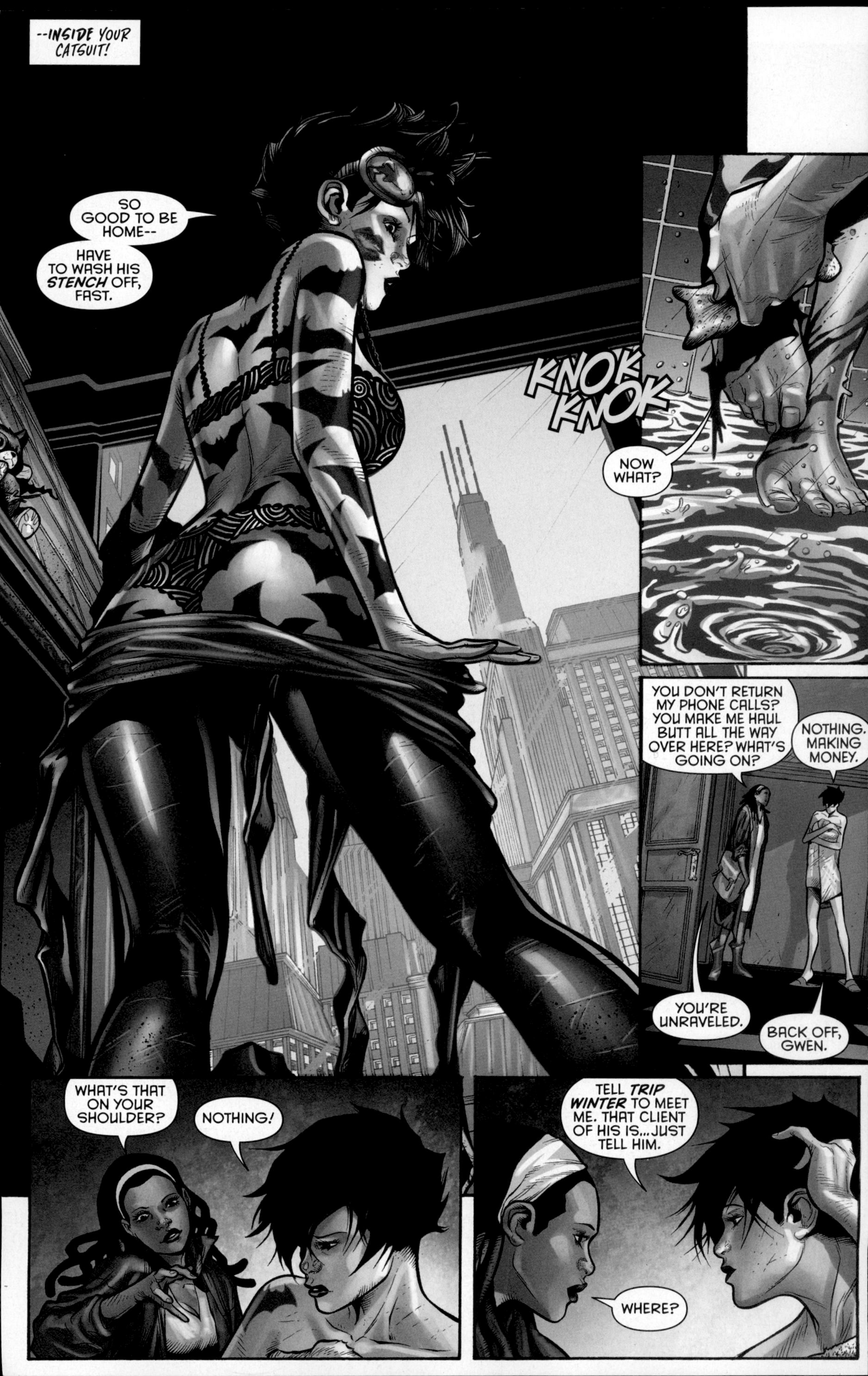
--INSIDE YOUR CATSUIT!
SO GOOD TO BE HOME--
HAVE TO WASH HIS STENCH OFF, FAST.
KNOK KNOK
NOW WHAT?
YOU DON'T RETURN MY PHONE CALLS? YOU MAKE ME HAUL BUTT ALL THE WAY OVER HERE? WHAT'S GOING ON?
NOTHING. MAKING MONEY.
YOU'RE UNRAVELED.
BACK OFF, GWEN.
WHAT'S THAT ON YOUR SHOULDER?
NOTHING!
TELL TRIP WINTER TO MEET ME. THAT CLIENT OF HIS IS...JUST TELL HIM.
WHERE?

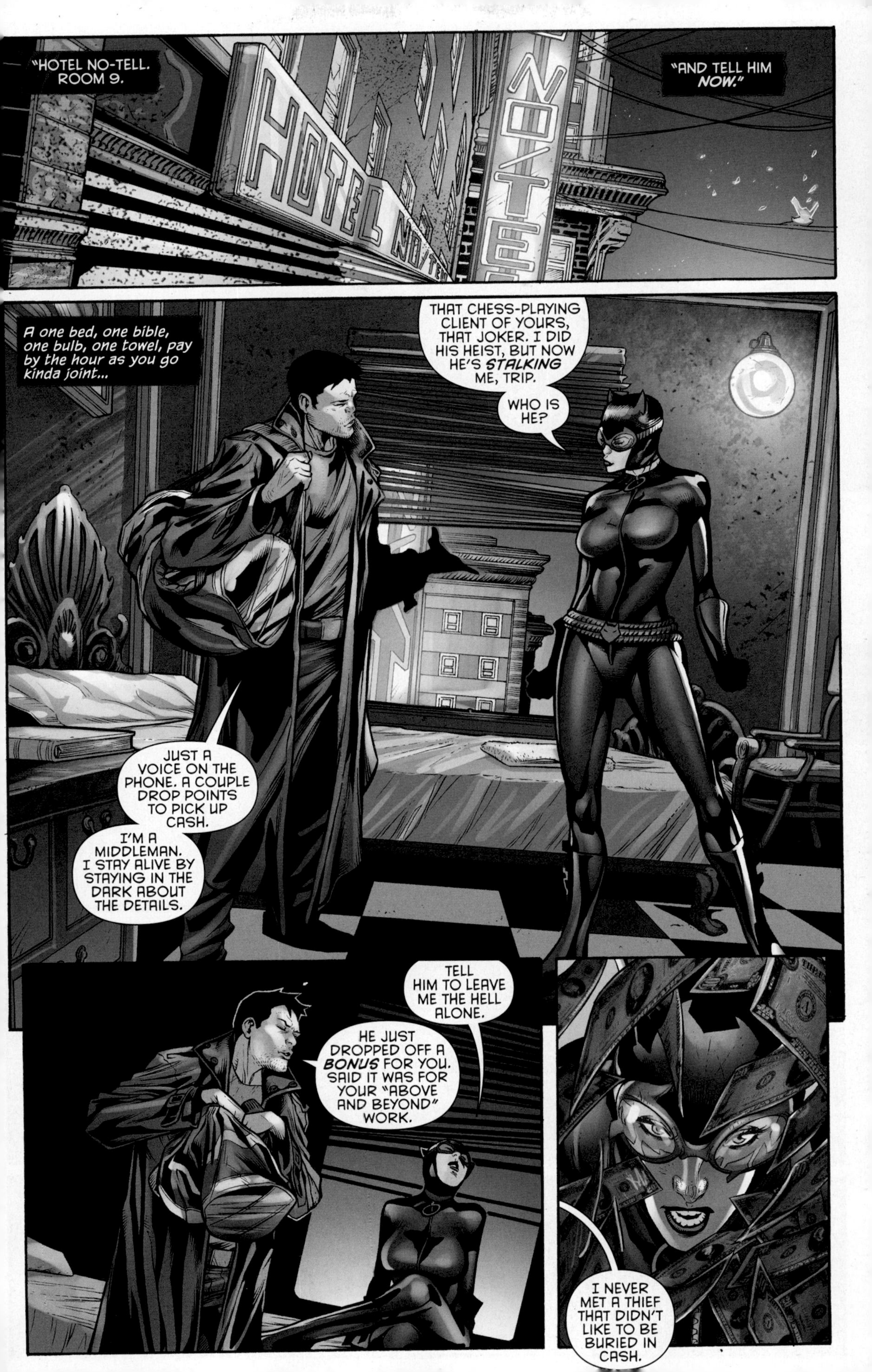
"HOTEL NO-TELL. ROOM 9.
"AND TELL HIM NOW."
A one bed, one bible, one bulb, one towel, pay by the hour as you go kinda joint...
THAT CHESS-PLAYING CLIENT OF YOURS, THAT JOKER. I DID HIS HEIST, BUT NOW HE'S STALKING ME, TRIP.
WHO IS HE?
JUST A VOICE ON THE PHONE. A COUPLE DROP POINTS TO PICK UP CASH.
I'M A MIDDLEMAN. I STAY ALIVE BY STAYING IN THE DARK ABOUT THE DETAILS.
TELL HIM TO LEAVE ME THE HELL ALONE.
HE JUST DROPPED OFF A BONUS FOR YOU. SAID IT WAS FOR YOUR "ABOVE AND BEYOND" WORK.
I NEVER MET A THIEF THAT DIDN'T LIKE TO BE BURIED IN CASH.

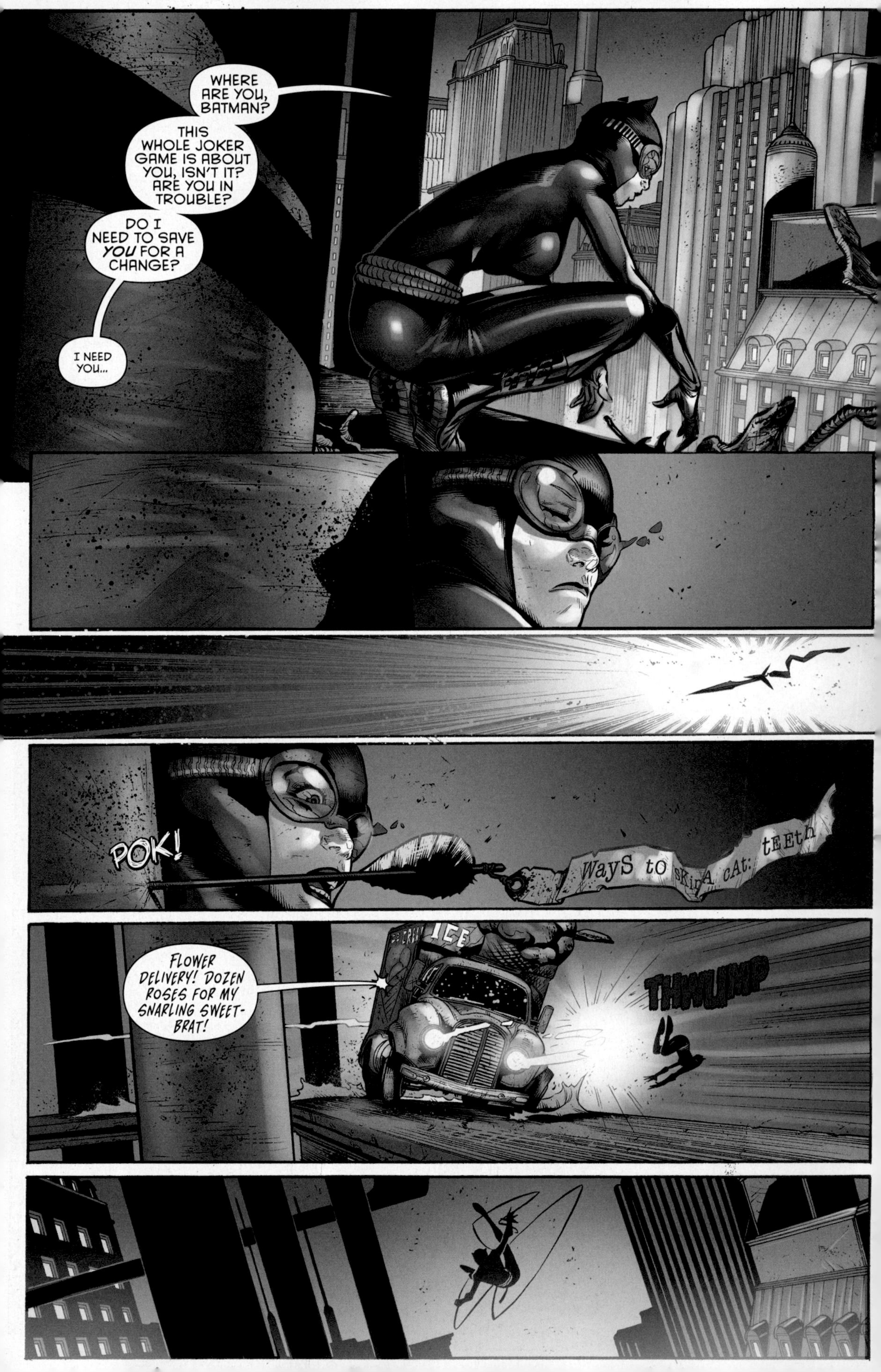
WHERE ARE YOU, BATMAN?
THIS WHOLE JOKER GAME IS ABOUT YOU, ISN'T IT? ARE YOU IN TROUBLE?
DO I NEED TO SAVE *YOU* FOR A CHANGE?
I NEED YOU...
POK!
WayS to skin A cAt: tEEth
FLOWER DELIVERY! DOZEN ROSES FOR MY SNARLING SWEET-BRAT!
ICE
THWUMP

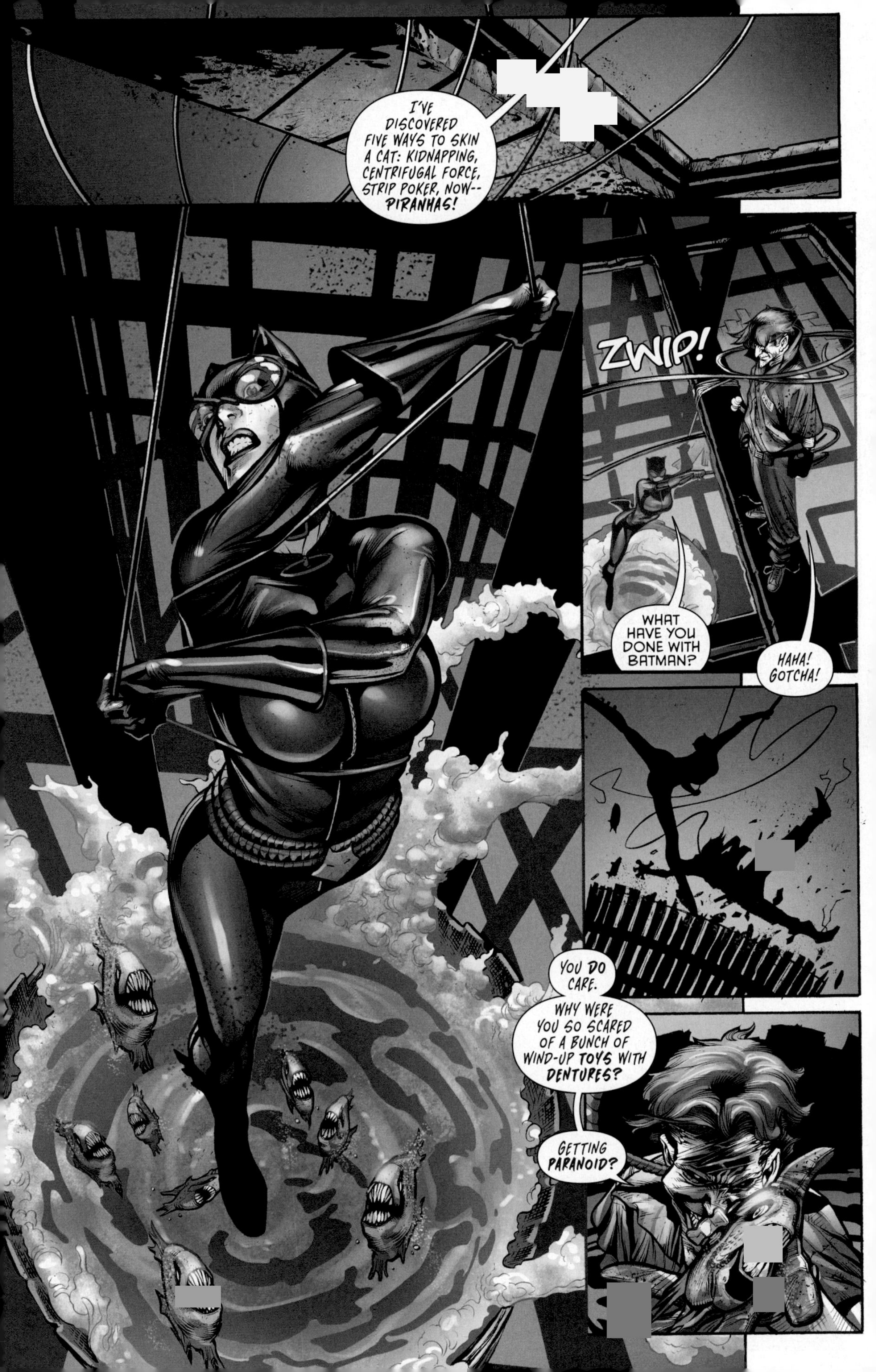

I'VE DISCOVERED FIVE WAYS TO SKIN A CAT: KIDNAPPING, CENTRIFUGAL FORCE, STRIP POKER, NOW-- PIRANHAS!
ZWIP!
WHAT HAVE YOU DONE WITH BATMAN?
HAHA! GOTCHA!
YOU DO CARE.
WHY WERE YOU SO SCARED OF A BUNCH OF WIND-UP TOYS WITH DENTURES?
GETTING PARANOID?

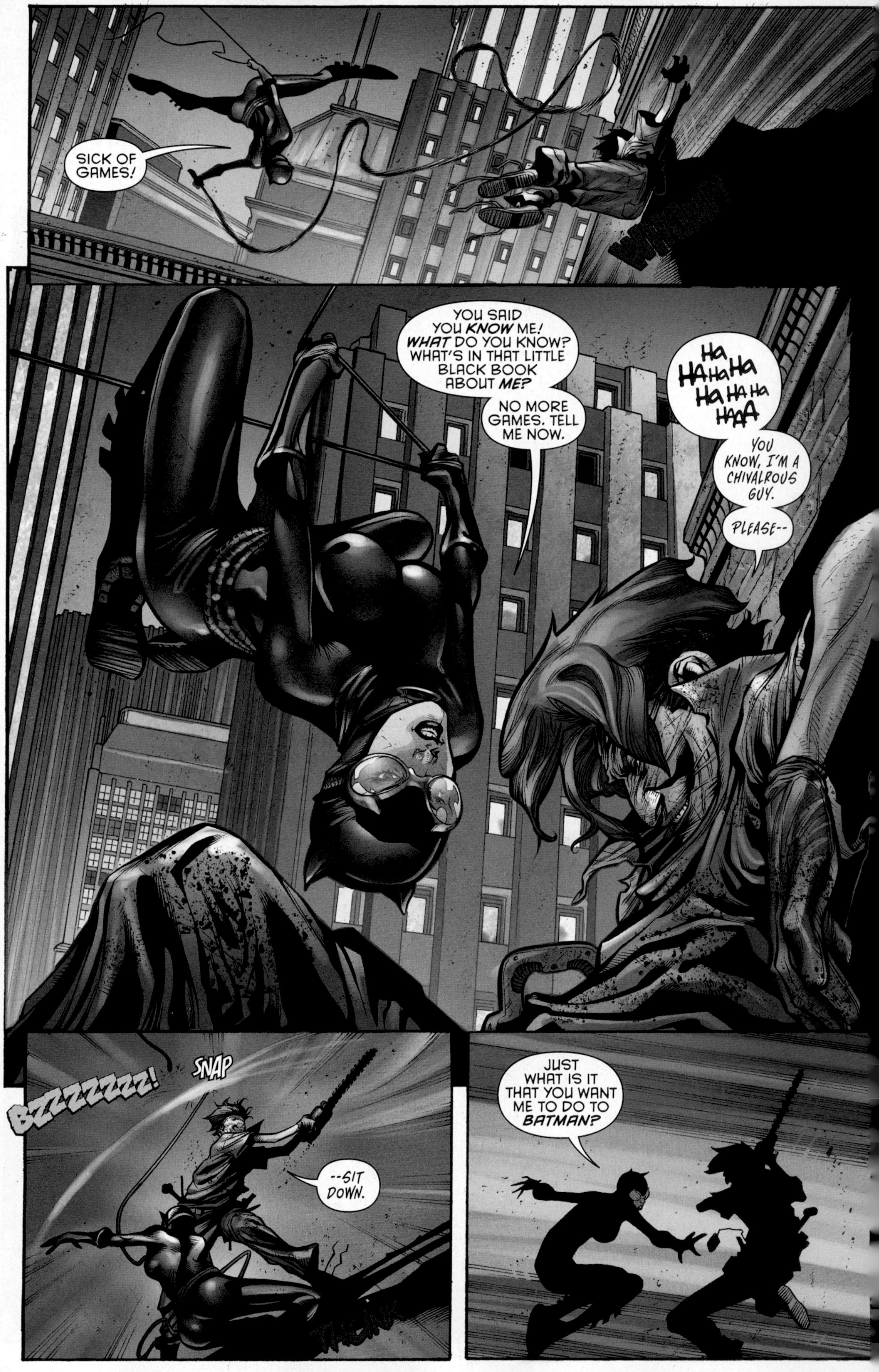
SICK OF GAMES!
YOU SAID YOU KNOW ME! WHAT DO YOU KNOW? WHAT'S IN THAT LITTLE BLACK BOOK ABOUT ME?
NO MORE GAMES. TELL ME NOW.
Ha HAHaHa HaHaHa HAAA
YOU KNOW, I'M A CHIVALROUS GUY.
PLEASE--
BZZZZZZZ!
SNAP
--SIT DOWN.
JUST WHAT IS IT THAT YOU WANT ME TO DO TO BATMAN?

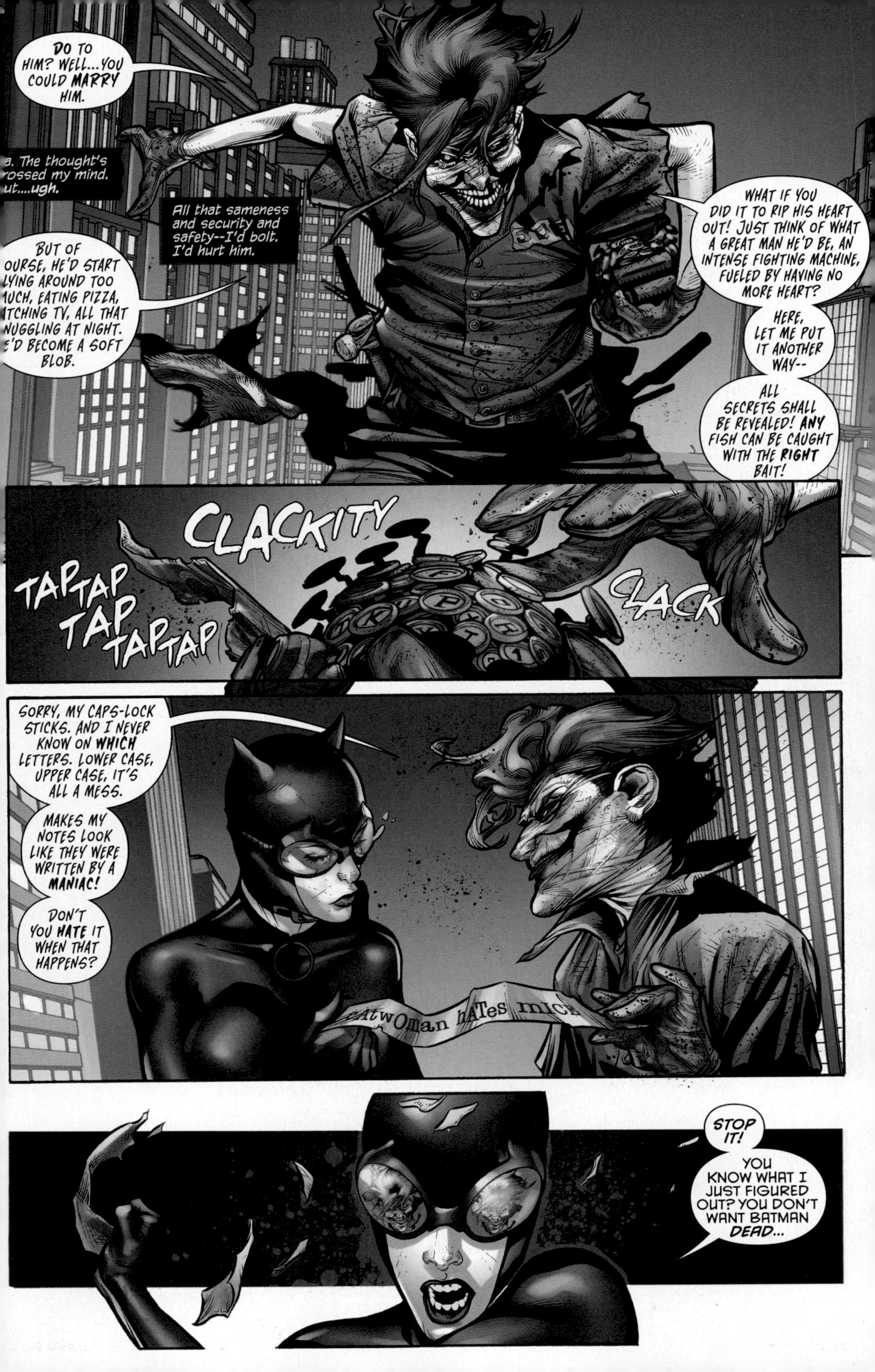
DO TO HIM? WELL...YOU COULD MARRY HIM.
a. The thought's rossed my mind. ut....ugh.
All that sameness and security and safety--I'd bolt. I'd hurt him.
BUT OF OURSE, HE'D START LYING AROUND TOO UCH, EATING PIZZA, TCHING TV, ALL THAT NUGGLING AT NIGHT. E'D BECOME A SOFT BLOB.
WHAT IF YOU DID IT TO RIP HIS HEART OUT! JUST THINK OF WHAT A GREAT MAN HE'D BE, AN INTENSE FIGHTING MACHINE, FUELED BY HAVING NO MORE HEART?
HERE, LET ME PUT IT ANOTHER WAY--
ALL SECRETS SHALL BE REVEALED! ANY FISH CAN BE CAUGHT WITH THE RIGHT BAIT!
CLACKITY
TAP TAP TAP TAP TAP
CLACK
SORRY, MY CAPS-LOCK STICKS. AND I NEVER KNOW ON WHICH LETTERS. LOWER CASE, UPPER CASE, IT'S ALL A MESS.
MAKES MY NOTES LOOK LIKE THEY WERE WRITTEN BY A MANIAC!
DON'T YOU HATE IT WHEN THAT HAPPENS?
cAtwOman hATes mICE
STOP IT!
YOU KNOW WHAT I JUST FIGURED OUT? YOU DON'T WANT BATMAN DEAD...

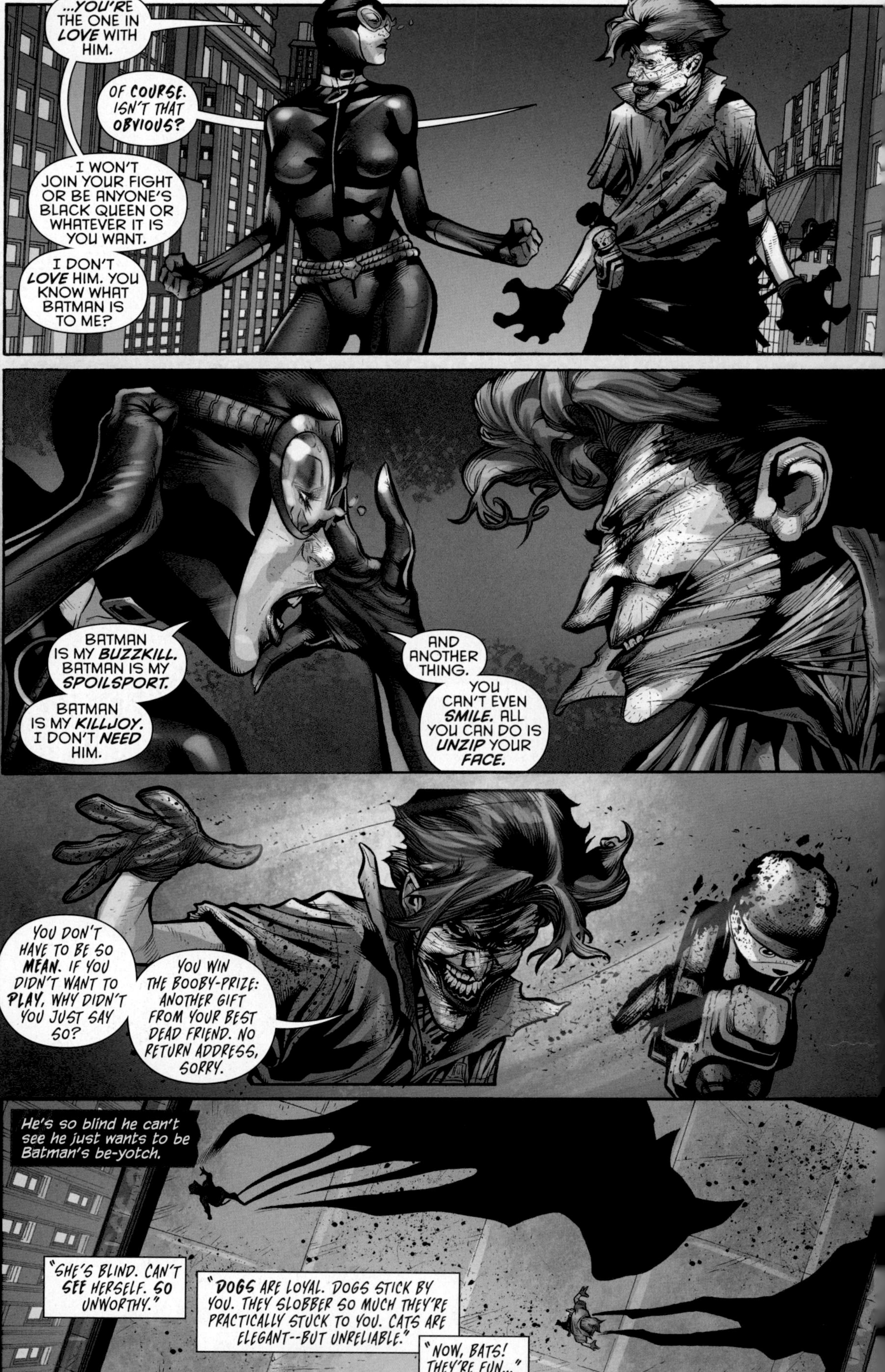
...YOU'RE THE ONE IN LOVE WITH HIM.
OF COURSE. ISN'T THAT OBVIOUS?
I WON'T JOIN YOUR FIGHT OR BE ANYONE'S BLACK QUEEN OR WHATEVER IT IS YOU WANT.
I DON'T LOVE HIM. YOU KNOW WHAT BATMAN IS TO ME?
BATMAN IS MY BUZZKILL. BATMAN IS MY SPOILSPORT.
BATMAN IS MY KILLJOY. I DON'T NEED HIM.
AND ANOTHER THING.
YOU CAN'T EVEN SMILE. ALL YOU CAN DO IS UNZIP YOUR FACE.
YOU DON'T HAVE TO BE SO MEAN. IF YOU DIDN'T WANT TO PLAY, WHY DIDN'T YOU JUST SAY SO?
YOU WIN THE BOOBY-PRIZE: ANOTHER GIFT FROM YOUR BEST DEAD FRIEND. NO RETURN ADDRESS, SORRY.
He's so blind he can't see he just wants to be Batman's be-yotch.
"SHE'S BLIND. CAN'T SEE HERSELF. SO UNWORTHY."
"DOGS ARE LOYAL. DOGS STICK BY YOU. THEY SLOBBER SO MUCH THEY'RE PRACTICALLY STUCK TO YOU. CATS ARE ELEGANT--BUT UNRELIABLE."
"NOW, BATS! THEY'RE FUN..."

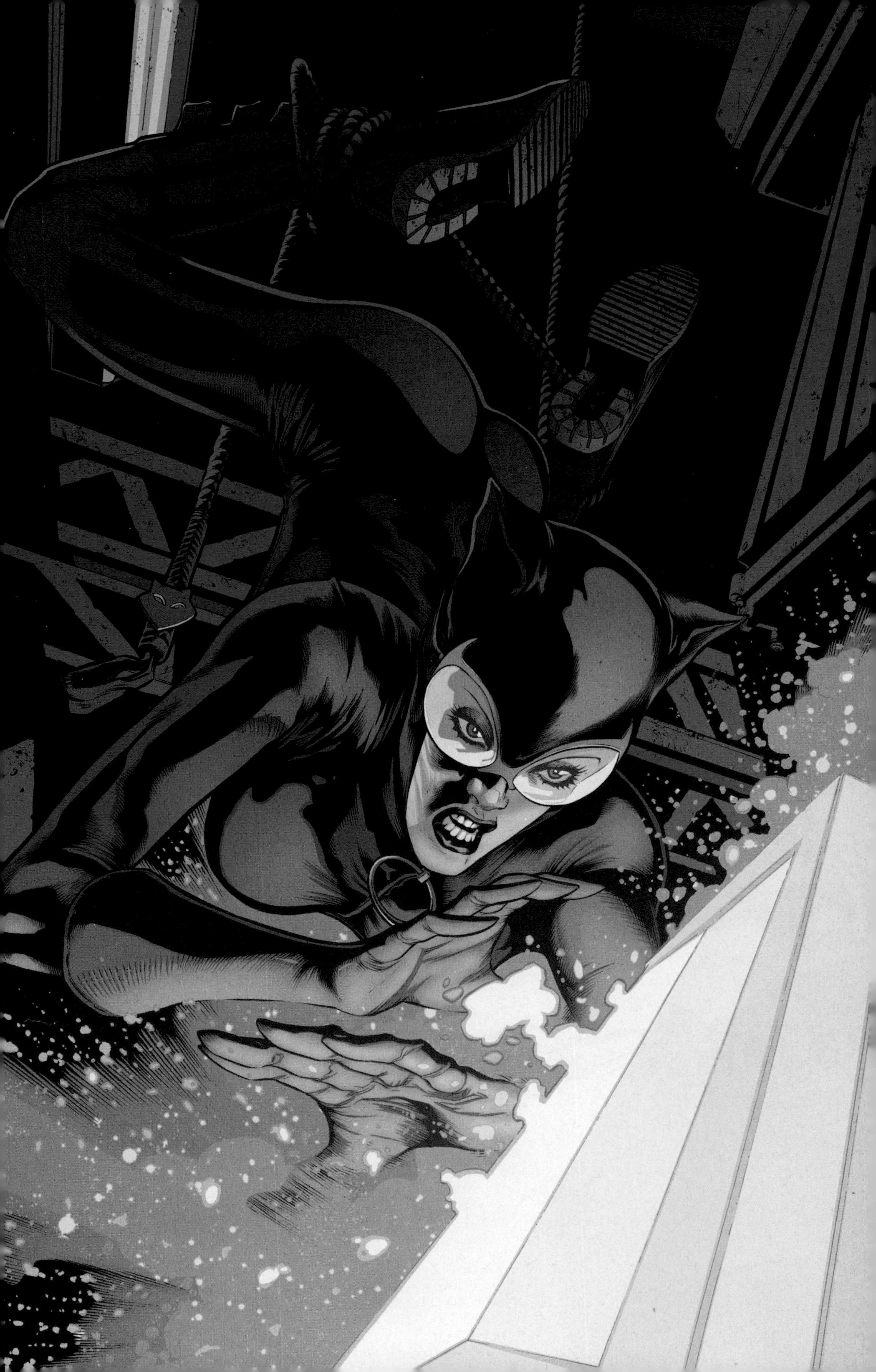

ANN NOCENTI writer RAFA SANDOVAL penciler JORDI TARRAGONA inker cover by RAFA SANDOVAL & JORDI TARRAGONA

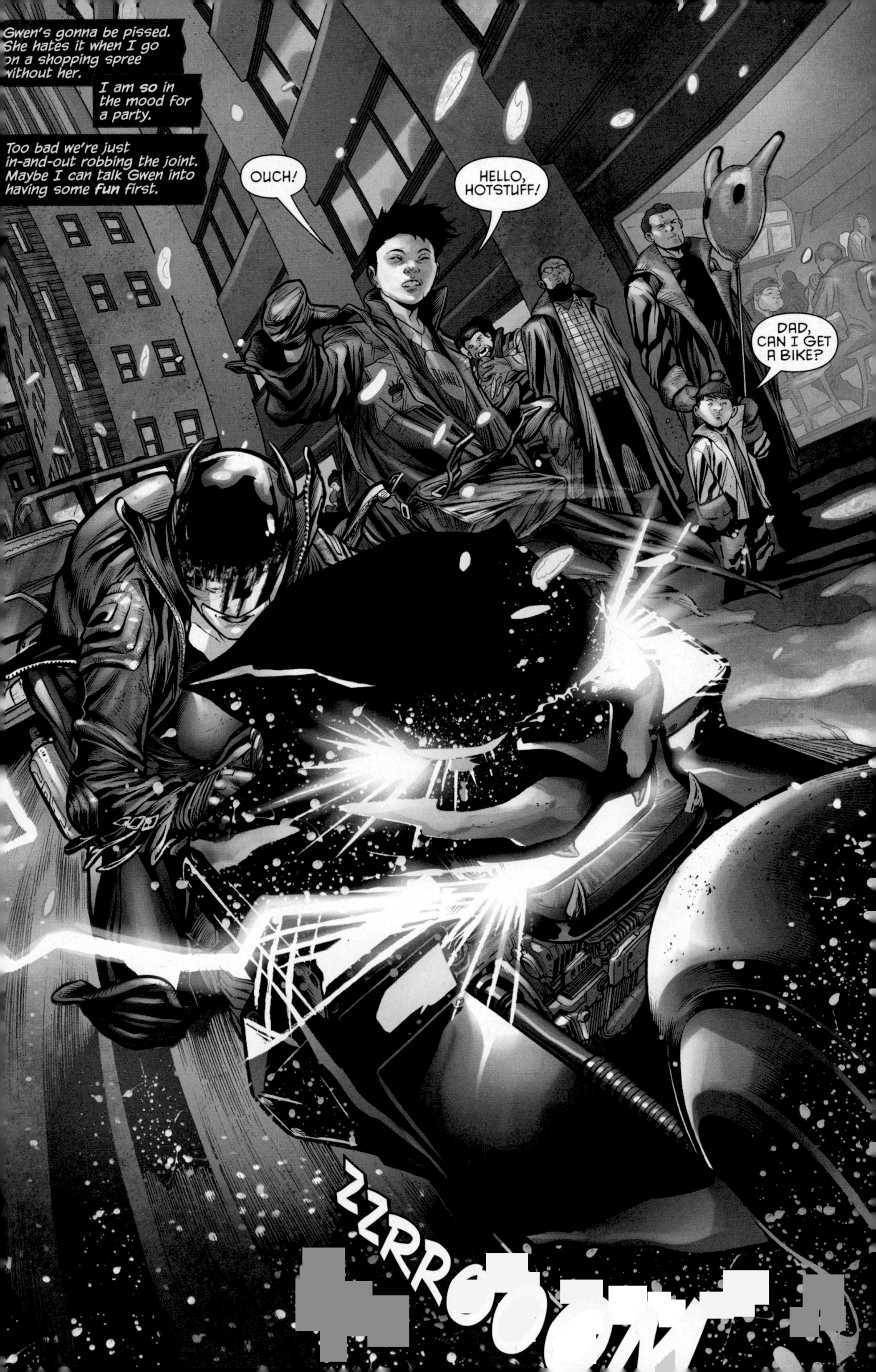
Gwen's gonna be pissed. She hates it when I go on a shopping spree without her.
I am so in the mood for a party.
Too bad we're just in-and-out robbing the joint. Maybe I can talk Gwen into having some **fun** first.
OUCH!
HELLO, HOTSTUFF!
DAD, CAN I GET A BIKE?
ZZRROOOM

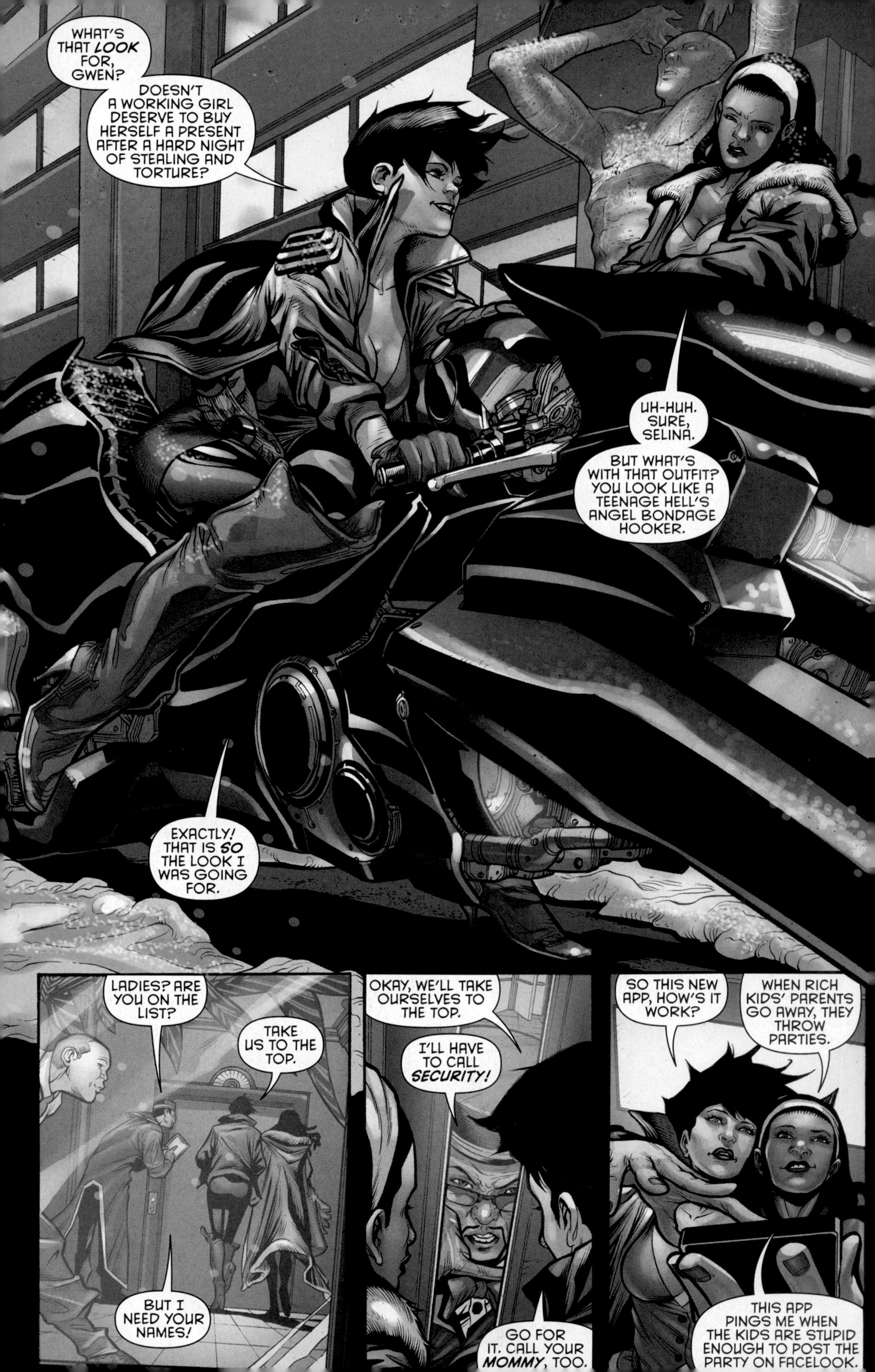
WHAT'S THAT LOOK FOR, GWEN?
DOESN'T A WORKING GIRL DESERVE TO BUY HERSELF A PRESENT AFTER A HARD NIGHT OF STEALING AND TORTURE?
UH-HUH. SURE, SELINA.
BUT WHAT'S WITH THAT OUTFIT? YOU LOOK LIKE A TEENAGE HELL'S ANGEL BONDAGE HOOKER.
EXACTLY! THAT IS SO THE LOOK I WAS GOING FOR.
LADIES? ARE YOU ON THE LIST?
TAKE US TO THE TOP.
BUT I NEED YOUR NAMES!
OKAY, WE'LL TAKE OURSELVES TO THE TOP.
I'LL HAVE TO CALL SECURITY!
GO FOR IT. CALL YOUR MOMMY, TOO.
SO THIS NEW APP, HOW'S IT WORK?
WHEN RICH KIDS' PARENTS GO AWAY, THEY THROW PARTIES.
THIS APP PINGS ME WHEN THE KIDS ARE STUPID ENOUGH TO POST THE PARTY ON FACELOOK.

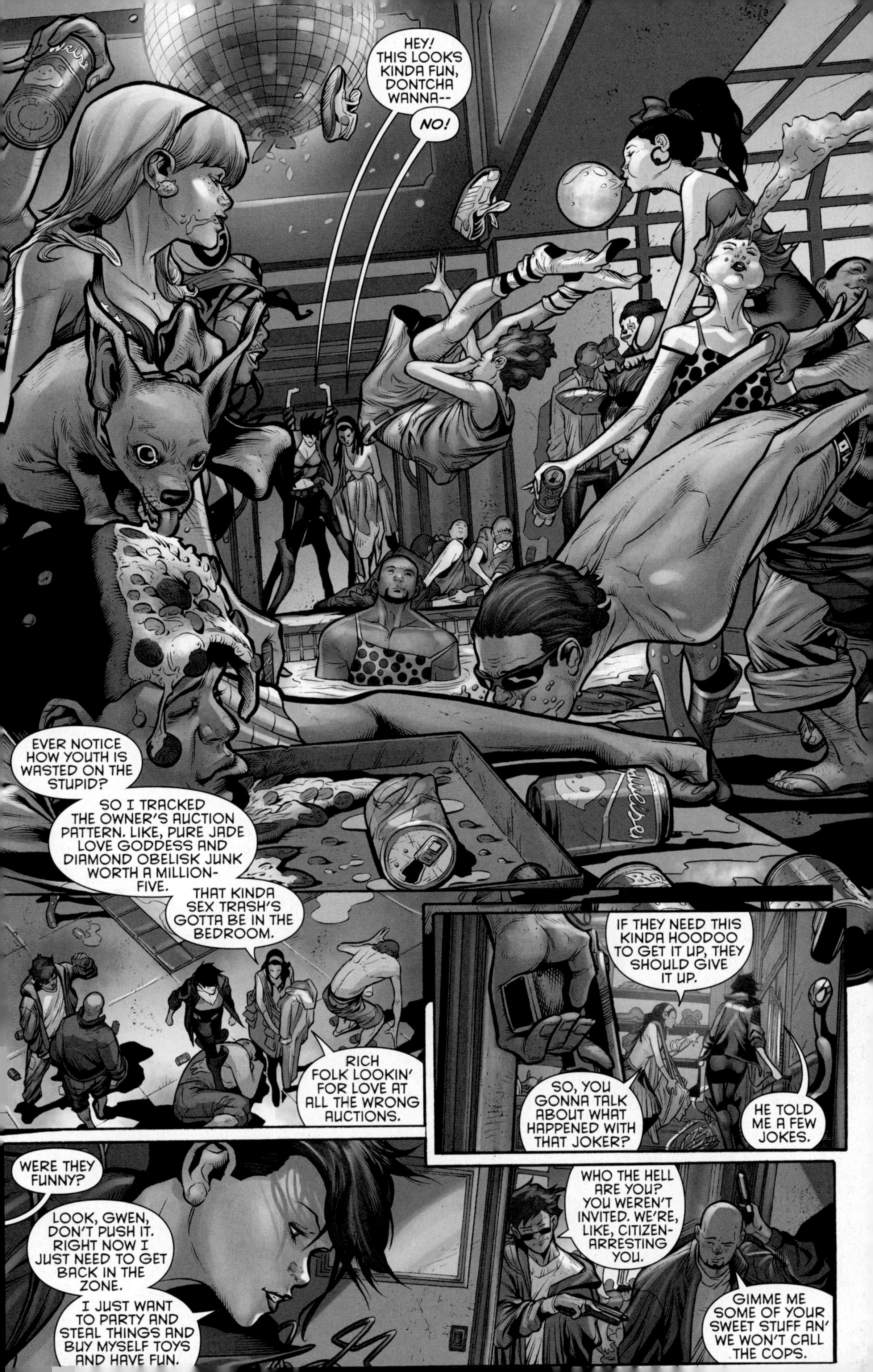
HEY! THIS LOOKS KINDA FUN, DONTCHA WANNA--
NO!
EVER NOTICE HOW YOUTH IS WASTED ON THE STUPID?
SO I TRACKED THE OWNER'S AUCTION PATTERN. LIKE, PURE JADE LOVE GODDESS AND DIAMOND OBELISK JUNK WORTH A MILLION-FIVE.
THAT KINDA SEX TRASH'S GOTTA BE IN THE BEDROOM.
RICH FOLK LOOKIN' FOR LOVE AT ALL THE WRONG AUCTIONS.
IF THEY NEED THIS KINDA HOODOO TO GET IT UP, THEY SHOULD GIVE IT UP.
SO, YOU GONNA TALK ABOUT WHAT HAPPENED WITH THAT JOKER?
HE TOLD ME A FEW JOKES.
WERE THEY FUNNY?
LOOK, GWEN, DON'T PUSH IT. RIGHT NOW I JUST NEED TO GET BACK IN THE ZONE.
I JUST WANT TO PARTY AND STEAL THINGS AND BUY MYSELF TOYS AND HAVE FUN.
WHO THE HELL ARE YOU? YOU WEREN'T INVITED. WE'RE, LIKE, CITIZEN-ARRESTING YOU.
GIMME ME SOME OF YOUR SWEET STUFF AN' WE WON'T CALL THE COPS.

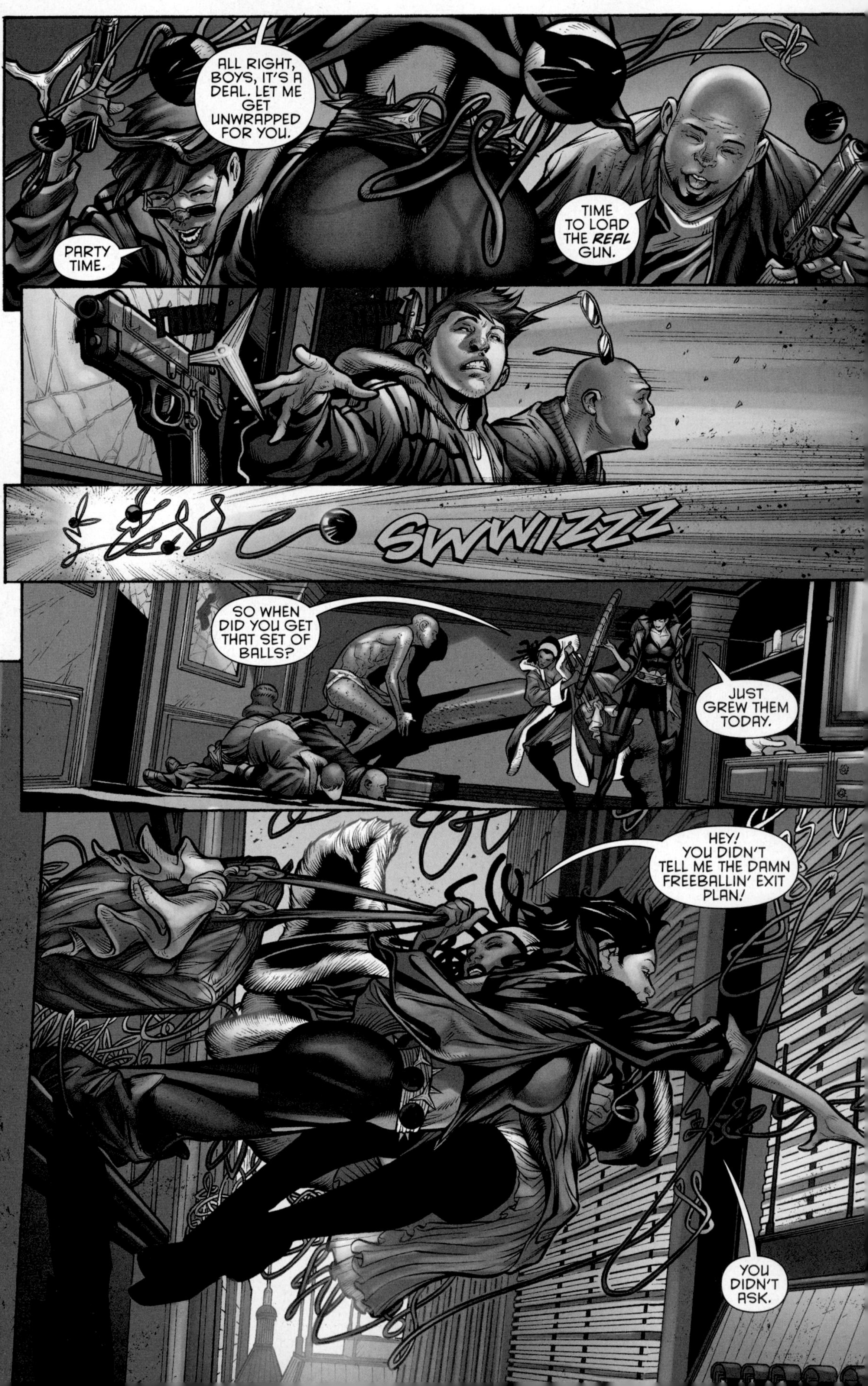
ALL RIGHT, BOYS, IT'S A DEAL. LET ME GET UNWRAPPED FOR YOU.
PARTY TIME.
TIME TO LOAD THE *REAL* GUN.
SWWIZZZ
SO WHEN DID YOU GET THAT SET OF BALLS?
JUST GREW THEM TODAY.
HEY! YOU DIDN'T TELL ME THE DAMN FREEBALLIN' EXIT PLAN!
YOU DIDN'T ASK.

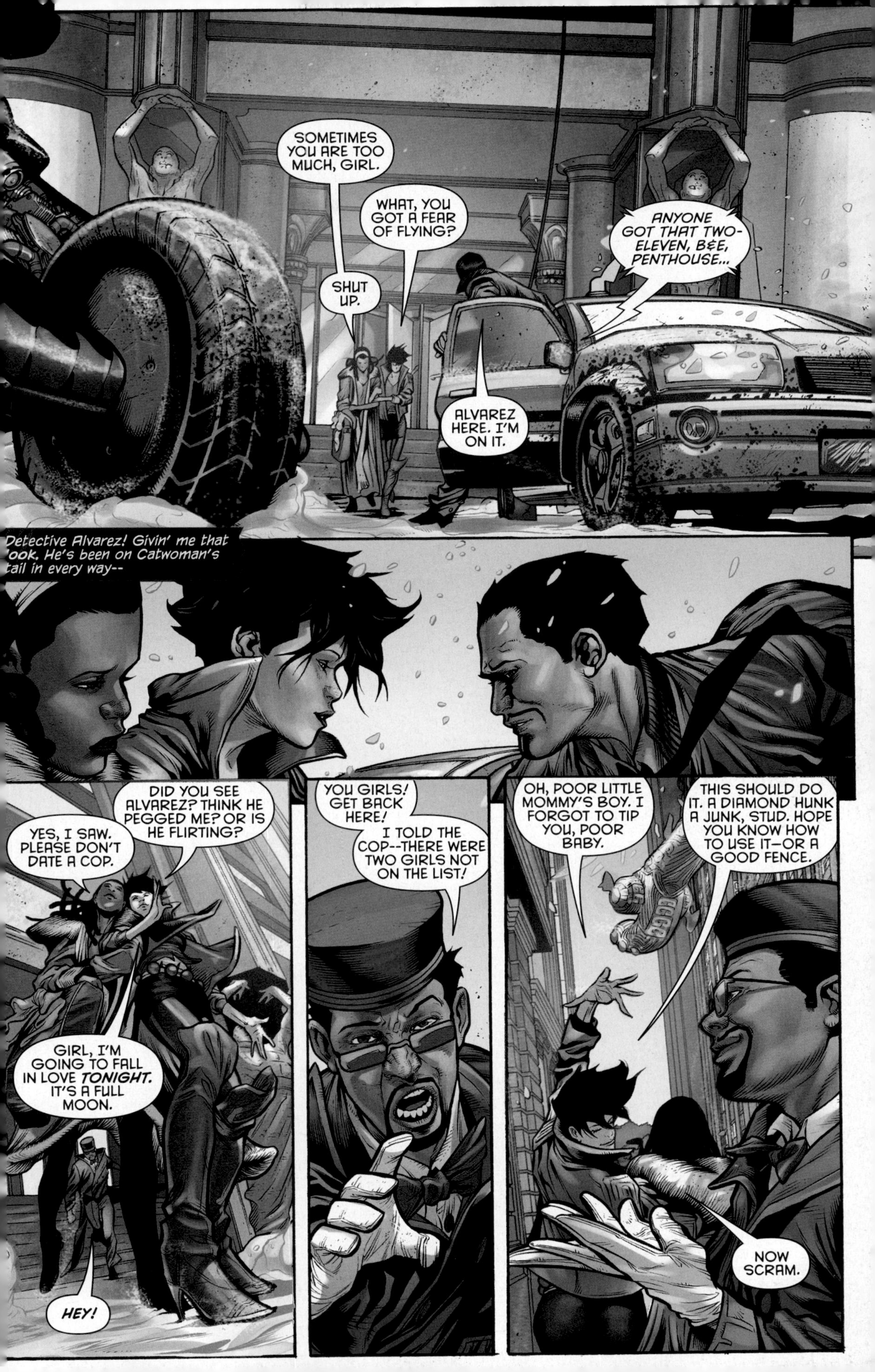
SOMETIMES YOU ARE TOO MUCH, GIRL.
WHAT, YOU GOT A FEAR OF FLYING?
SHUT UP.
ANYONE GOT THAT TWO-ELEVEN, B&E, PENTHOUSE...
ALVAREZ HERE. I'M ON IT.
Detective Alvarez! Givin' me that look. He's been on Catwoman's tail in every way--
DID YOU SEE ALVAREZ? THINK HE PEGGED ME? OR IS HE FLIRTING?
YES, I SAW. PLEASE DON'T DATE A COP.
GIRL, I'M GOING TO FALL IN LOVE TONIGHT. IT'S A FULL MOON.
HEY!
YOU GIRLS! GET BACK HERE!
I TOLD THE COP--THERE WERE TWO GIRLS NOT ON THE LIST!
OH, POOR LITTLE MOMMY'S BOY. I FORGOT TO TIP YOU, POOR BABY.
THIS SHOULD DO IT. A DIAMOND HUNK A JUNK, STUD. HOPE YOU KNOW HOW TO USE IT--OR A GOOD FENCE.
NOW SCRAM.

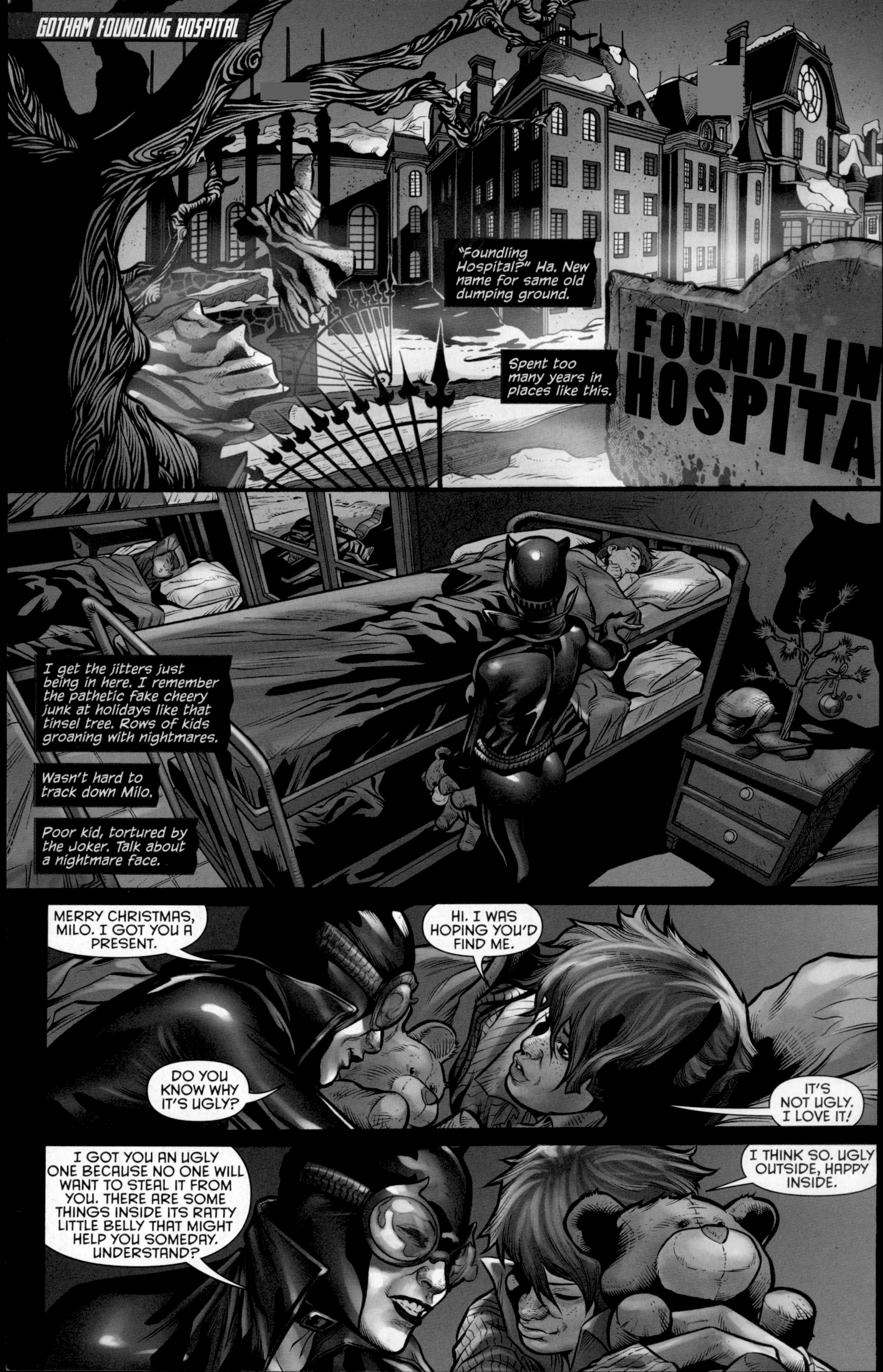
GOTHAM FOUNDLING HOSPITAL
"Foundling Hospital?" Ha. New name for same old dumping ground.
FOUNDLIN HOSPITA
Spent too many years in places like this.
I get the jitters just being in here. I remember the pathetic fake cheery junk at holidays like that tinsel tree. Rows of kids groaning with nightmares.
Wasn't hard to track down Milo.
Poor kid, tortured by the Joker. Talk about a nightmare face.
MERRY CHRISTMAS, MILO. I GOT YOU A PRESENT.
HI. I WAS HOPING YOU'D FIND ME.
DO YOU KNOW WHY IT'S UGLY?
IT'S NOT UGLY. I LOVE IT!
I GOT YOU AN UGLY ONE BECAUSE NO ONE WILL WANT TO STEAL IT FROM YOU. THERE ARE SOME THINGS INSIDE ITS RATTY LITTLE BELLY THAT MIGHT HELP YOU SOMEDAY. UNDERSTAND?
I THINK SO. UGLY OUTSIDE, HAPPY INSIDE.

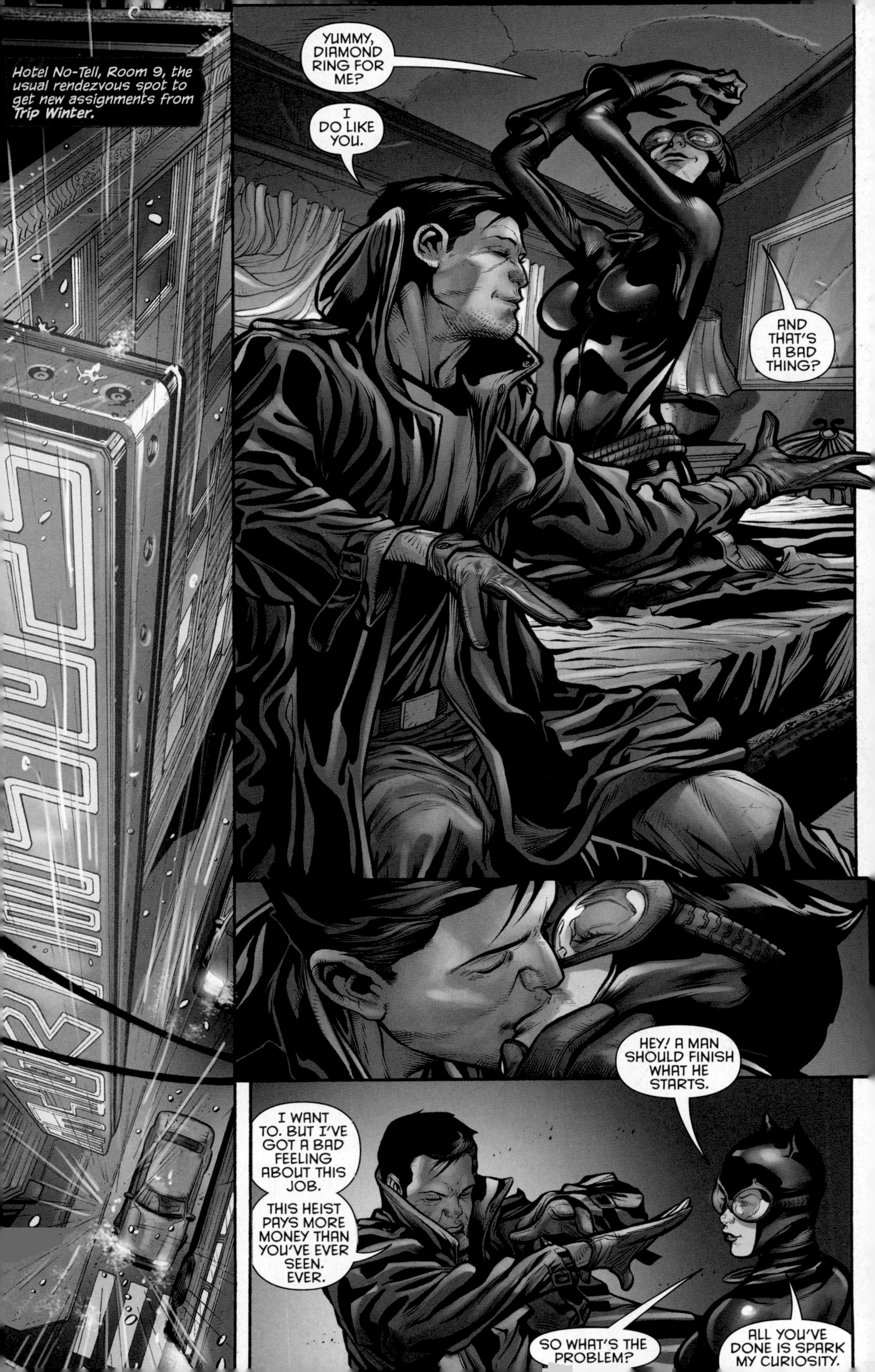

Hotel No-Tell, Room 9, the usual rendezvous spot to get new assignments from Trip Winter.
YUMMY, DIAMOND RING FOR ME?
I DO LIKE YOU.
AND THAT'S A BAD THING?
HEY! A MAN SHOULD FINISH WHAT HE STARTS.
I WANT TO. BUT I'VE GOT A BAD FEELING ABOUT THIS JOB.
THIS HEIST PAYS MORE MONEY THAN YOU'VE EVER SEEN. EVER.
SO WHAT'S THE PROBLEM?
ALL YOU'VE DONE IS SPARK MY CURIOSITY.

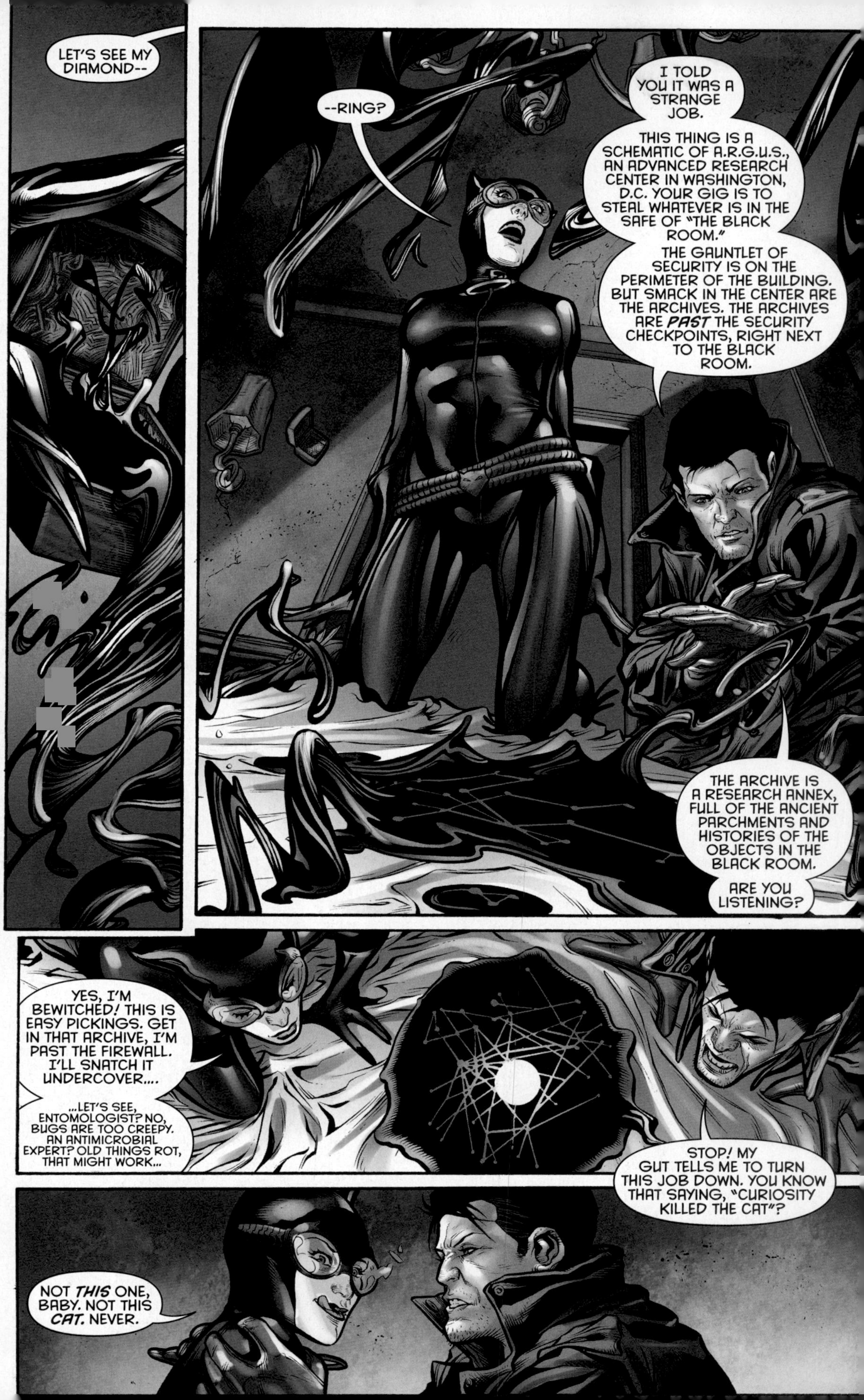
LET'S SEE MY DIAMOND--
--RING?
I TOLD YOU IT WAS A STRANGE JOB.
THIS THING IS A SCHEMATIC OF A.R.G.U.S., AN ADVANCED RESEARCH CENTER IN WASHINGTON, D.C. YOUR GIG IS TO STEAL WHATEVER IS IN THE SAFE OF "THE BLACK ROOM."
THE GAUNTLET OF SECURITY IS ON THE PERIMETER OF THE BUILDING. BUT SMACK IN THE CENTER ARE THE ARCHIVES. THE ARCHIVES ARE PAST THE SECURITY CHECKPOINTS, RIGHT NEXT TO THE BLACK ROOM.
THE ARCHIVE IS A RESEARCH ANNEX, FULL OF THE ANCIENT PARCHMENTS AND HISTORIES OF THE OBJECTS IN THE BLACK ROOM.
ARE YOU LISTENING?
YES, I'M BEWITCHED! THIS IS EASY PICKINGS. GET IN THAT ARCHIVE, I'M PAST THE FIREWALL. I'LL SNATCH IT UNDERCOVER....
...LET'S SEE, ENTOMOLOGIST? NO, BUGS ARE TOO CREEPY. AN ANTIMICROBIAL EXPERT? OLD THINGS ROT, THAT MIGHT WORK...
STOP! MY GUT TELLS ME TO TURN THIS JOB DOWN. YOU KNOW THAT SAYING, "CURIOSITY KILLED THE CAT"?
NOT THIS ONE, BABY. NOT THIS CAT. NEVER.

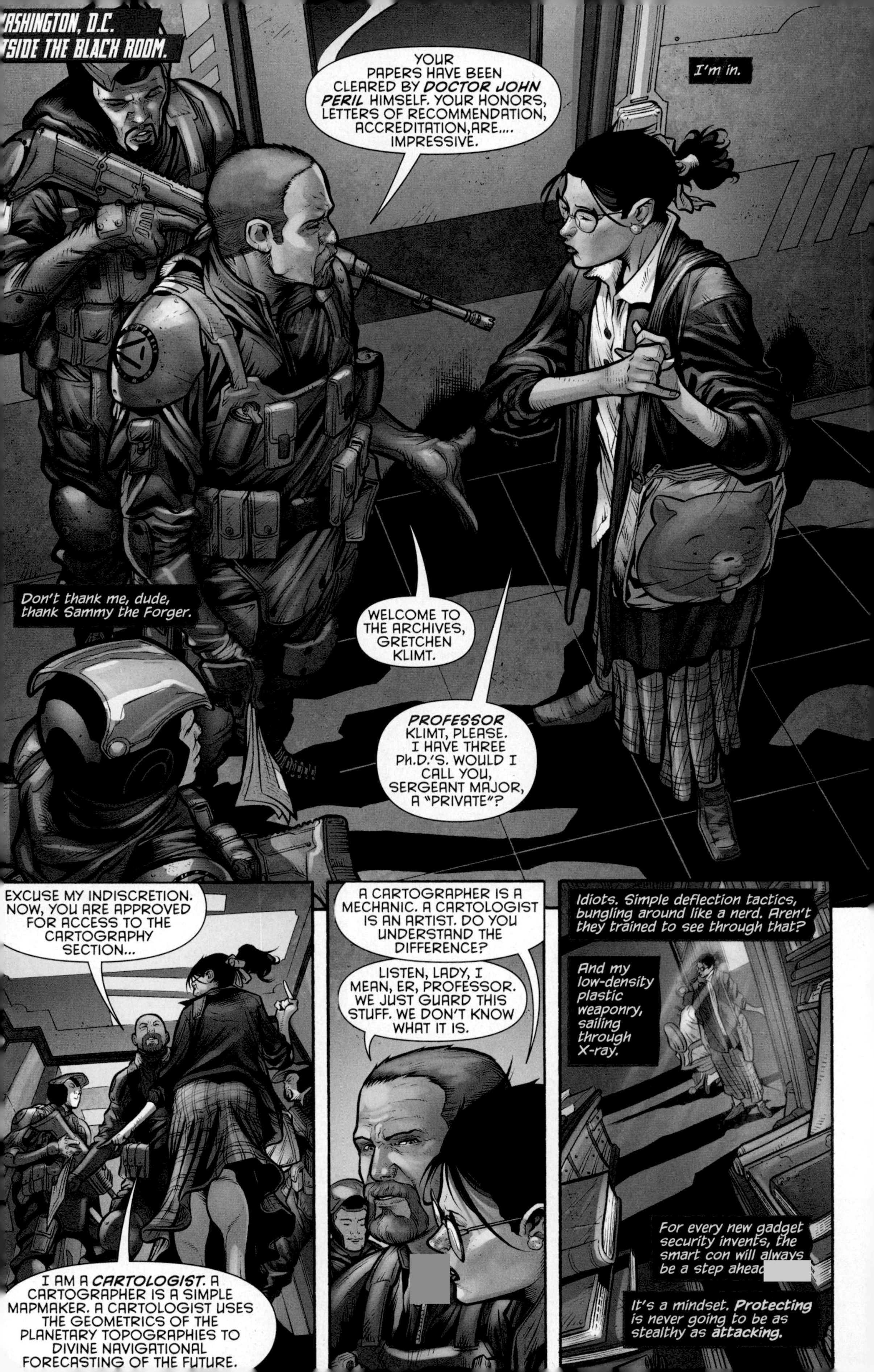
ASHINGTON, D.C.
TSIDE THE BLACK ROOM.
YOUR PAPERS HAVE BEEN CLEARED BY DOCTOR JOHN PERIL HIMSELF. YOUR HONORS, LETTERS OF RECOMMENDATION, ACCREDITATION, ARE.... IMPRESSIVE.
I'm in.
Don't thank me, dude, thank Sammy the Forger.
WELCOME TO THE ARCHIVES, GRETCHEN KLIMT.
PROFESSOR KLIMT, PLEASE. I HAVE THREE Ph.D.'S. WOULD I CALL YOU, SERGEANT MAJOR, A "PRIVATE"?
EXCUSE MY INDISCRETION. NOW, YOU ARE APPROVED FOR ACCESS TO THE CARTOGRAPHY SECTION...
I AM A CARTOLOGIST. A CARTOGRAPHER IS A SIMPLE MAPMAKER. A CARTOLOGIST USES THE GEOMETRICS OF THE PLANETARY TOPOGRAPHIES TO DIVINE NAVIGATIONAL FORECASTING OF THE FUTURE.
A CARTOGRAPHER IS A MECHANIC. A CARTOLOGIST IS AN ARTIST. DO YOU UNDERSTAND THE DIFFERENCE?
LISTEN, LADY, I MEAN, ER, PROFESSOR. WE JUST GUARD THIS STUFF. WE DON'T KNOW WHAT IT IS.
Idiots. Simple deflection tactics, bungling around like a nerd. Aren't they trained to see through that?
And my low-density plastic weaponry, sailing through X-ray.
For every new gadget security invents, the smart con will always be a step ahead
It's a mindset. Protecting is never going to be as stealthy as attacking.

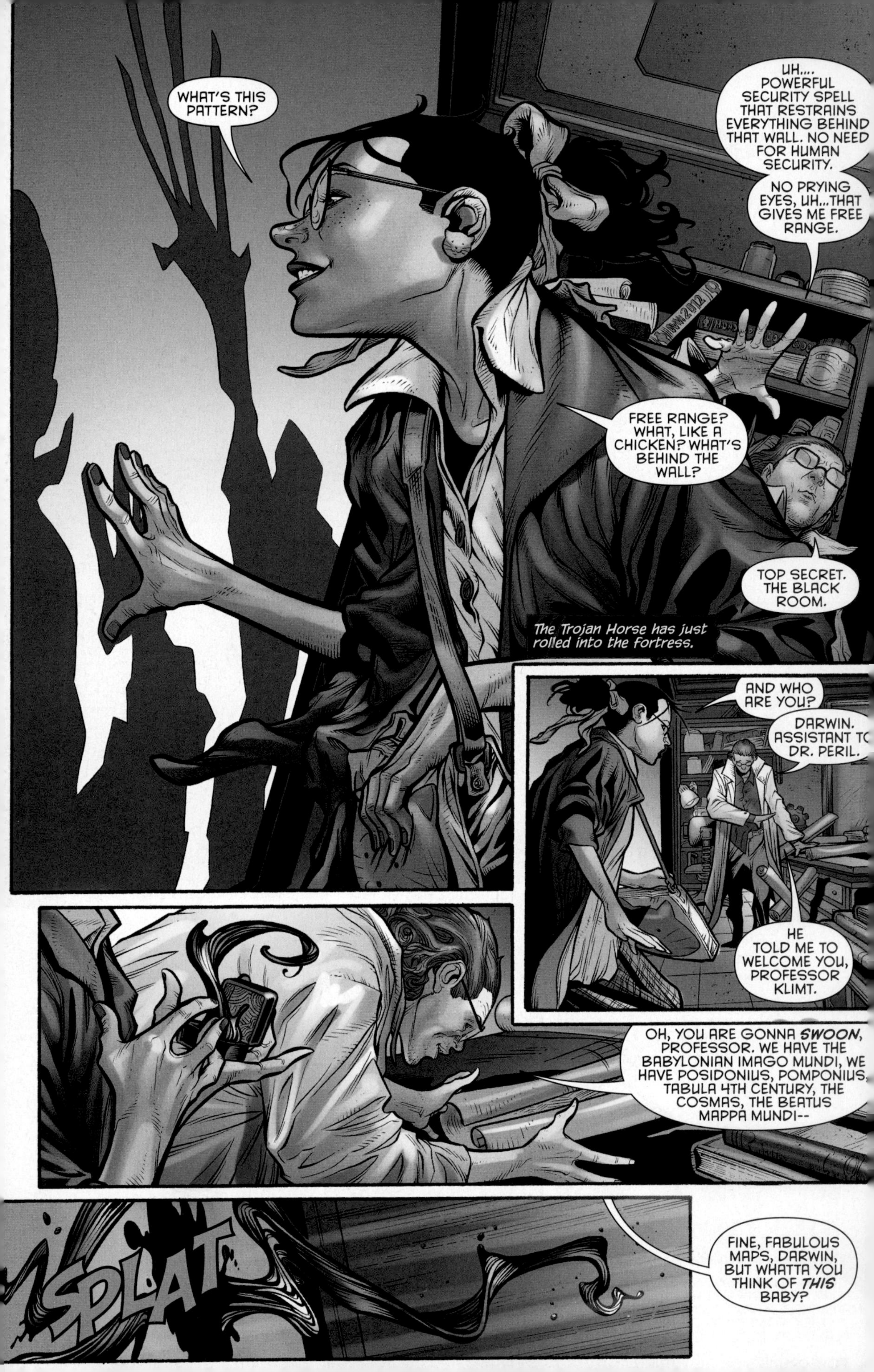
WHAT'S THIS PATTERN?
UH.... POWERFUL SECURITY SPELL THAT RESTRAINS EVERYTHING BEHIND THAT WALL. NO NEED FOR HUMAN SECURITY.
NO PRYING EYES, UH...THAT GIVES ME FREE RANGE.
FREE RANGE? WHAT, LIKE A CHICKEN? WHAT'S BEHIND THE WALL?
TOP SECRET. THE BLACK ROOM.
The Trojan Horse has just rolled into the fortress.
AND WHO ARE YOU?
DARWIN. ASSISTANT TO DR. PERIL.
HE TOLD ME TO WELCOME YOU, PROFESSOR KLIMT.
OH, YOU ARE GONNA *SWOON*, PROFESSOR. WE HAVE THE BABYLONIAN IMAGO MUNDI, WE HAVE POSIDONIUS, POMPONIUS, TABULA 4TH CENTURY, THE COSMAS, THE BEATUS MAPPA MUNDI--
SPLAT
FINE, FABULOUS MAPS, DARWIN, BUT WHATTA YOU THINK OF *THIS* BABY?

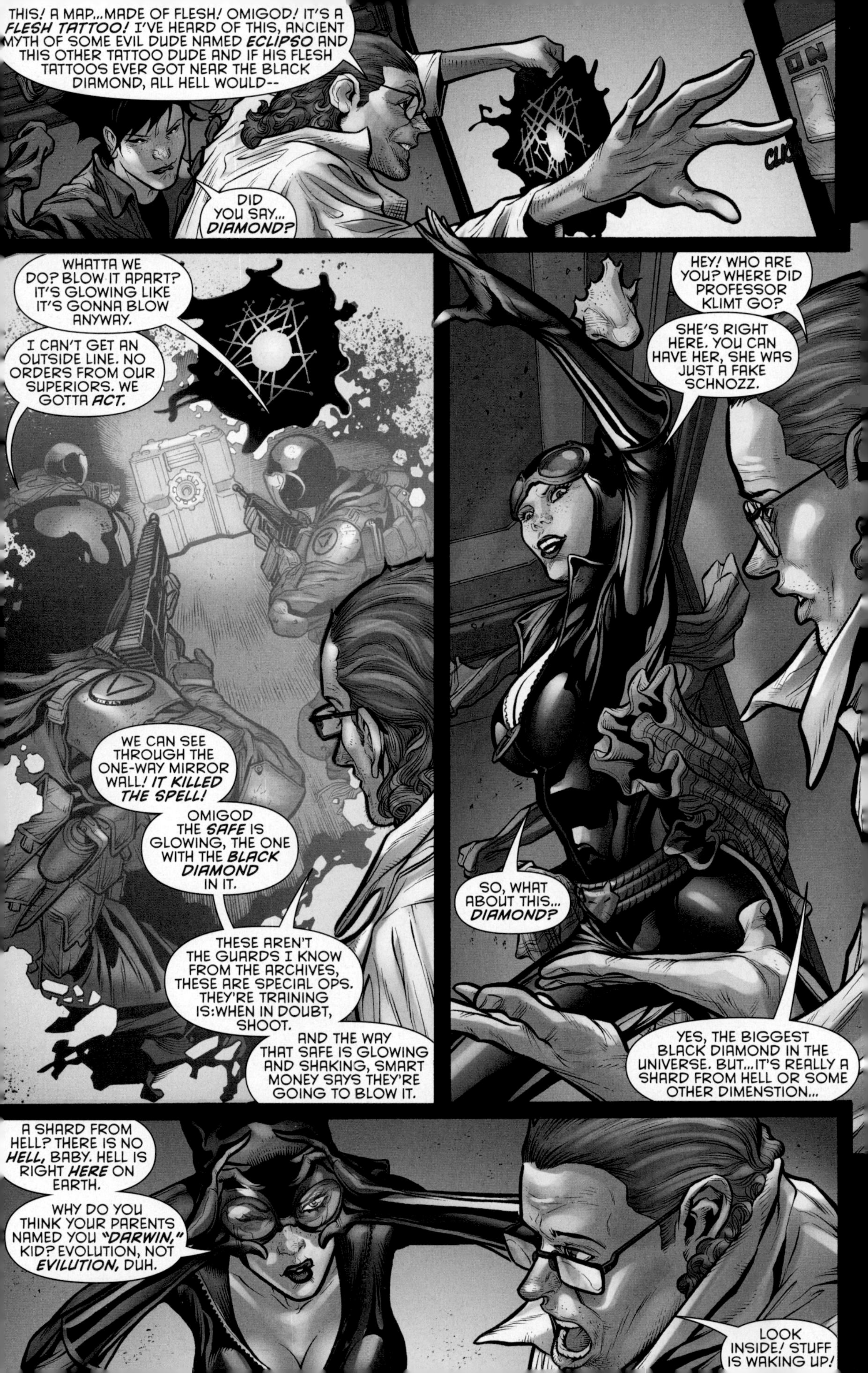
THIS! A MAP...MADE OF FLESH! OMIGOD! IT'S A FLESH TATTOO! I'VE HEARD OF THIS, ANCIENT MYTH OF SOME EVIL DUDE NAMED ECLIPSO AND THIS OTHER TATTOO DUDE AND IF HIS FLESH TATTOOS EVER GOT NEAR THE BLACK DIAMOND, ALL HELL WOULD--
DID YOU SAY... DIAMOND?
WHATTA WE DO? BLOW IT APART? IT'S GLOWING LIKE IT'S GONNA BLOW ANYWAY.
I CAN'T GET AN OUTSIDE LINE. NO ORDERS FROM OUR SUPERIORS. WE GOTTA ACT.
WE CAN SEE THROUGH THE ONE-WAY MIRROR WALL! IT KILLED THE SPELL!
OMIGOD THE SAFE IS GLOWING, THE ONE WITH THE BLACK DIAMOND IN IT.
THESE AREN'T THE GUARDS I KNOW FROM THE ARCHIVES, THESE ARE SPECIAL OPS. THEY'RE TRAINING IS:WHEN IN DOUBT, SHOOT.
AND THE WAY THAT SAFE IS GLOWING AND SHAKING, SMART MONEY SAYS THEY'RE GOING TO BLOW IT.
HEY! WHO ARE YOU? WHERE DID PROFESSOR KLIMT GO?
SHE'S RIGHT HERE. YOU CAN HAVE HER, SHE WAS JUST A FAKE SCHNOZZ.
SO, WHAT ABOUT THIS... DIAMOND?
YES, THE BIGGEST BLACK DIAMOND IN THE UNIVERSE. BUT...IT'S REALLY A SHARD FROM HELL OR SOME OTHER DIMENSTION...
A SHARD FROM HELL? THERE IS NO HELL, BABY. HELL IS RIGHT HERE ON EARTH.
WHY DO YOU THINK YOUR PARENTS NAMED YOU "DARWIN," KID? EVOLUTION, NOT EVILUTION, DUH.
LOOK INSIDE! STUFF IS WAKING UP!

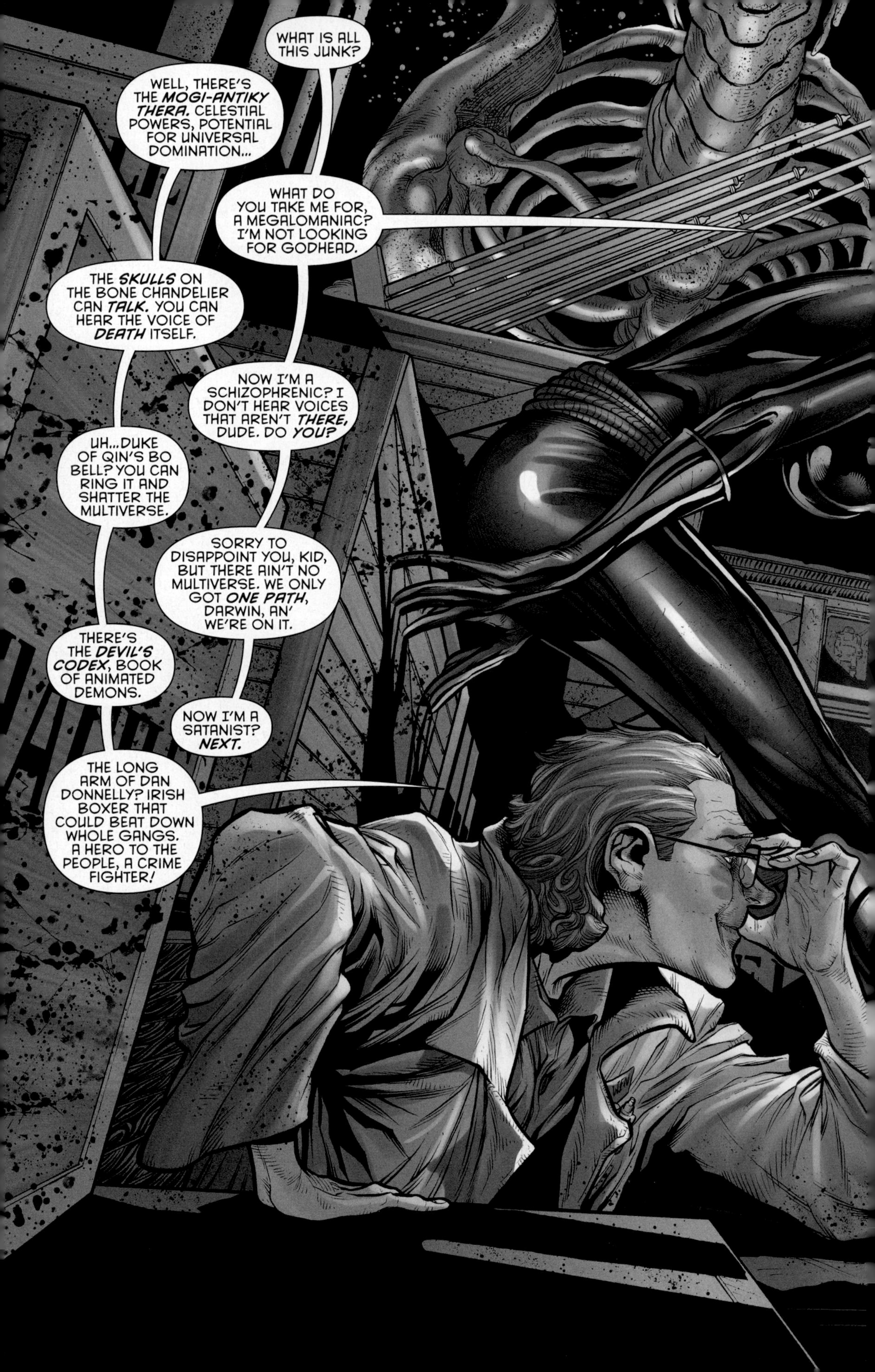
WHAT IS ALL THIS JUNK?
WELL, THERE'S THE MOGI-ANTIKY THERA. CELESTIAL POWERS, POTENTIAL FOR UNIVERSAL DOMINATION...
WHAT DO YOU TAKE ME FOR, A MEGALOMANIAC? I'M NOT LOOKING FOR GODHEAD.
THE SKULLS ON THE BONE CHANDELIER CAN TALK. YOU CAN HEAR THE VOICE OF DEATH ITSELF.
NOW I'M A SCHIZOPHRENIC? I DON'T HEAR VOICES THAT AREN'T THERE, DUDE. DO YOU?
UH...DUKE OF QIN'S BO BELL? YOU CAN RING IT AND SHATTER THE MULTIVERSE.
SORRY TO DISAPPOINT YOU, KID, BUT THERE AIN'T NO MULTIVERSE. WE ONLY GOT ONE PATH, DARWIN, AN' WE'RE ON IT.
THERE'S THE DEVIL'S CODEX, BOOK OF ANIMATED DEMONS.
NOW I'M A SATANIST? NEXT.
THE LONG ARM OF DAN DONNELLY? IRISH BOXER THAT COULD BEAT DOWN WHOLE GANGS. A HERO TO THE PEOPLE, A CRIME FIGHTER!

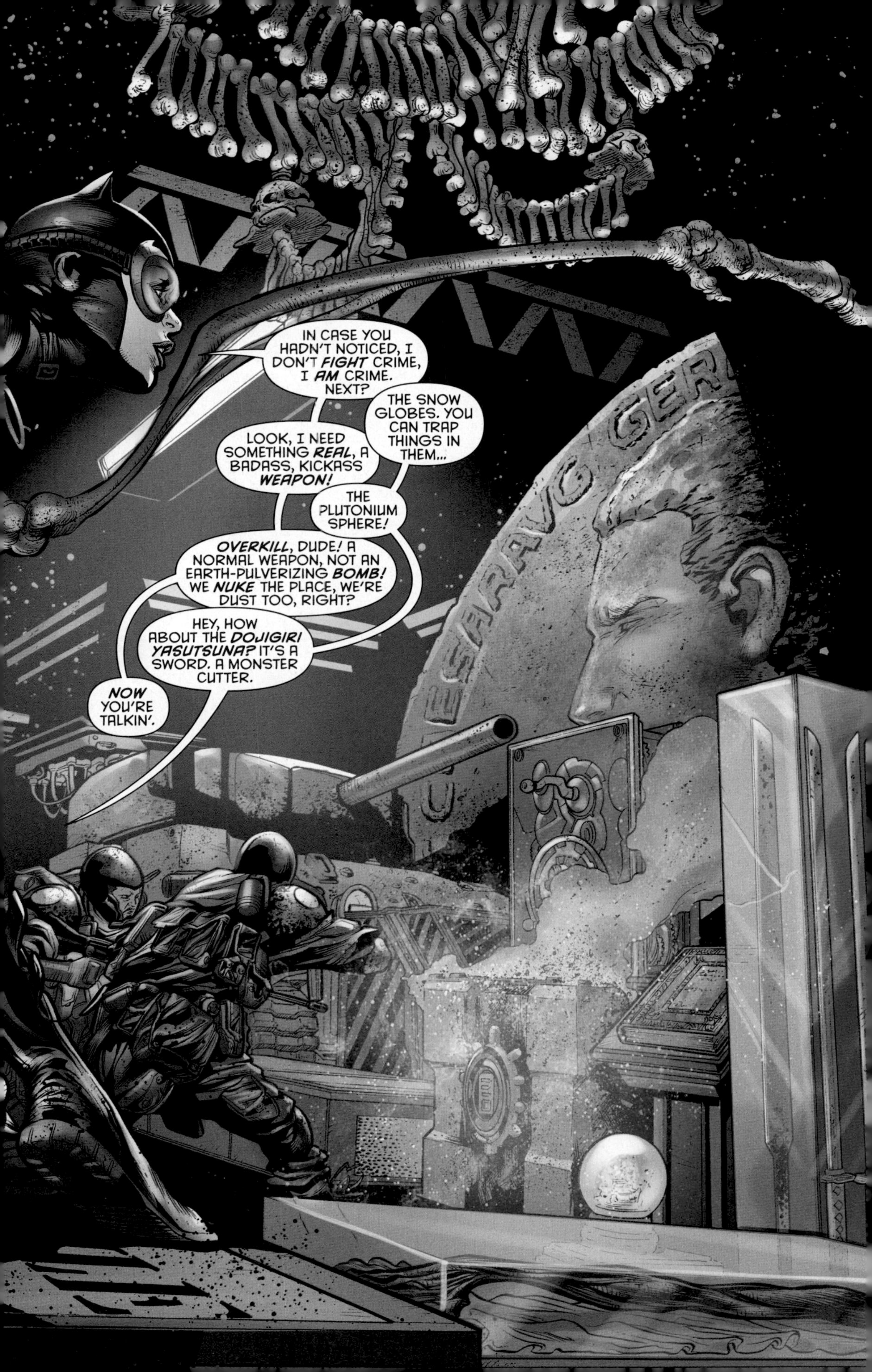
IN CASE YOU HADN'T NOTICED, I DON'T FIGHT CRIME, I AM CRIME. NEXT?
THE SNOW GLOBES. YOU CAN TRAP THINGS IN THEM...
LOOK, I NEED SOMETHING REAL, A BADASS, KICKASS WEAPON!
THE PLUTONIUM SPHERE!
OVERKILL, DUDE! A NORMAL WEAPON, NOT AN EARTH-PULVERIZING BOMB! WE NUKE THE PLACE, WE'RE DUST TOO, RIGHT?
HEY, HOW ABOUT THE DOJIGIRI YASUTSUNA? IT'S A SWORD. A MONSTER CUTTER.
NOW YOU'RE TALKIN'.

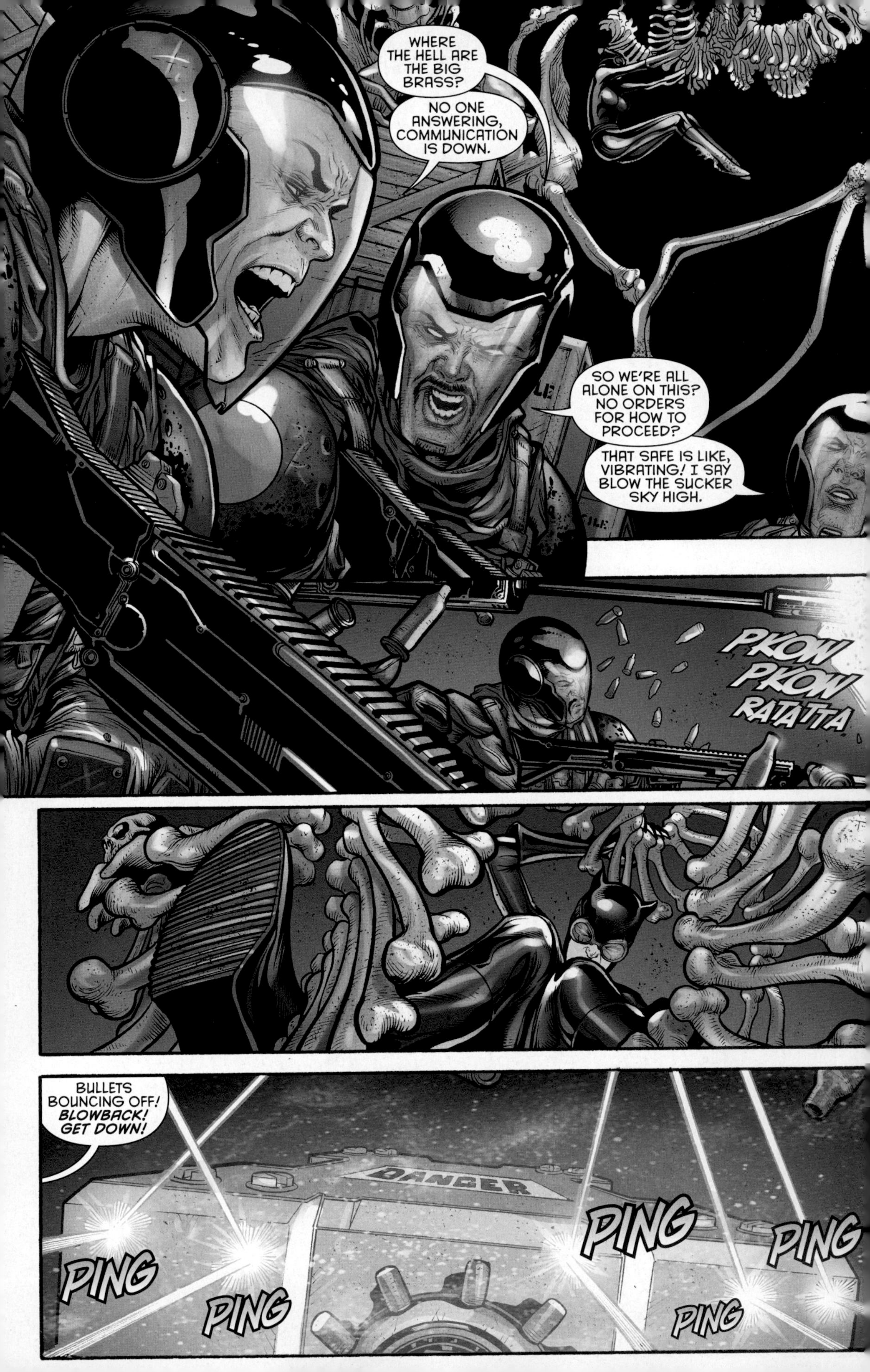
WHERE THE HELL ARE THE BIG BRASS?
NO ONE ANSWERING, COMMUNICATION IS DOWN.
SO WE'RE ALL ALONE ON THIS? NO ORDERS FOR HOW TO PROCEED?
THAT SAFE IS LIKE, VIBRATING! I SAY BLOW THE SUCKER SKY HIGH.
PKOW PKOW RATATTA
BULLETS BOUNCING OFF! BLOWBACK! GET DOWN!
DANGER
PING
PING
PING
PING
PING

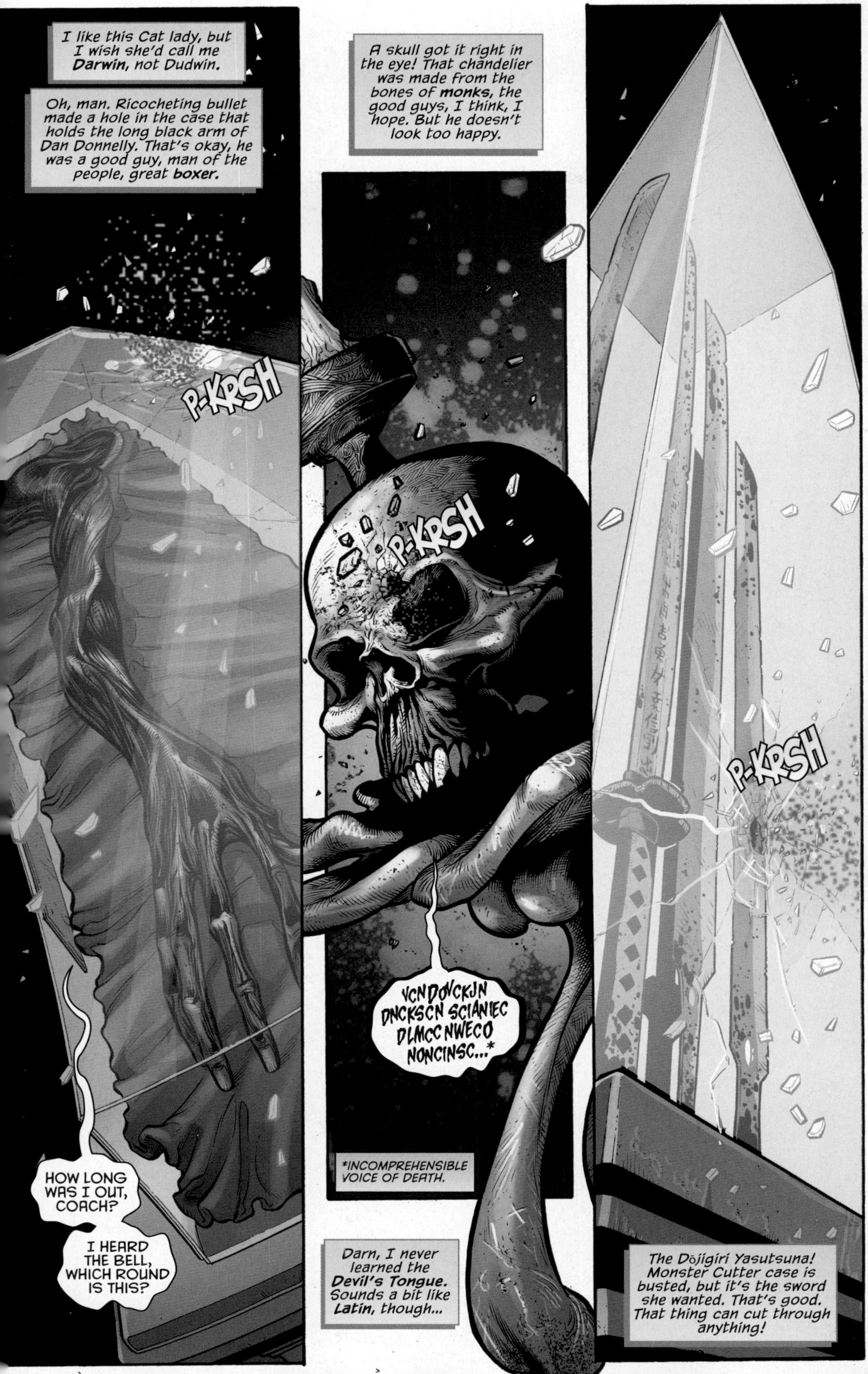
I like this Cat lady, but I wish she'd call me **Darwin**, not Dudwin.
Oh, man. Ricocheting bullet made a hole in the case that holds the long black arm of Dan Donnelly. That's okay, he was a good guy, man of the people, great **boxer.**
P-KRSH
HOW LONG WAS I OUT, COACH?
I HEARD THE BELL, WHICH ROUND IS THIS?
A skull got it right in the eye! That chandelier was made from the bones of **monks**, the good guys, I think, I hope. But he doesn't look too happy.
P-KRSH
VCNDOVCKJN DNCKSCN SCIANIEC DLMCCNWECO NONCINSC...*
*INCOMPREHENSIBLE VOICE OF DEATH.
Darn, I never learned the **Devil's Tongue.** Sounds a bit like **Latin**, though...
P-KRSH
The Dōjigiri Yasutsuna! Monster Cutter case is busted, but it's the sword she wanted. That's good. That thing can cut through anything!

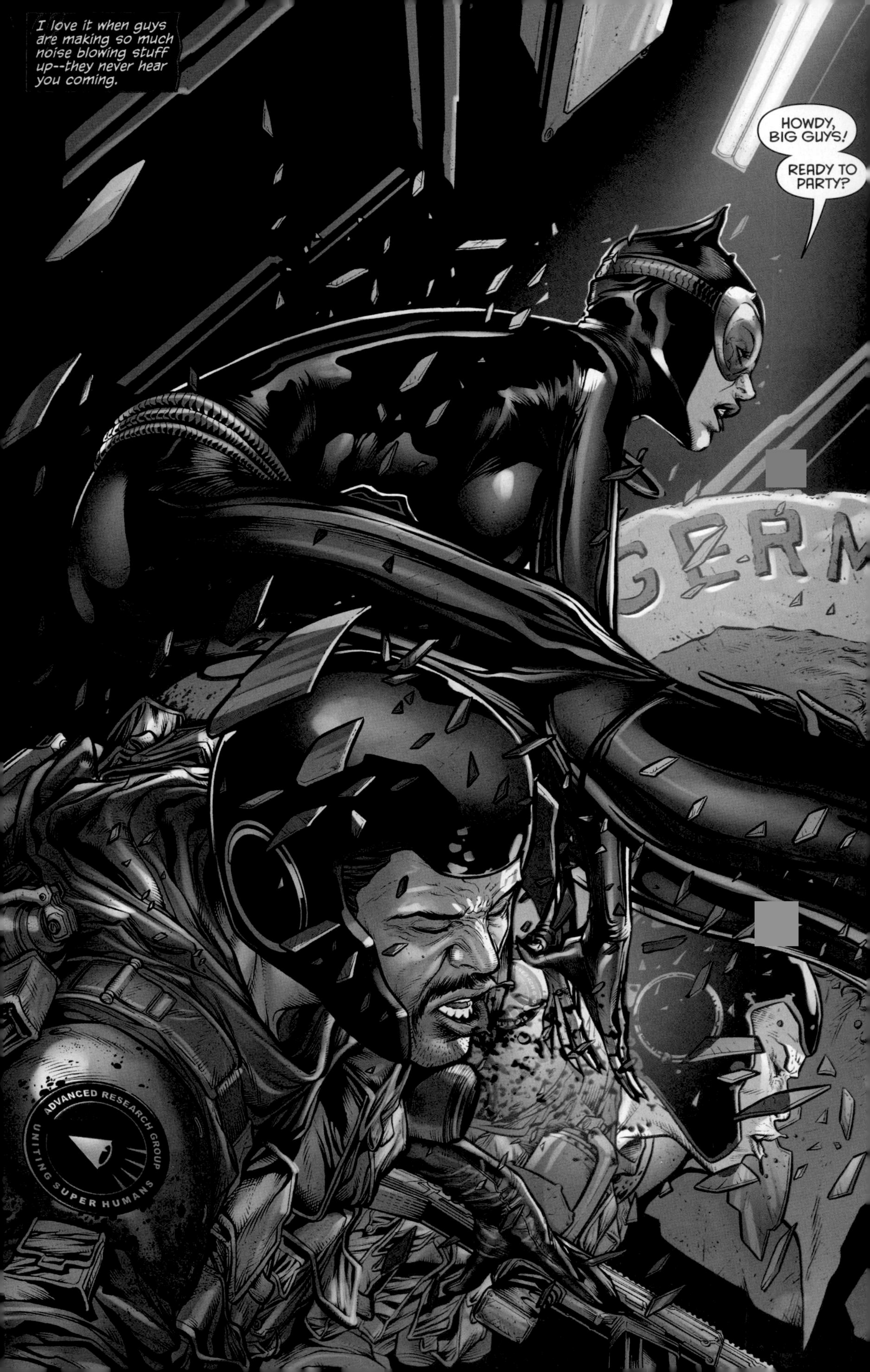
I love it when guys are making so much noise blowing stuff up--they never hear you coming.
HOWDY, BIG GUYS!
READY TO PARTY?
GERM
ADVANCED RESEARCH GROUP
UNITING SUPER HUMANS

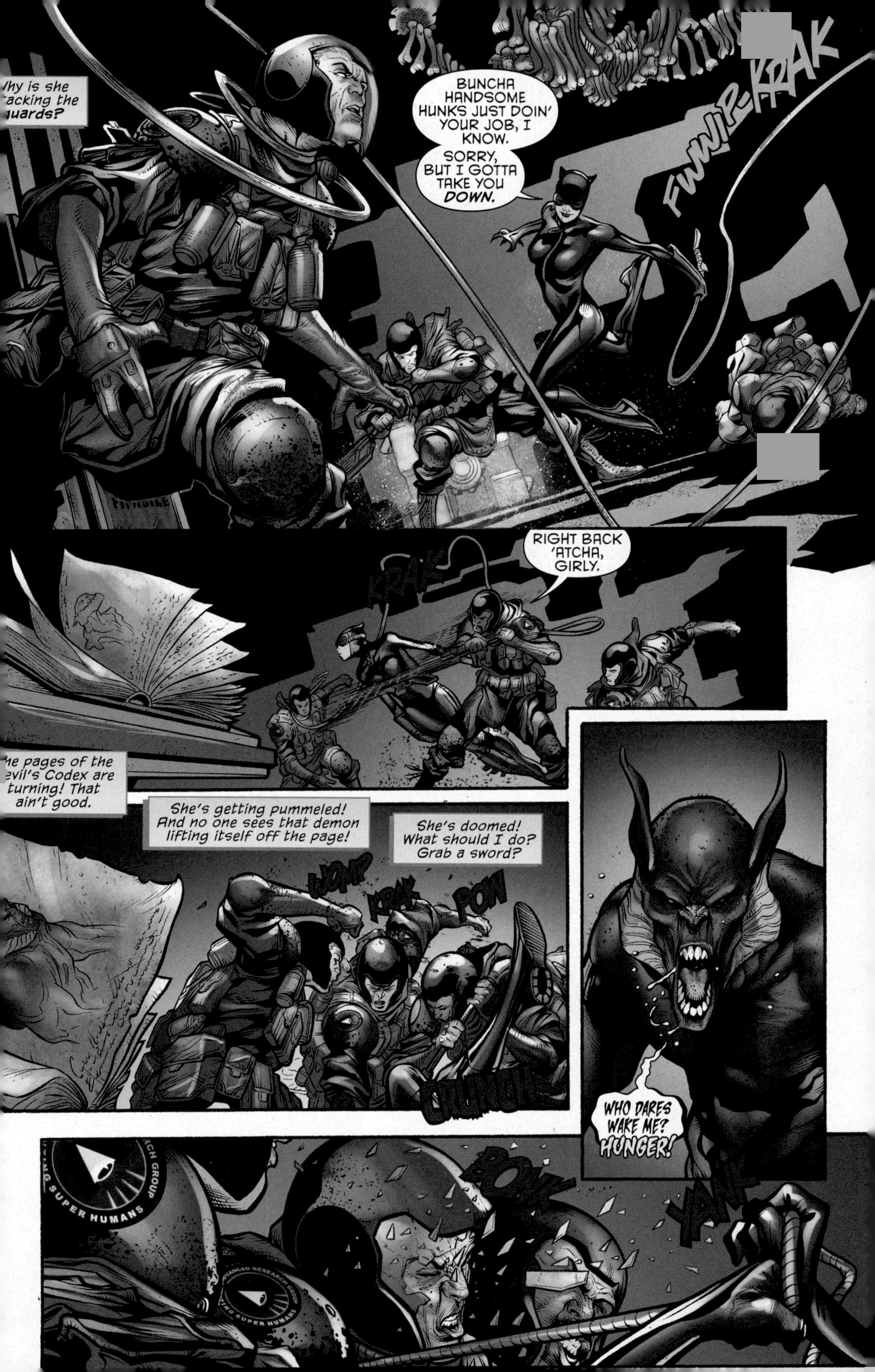

hy is she
tacking the
uards?
BUNCHA HANDSOME HUNKS JUST DOIN' YOUR JOB, I KNOW.
SORRY, BUT I GOTTA TAKE YOU DOWN.
FWWIP-KRAK
KRAK
RIGHT BACK 'ATCHA, GIRLY.
he pages of the
evil's Codex are
turning! That
ain't good.
She's getting pummeled! And no one sees that demon lifting itself off the page!
She's doomed! What should I do? Grab a sword?
WOMP
KRAK
POW
CRUNCH
WHO DARES WAKE ME? HUNGER!
SUPER HUMANS
YANK

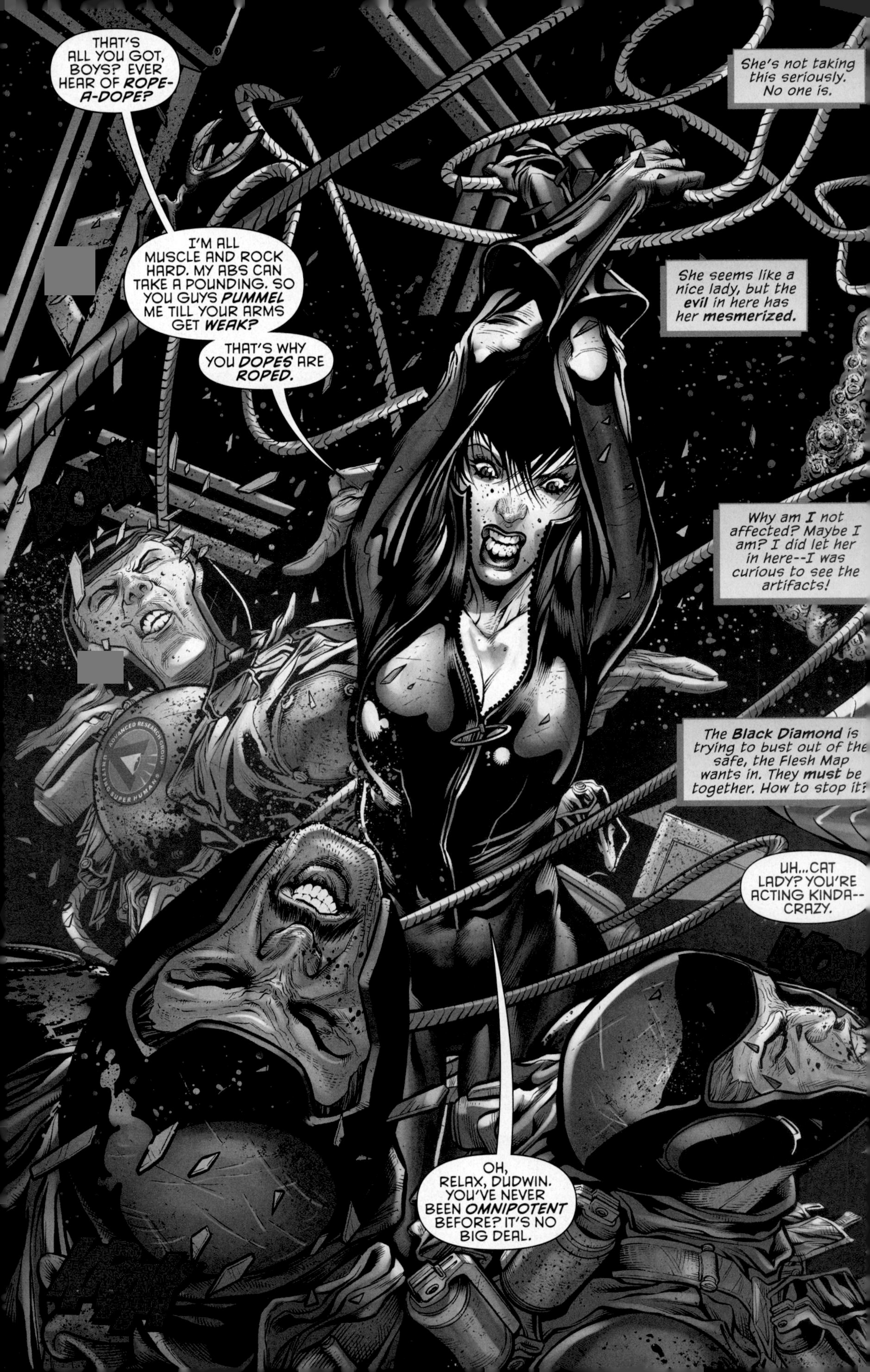
THAT'S ALL YOU GOT, BOYS? EVER HEAR OF ROPE-A-DOPE?
She's not taking this seriously. No one is.
I'M ALL MUSCLE AND ROCK HARD. MY ABS CAN TAKE A POUNDING. SO YOU GUYS PUMMEL ME TILL YOUR ARMS GET WEAK?
THAT'S WHY YOU DOPES ARE ROPED.
She seems like a nice lady, but the evil in here has her mesmerized.
Why am I not affected? Maybe I am? I did let her in here--I was curious to see the artifacts!
The Black Diamond is trying to bust out of the safe, the Flesh Map wants in. They must be together. How to stop it?
UH...CAT LADY? YOU'RE ACTING KINDA--CRAZY.
OH, RELAX, DUDWIN. YOU'VE NEVER BEEN OMNIPOTENT BEFORE? IT'S NO BIG DEAL.

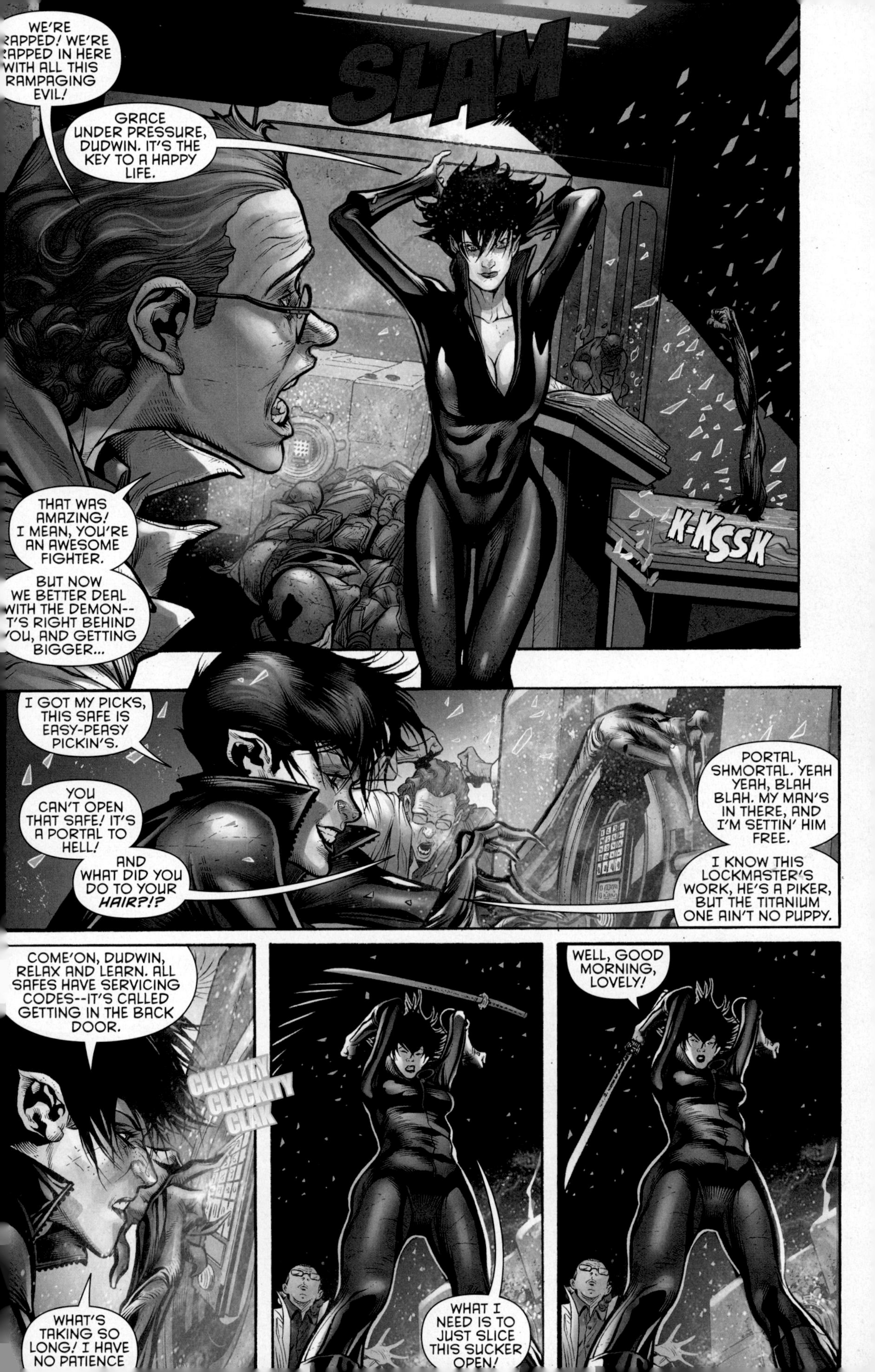

SLAM
WE'RE RAPPED! WE'RE RAPPED IN HERE WITH ALL THIS RAMPAGING EVIL!
GRACE UNDER PRESSURE, DUDWIN. IT'S THE KEY TO A HAPPY LIFE.
THAT WAS AMAZING! I MEAN, YOU'RE AN AWESOME FIGHTER.
BUT NOW WE BETTER DEAL WITH THE DEMON-- 'T'S RIGHT BEHIND YOU, AND GETTING BIGGER...
K-KSSK
I GOT MY PICKS, THIS SAFE IS EASY-PEASY PICKIN'S.
YOU CAN'T OPEN THAT SAFE! IT'S A PORTAL TO HELL!
AND WHAT DID YOU DO TO YOUR HAIR?!?
PORTAL, SHMORTAL. YEAH YEAH, BLAH BLAH. MY MAN'S IN THERE, AND I'M SETTIN' HIM FREE.
I KNOW THIS LOCKMASTER'S WORK, HE'S A PIKER, BUT THE TITANIUM ONE AIN'T NO PUPPY.
COME'ON, DUDWIN, RELAX AND LEARN. ALL SAFES HAVE SERVICING CODES--IT'S CALLED GETTING IN THE BACK DOOR.
CLICKITY CLACKITY CLAK
WHAT'S TAKING SO LONG! I HAVE NO PATIENCE
WHAT I NEED IS TO JUST SLICE THIS SUCKER OPEN!
WELL, GOOD MORNING, LOVELY!

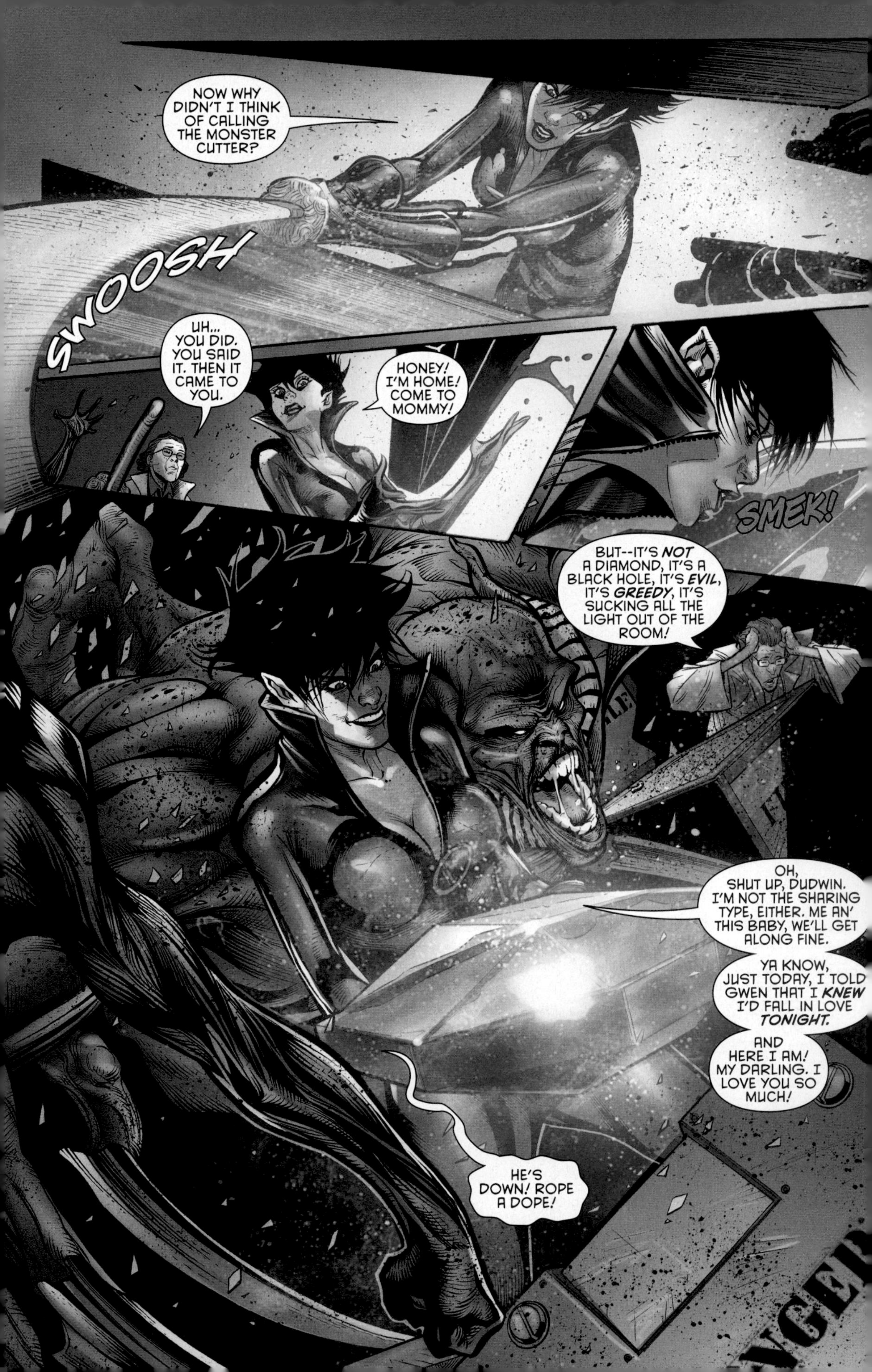
NOW WHY DIDN'T I THINK OF CALLING THE MONSTER CUTTER?
SWOOSH
UH... YOU DID. YOU SAID IT. THEN IT CAME TO YOU.
HONEY! I'M HOME! COME TO MOMMY!
SMEK!
BUT--IT'S NOT A DIAMOND, IT'S A BLACK HOLE, IT'S EVIL, IT'S GREEDY, IT'S SUCKING ALL THE LIGHT OUT OF THE ROOM!
OH, SHUT UP, DUDWIN. I'M NOT THE SHARING TYPE, EITHER. ME AN' THIS BABY, WE'LL GET ALONG FINE.
YA KNOW, JUST TODAY, I TOLD GWEN THAT I KNEW I'D FALL IN LOVE TONIGHT.
AND HERE I AM! MY DARLING. I LOVE YOU SO MUCH!
HE'S DOWN! ROPE A DOPE!

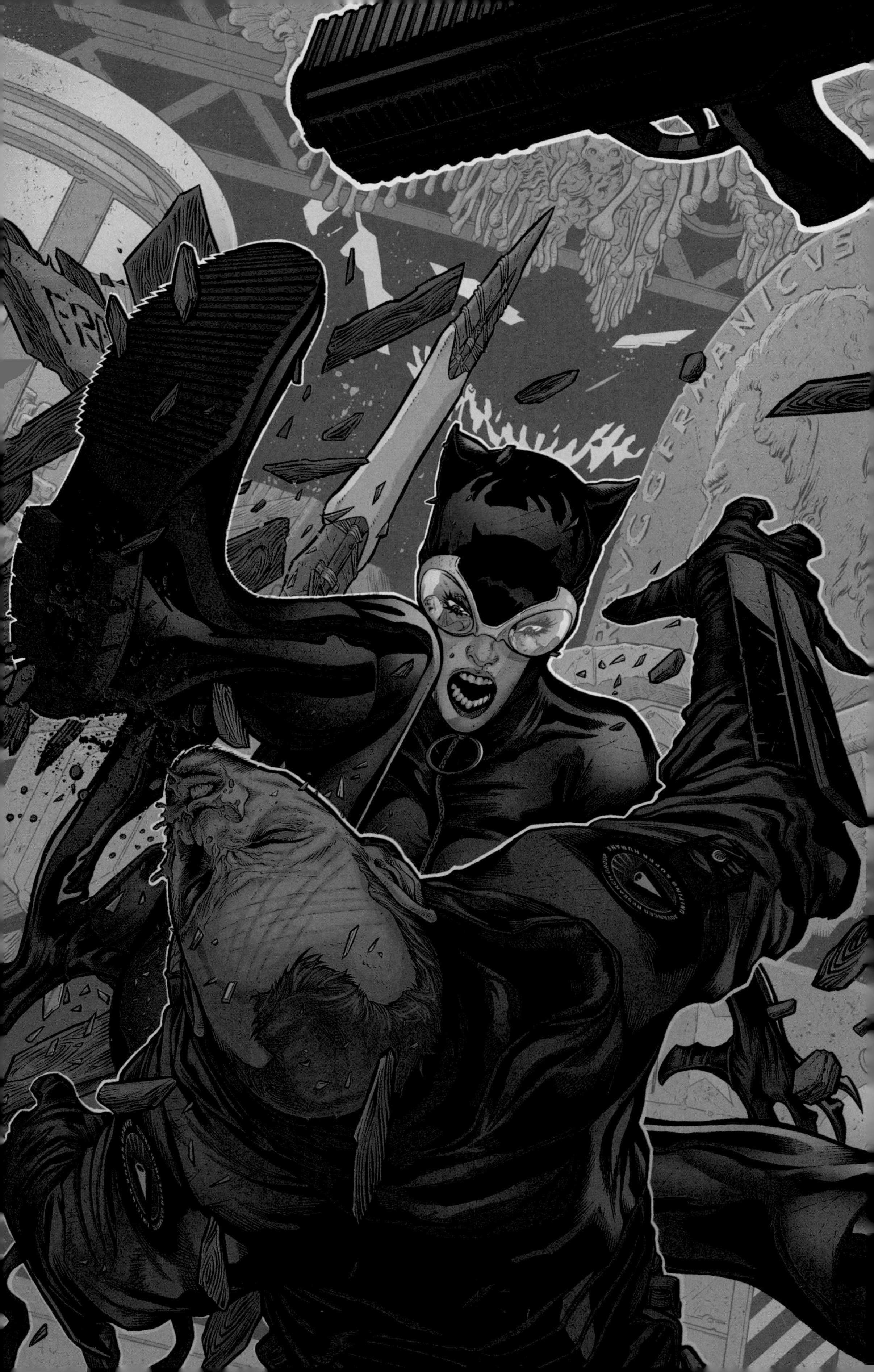

ANN NOCENTI writer RAFA SANDOVAL penciller JORDI TARRAGONA inker cover by RAFA SANDOVAL & JORDI TARRAGONA

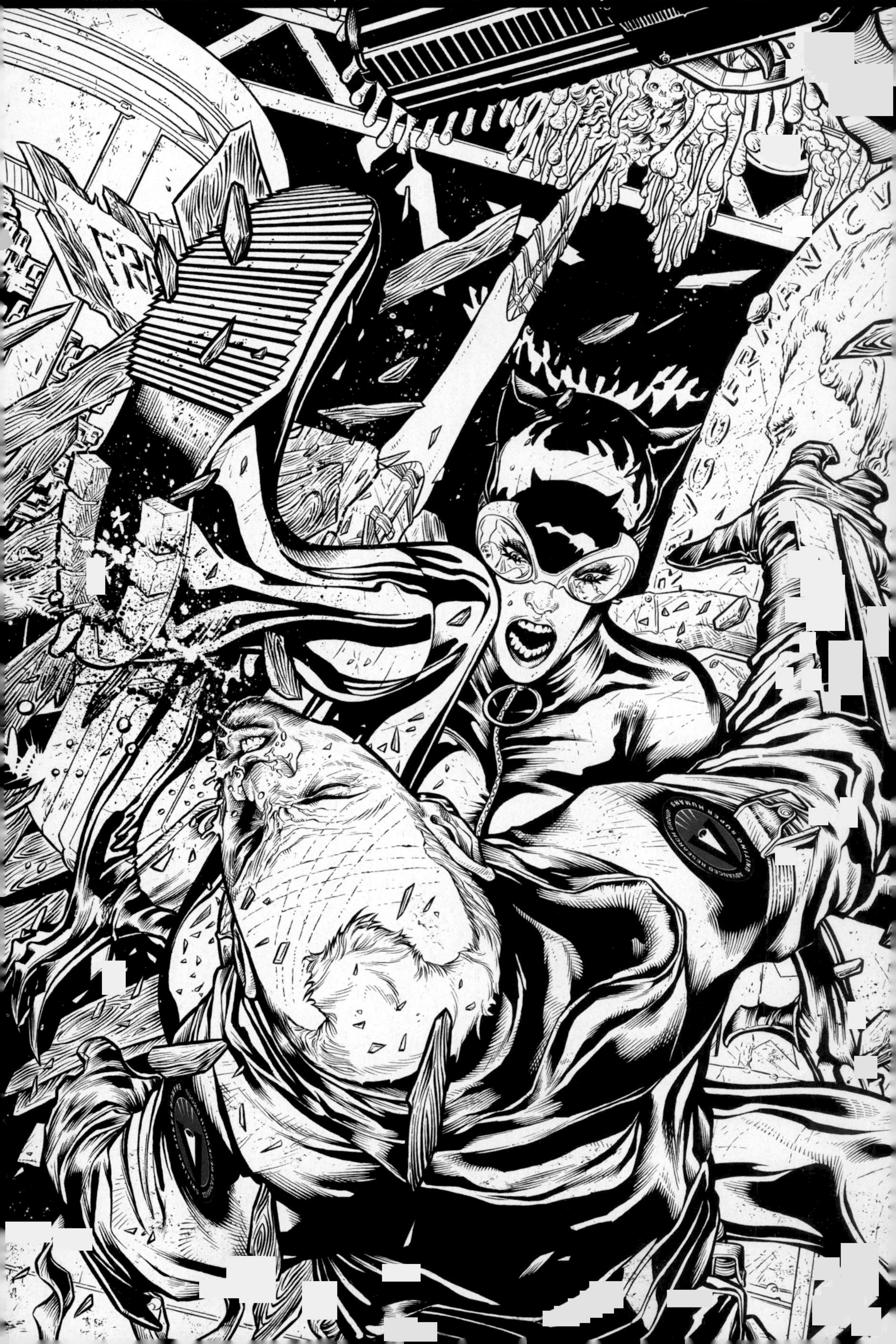
ADVANCED RESEARCH GROUP UNITING SUPER HUMANS

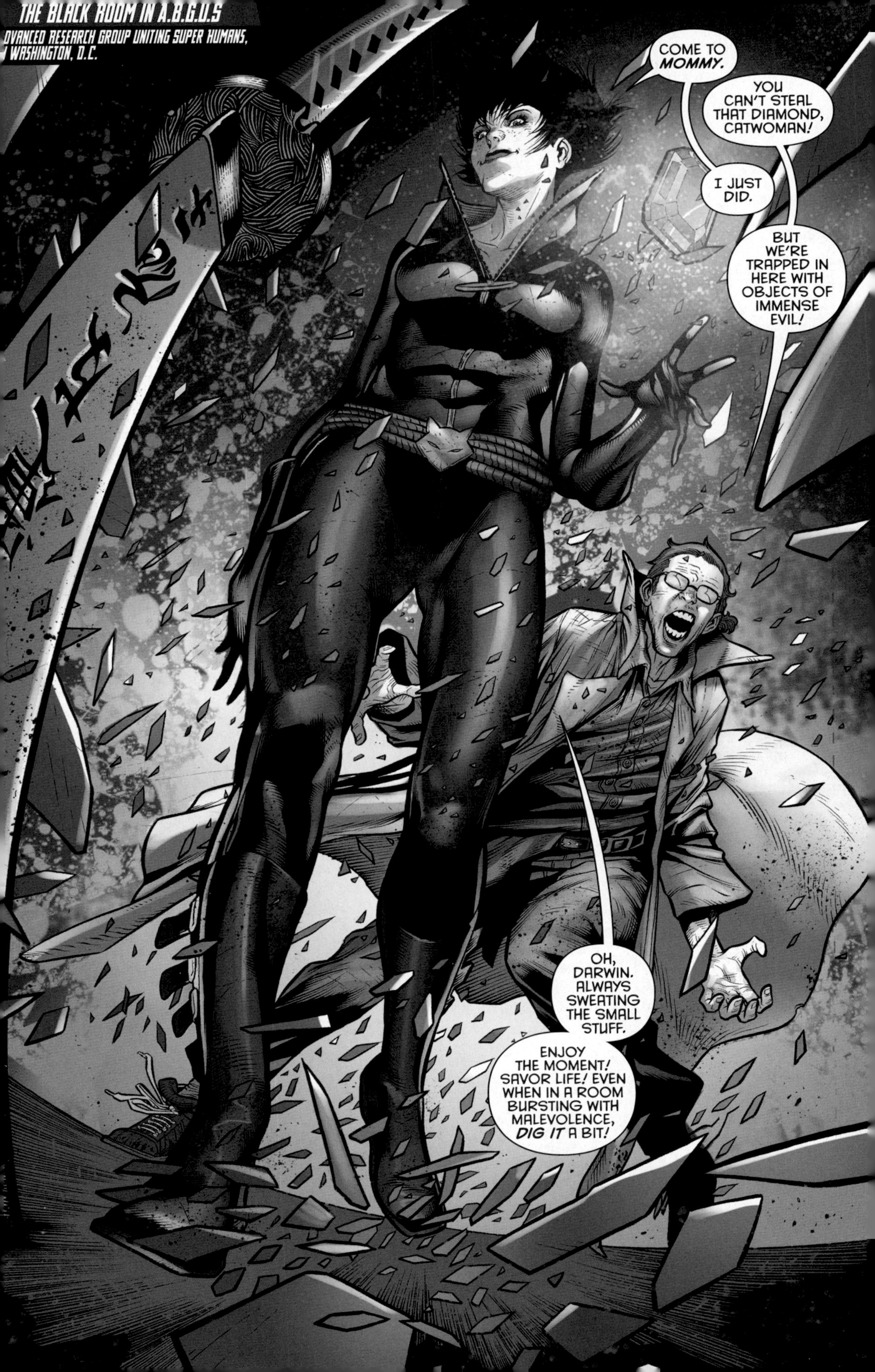
THE BLACK ROOM IN A.R.G.U.S
DVANCED RESEARCH GROUP UNITING SUPER HUMANS,
WASHINGTON, D.C.
COME TO MOMMY.
YOU CAN'T STEAL THAT DIAMOND, CATWOMAN!
I JUST DID.
BUT WE'RE TRAPPED IN HERE WITH OBJECTS OF IMMENSE EVIL!
OH, DARWIN. ALWAYS SWEATING THE SMALL STUFF.
ENJOY THE MOMENT! SAVOR LIFE! EVEN WHEN IN A ROOM BURSTING WITH MALEVOLENCE, DIG IT A BIT!

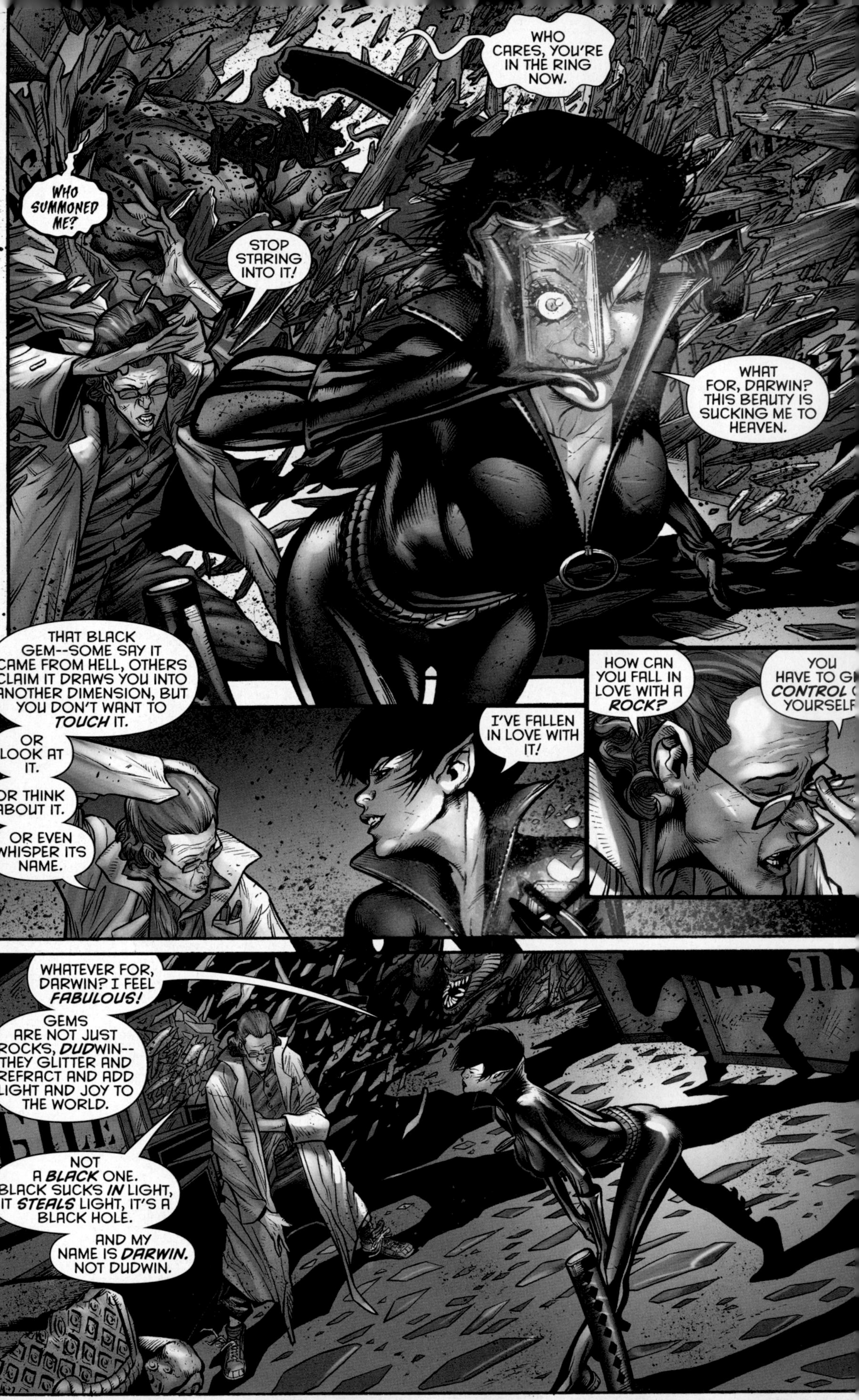
WHO CARES, YOU'RE IN THE RING NOW.
WHO SUMMONED ME?
STOP STARING INTO IT!
WHAT FOR, DARWIN? THIS BEAUTY IS SUCKING ME TO HEAVEN.
THAT BLACK GEM--SOME SAY IT CAME FROM HELL, OTHERS CLAIM IT DRAWS YOU INTO ANOTHER DIMENSION, BUT YOU DON'T WANT TO TOUCH IT.
OR LOOK AT IT.
OR THINK ABOUT IT.
OR EVEN WHISPER ITS NAME.
I'VE FALLEN IN LOVE WITH IT!
HOW CAN YOU FALL IN LOVE WITH A ROCK?
YOU HAVE TO G CONTROL YOURSELF
WHATEVER FOR, DARWIN? I FEEL FABULOUS!
GEMS ARE NOT JUST ROCKS, DUDWIN--THEY GLITTER AND REFRACT AND ADD LIGHT AND JOY TO THE WORLD.
NOT A BLACK ONE. BLACK SUCKS IN LIGHT, IT STEALS LIGHT, IT'S A BLACK HOLE.
AND MY NAME IS DARWIN. NOT DUDWIN.

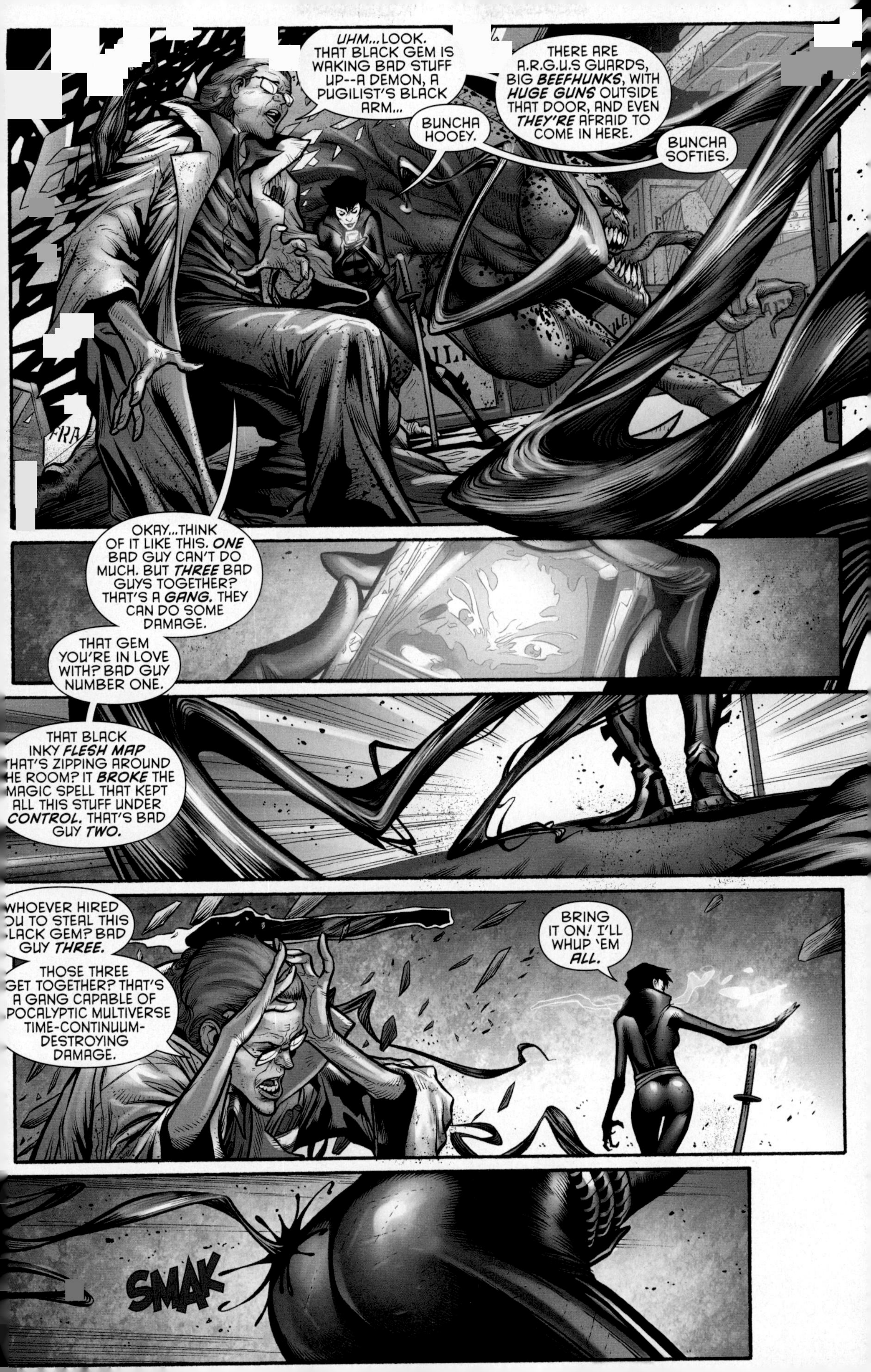
UHM... LOOK. THAT BLACK GEM IS WAKING BAD STUFF UP--A DEMON, A PUGILIST'S BLACK ARM...
BUNCHA HOOEY.
THERE ARE A.R.G.U.S GUARDS, BIG BEEFHUNKS, WITH HUGE GUNS OUTSIDE THAT DOOR, AND EVEN THEY'RE AFRAID TO COME IN HERE.
BUNCHA SOFTIES.
OKAY...THINK OF IT LIKE THIS. ONE BAD GUY CAN'T DO MUCH. BUT THREE BAD GUYS TOGETHER? THAT'S A GANG. THEY CAN DO SOME DAMAGE.
THAT GEM YOU'RE IN LOVE WITH? BAD GUY NUMBER ONE.
THAT BLACK INKY FLESH MAP THAT'S ZIPPING AROUND HE ROOM? IT BROKE THE MAGIC SPELL THAT KEPT ALL THIS STUFF UNDER CONTROL. THAT'S BAD GUY TWO.
WHOEVER HIRED OU TO STEAL THIS LACK GEM? BAD GUY THREE.
THOSE THREE GET TOGETHER? THAT'S A GANG CAPABLE OF POCALYPTIC MULTIVERSE TIME-CONTINUUM-DESTROYING DAMAGE.
BRING IT ON! I'LL WHUP 'EM ALL.
SMAK

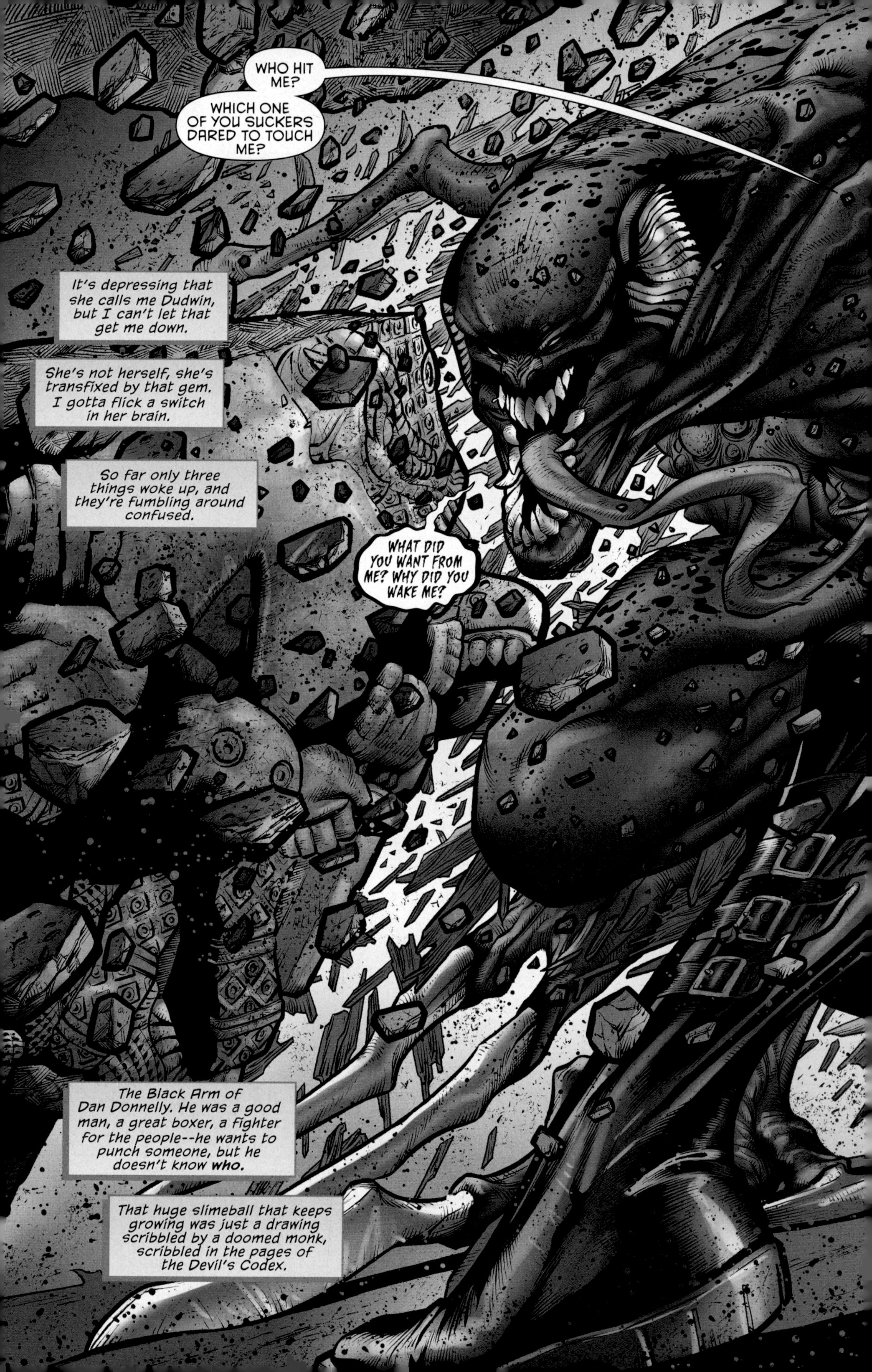
WHO HIT ME?
WHICH ONE OF YOU SUCKERS DARED TO TOUCH ME?
It's depressing that she calls me Dudwin, but I can't let that get me down.
She's not herself, she's transfixed by that gem. I gotta flick a switch in her brain.
So far only three things woke up, and they're fumbling around confused.
WHAT DID YOU WANT FROM ME? WHY DID YOU WAKE ME?
The Black Arm of Dan Donnelly. He was a good man, a great boxer, a fighter for the people--he wants to punch someone, but he doesn't know **who.**
That huge slimeball that keeps growing was just a drawing scribbled by a doomed monk, scribbled in the pages of the Devil's Codex.

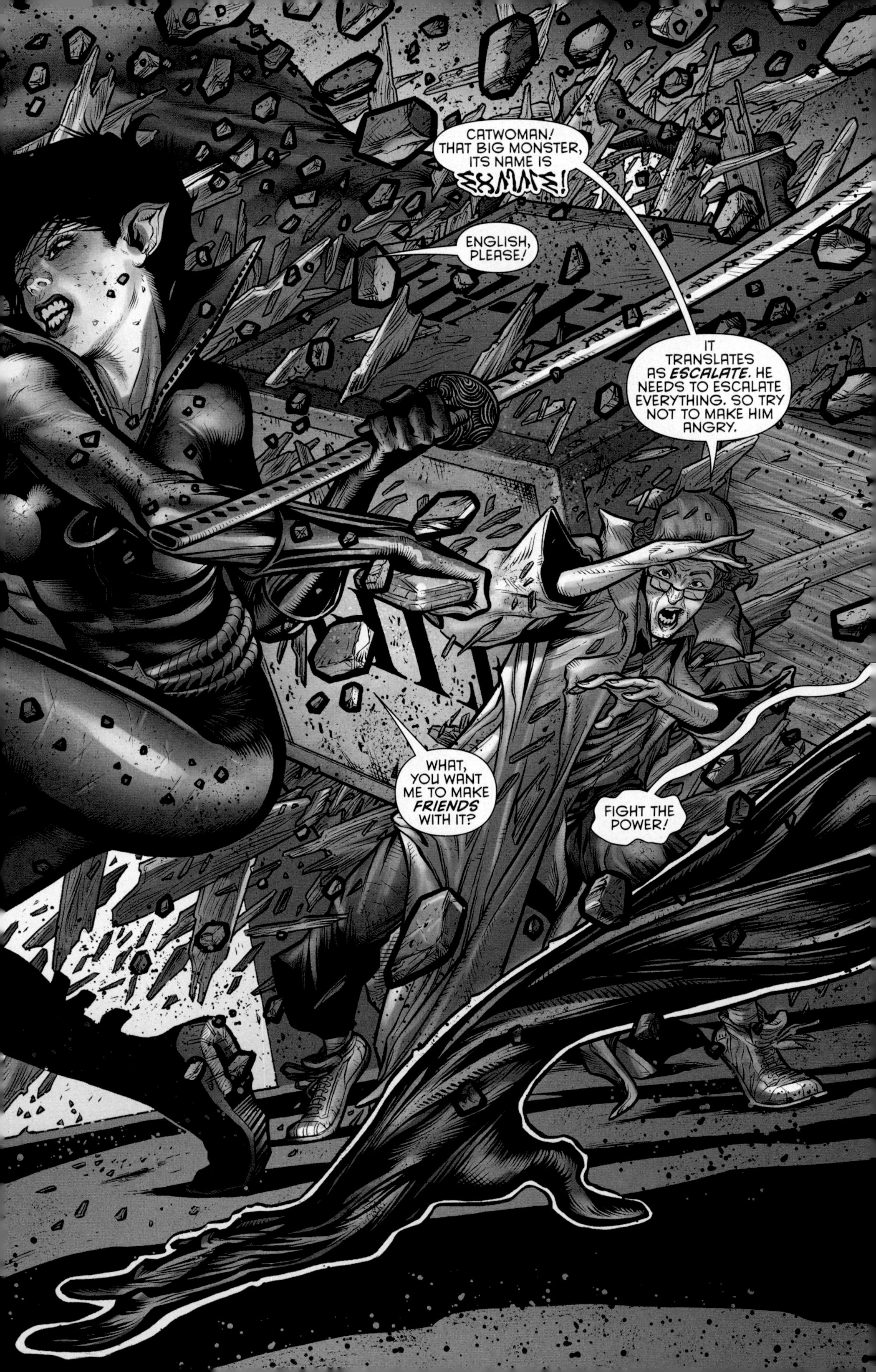
CATWOMAN! THAT BIG MONSTER, ITS NAME IS
ENGLISH, PLEASE!
IT TRANSLATES AS ESCALATE. HE NEEDS TO ESCALATE EVERYTHING. SO TRY NOT TO MAKE HIM ANGRY.
WHAT, YOU WANT ME TO MAKE FRIENDS WITH IT?
FIGHT THE POWER!

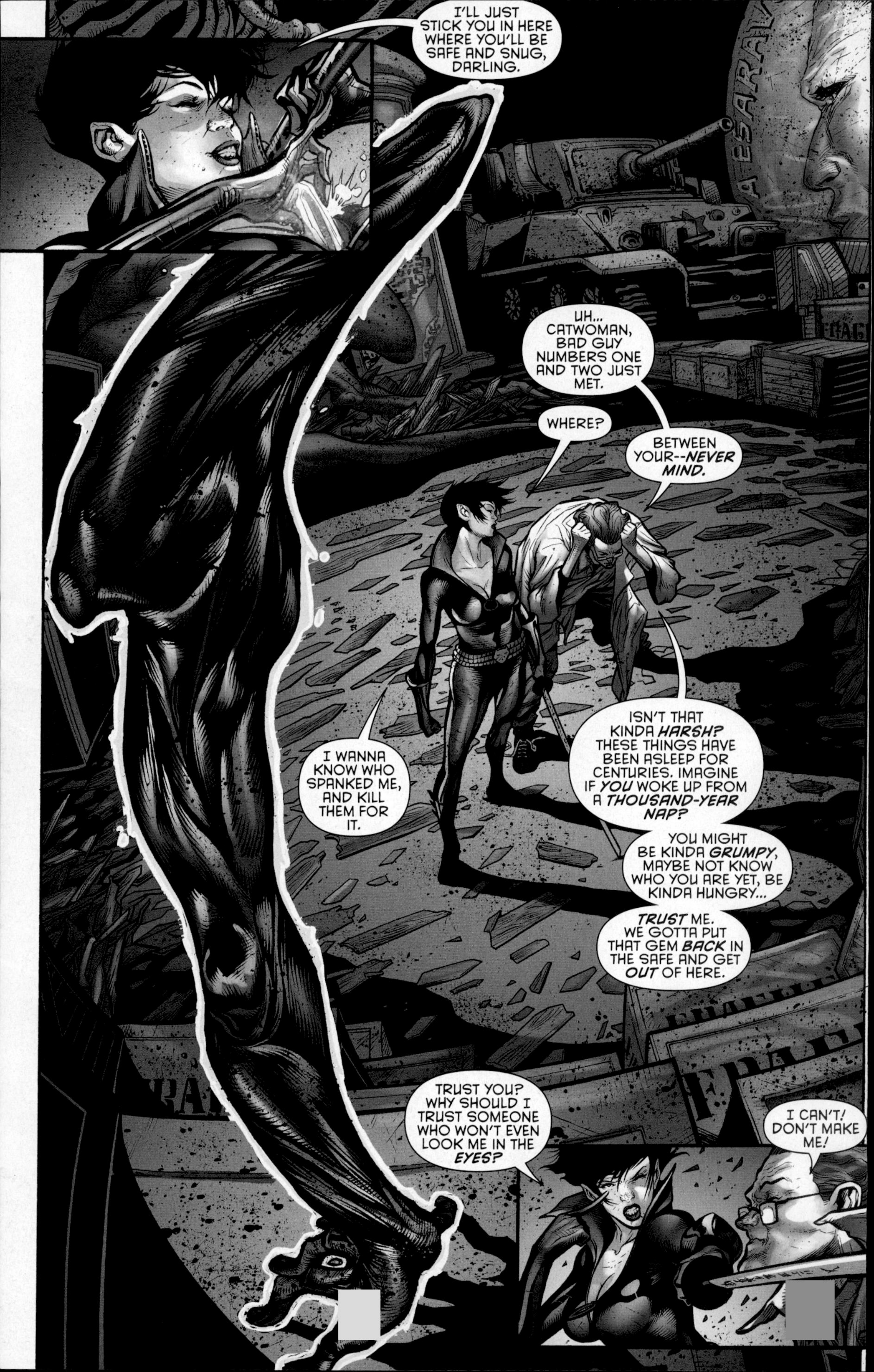

I'LL JUST STICK YOU IN HERE WHERE YOU'LL BE SAFE AND SNUG, DARLING.
UH... CATWOMAN, BAD GUY NUMBERS ONE AND TWO JUST MET.
WHERE?
BETWEEN YOUR--NEVER MIND.
I WANNA KNOW WHO SPANKED ME, AND KILL THEM FOR IT.
ISN'T THAT KINDA HARSH? THESE THINGS HAVE BEEN ASLEEP FOR CENTURIES. IMAGINE IF YOU WOKE UP FROM A THOUSAND-YEAR NAP?
YOU MIGHT BE KINDA GRUMPY, MAYBE NOT KNOW WHO YOU ARE YET, BE KINDA HUNGRY...
TRUST ME. WE GOTTA PUT THAT GEM BACK IN THE SAFE AND GET OUT OF HERE.
TRUST YOU? WHY SHOULD I TRUST SOMEONE WHO WON'T EVEN LOOK ME IN THE EYES?
I CAN'T! DON'T MAKE ME!

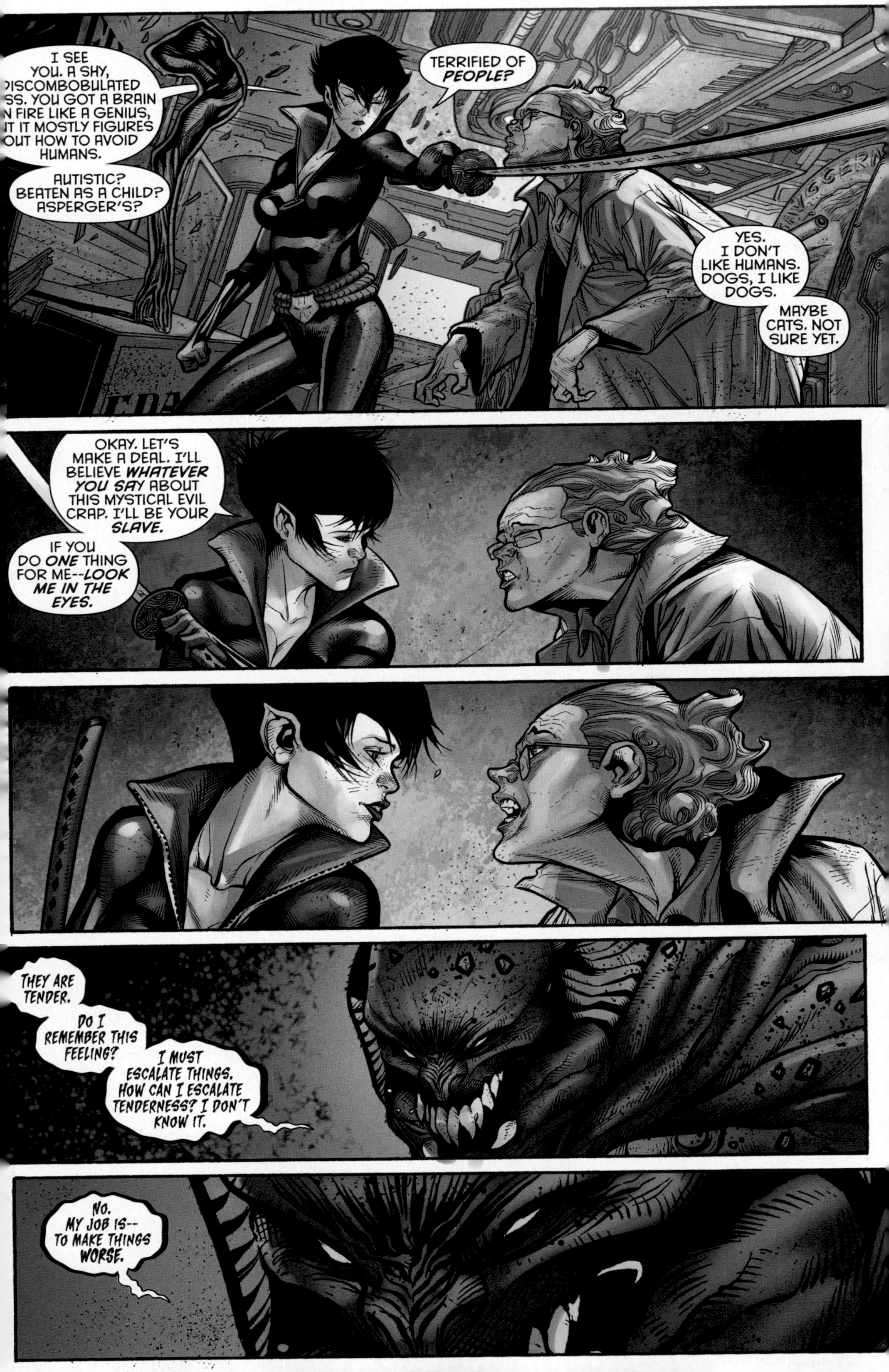
I SEE YOU. A SHY, DISCOMBOBULATED SS. YOU GOT A BRAIN N FIRE LIKE A GENIUS, IT IT MOSTLY FIGURES OUT HOW TO AVOID HUMANS.
AUTISTIC? BEATEN AS A CHILD? ASPERGER'S?
TERRIFIED OF PEOPLE?
YES. I DON'T LIKE HUMANS. DOGS, I LIKE DOGS.
MAYBE CATS. NOT SURE YET.
OKAY. LET'S MAKE A DEAL. I'LL BELIEVE WHATEVER YOU SAY ABOUT THIS MYSTICAL EVIL CRAP. I'LL BE YOUR SLAVE.
IF YOU DO ONE THING FOR ME--LOOK ME IN THE EYES.
THEY ARE TENDER.
DO I REMEMBER THIS FEELING?
I MUST ESCALATE THINGS. HOW CAN I ESCALATE TENDERNESS? I DON'T KNOW IT.
NO. MY JOB IS-- TO MAKE THINGS WORSE.

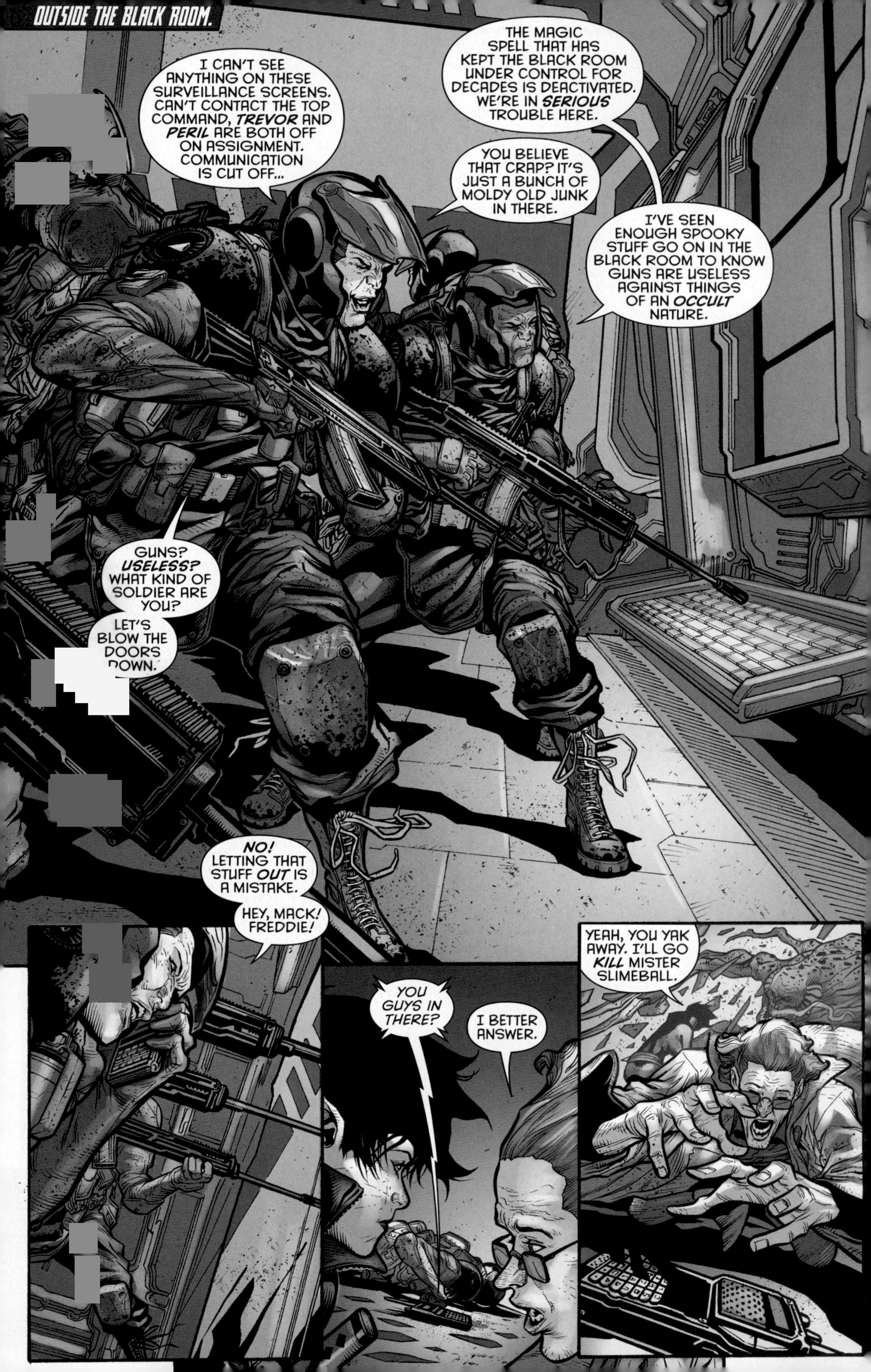

OUTSIDE THE BLACK ROOM.
I CAN'T SEE ANYTHING ON THESE SURVEILLANCE SCREENS. CAN'T CONTACT THE TOP COMMAND, TREVOR AND PERIL ARE BOTH OFF ON ASSIGNMENT. COMMUNICATION IS CUT OFF...
THE MAGIC SPELL THAT HAS KEPT THE BLACK ROOM UNDER CONTROL FOR DECADES IS DEACTIVATED. WE'RE IN SERIOUS TROUBLE HERE.
YOU BELIEVE THAT CRAP? IT'S JUST A BUNCH OF MOLDY OLD JUNK IN THERE.
I'VE SEEN ENOUGH SPOOKY STUFF GO ON IN THE BLACK ROOM TO KNOW GUNS ARE USELESS AGAINST THINGS OF AN OCCULT NATURE.
GUNS? USELESS? WHAT KIND OF SOLDIER ARE YOU?
LET'S BLOW THE DOORS DOWN.
NO! LETTING THAT STUFF OUT IS A MISTAKE.
HEY, MACK! FREDDIE!
YOU GUYS IN THERE?
I BETTER ANSWER.
YEAH, YOU YAK AWAY. I'LL GO KILL MISTER SLIMEBALL.

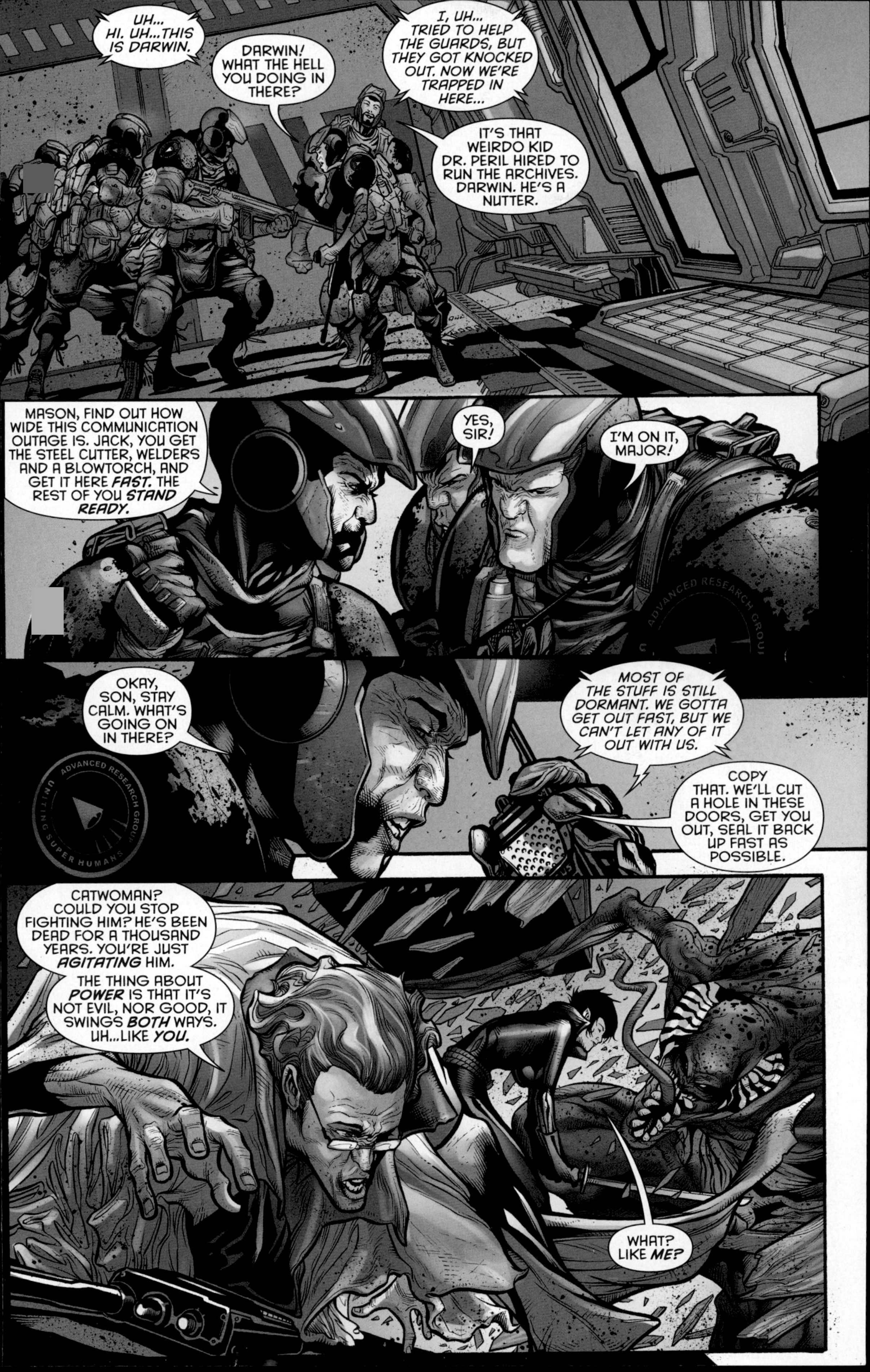
UH... HI. UH...THIS IS DARWIN.
DARWIN! WHAT THE HELL YOU DOING IN THERE?
I, UH... TRIED TO HELP THE GUARDS, BUT THEY GOT KNOCKED OUT. NOW WE'RE TRAPPED IN HERE...
IT'S THAT WEIRDO KID DR. PERIL HIRED TO RUN THE ARCHIVES. DARWIN. HE'S A NUTTER.
MASON, FIND OUT HOW WIDE THIS COMMUNICATION OUTAGE IS. JACK, YOU GET THE STEEL CUTTER, WELDERS AND A BLOWTORCH, AND GET IT HERE FAST. THE REST OF YOU STAND READY.
YES, SIR!
I'M ON IT, MAJOR!
ADVANCED RESEARCH GROUP
OKAY, SON, STAY CALM. WHAT'S GOING ON IN THERE?
MOST OF THE STUFF IS STILL DORMANT. WE GOTTA GET OUT FAST, BUT WE CAN'T LET ANY OF IT OUT WITH US.
COPY THAT. WE'LL CUT A HOLE IN THESE DOORS, GET YOU OUT, SEAL IT BACK UP FAST AS POSSIBLE.
ADVANCED RESEARCH GROUP UNITING SUPER HUMANS
CATWOMAN? COULD YOU STOP FIGHTING HIM? HE'S BEEN DEAD FOR A THOUSAND YEARS. YOU'RE JUST AGITATING HIM.
THE THING ABOUT POWER IS THAT IT'S NOT EVIL, NOR GOOD, IT SWINGS BOTH WAYS. UH...LIKE YOU.
WHAT? LIKE ME?

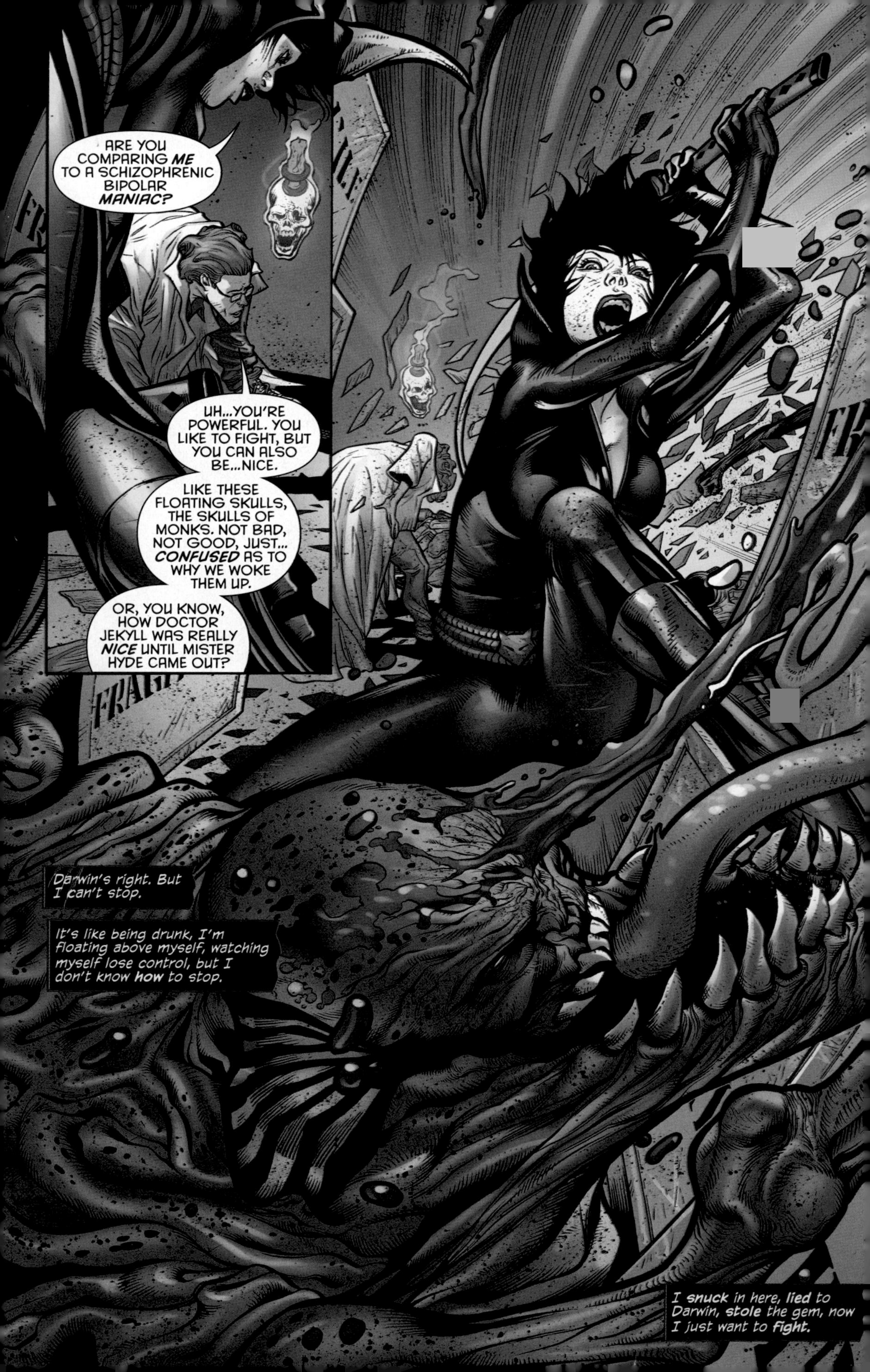
ARE YOU COMPARING ME TO A SCHIZOPHRENIC BIPOLAR MANIAC?
UH...YOU'RE POWERFUL. YOU LIKE TO FIGHT, BUT YOU CAN ALSO BE...NICE.
LIKE THESE FLOATING SKULLS, THE SKULLS OF MONKS. NOT BAD, NOT GOOD, JUST... CONFUSED AS TO WHY WE WOKE THEM UP.
OR, YOU KNOW, HOW DOCTOR JEKYLL WAS REALLY NICE UNTIL MISTER HYDE CAME OUT?
Darwin's right. But I can't stop.
It's like being drunk, I'm floating above myself, watching myself lose control, but I don't know how to stop.
I snuck in here, lied to Darwin, stole the gem, now I just want to fight.

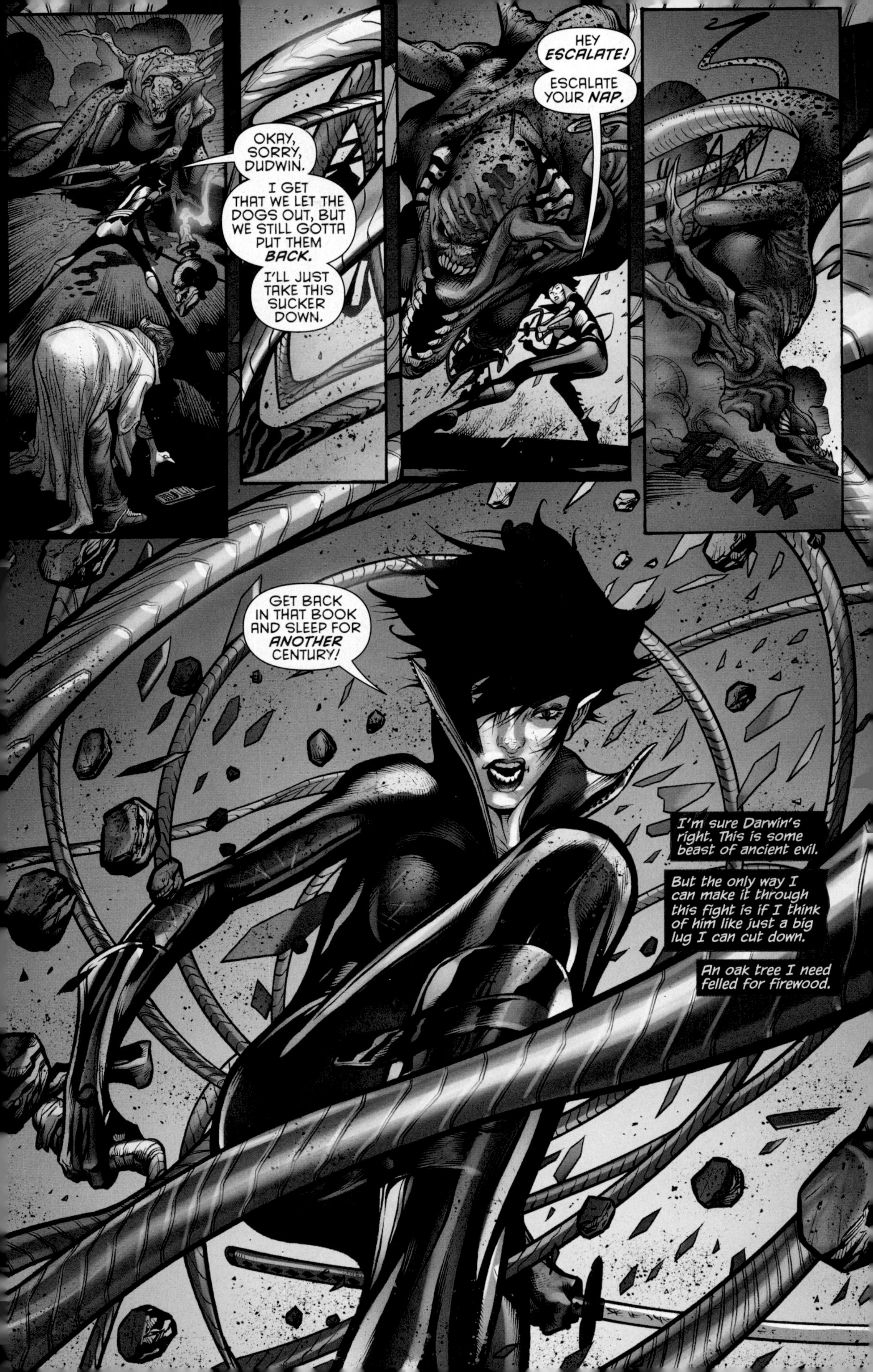
OKAY, SORRY, DUDWIN.
I GET THAT WE LET THE DOGS OUT, BUT WE STILL GOTTA PUT THEM BACK.
I'LL JUST TAKE THIS SUCKER DOWN.
HEY ESCALATE!
ESCALATE YOUR NAP.
THUNK
GET BACK IN THAT BOOK AND SLEEP FOR ANOTHER CENTURY!
I'm sure Darwin's right. This is some beast of ancient evil.
But the only way I can make it through this fight is if I think of him like just a big lug I can cut down.
An oak tree I need felled for firewood.

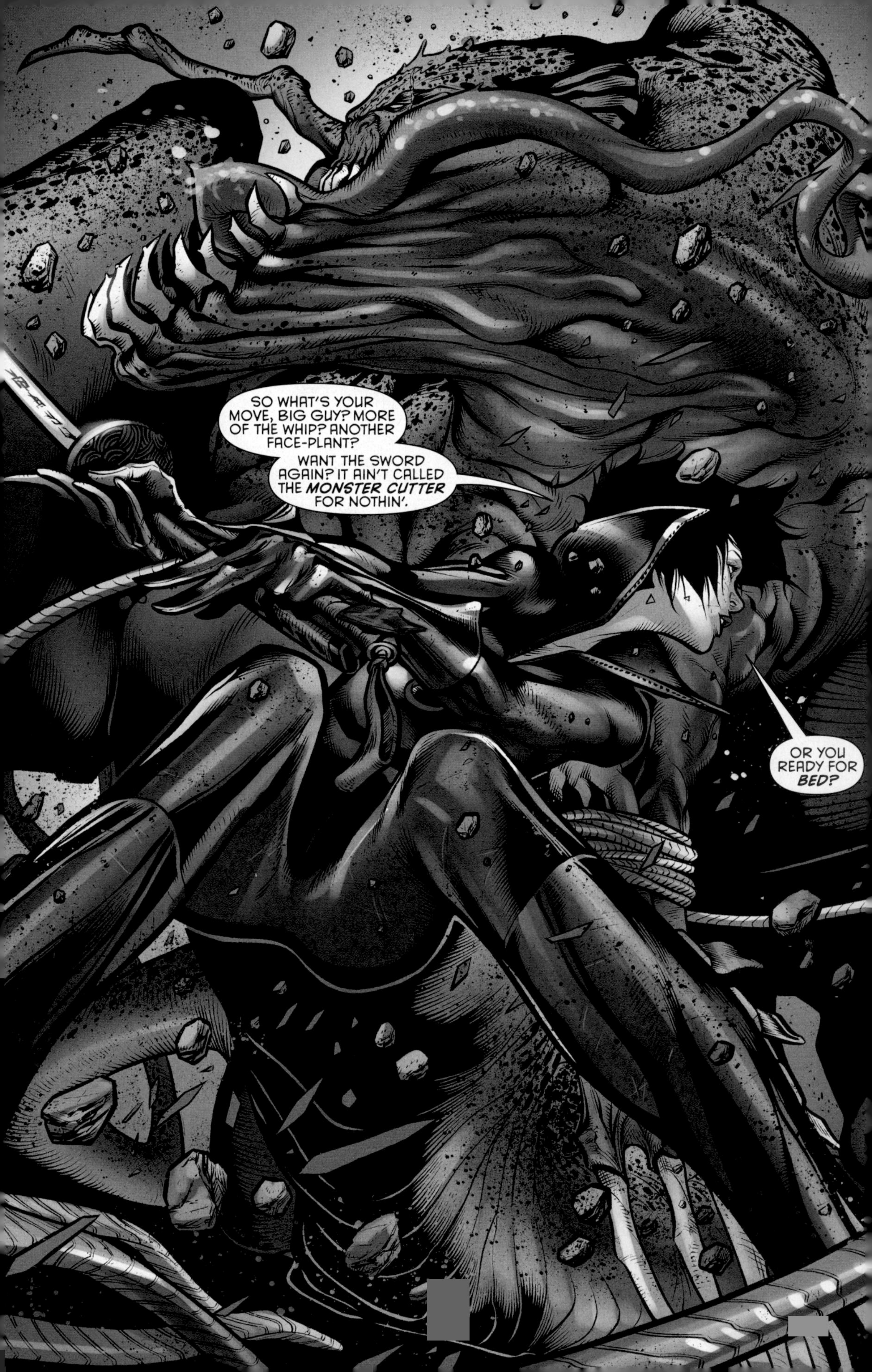
SO WHAT'S YOUR MOVE, BIG GUY? MORE OF THE WHIP? ANOTHER FACE-PLANT?
WANT THE SWORD AGAIN? IT AIN'T CALLED THE *MONSTER CUTTER* FOR NOTHIN'.
OR YOU READY FOR *BED?*

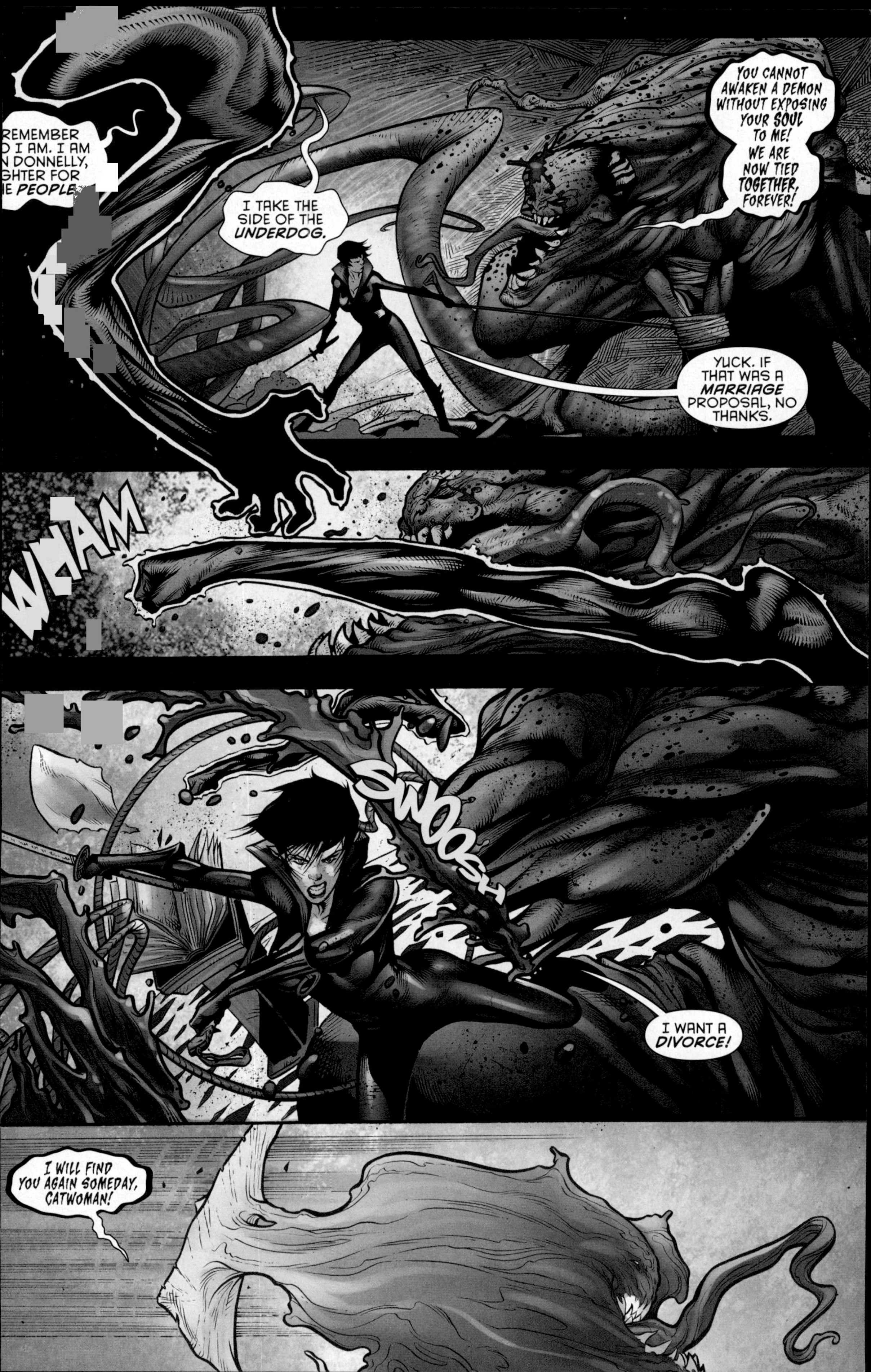
REMEMBER D I AM. I AM N DONNELLY, GHTER FOR IE PEOPLE
I TAKE THE SIDE OF THE UNDERDOG.
YOU CANNOT AWAKEN A DEMON WITHOUT EXPOSING YOUR SOUL TO ME! WE ARE NOW TIED TOGETHER, FOREVER!
YUCK. IF THAT WAS A MARRIAGE PROPOSAL, NO THANKS.
WHAM
SWOOSH
I WANT A DIVORCE!
I WILL FIND YOU AGAIN SOMEDAY, CATWOMAN!

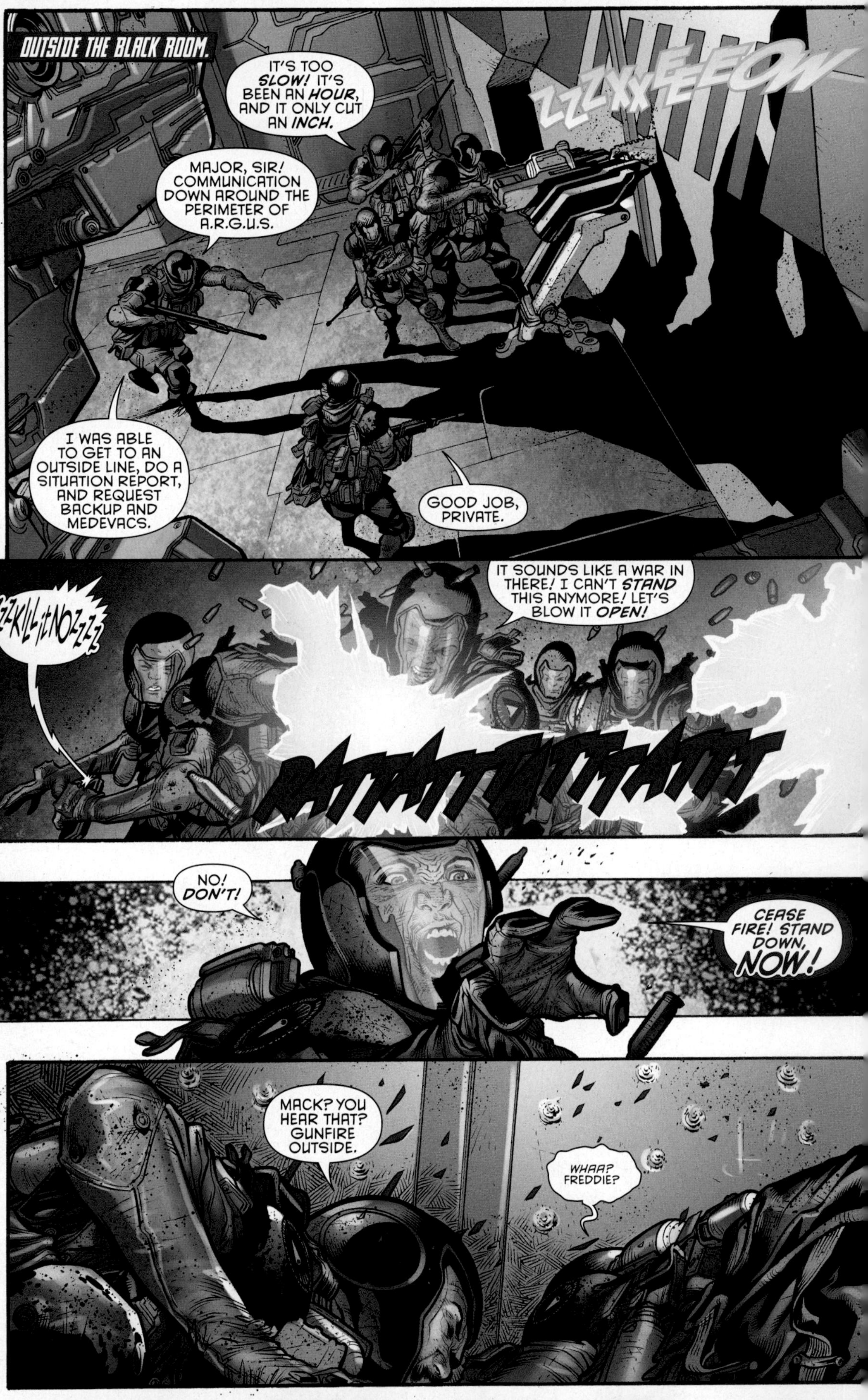
OUTSIDE THE BLACK ROOM.
IT'S TOO SLOW! IT'S BEEN AN HOUR, AND IT ONLY CUT AN INCH.
ZZZXXEEEEOW
MAJOR, SIR! COMMUNICATION DOWN AROUND THE PERIMETER OF A.R.G.U.S.
I WAS ABLE TO GET TO AN OUTSIDE LINE, DO A SITUATION REPORT, AND REQUEST BACKUP AND MEDEVACS.
GOOD JOB, PRIVATE.
ZZZ-KILL-it NOZZZZ
IT SOUNDS LIKE A WAR IN THERE! I CAN'T STAND THIS ANYMORE! LET'S BLOW IT OPEN!
RATATATTATTATATT
NO! DON'T!
CEASE FIRE! STAND DOWN, NOW!
MACK? YOU HEAR THAT? GUNFIRE OUTSIDE.
WHAA? FREDDIE?

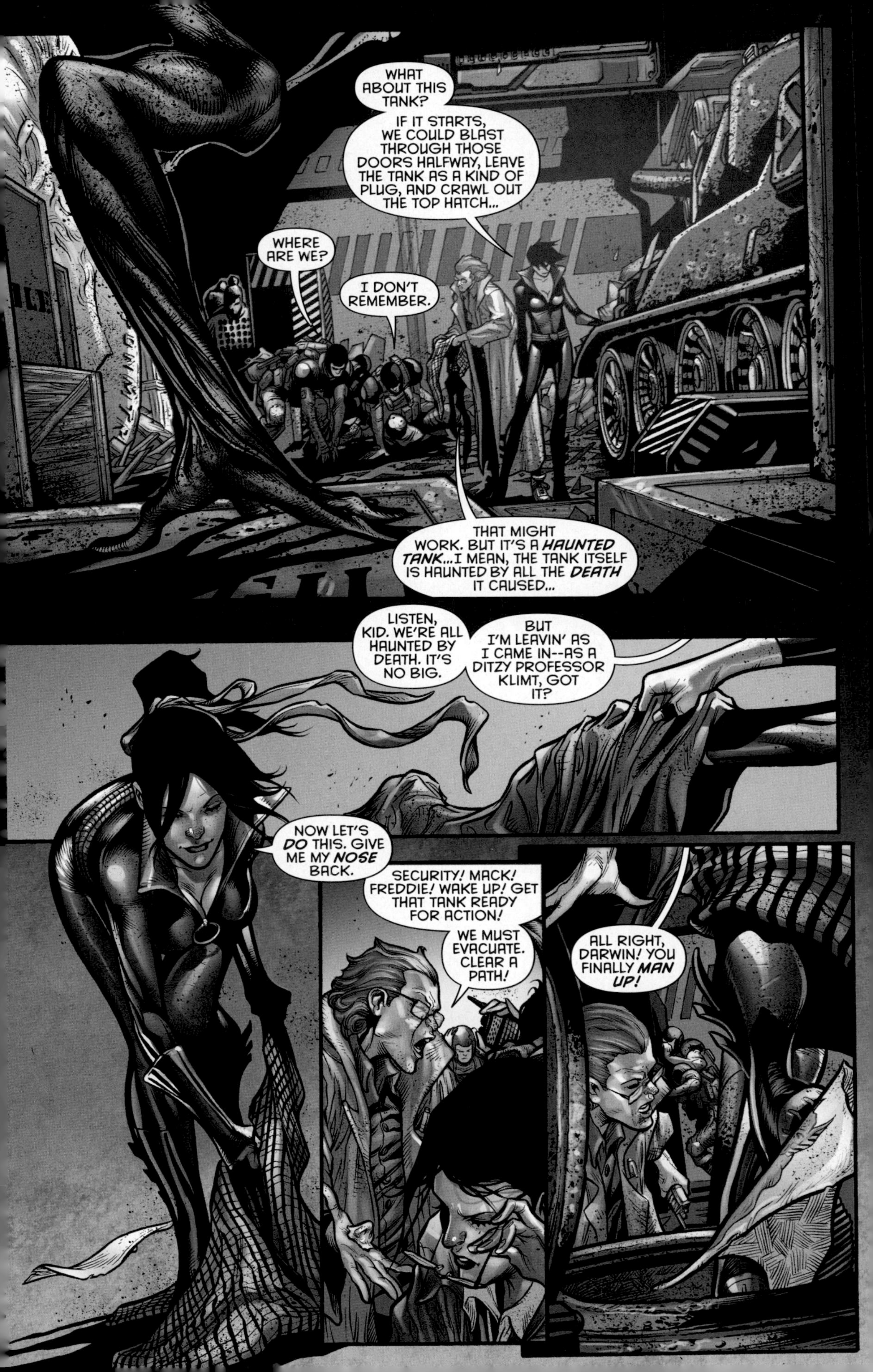
WHAT ABOUT THIS TANK?
IF IT STARTS, WE COULD BLAST THROUGH THOSE DOORS HALFWAY, LEAVE THE TANK AS A KIND OF PLUG, AND CRAWL OUT THE TOP HATCH...
WHERE ARE WE?
I DON'T REMEMBER.
THAT MIGHT WORK. BUT IT'S A *HAUNTED TANK*...I MEAN, THE TANK ITSELF IS HAUNTED BY ALL THE *DEATH* IT CAUSED...
LISTEN, KID. WE'RE ALL HAUNTED BY DEATH. IT'S NO BIG.
BUT I'M LEAVIN' AS I CAME IN--AS A DITZY PROFESSOR KLIMT, GOT IT?
NOW LET'S *DO* THIS. GIVE ME MY *NOSE* BACK.
SECURITY! MACK! FREDDIE! WAKE UP! GET THAT TANK READY FOR ACTION!
WE MUST EVACUATE. CLEAR A PATH!
ALL RIGHT, DARWIN! YOU FINALLY *MAN UP!*

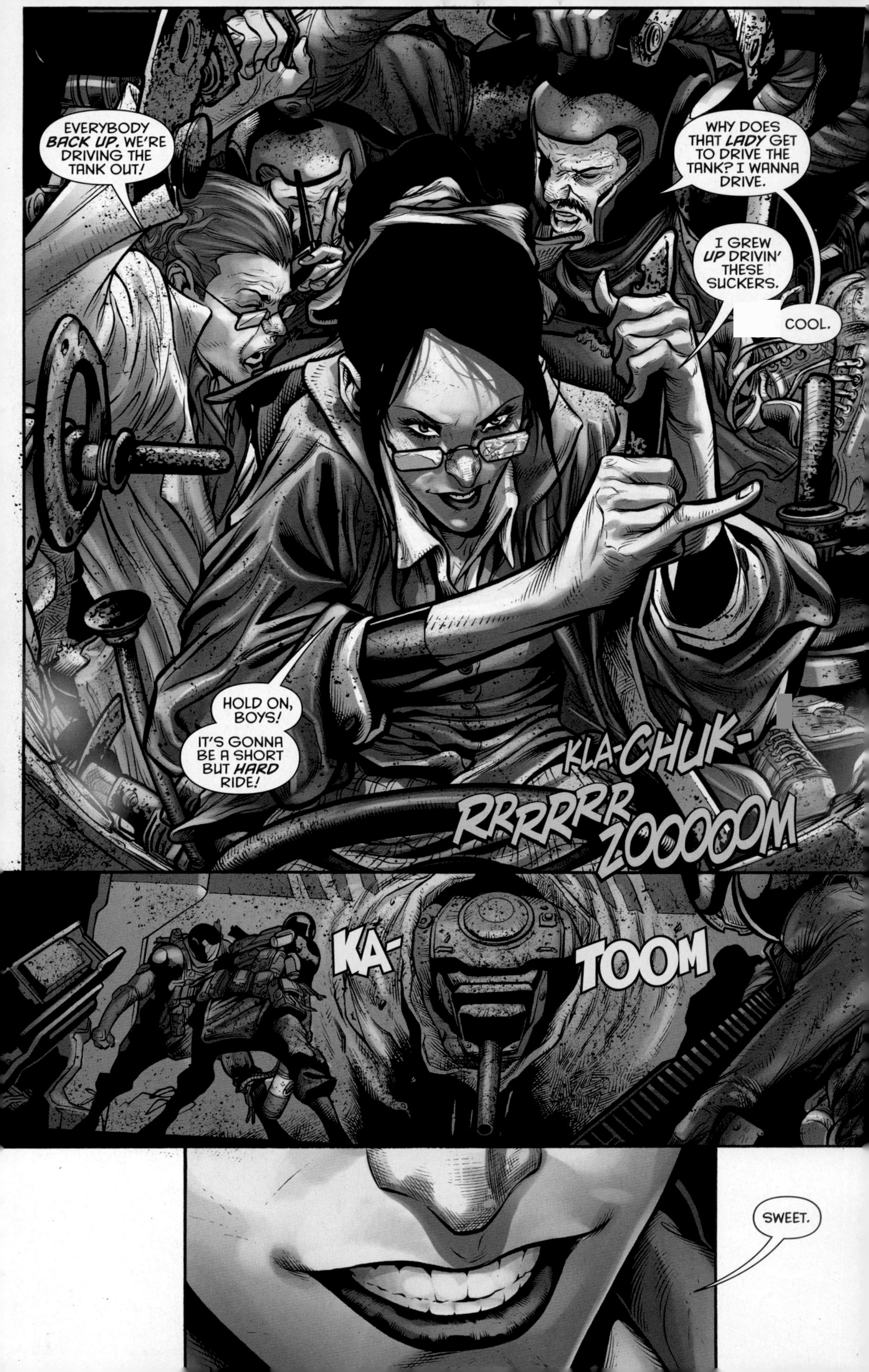
EVERYBODY BACK UP. WE'RE DRIVING THE TANK OUT!
WHY DOES THAT LADY GET TO DRIVE THE TANK? I WANNA DRIVE.
I GREW UP DRIVIN' THESE SUCKERS.
COOL.
HOLD ON, BOYS!
IT'S GONNA BE A SHORT BUT HARD RIDE!
KLA-CHUK-
RRRRRR ZOOOOOOM
KA- TOOM
SWEET.

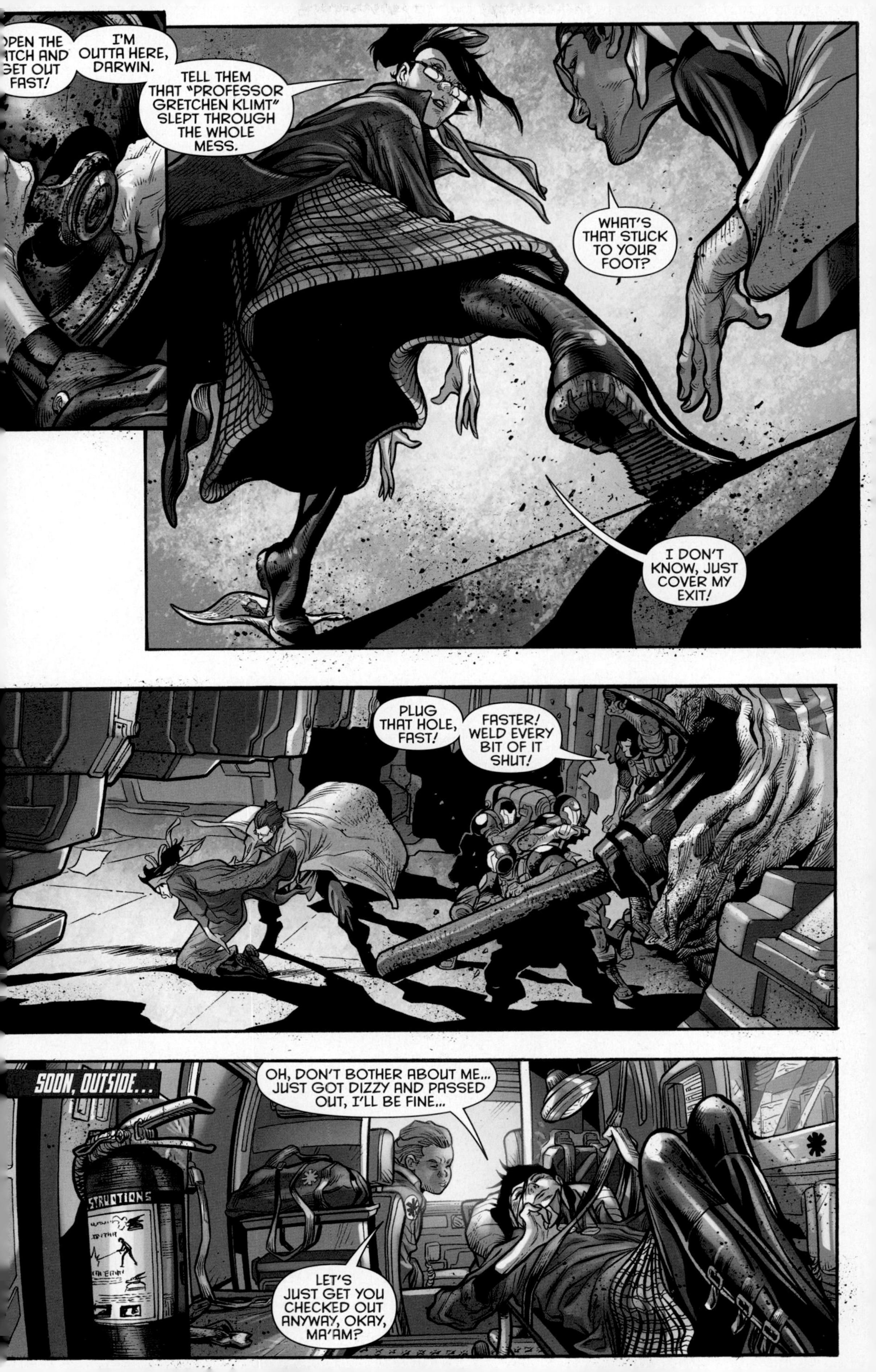
OPEN THE HATCH AND GET OUT FAST!
I'M OUTTA HERE, DARWIN.
TELL THEM THAT "PROFESSOR GRETCHEN KLIMT" SLEPT THROUGH THE WHOLE MESS.
WHAT'S THAT STUCK TO YOUR FOOT?
I DON'T KNOW, JUST COVER MY EXIT!
PLUG THAT HOLE, FAST!
FASTER! WELD EVERY BIT OF IT SHUT!
SOON, OUTSIDE...
OH, DON'T BOTHER ABOUT ME... JUST GOT DIZZY AND PASSED OUT, I'LL BE FINE...
LET'S JUST GET YOU CHECKED OUT ANYWAY, OKAY, MA'AM?

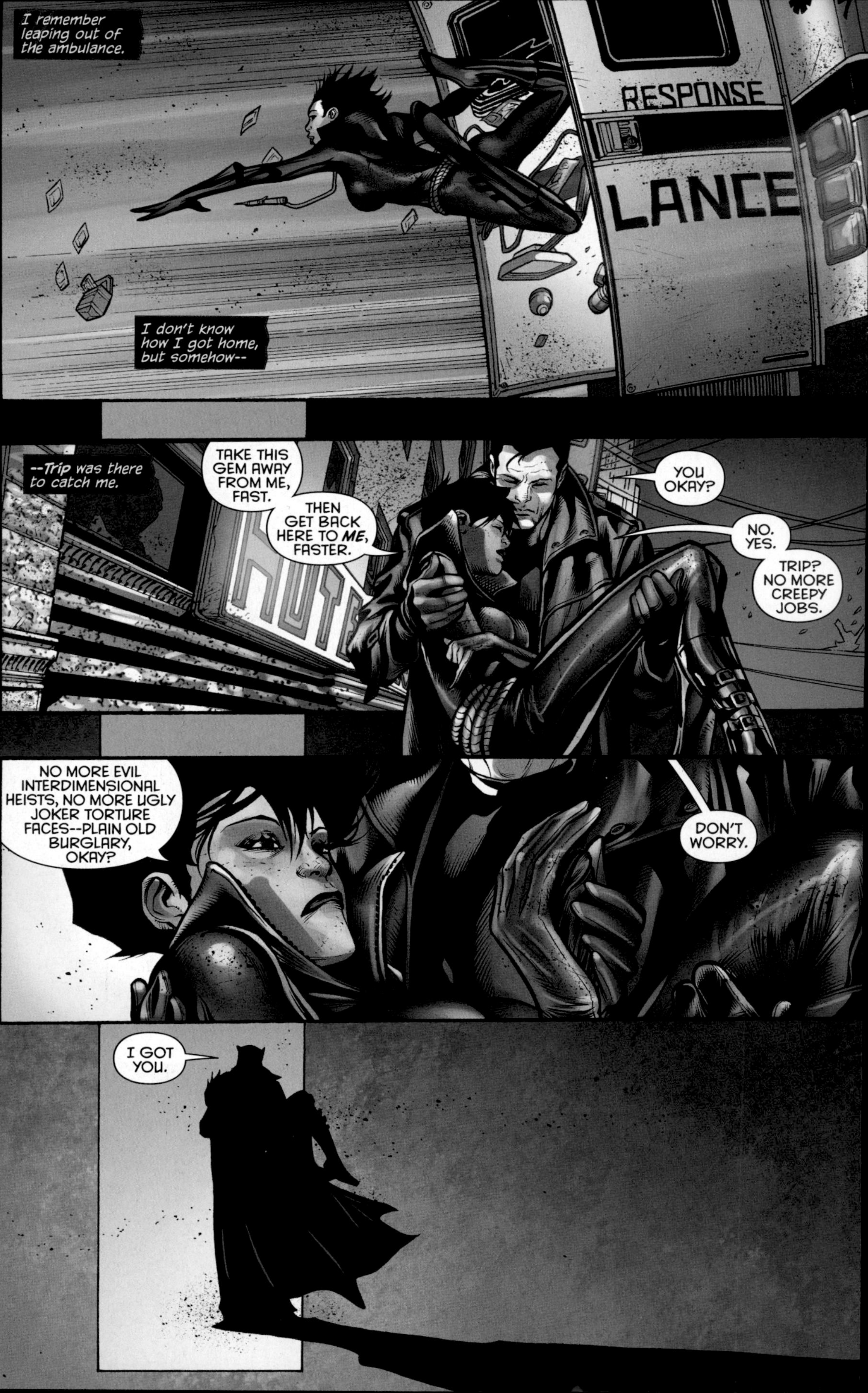
I remember leaping out of the ambulance.
RESPONSE
LANCE
I don't know how I got home, but somehow--
--Trip was there to catch me.
TAKE THIS GEM AWAY FROM ME, FAST.
THEN GET BACK HERE TO ME, FASTER.
YOU OKAY?
NO. YES.
TRIP? NO MORE CREEPY JOBS.
NO MORE EVIL INTERDIMENSIONAL HEISTS, NO MORE UGLY JOKER TORTURE FACES--PLAIN OLD BURGLARY, OKAY?
DON'T WORRY.
I GOT YOU.

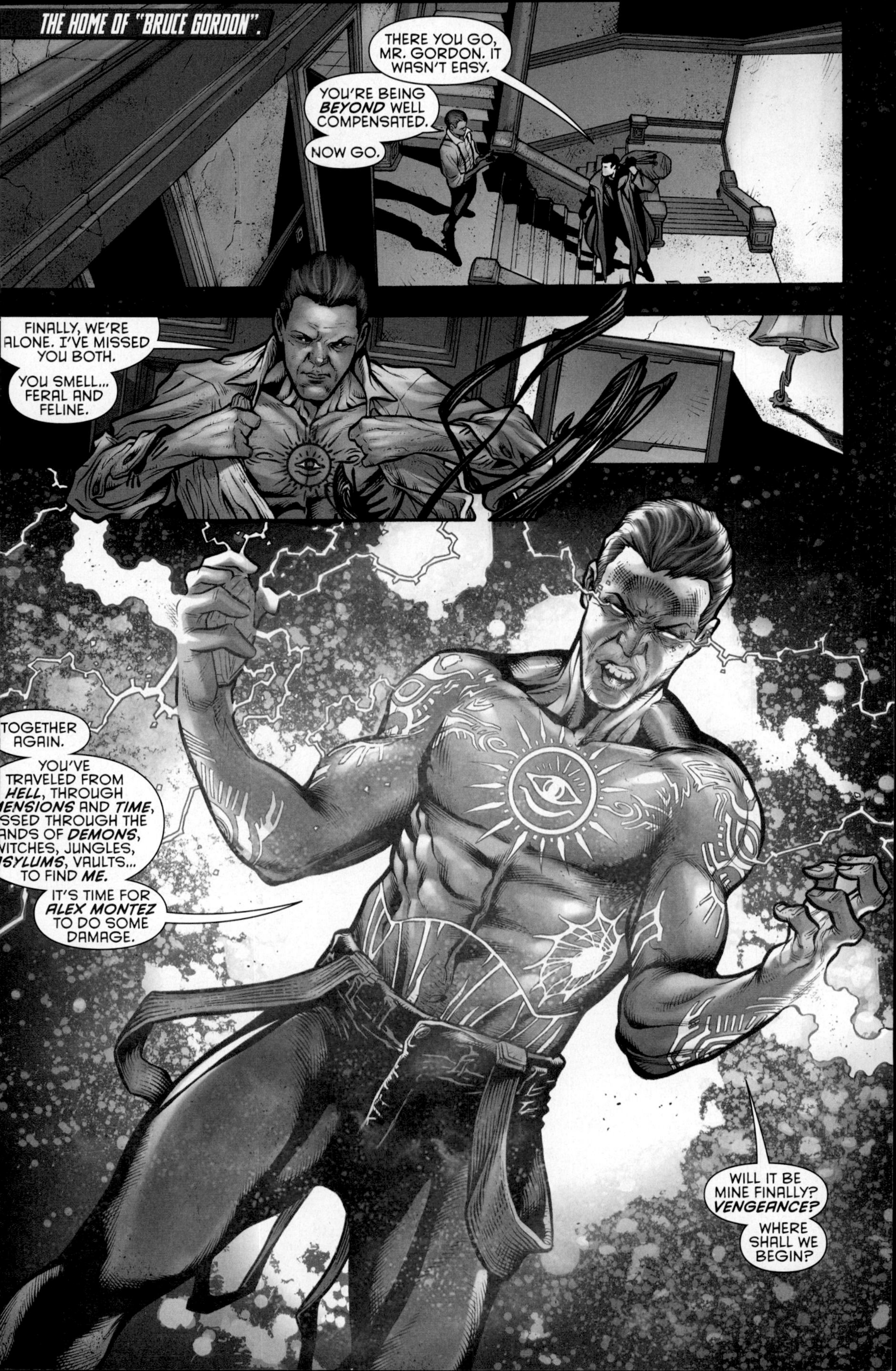
THE HOME OF "BRUCE GORDON".
THERE YOU GO, MR. GORDON. IT WASN'T EASY.
YOU'RE BEING **BEYOND** WELL COMPENSATED.
NOW GO.
FINALLY, WE'RE ALONE. I'VE MISSED YOU BOTH.
YOU SMELL... FERAL AND FELINE.
TOGETHER AGAIN.
YOU'VE TRAVELED FROM **HELL**, THROUGH **IENSIONS** AND **TIME**, SSED THROUGH THE ANDS OF **DEMONS**, WITCHES, JUNGLES, **SYLUMS**, VAULTS... TO FIND **ME**.
IT'S TIME FOR **ALEX MONTEZ** TO DO SOME DAMAGE.
WILL IT BE MINE FINALLY? **VENGEANCE?**
WHERE SHALL WE BEGIN?

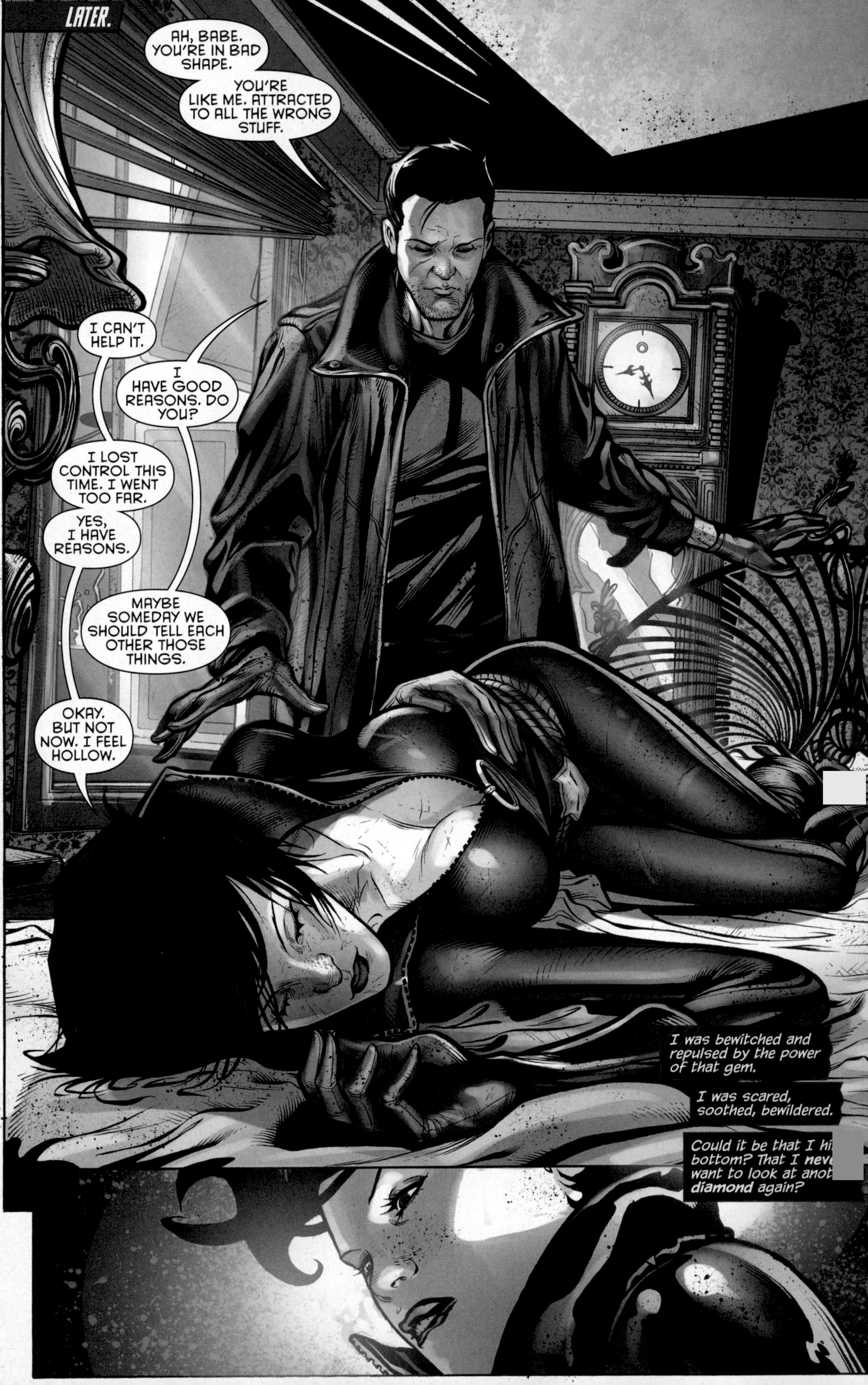
LATER.
AH, BABE. YOU'RE IN BAD SHAPE.
YOU'RE LIKE ME. ATTRACTED TO ALL THE WRONG STUFF.
I CAN'T HELP IT.
I HAVE GOOD REASONS. DO YOU?
I LOST CONTROL THIS TIME. I WENT TOO FAR.
YES, I HAVE REASONS.
MAYBE SOMEDAY WE SHOULD TELL EACH OTHER THOSE THINGS.
OKAY. BUT NOT NOW. I FEEL HOLLOW.
I was bewitched and repulsed by the power of that gem.
I was scared, soothed, bewildered.
Could it be that I hi bottom? That I neve want to look at anot diamond again?

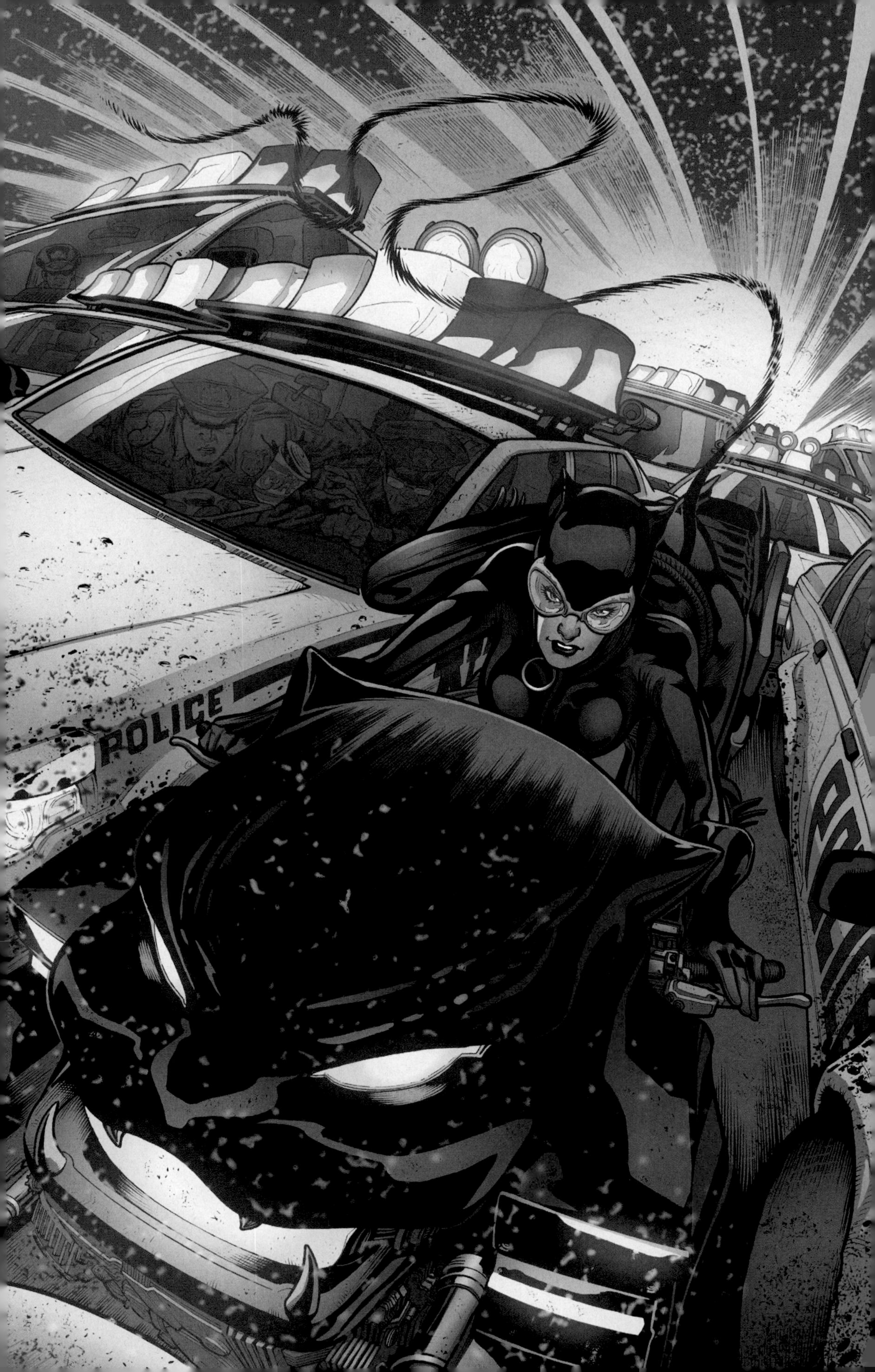
POLICE

ANN NOCENTI writer RAFA SANDOVAL penciller JORDI TARRAGONA inker cover by RAFA SANDOVAL & JORDI TARRAGONA

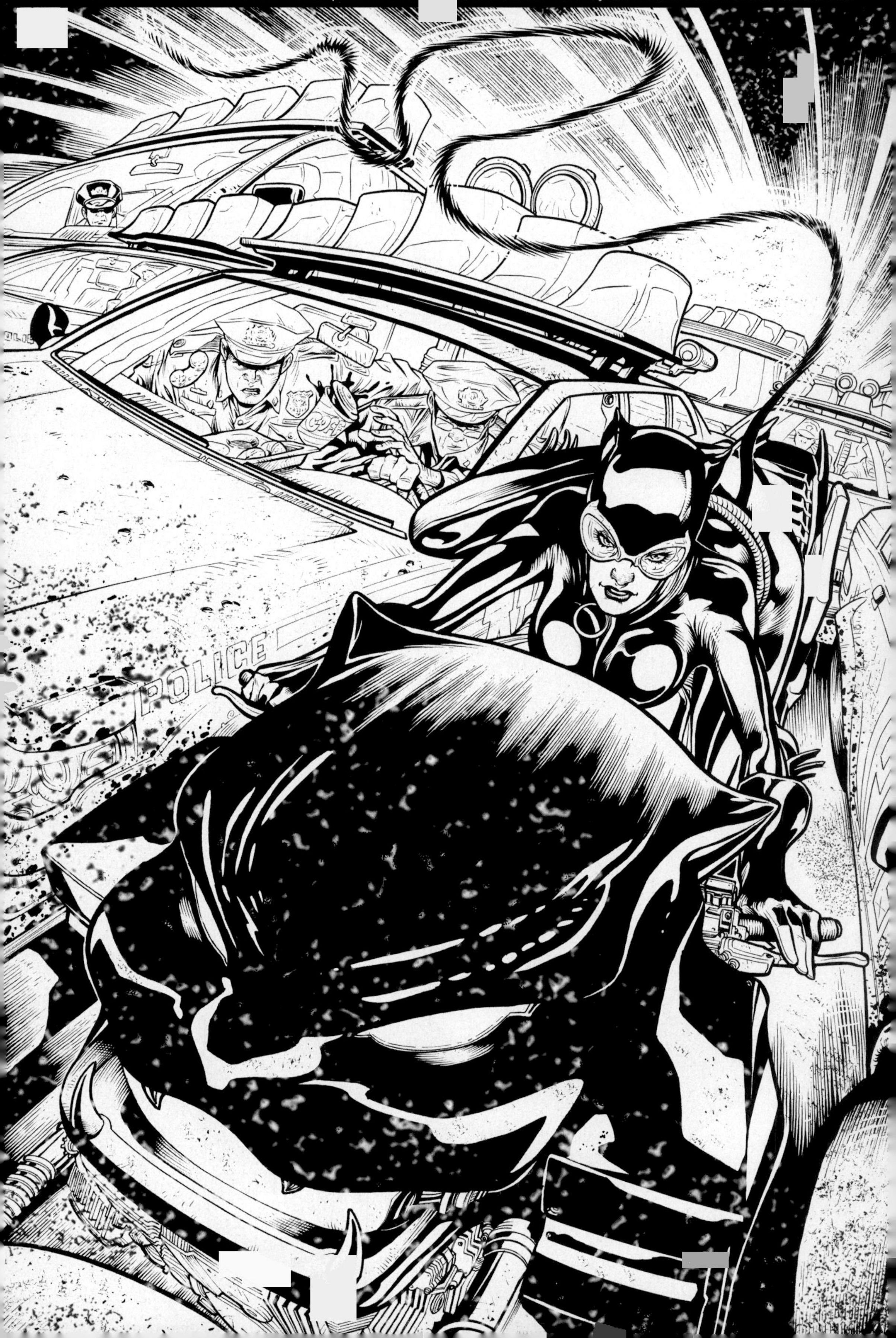

POLICE

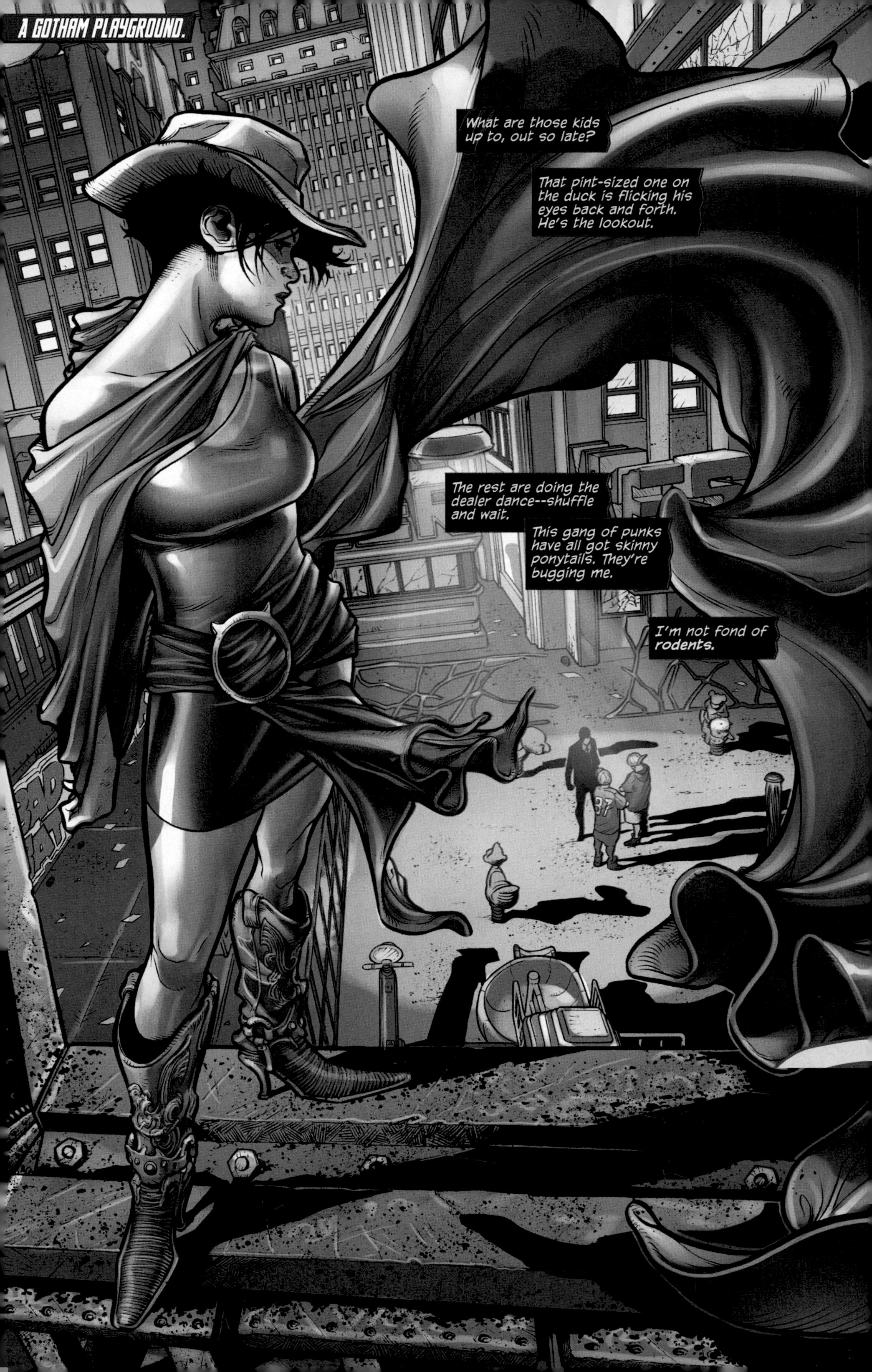
A GOTHAM PLAYGROUND.
What are those kids up to, out so late?
That pint-sized one on the duck is flicking his eyes back and forth. He's the lookout.
The rest are doing the dealer dance--shuffle and wait.
This gang of punks have all got skinny ponytails. They're bugging me.
I'm not fond of **rodents.**

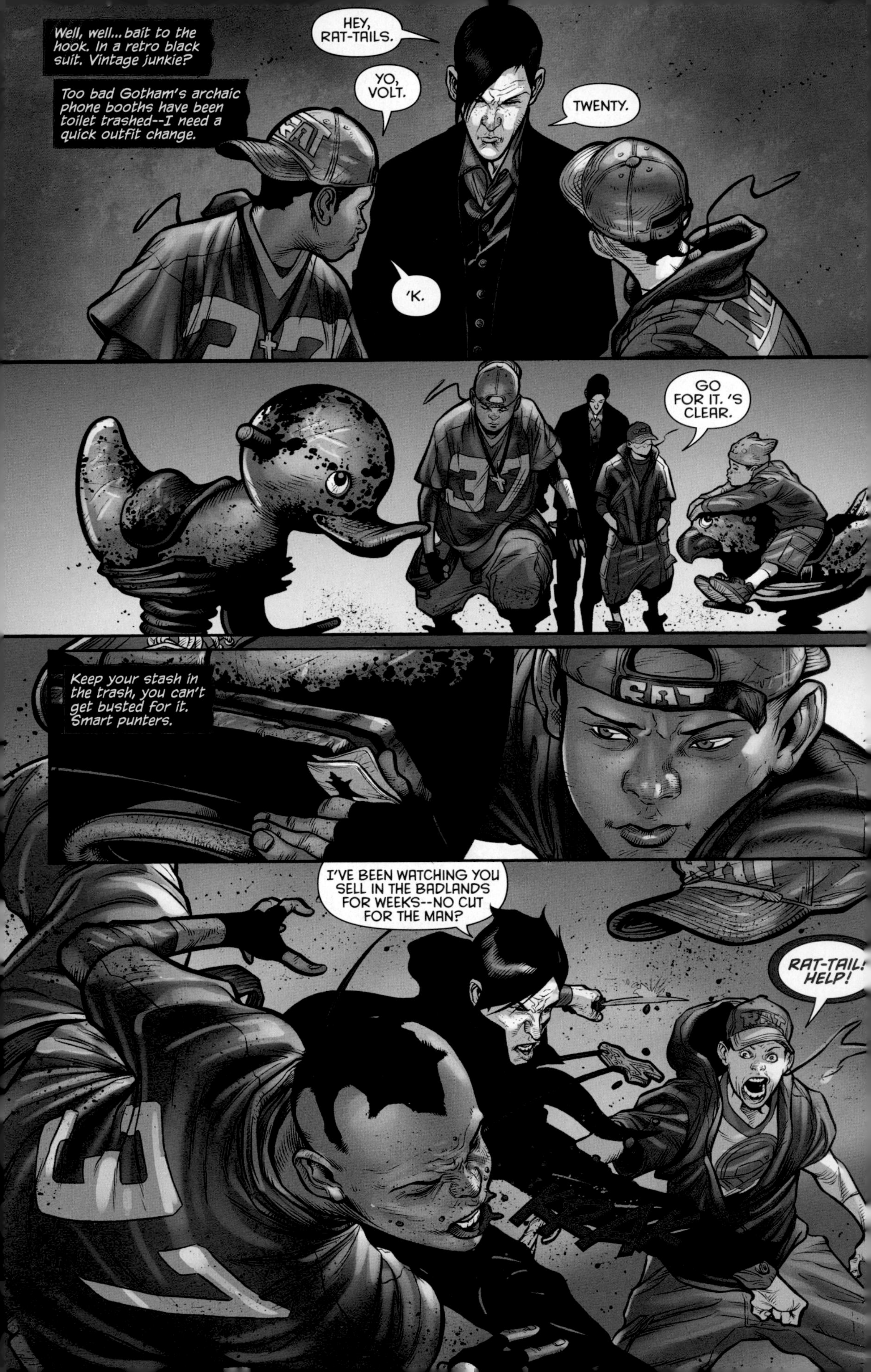
Well, well...bait to the hook. In a retro black suit. Vintage junkie?
HEY, RAT-TAILS.
Too bad Gotham's archaic phone booths have been toilet trashed--I need a quick outfit change.
YO, VOLT.
TWENTY.
'K.
GO FOR IT. 'S CLEAR.
Keep your stash in the trash, you can't get busted for it. Smart punters.
I'VE BEEN WATCHING YOU SELL IN THE BADLANDS FOR WEEKS--NO CUT FOR THE MAN?
RAT-TAIL! HELP!

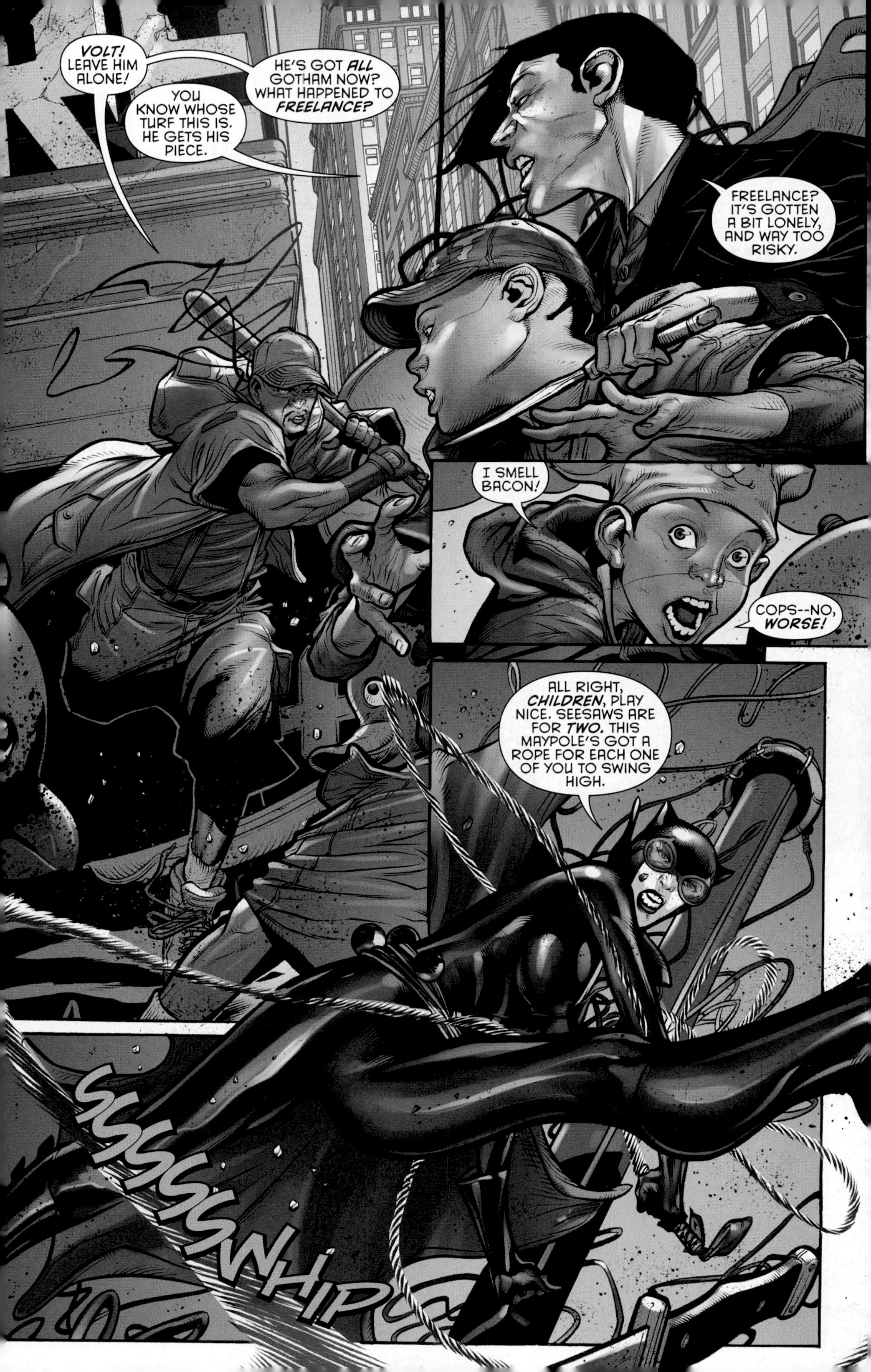
VOLT! LEAVE HIM ALONE!
HE'S GOT ALL GOTHAM NOW? WHAT HAPPENED TO FREELANCE?
YOU KNOW WHOSE TURF THIS IS. HE GETS HIS PIECE.
FREELANCE? IT'S GOTTEN A BIT LONELY, AND WAY TOO RISKY.
I SMELL BACON!
COPS--NO, WORSE!
ALL RIGHT, CHILDREN, PLAY NICE. SEESAWS ARE FOR TWO. THIS MAYPOLE'S GOT A ROPE FOR EACH ONE OF YOU TO SWING HIGH.
SSSSSSWHIP

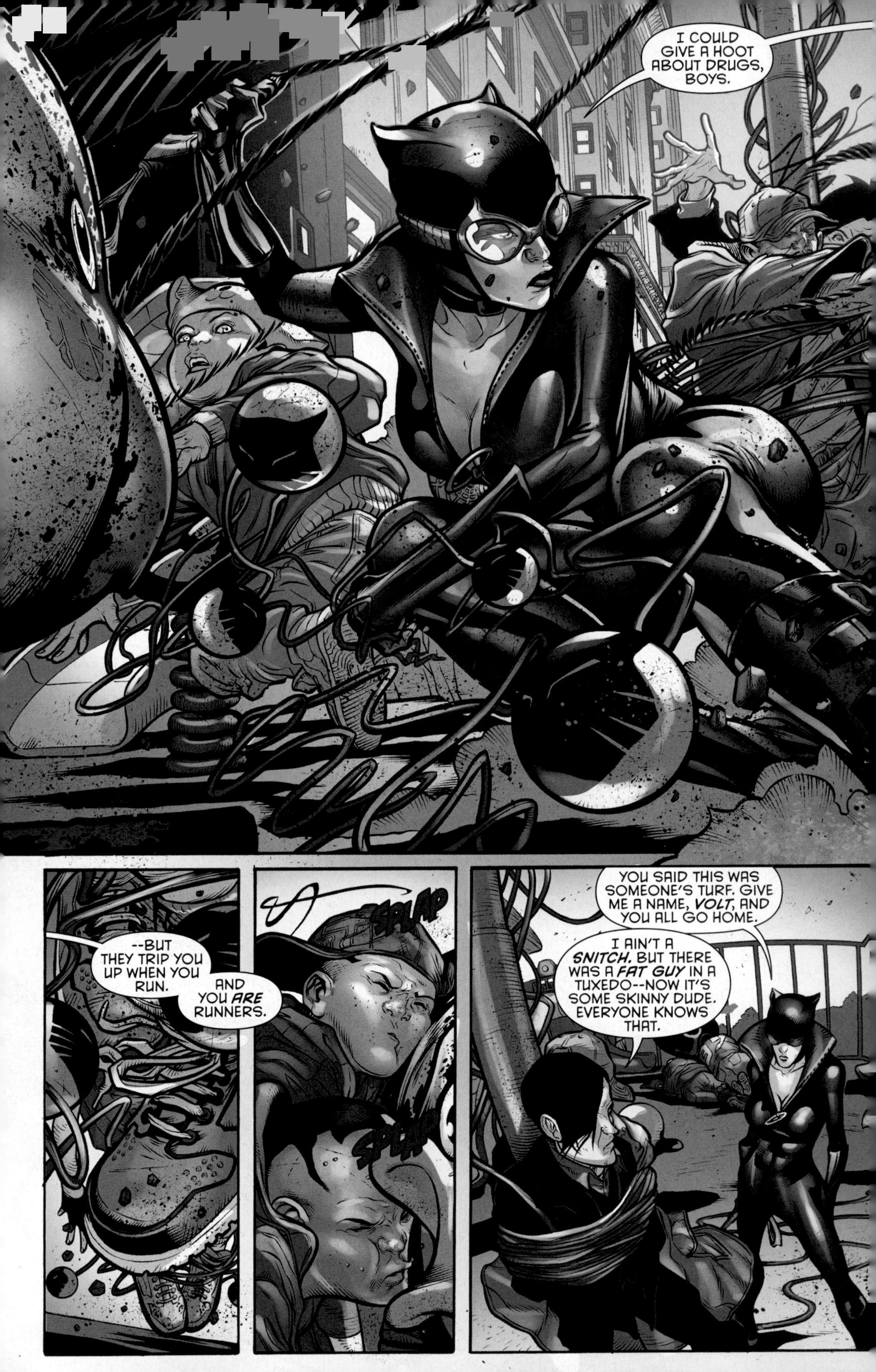
I COULD GIVE A HOOT ABOUT DRUGS, BOYS.
--BUT THEY TRIP YOU UP WHEN YOU RUN.
AND YOU *ARE* RUNNERS.
SPLAP
SPLAP
YOU SAID THIS WAS SOMEONE'S TURF. GIVE ME A NAME, *VOLT*, AND YOU ALL GO HOME.
I AIN'T A *SNITCH*. BUT THERE WAS A *FAT GUY* IN A TUXEDO--NOW IT'S SOME SKINNY DUDE. EVERYONE KNOWS THAT.

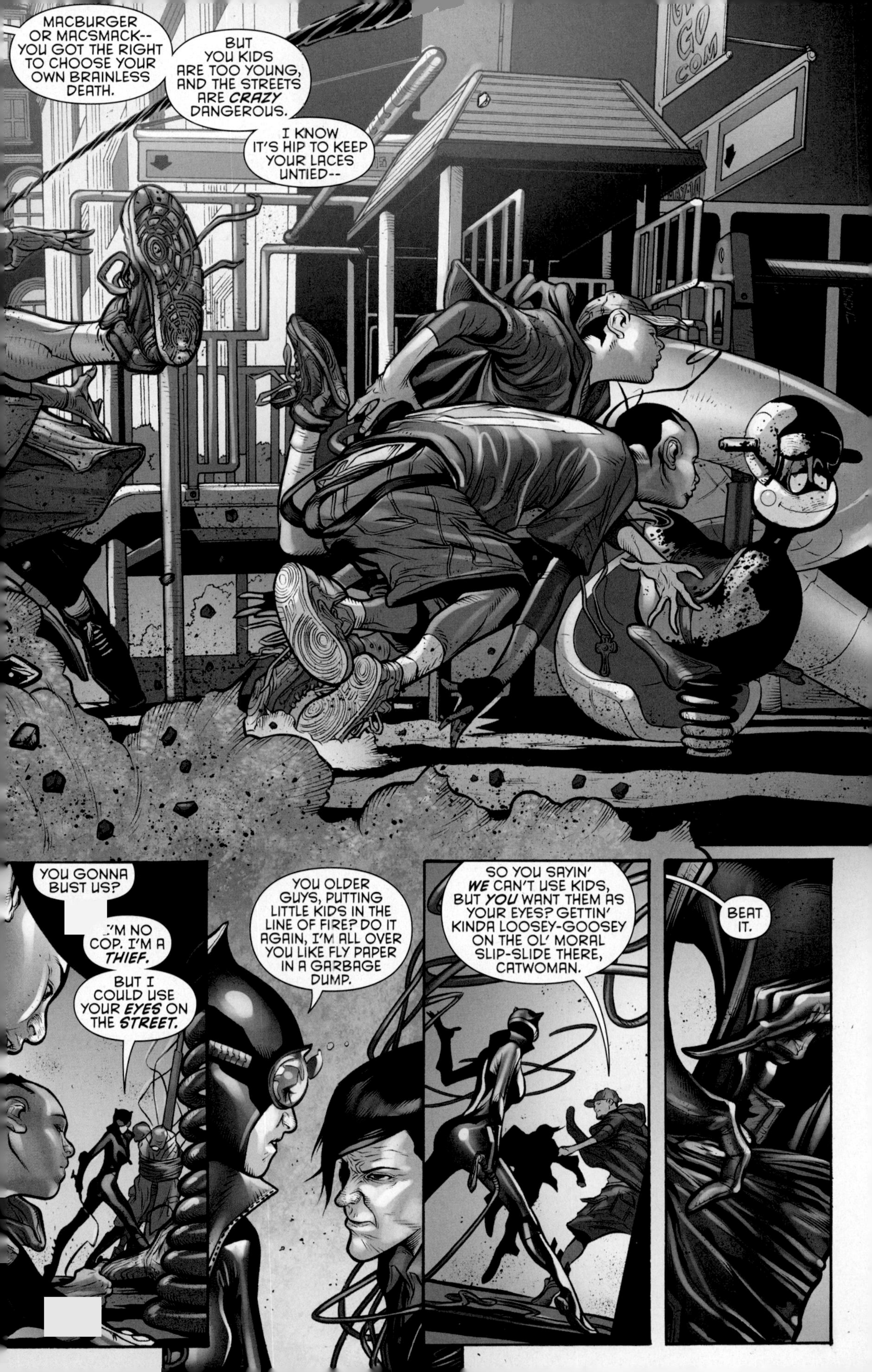
MACBURGER OR MACSMACK-- YOU GOT THE RIGHT TO CHOOSE YOUR OWN BRAINLESS DEATH.
BUT YOU KIDS ARE TOO YOUNG, AND THE STREETS ARE *CRAZY* DANGEROUS.
I KNOW IT'S HIP TO KEEP YOUR LACES UNTIED--
YOU GONNA BUST US?
'M NO COP. I'M A *THIEF.*
BUT I COULD USE YOUR *EYES* ON THE *STREET.*
YOU OLDER GUYS, PUTTING LITTLE KIDS IN THE LINE OF FIRE? DO IT AGAIN, I'M ALL OVER YOU LIKE FLY PAPER IN A GARBAGE DUMP.
SO YOU SAYIN' *WE* CAN'T USE KIDS, BUT *YOU* WANT THEM AS YOUR EYES? GETTIN' KINDA LOOSEY-GOOSEY ON THE OL' MORAL SLIP-SLIDE THERE, CATWOMAN.
BEAT IT.

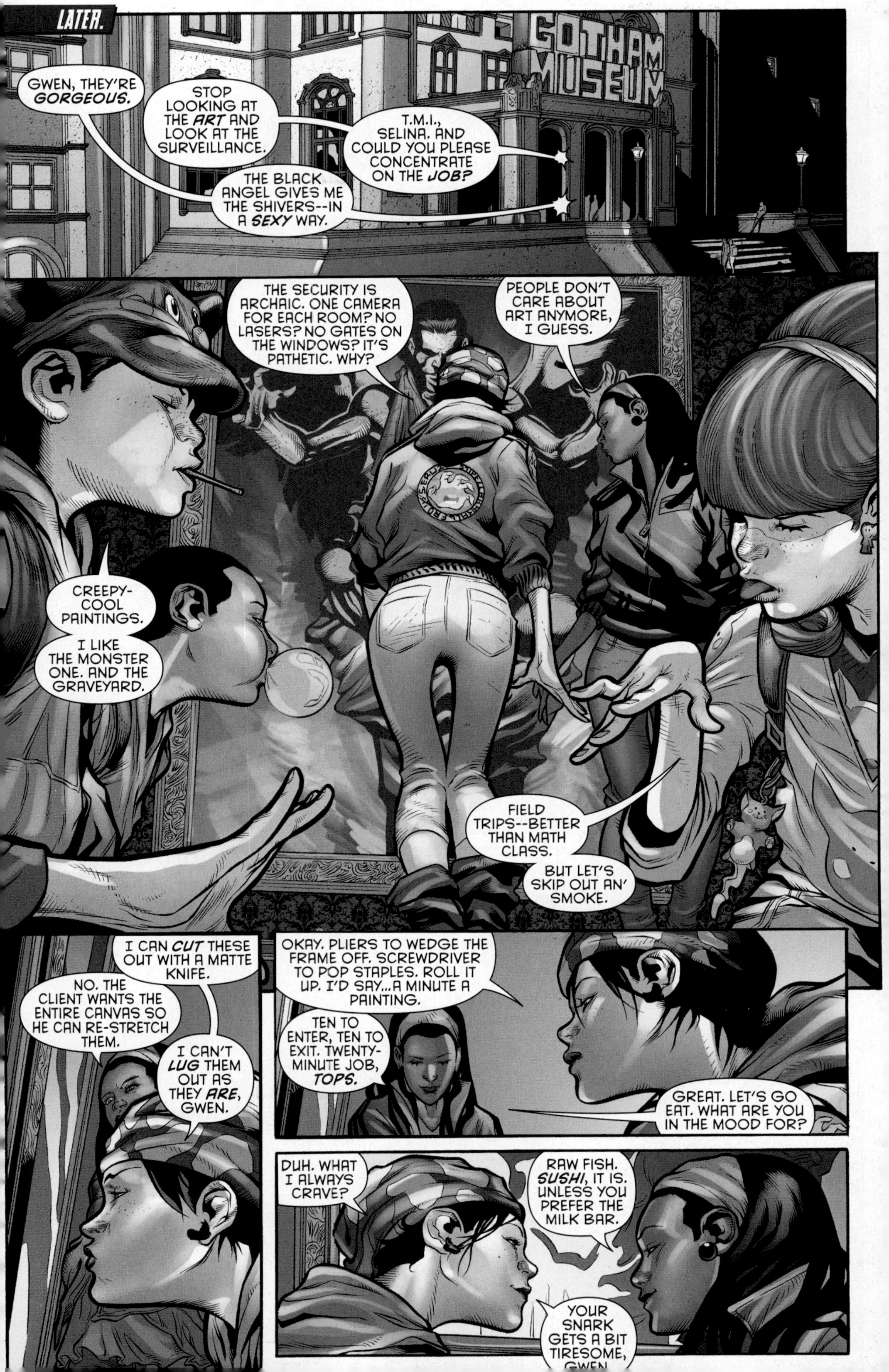

LATER.
GOTHAM MUSEUM
GWEN, THEY'RE *GORGEOUS.*
STOP LOOKING AT THE *ART* AND LOOK AT THE SURVEILLANCE.
T.M.I., SELINA. AND COULD YOU PLEASE CONCENTRATE ON THE *JOB?*
THE BLACK ANGEL GIVES ME THE SHIVERS--IN A *SEXY* WAY.
THE SECURITY IS ARCHAIC. ONE CAMERA FOR EACH ROOM? NO LASERS? NO GATES ON THE WINDOWS? IT'S PATHETIC. WHY?
PEOPLE DON'T CARE ABOUT ART ANYMORE, I GUESS.
CREEPY-COOL PAINTINGS.
I LIKE THE MONSTER ONE. AND THE GRAVEYARD.
FIELD TRIPS--BETTER THAN MATH CLASS.
BUT LET'S SKIP OUT AN' SMOKE.
I CAN *CUT* THESE OUT WITH A MATTE KNIFE.
NO. THE CLIENT WANTS THE ENTIRE CANVAS SO HE CAN RE-STRETCH THEM.
I CAN'T *LUG* THEM OUT AS THEY *ARE,* GWEN.
OKAY. PLIERS TO WEDGE THE FRAME OFF. SCREWDRIVER TO POP STAPLES. ROLL IT UP. I'D SAY...A MINUTE A PAINTING.
TEN TO ENTER, TEN TO EXIT. TWENTY-MINUTE JOB, *TOPS.*
GREAT. LET'S GO EAT. WHAT ARE YOU IN THE MOOD FOR?
DUH. WHAT I ALWAYS CRAVE?
RAW FISH. *SUSHI,* IT IS. UNLESS YOU PREFER THE MILK BAR.
YOUR SNARK GETS A BIT TIRESOME, GWEN.

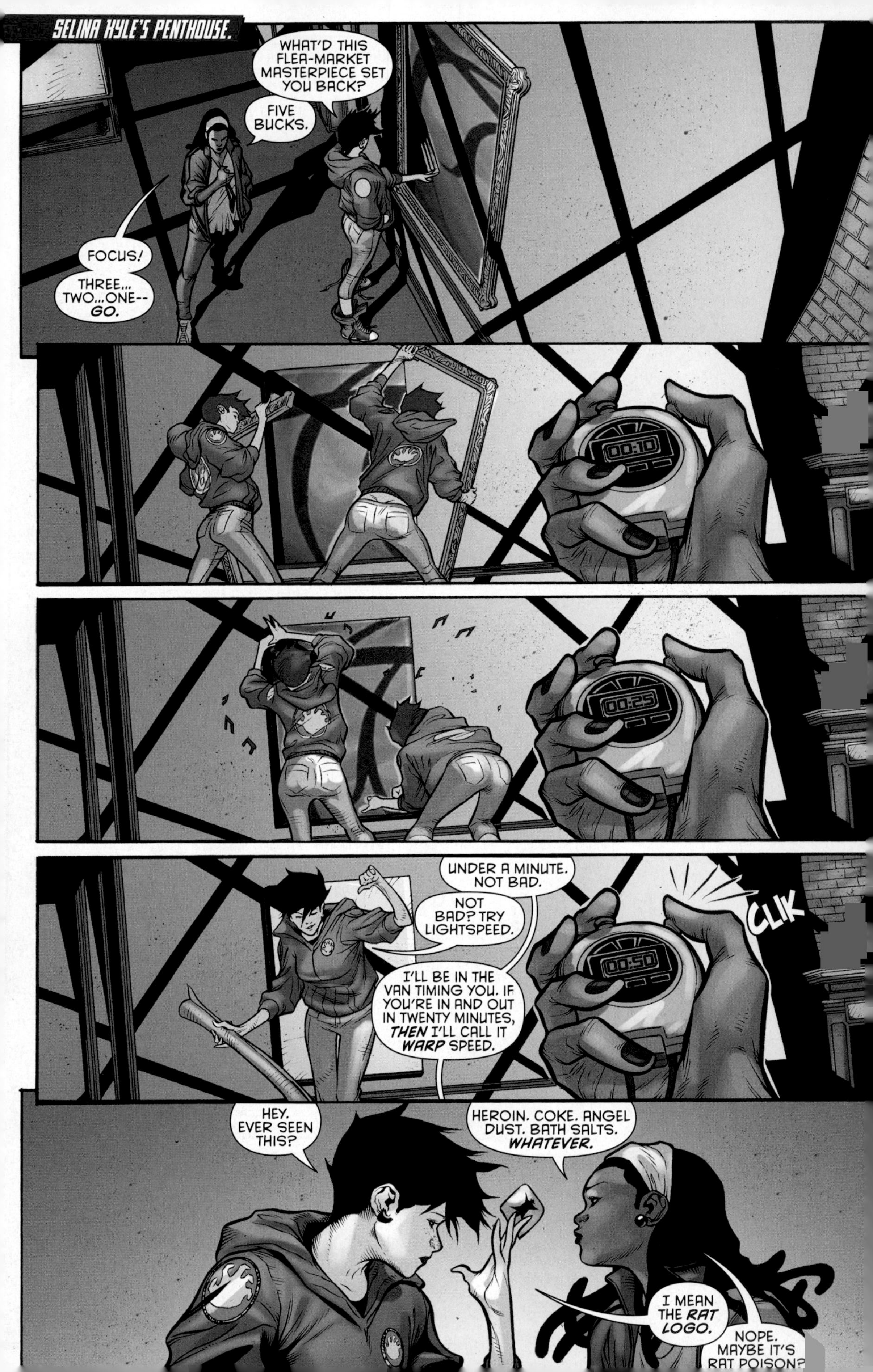

SELINA KYLE'S PENTHOUSE.
WHAT'D THIS FLEA-MARKET MASTERPIECE SET YOU BACK?
FIVE BUCKS.
FOCUS! THREE... TWO...ONE-- GO.
00:10
00:25
UNDER A MINUTE. NOT BAD.
NOT BAD? TRY LIGHTSPEED.
I'LL BE IN THE VAN TIMING YOU. IF YOU'RE IN AND OUT IN TWENTY MINUTES, THEN I'LL CALL IT WARP SPEED.
CLIK
00:50
HEY. EVER SEEN THIS?
HEROIN. COKE. ANGEL DUST. BATH SALTS. WHATEVER.
I MEAN THE RAT LOGO.
NOPE. MAYBE IT'S RAT POISON?

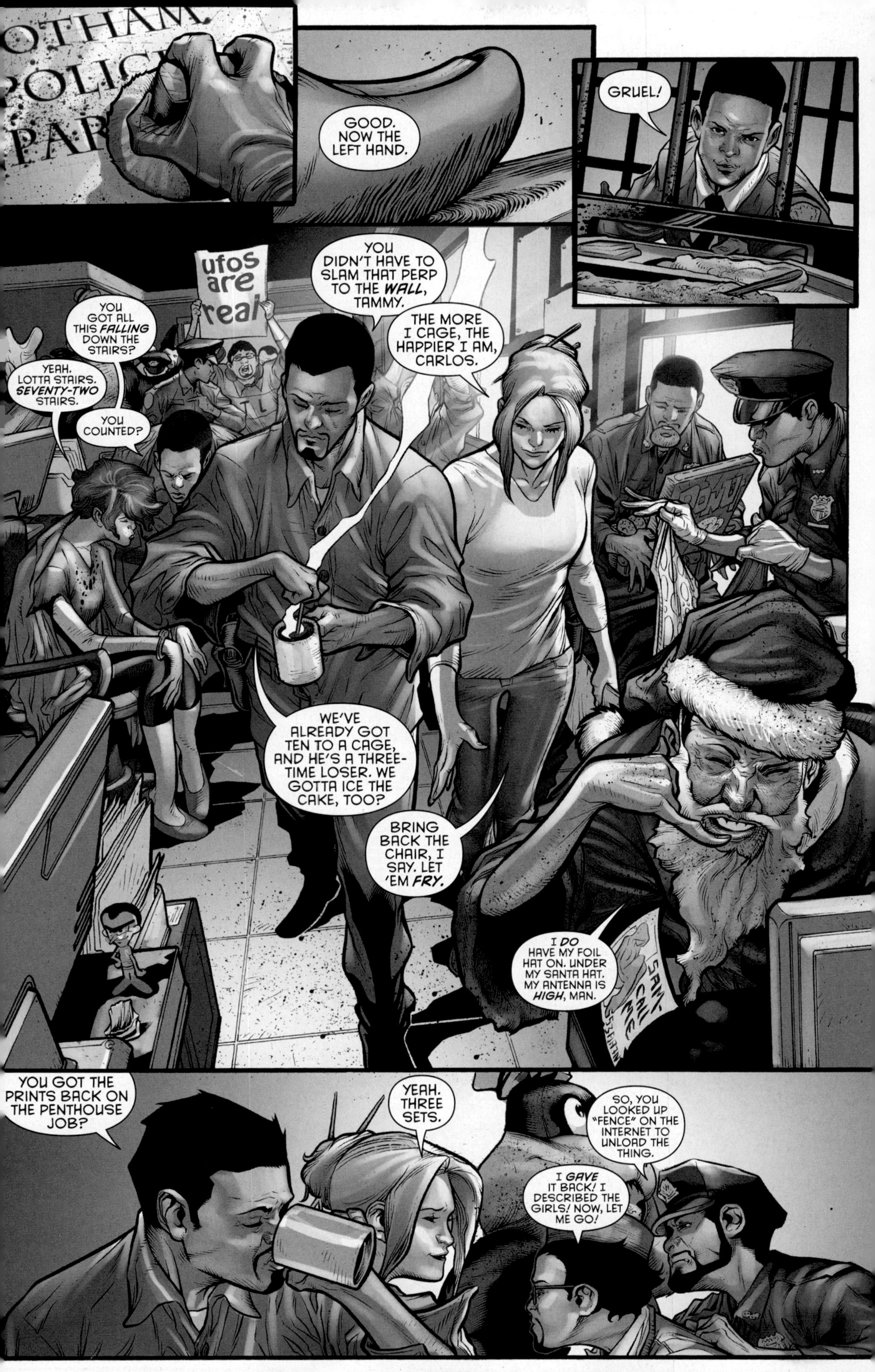

OTHAM POLIC PAR
GOOD. NOW THE LEFT HAND.
GRUEL!
ufos are real
YOU DIDN'T HAVE TO SLAM THAT PERP TO THE WALL, TAMMY.
THE MORE I CAGE, THE HAPPIER I AM, CARLOS.
YOU GOT ALL THIS FALLING DOWN THE STAIRS?
YEAH. LOTTA STAIRS. SEVENTY-TWO STAIRS.
YOU COUNTED?
WE'VE ALREADY GOT TEN TO A CAGE, AND HE'S A THREE-TIME LOSER. WE GOTTA ICE THE CAKE, TOO?
BRING BACK THE CHAIR, I SAY. LET 'EM FRY.
I DO HAVE MY FOIL HAT ON. UNDER MY SANTA HAT. MY ANTENNA IS HIGH, MAN.
YOU GOT THE PRINTS BACK ON THE PENTHOUSE JOB?
YEAH. THREE SETS.
SO, YOU LOOKED UP "FENCE" ON THE INTERNET TO UNLOAD THE THING.
I GAVE IT BACK! I DESCRIBED THE GIRLS! NOW, LET ME GO!

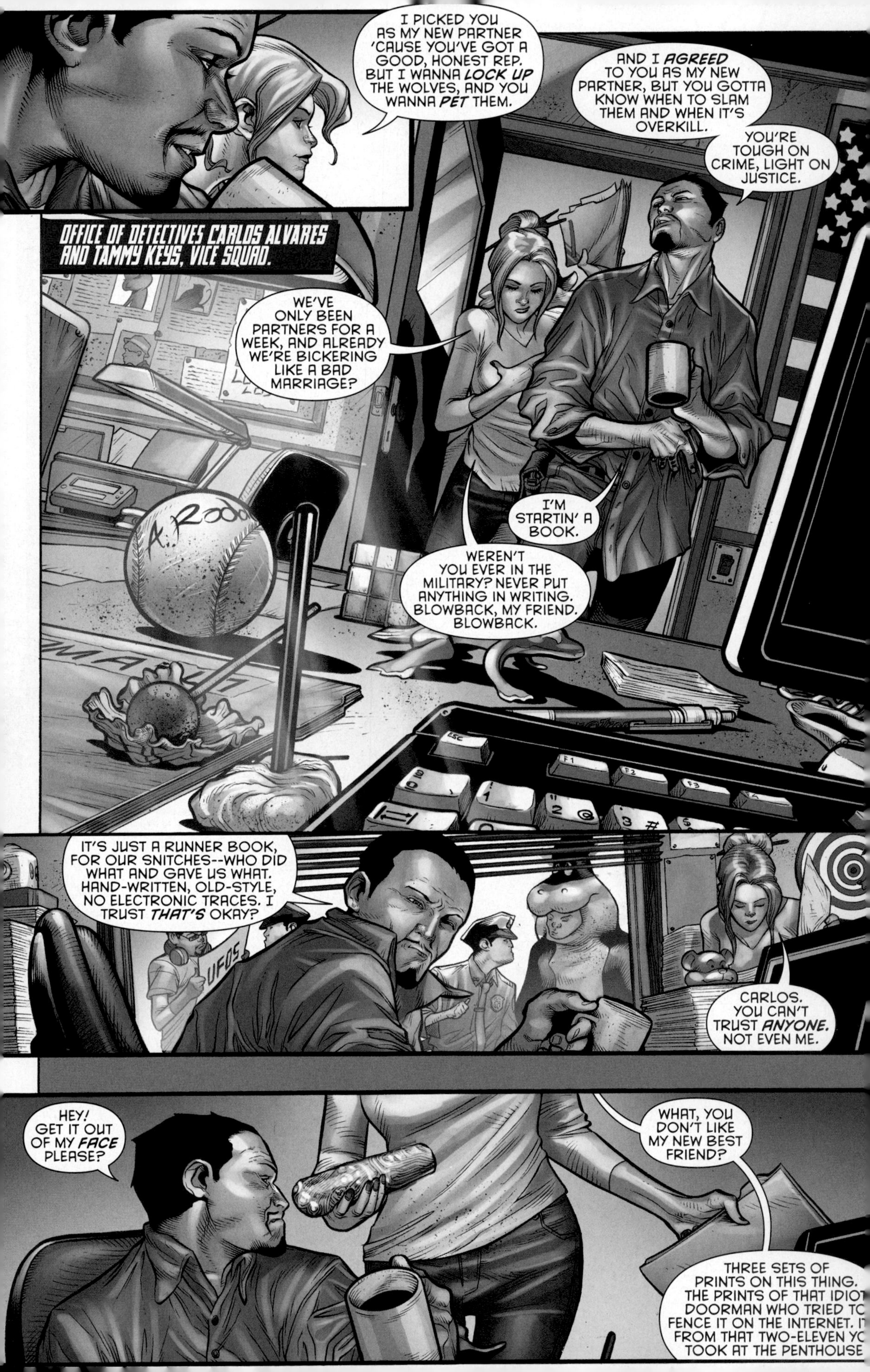
I PICKED YOU AS MY NEW PARTNER 'CAUSE YOU'VE GOT A GOOD, HONEST REP. BUT I WANNA LOCK UP THE WOLVES, AND YOU WANNA PET THEM.
AND I AGREED TO YOU AS MY NEW PARTNER, BUT YOU GOTTA KNOW WHEN TO SLAM THEM AND WHEN IT'S OVERKILL.
YOU'RE TOUGH ON CRIME, LIGHT ON JUSTICE.
OFFICE OF DETECTIVES CARLOS ALVARES AND TAMMY KEYS, VICE SQUAD.
WE'VE ONLY BEEN PARTNERS FOR A WEEK, AND ALREADY WE'RE BICKERING LIKE A BAD MARRIAGE?
I'M STARTIN' A BOOK.
WEREN'T YOU EVER IN THE MILITARY? NEVER PUT ANYTHING IN WRITING. BLOWBACK, MY FRIEND. BLOWBACK.
IT'S JUST A RUNNER BOOK, FOR OUR SNITCHES--WHO DID WHAT AND GAVE US WHAT. HAND-WRITTEN, OLD-STYLE, NO ELECTRONIC TRACES. I TRUST THAT'S OKAY?
CARLOS. YOU CAN'T TRUST ANYONE. NOT EVEN ME.
HEY! GET IT OUT OF MY FACE PLEASE?
WHAT, YOU DON'T LIKE MY NEW BEST FRIEND?
THREE SETS OF PRINTS ON THIS THING. THE PRINTS OF THAT IDIOT DOORMAN WHO TRIED TO FENCE IT ON THE INTERNET. IT FROM THAT TWO-ELEVEN YO TOOK AT THE PENTHOUSE

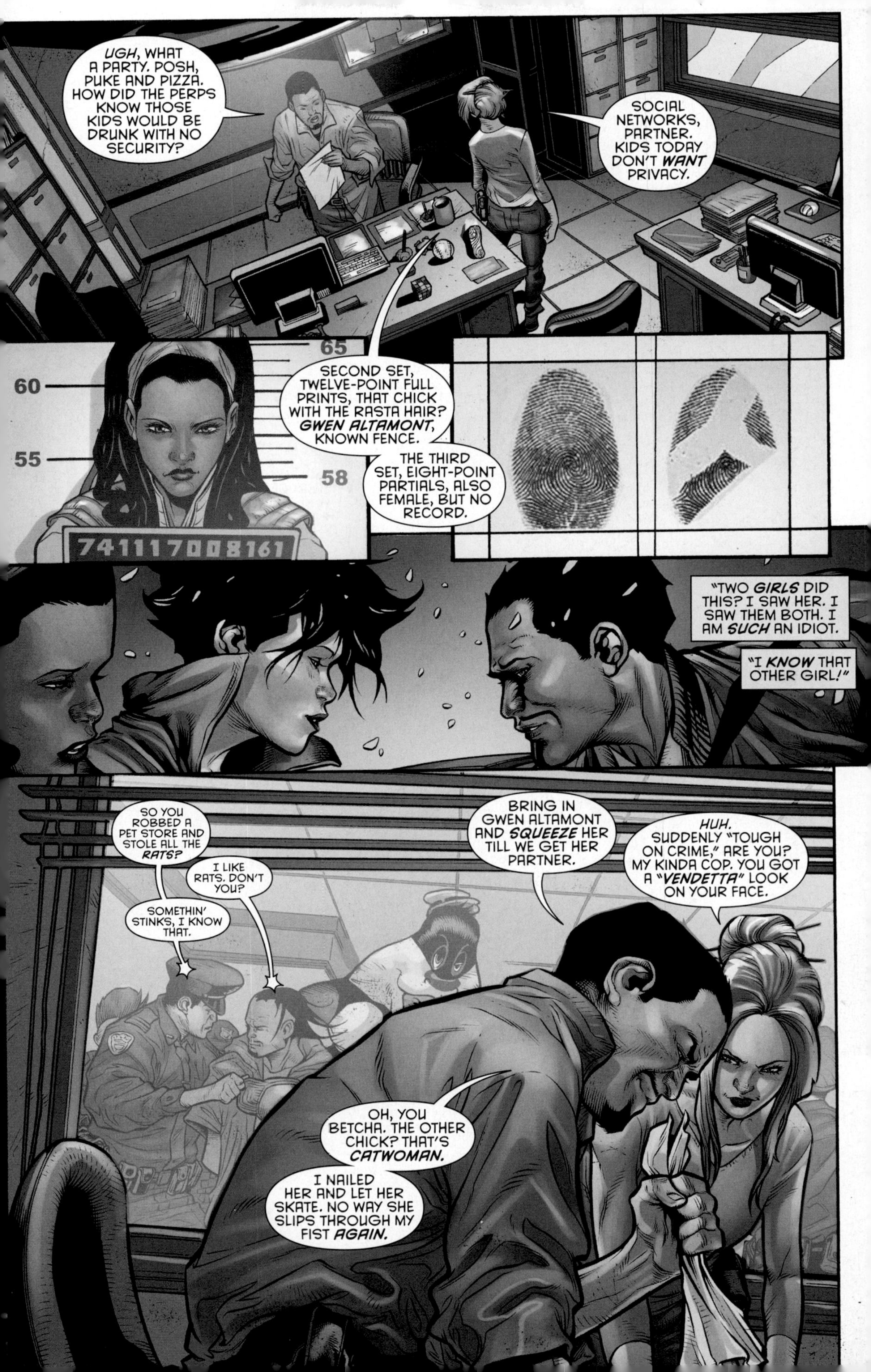
UGH, WHAT A PARTY. POSH, PUKE AND PIZZA. HOW DID THE PERPS KNOW THOSE KIDS WOULD BE DRUNK WITH NO SECURITY?
SOCIAL NETWORKS, PARTNER. KIDS TODAY DON'T WANT PRIVACY.
60
55
65
58
741117008161
SECOND SET, TWELVE-POINT FULL PRINTS, THAT CHICK WITH THE RASTA HAIR? GWEN ALTAMONT, KNOWN FENCE.
THE THIRD SET, EIGHT-POINT PARTIALS, ALSO FEMALE, BUT NO RECORD.
"TWO GIRLS DID THIS? I SAW HER. I SAW THEM BOTH. I AM SUCH AN IDIOT.
"I KNOW THAT OTHER GIRL!"
SO YOU ROBBED A PET STORE AND STOLE ALL THE RATS?
I LIKE RATS. DON'T YOU?
SOMETHIN' STINKS, I KNOW THAT.
BRING IN GWEN ALTAMONT AND SQUEEZE HER TILL WE GET HER PARTNER.
HUH. SUDDENLY "TOUGH ON CRIME," ARE YOU? MY KINDA COP. YOU GOT A "VENDETTA" LOOK ON YOUR FACE.
OH, YOU BETCHA. THE OTHER CHICK? THAT'S CATWOMAN.
I NAILED HER AND LET HER SKATE. NO WAY SHE SLIPS THROUGH MY FIST AGAIN.

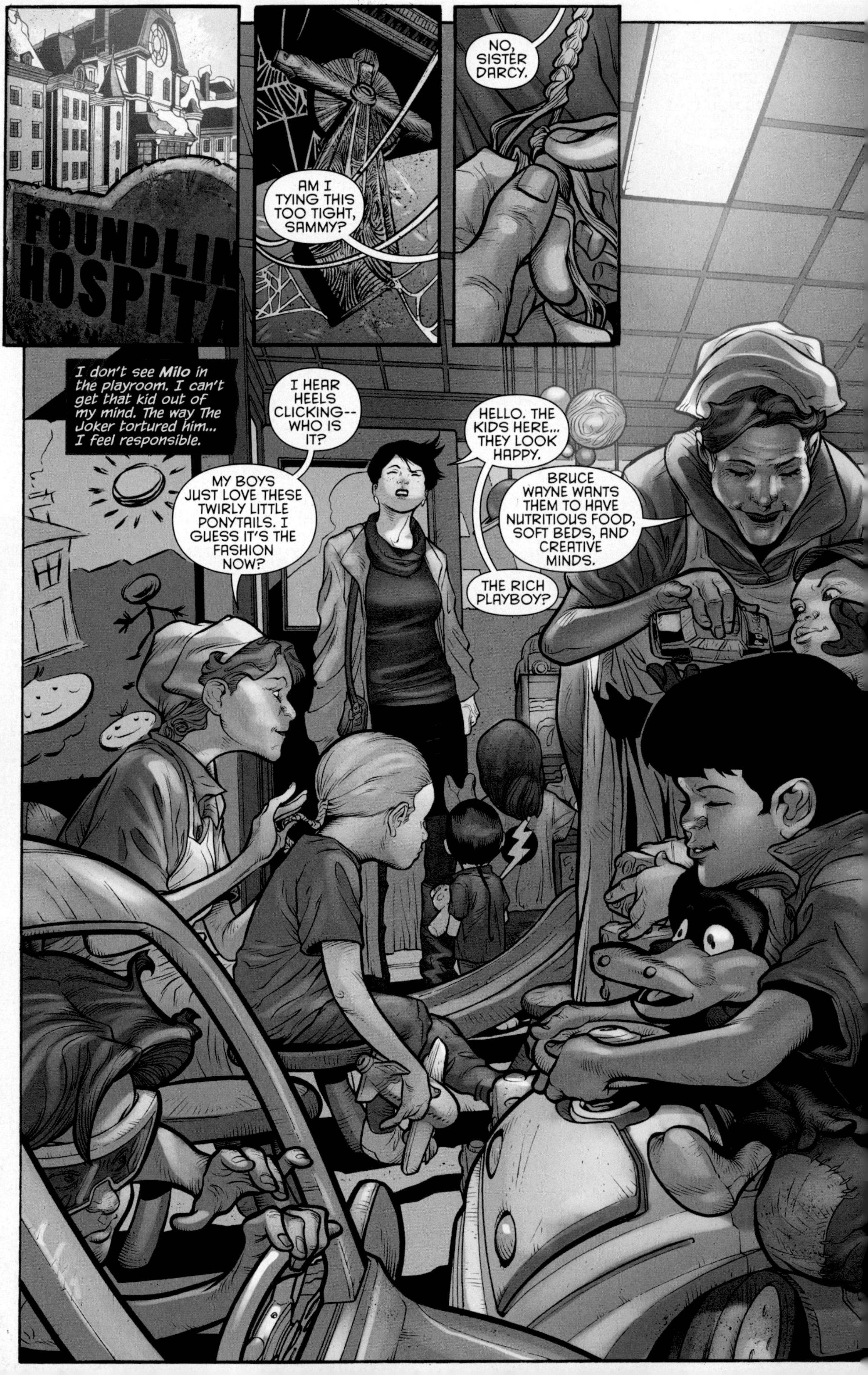

FOUNDLING HOSPITAL
AM I TYING THIS TOO TIGHT, SAMMY?
NO, SISTER DARCY.
I don't see Milo in the playroom. I can't get that kid out of my mind. The way The Joker tortured him... I feel responsible.
I HEAR HEELS CLICKING-- WHO IS IT?
MY BOYS JUST LOVE THESE TWIRLY LITTLE PONYTAILS. I GUESS IT'S THE FASHION NOW?
HELLO. THE KIDS HERE... THEY LOOK HAPPY.
BRUCE WAYNE WANTS THEM TO HAVE NUTRITIOUS FOOD, SOFT BEDS, AND CREATIVE MINDS.
THE RICH PLAYBOY?

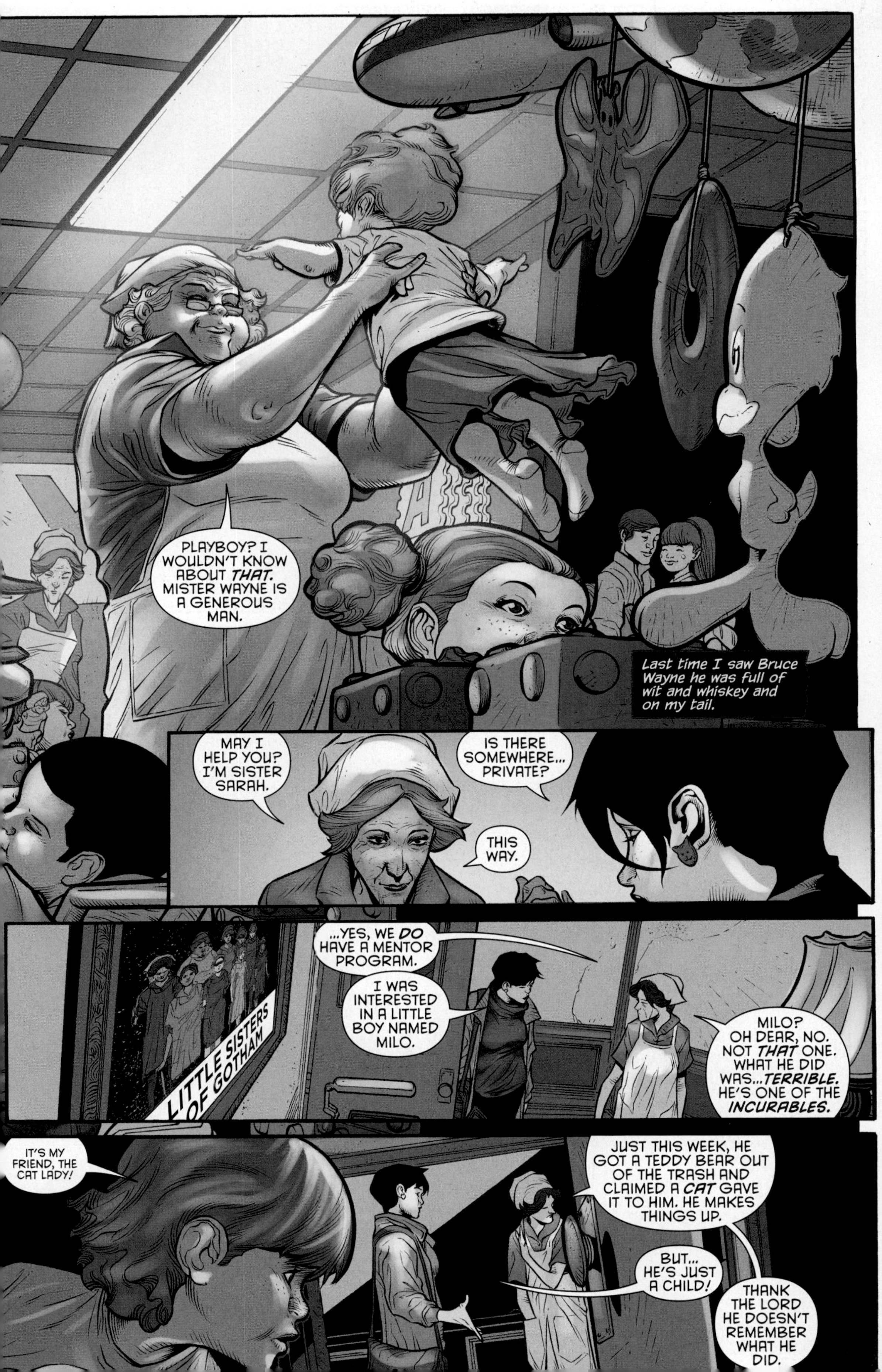
PLAYBOY? I WOULDN'T KNOW ABOUT *THAT.* MISTER WAYNE IS A GENEROUS MAN.
Last time I saw Bruce Wayne he was full of wit and whiskey and on my tail.
MAY I HELP YOU? I'M SISTER SARAH.
IS THERE SOMEWHERE... PRIVATE?
THIS WAY.
LITTLE SISTERS OF GOTHAM
...YES, WE *DO* HAVE A MENTOR PROGRAM.
I WAS INTERESTED IN A LITTLE BOY NAMED MILO.
MILO? OH DEAR, NO. NOT *THAT* ONE. WHAT HE DID WAS...*TERRIBLE.* HE'S ONE OF THE *INCURABLES.*
IT'S MY FRIEND, THE CAT LADY!
JUST THIS WEEK, HE GOT A TEDDY BEAR OUT OF THE TRASH AND CLAIMED A *CAT* GAVE IT TO HIM. HE MAKES THINGS UP.
BUT... HE'S JUST A CHILD!
THANK THE LORD HE DOESN'T REMEMBER WHAT HE DID.

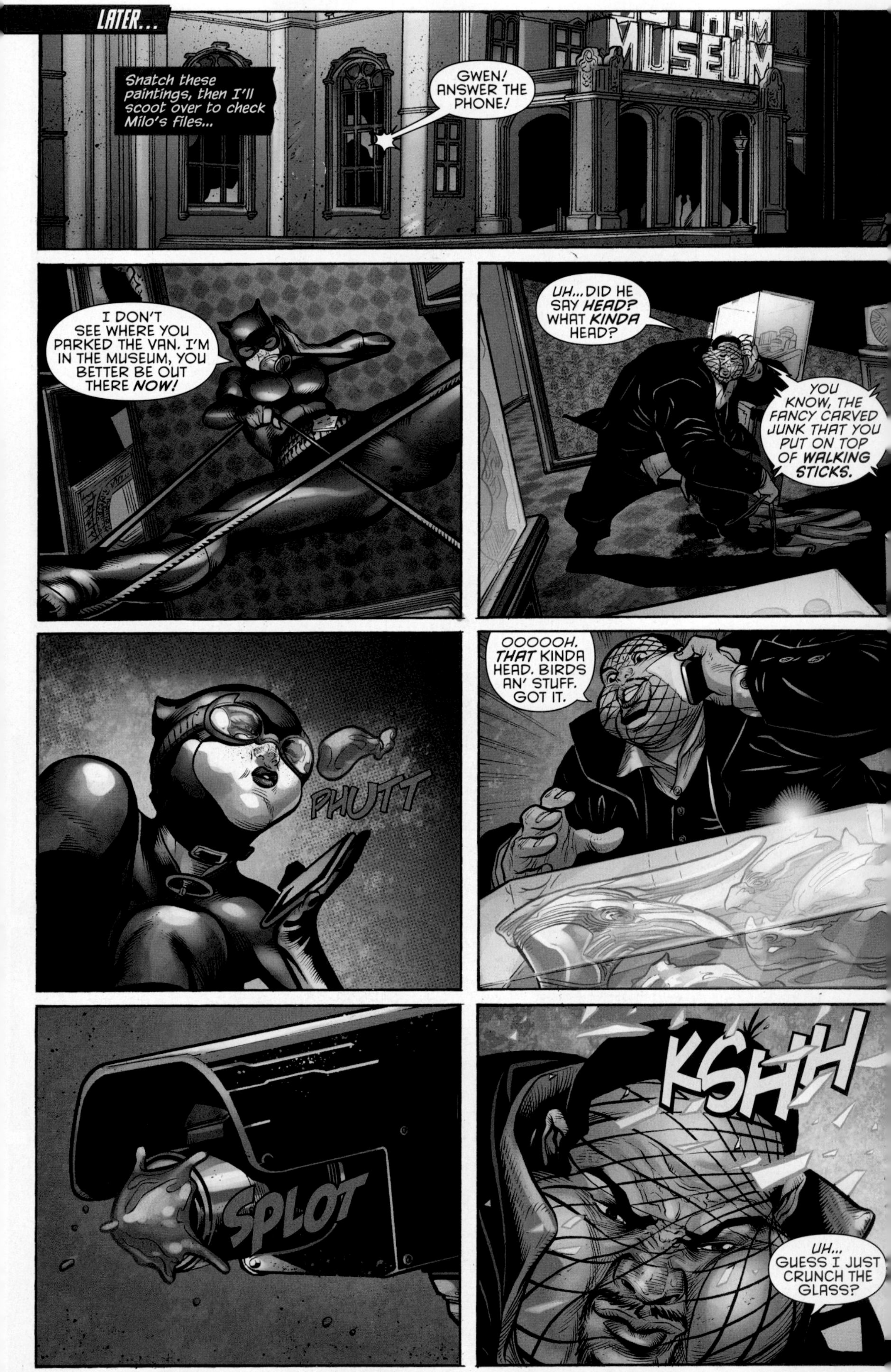
LATER...
Snatch these paintings, then I'll scoot over to check Milo's files...
GWEN! ANSWER THE PHONE!
GOTHAM MUSEUM
I DON'T SEE WHERE YOU PARKED THE VAN. I'M IN THE MUSEUM, YOU BETTER BE OUT THERE NOW!
UH...DID HE SAY HEAD? WHAT KINDA HEAD?
YOU KNOW, THE FANCY CARVED JUNK THAT YOU PUT ON TOP OF WALKING STICKS.
PHUTT
OOOOOH. THAT KINDA HEAD. BIRDS AN' STUFF. GOT IT.
SPLOT
KSHH
UH... GUESS I JUST CRUNCH THE GLASS?

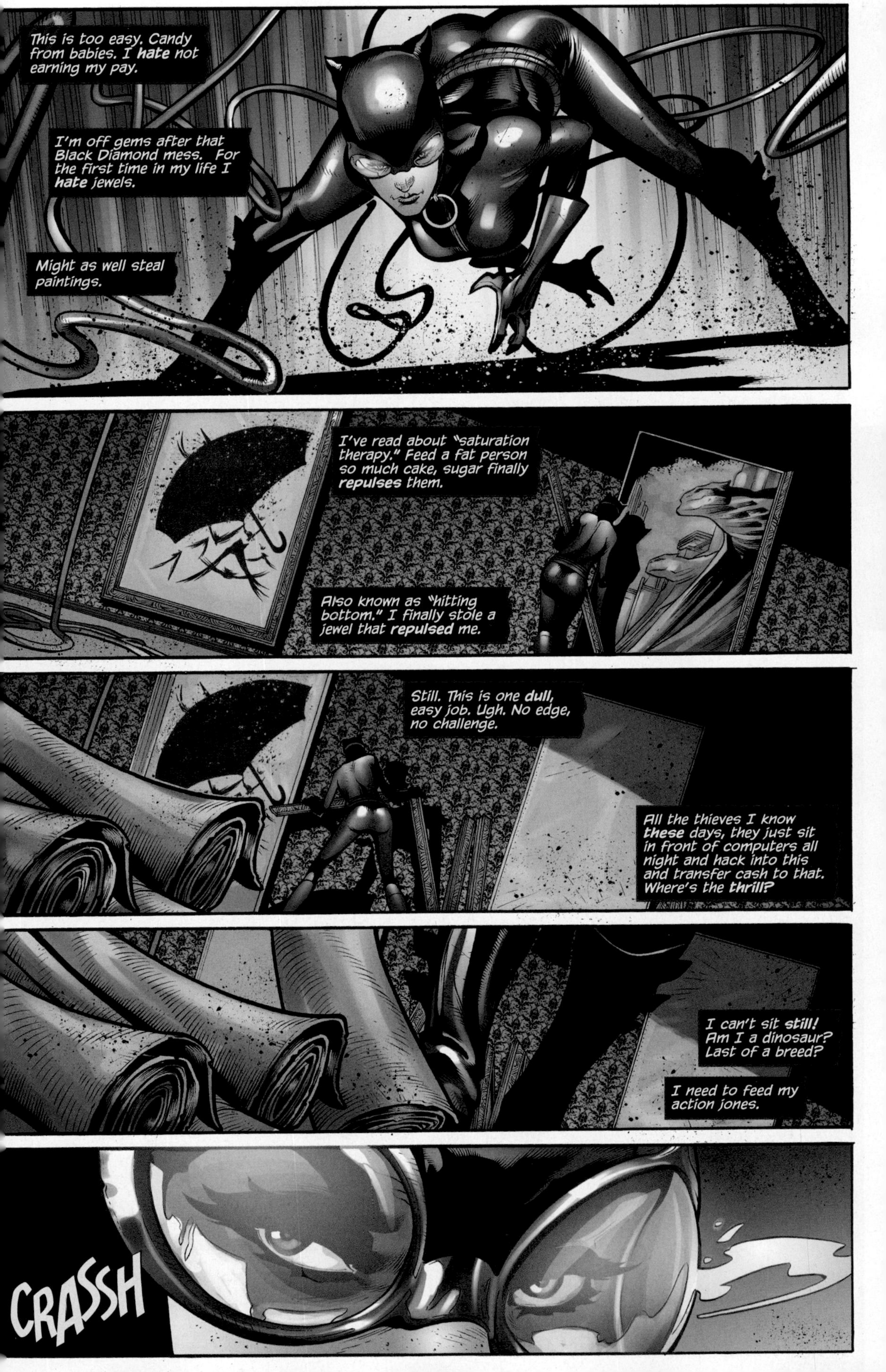
This is too easy. Candy from babies. I hate not earning my pay.
I'm off gems after that Black Diamond mess. For the first time in my life I hate jewels.
Might as well steal paintings.
I've read about "saturation therapy." Feed a fat person so much cake, sugar finally repulses them.
Also known as "hitting bottom." I finally stole a jewel that repulsed me.
Still. This is one dull, easy job. Ugh. No edge, no challenge.
All the thieves I know these days, they just sit in front of computers all night and hack into this and transfer cash to that. Where's the thrill?
I can't sit still! Am I a dinosaur? Last of a breed?
I need to feed my action jones.
CRASSH

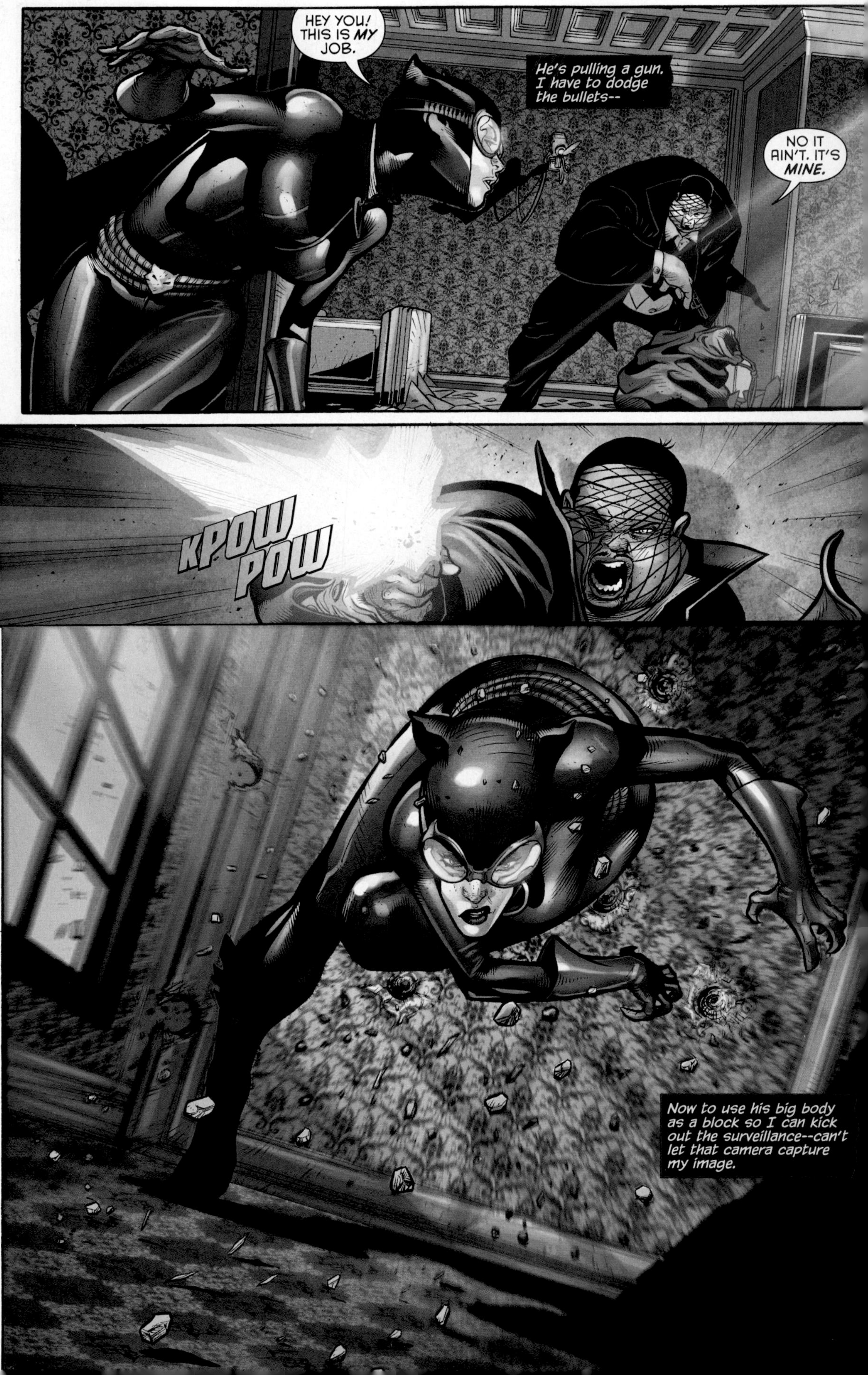
HEY YOU! THIS IS *MY* JOB.
He's pulling a gun. I have to dodge the bullets--
NO IT AIN'T. IT'S *MINE.*
KPOW POW
Now to use his big body as a block so I can kick out the surveillance--can't let that camera capture my image.

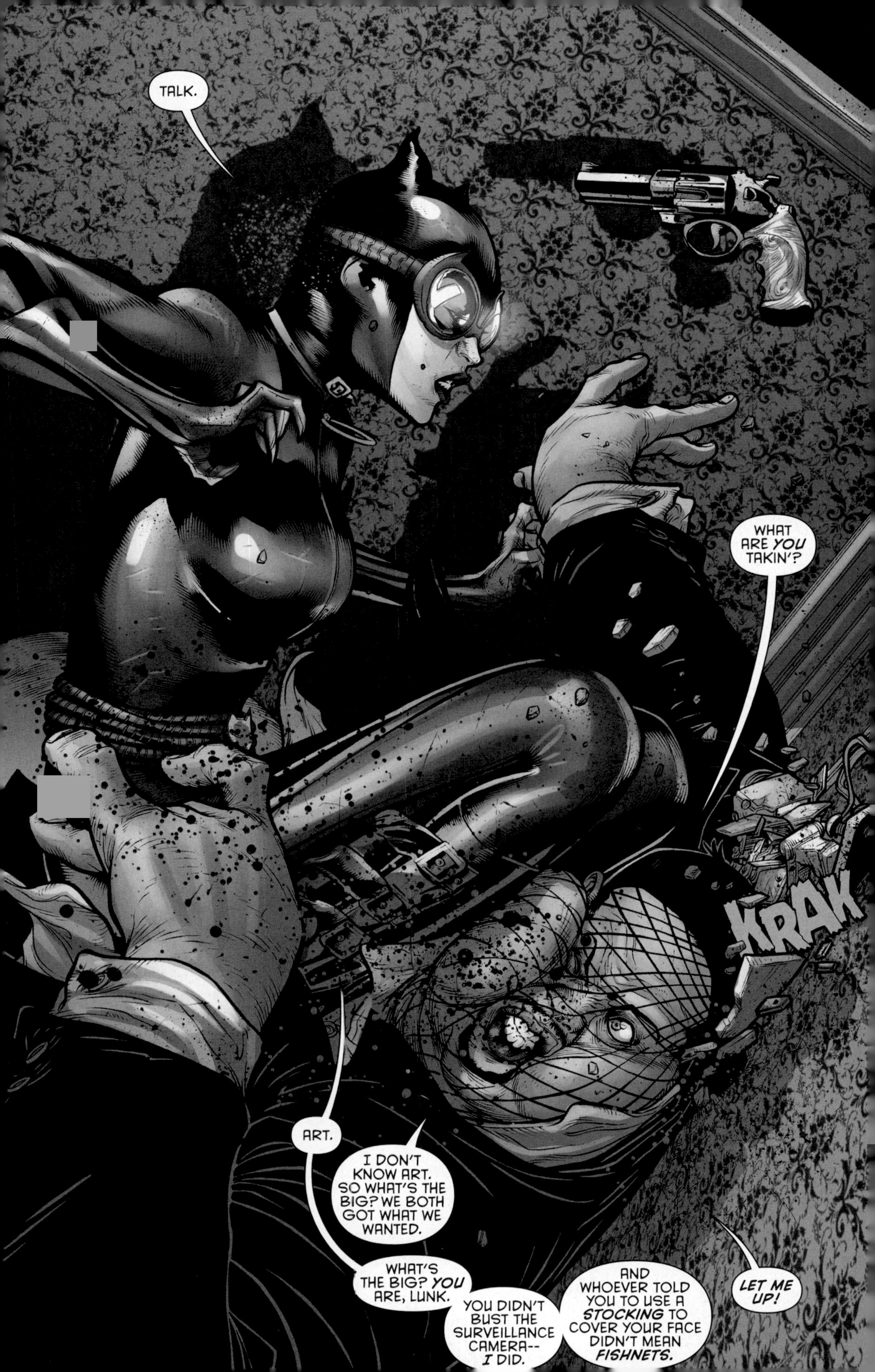
TALK.
WHAT ARE YOU TAKIN'?
KRAK
ART.
I DON'T KNOW ART. SO WHAT'S THE BIG? WE BOTH GOT WHAT WE WANTED.
WHAT'S THE BIG? YOU ARE, LUNK.
YOU DIDN'T BUST THE SURVEILLANCE CAMERA-- I DID.
AND WHOEVER TOLD YOU TO USE A STOCKING TO COVER YOUR FACE DIDN'T MEAN FISHNETS.
LET ME UP!

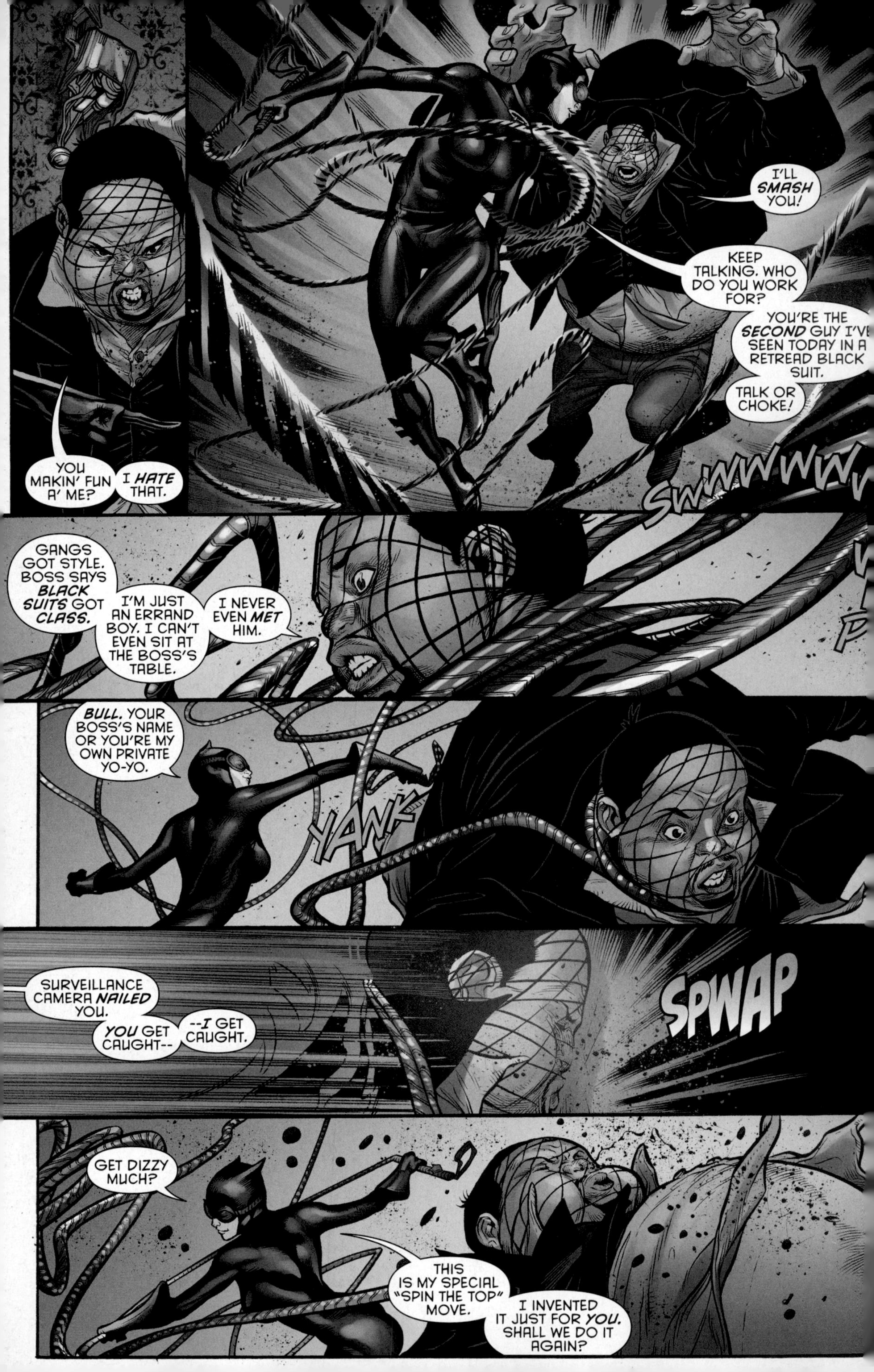
I'LL SMASH YOU!
KEEP TALKING. WHO DO YOU WORK FOR?
YOU'RE THE SECOND GUY I'VE SEEN TODAY IN A RETREAD BLACK SUIT.
TALK OR CHOKE!
YOU MAKIN' FUN A' ME?
I HATE THAT.
SWWWWWW
GANGS GOT STYLE. BOSS SAYS BLACK SUITS GOT CLASS.
I'M JUST AN ERRAND BOY. I CAN'T EVEN SIT AT THE BOSS'S TABLE.
I NEVER EVEN MET HIM.
BULL. YOUR BOSS'S NAME OR YOU'RE MY OWN PRIVATE YO-YO.
YANK
SURVEILLANCE CAMERA NAILED YOU.
YOU GET CAUGHT--
--I GET CAUGHT.
SPWAP
GET DIZZY MUCH?
THIS IS MY SPECIAL "SPIN THE TOP" MOVE.
I INVENTED IT JUST FOR YOU. SHALL WE DO IT AGAIN?

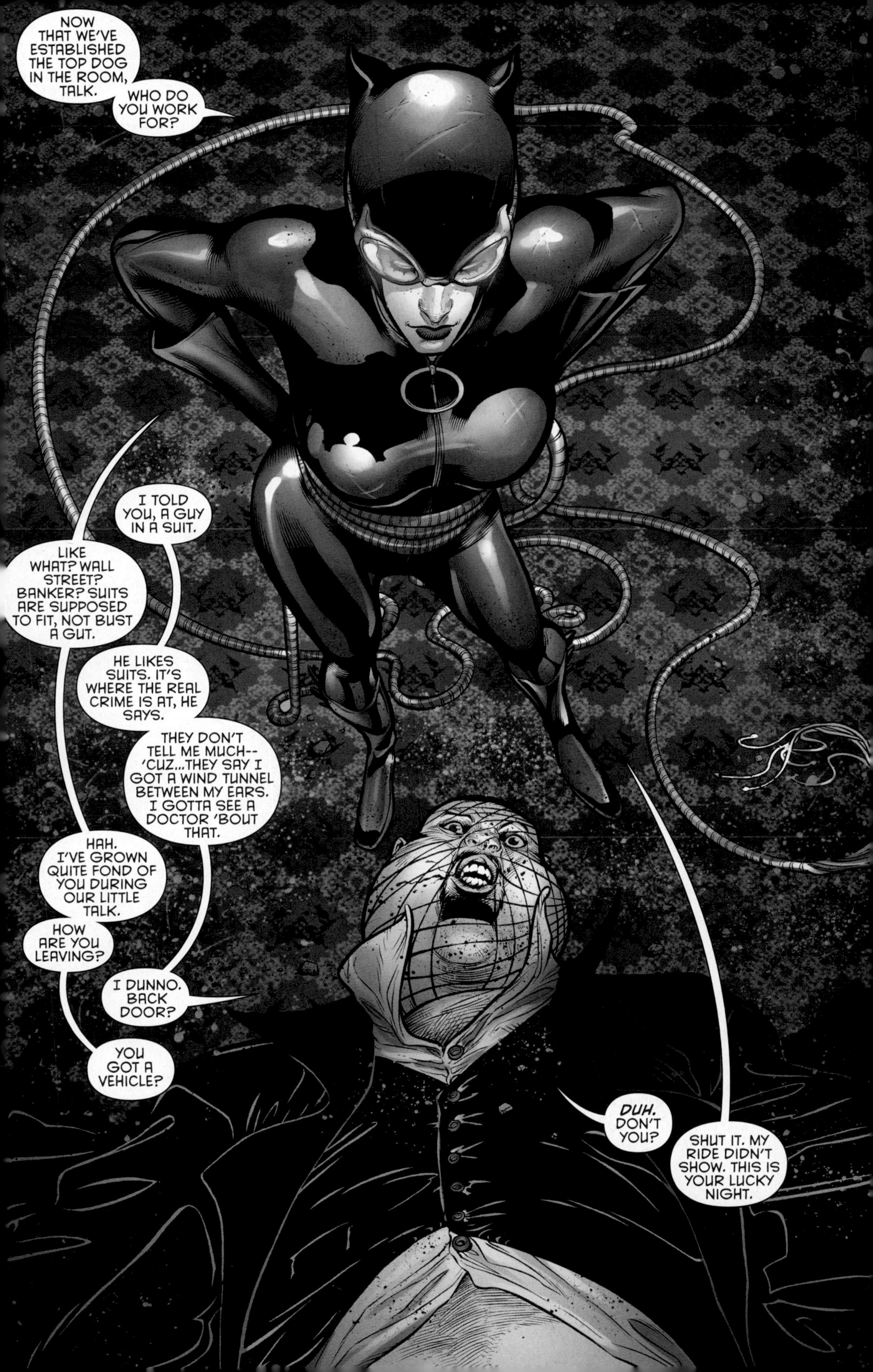
NOW THAT WE'VE ESTABLISHED THE TOP DOG IN THE ROOM, TALK.
WHO DO YOU WORK FOR?
I TOLD YOU, A GUY IN A SUIT.
LIKE WHAT? WALL STREET? BANKER? SUITS ARE SUPPOSED TO FIT, NOT BUST A GUT.
HE LIKES SUITS. IT'S WHERE THE REAL CRIME IS AT, HE SAYS.
THEY DON'T TELL ME MUCH-- 'CUZ...THEY SAY I GOT A WIND TUNNEL BETWEEN MY EARS. I GOTTA SEE A DOCTOR 'BOUT THAT.
HAH. I'VE GROWN QUITE FOND OF YOU DURING OUR LITTLE TALK.
HOW ARE YOU LEAVING?
I DUNNO. BACK DOOR?
YOU GOT A VEHICLE?
DUH. DON'T YOU?
SHUT IT. MY RIDE DIDN'T SHOW. THIS IS YOUR LUCKY NIGHT.

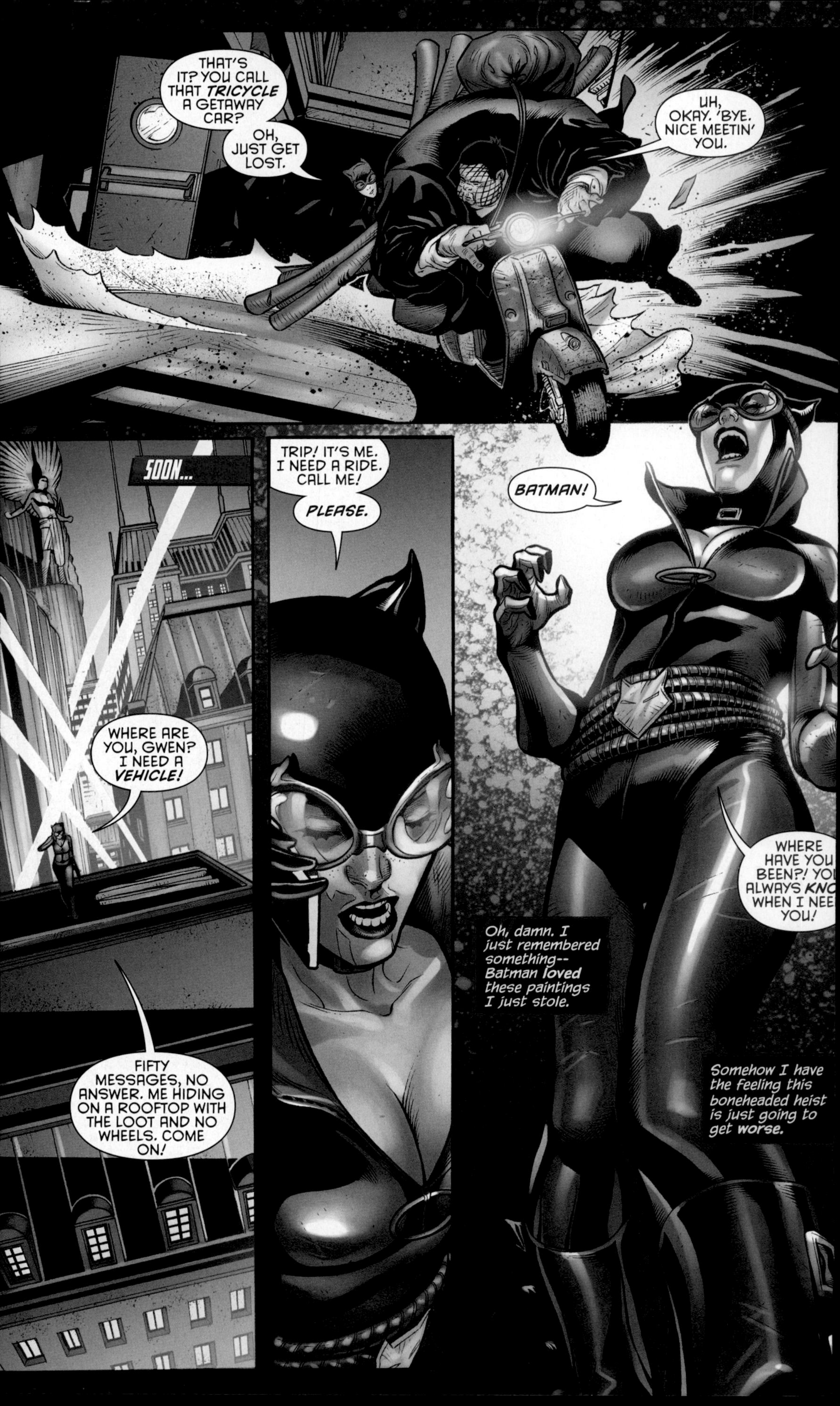

THAT'S IT? YOU CALL THAT TRICYCLE A GETAWAY CAR?
OH, JUST GET LOST.
UH, OKAY. 'BYE. NICE MEETIN' YOU.
SOON...
WHERE ARE YOU, GWEN? I NEED A VEHICLE!
FIFTY MESSAGES, NO ANSWER. ME HIDING ON A ROOFTOP WITH THE LOOT AND NO WHEELS. COME ON!
TRIP! IT'S ME. I NEED A RIDE. CALL ME!
PLEASE.
BATMAN!
Oh, damn. I just remembered something-- Batman loved these paintings I just stole.
WHERE HAVE YOU BEEN?! YO ALWAYS KNO WHEN I NEE YOU!
Somehow I have the feeling this boneheaded heist is just going to get worse.

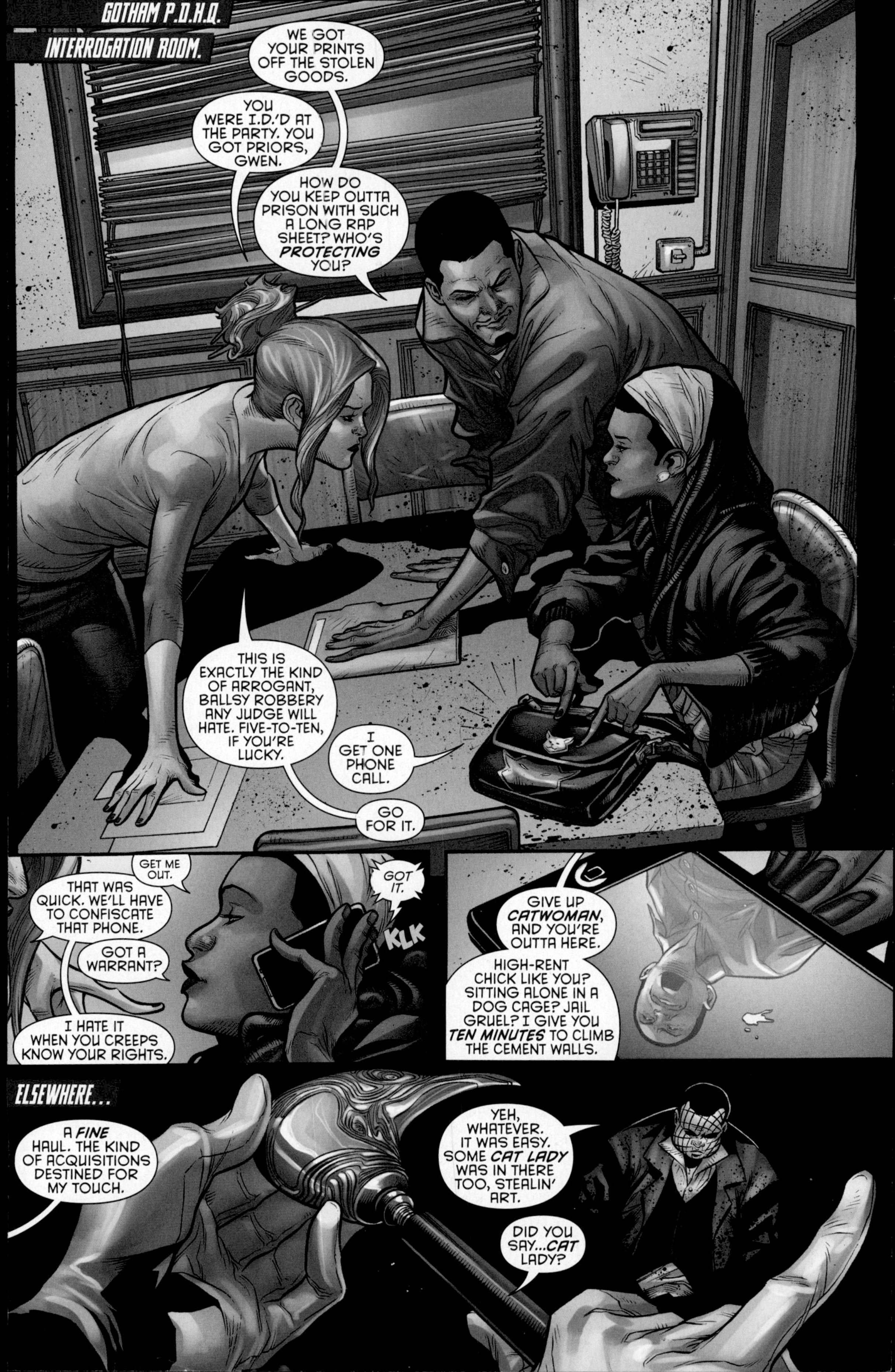
GOTHAM P.D.H.Q.
INTERROGATION ROOM.
WE GOT YOUR PRINTS OFF THE STOLEN GOODS.
YOU WERE I.D.'D AT THE PARTY. YOU GOT PRIORS, GWEN.
HOW DO YOU KEEP OUTTA PRISON WITH SUCH A LONG RAP SHEET? WHO'S *PROTECTING* YOU?
THIS IS EXACTLY THE KIND OF ARROGANT, BALLSY ROBBERY ANY JUDGE WILL HATE. FIVE-TO-TEN, IF YOU'RE LUCKY.
I GET ONE PHONE CALL.
GO FOR IT.
GET ME OUT.
GOT IT.
KLK
THAT WAS QUICK. WE'LL HAVE TO CONFISCATE THAT PHONE.
GOT A WARRANT?
I HATE IT WHEN YOU CREEPS KNOW YOUR RIGHTS.
GIVE UP *CATWOMAN*, AND YOU'RE OUTTA HERE.
HIGH-RENT CHICK LIKE YOU? SITTING ALONE IN A DOG CAGE? JAIL GRUEL? I GIVE YOU *TEN MINUTES* TO CLIMB THE CEMENT WALLS.
ELSEWHERE...
A *FINE* HAUL. THE KIND OF ACQUISITIONS DESTINED FOR MY TOUCH.
YEH, WHATEVER. IT WAS EASY. SOME *CAT LADY* WAS IN THERE TOO, STEALIN' ART.
DID YOU SAY...*CAT* LADY?

ANN NOCENTI
writer

EMANUELA LUPACCHINO
penciller

JAIME MENDOZA
inker

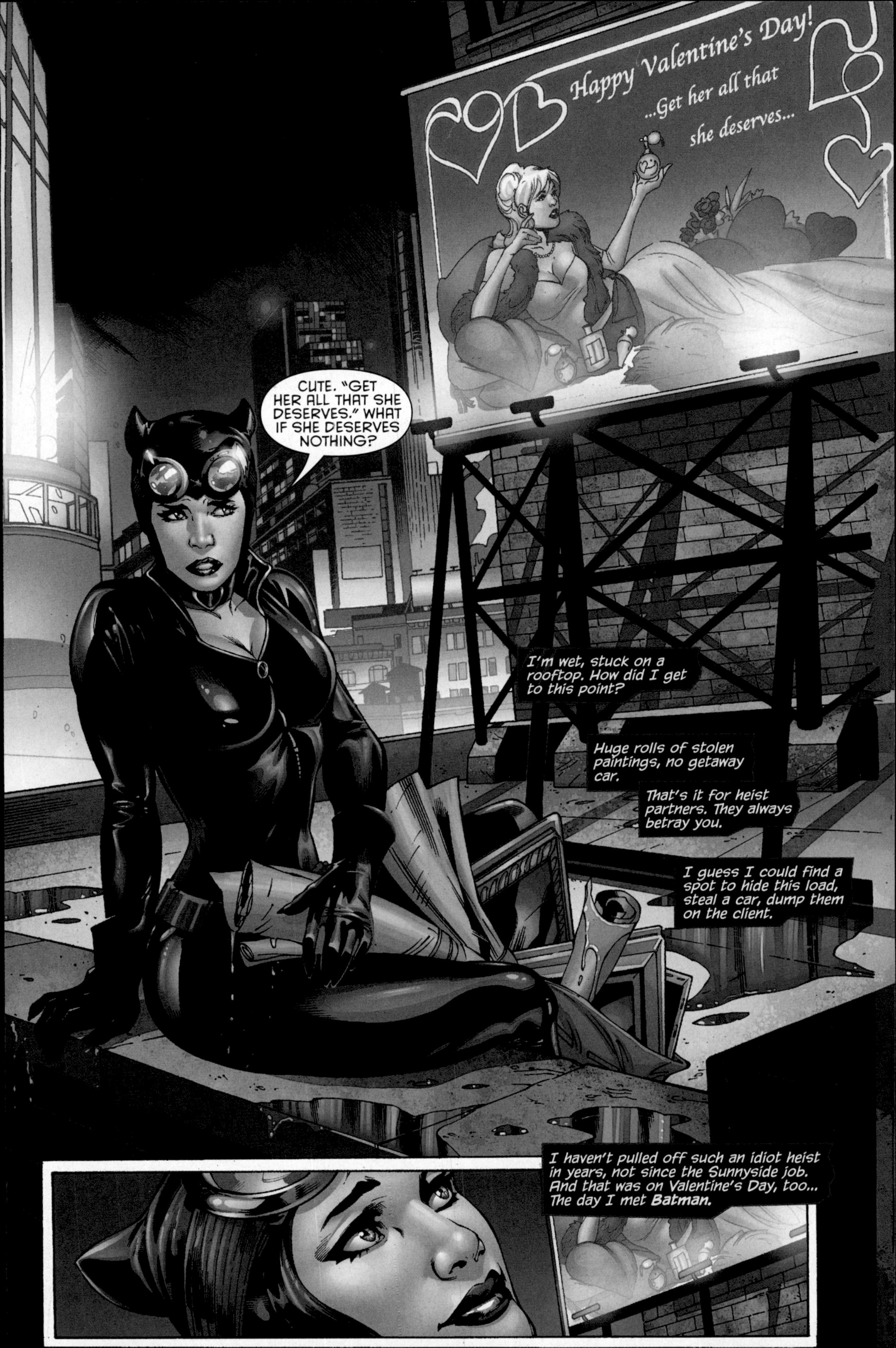
Happy Valentine's Day!
...Get her all that she deserves...
CUTE. "GET HER ALL THAT SHE DESERVES." WHAT IF SHE DESERVES NOTHING?
I'm wet, stuck on a rooftop. How did I get to this point?
Huge rolls of stolen paintings, no getaway car.
That's it for heist partners. They always betray you.
I guess I could find a spot to hide this load, steal a car, dump them on the client.
I haven't pulled off such an idiot heist in years, not since the Sunnyside job. And that was on Valentine's Day, too... The day I met Batman.

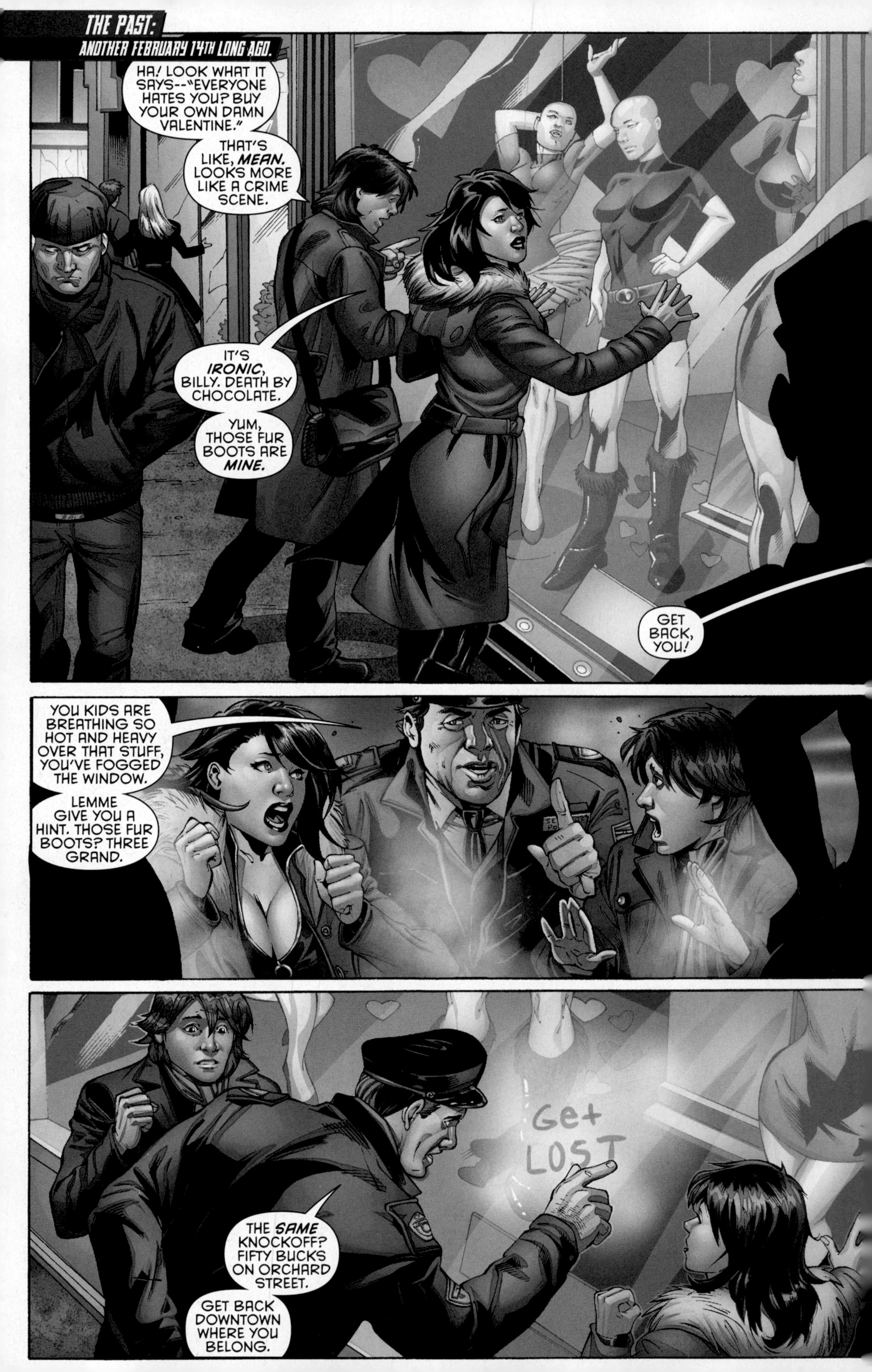
THE PAST:
ANOTHER FEBRUARY 14TH LONG AGO.
HA! LOOK WHAT IT SAYS--"EVERYONE HATES YOU? BUY YOUR OWN DAMN VALENTINE."
THAT'S LIKE, MEAN. LOOKS MORE LIKE A CRIME SCENE.
IT'S IRONIC, BILLY. DEATH BY CHOCOLATE.
YUM, THOSE FUR BOOTS ARE MINE.
GET BACK, YOU!
YOU KIDS ARE BREATHING SO HOT AND HEAVY OVER THAT STUFF, YOU'VE FOGGED THE WINDOW.
LEMME GIVE YOU A HINT. THOSE FUR BOOTS? THREE GRAND.
Get LOST
THE SAME KNOCKOFF? FIFTY BUCKS ON ORCHARD STREET.
GET BACK DOWNTOWN WHERE YOU BELONG.

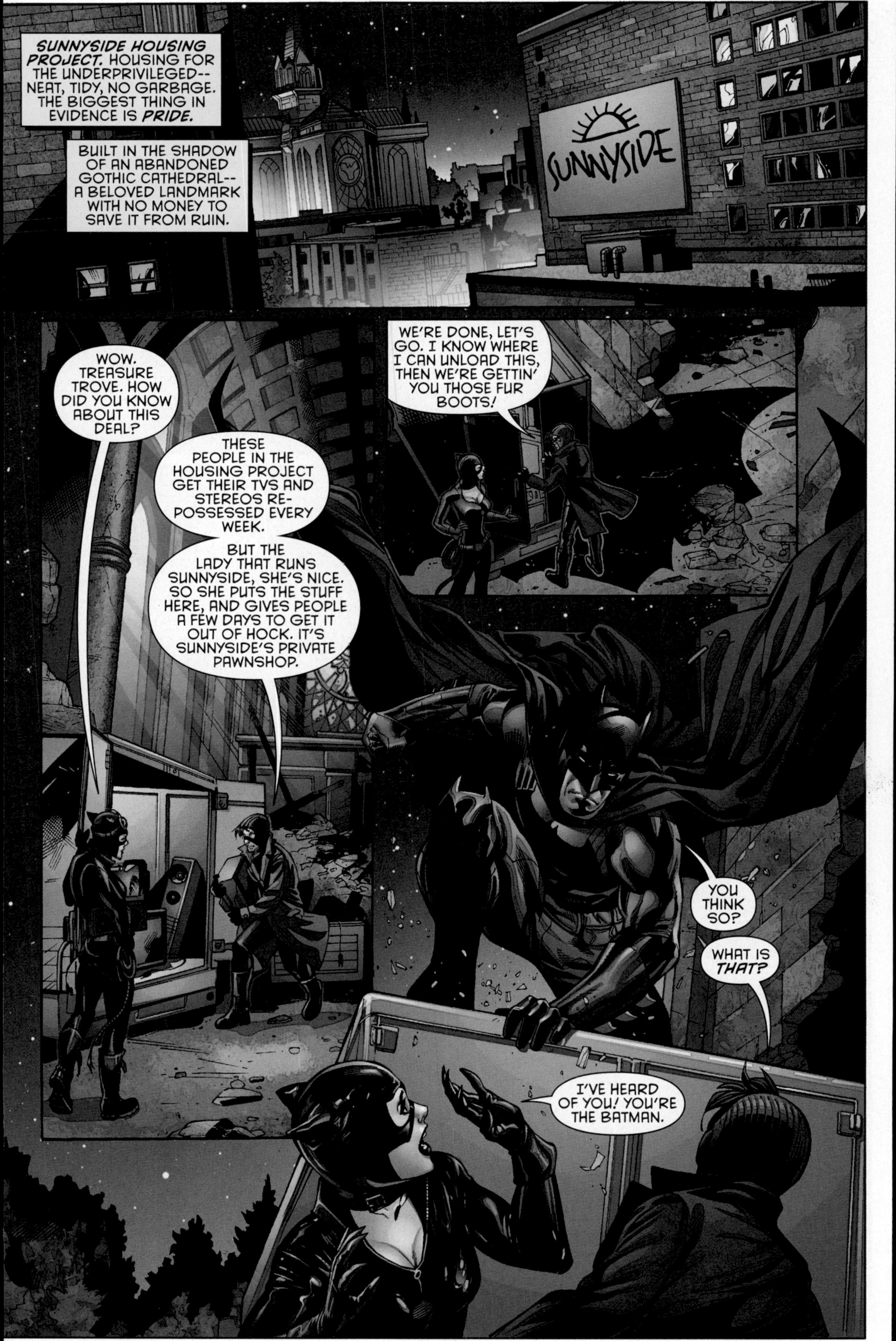
SUNNYSIDE HOUSING PROJECT. HOUSING FOR THE UNDERPRIVILEGED-- NEAT, TIDY, NO GARBAGE. THE BIGGEST THING IN EVIDENCE IS PRIDE.
BUILT IN THE SHADOW OF AN ABANDONED GOTHIC CATHEDRAL-- A BELOVED LANDMARK WITH NO MONEY TO SAVE IT FROM RUIN.
SUNNYSIDE
WOW. TREASURE TROVE. HOW DID YOU KNOW ABOUT THIS DEAL?
THESE PEOPLE IN THE HOUSING PROJECT GET THEIR TVS AND STEREOS RE-POSSESSED EVERY WEEK.
BUT THE LADY THAT RUNS SUNNYSIDE, SHE'S NICE. SO SHE PUTS THE STUFF HERE, AND GIVES PEOPLE A FEW DAYS TO GET IT OUT OF HOCK. IT'S SUNNYSIDE'S PRIVATE PAWNSHOP.
WE'RE DONE, LET'S GO. I KNOW WHERE I CAN UNLOAD THIS, THEN WE'RE GETTIN' YOU THOSE FUR BOOTS!
YOU THINK SO?
WHAT IS THAT?
I'VE HEARD OF YOU! YOU'RE THE BATMAN.

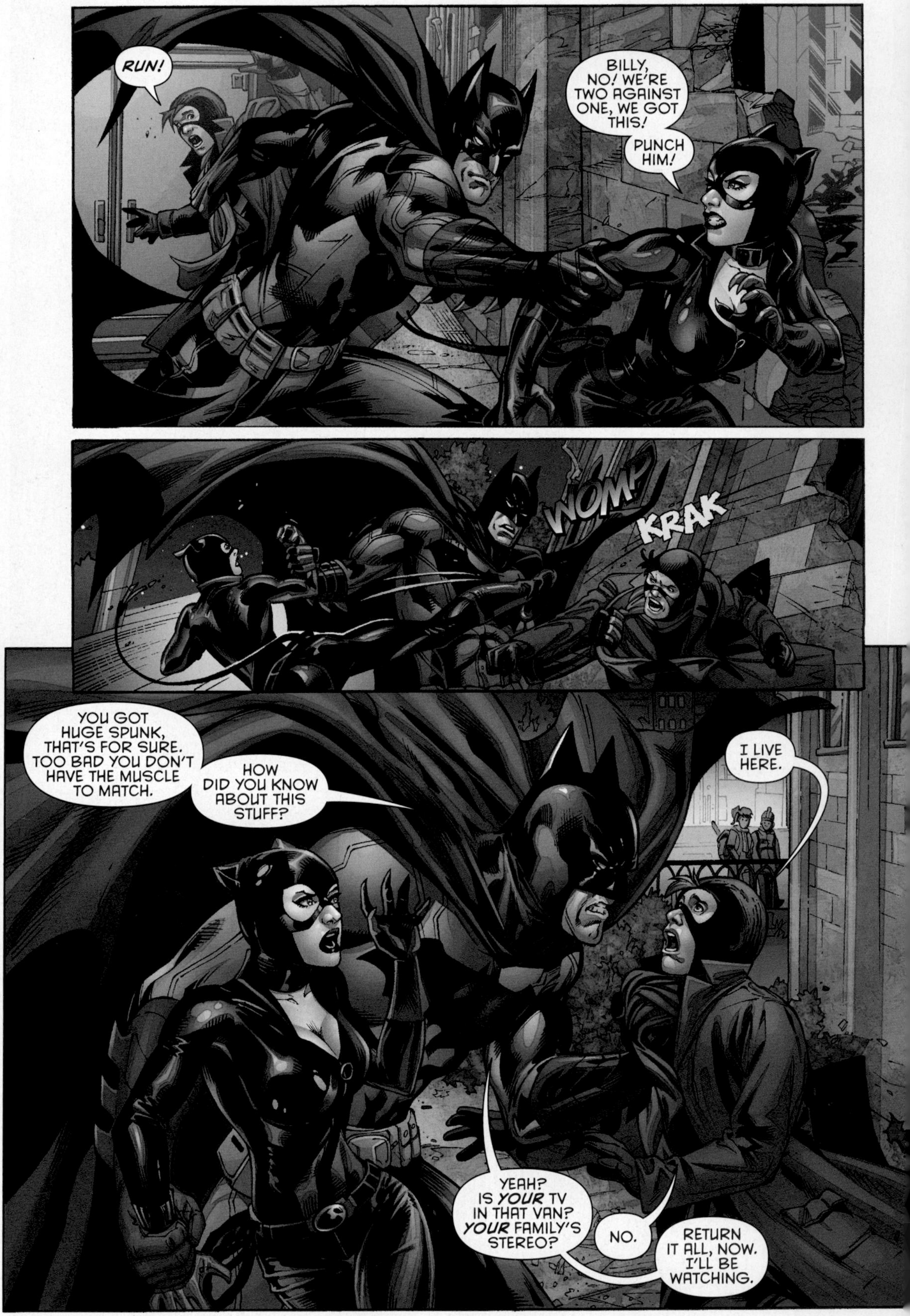
RUN!
BILLY, NO! WE'RE TWO AGAINST ONE, WE GOT THIS!
PUNCH HIM!
WOMP
KRAK
YOU GOT HUGE SPUNK, THAT'S FOR SURE. TOO BAD YOU DON'T HAVE THE MUSCLE TO MATCH.
HOW DID YOU KNOW ABOUT THIS STUFF?
I LIVE HERE.
YEAH? IS YOUR TV IN THAT VAN? YOUR FAMILY'S STEREO?
NO.
RETURN IT ALL, NOW. I'LL BE WATCHING.

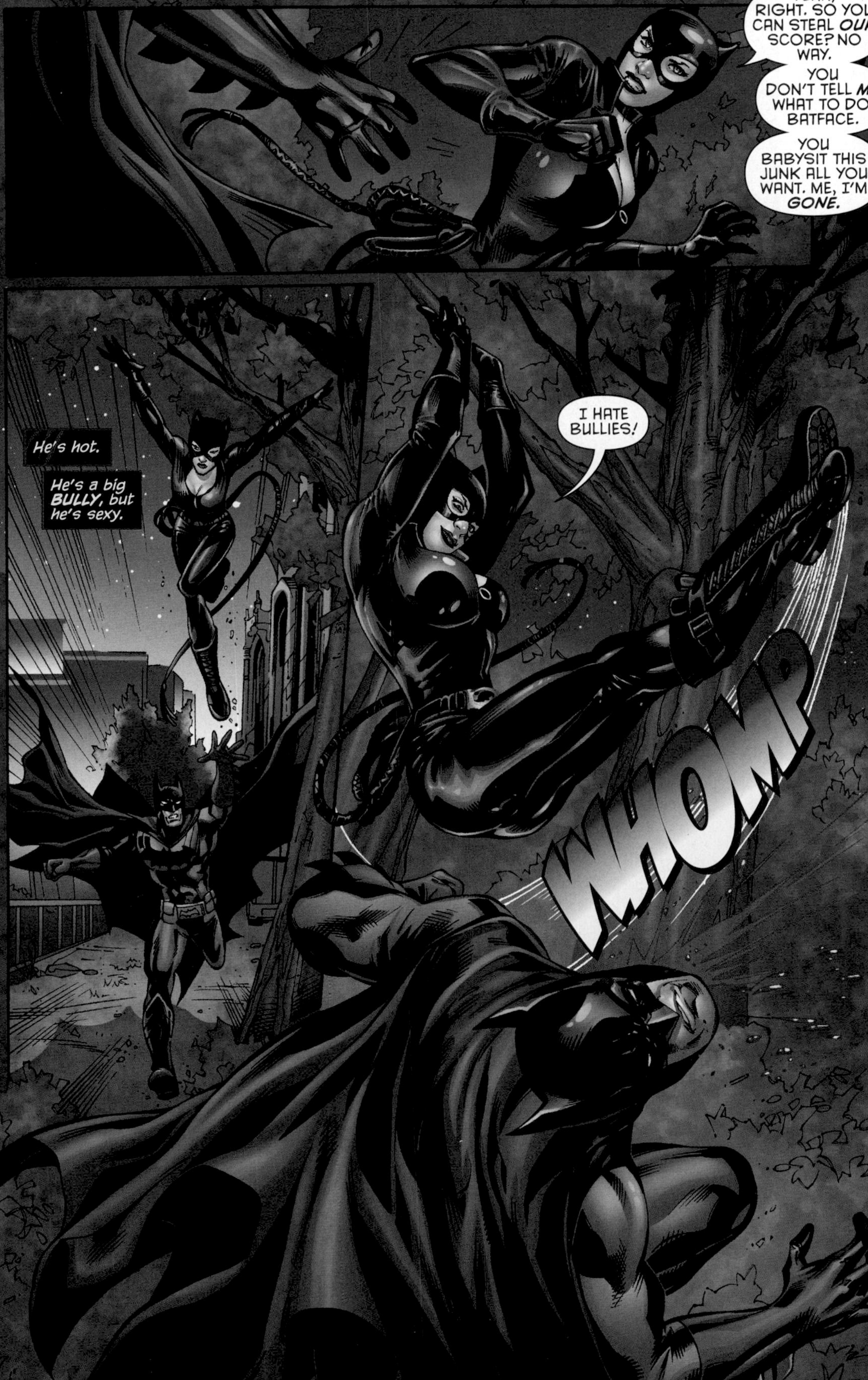
YEAH, RIGHT. SO YOU CAN STEAL OUR SCORE? NO WAY.
YOU DON'T TELL ME WHAT TO DO, BATFACE.
YOU BABYSIT THIS JUNK ALL YOU WANT. ME, I'M GONE.
He's hot.
He's a big BULLY, but he's sexy.
I HATE BULLIES!
WHOMP

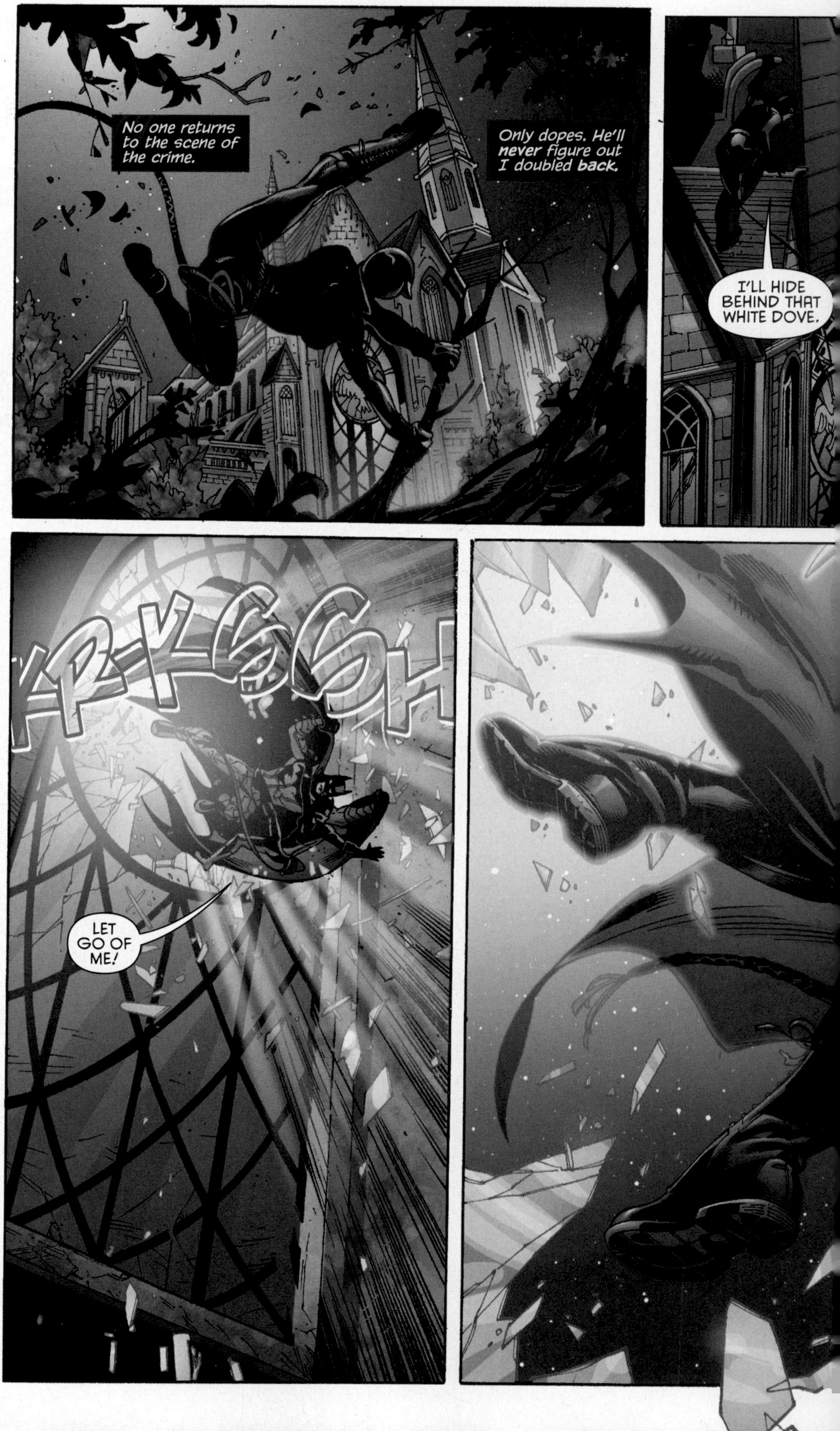
No one returns to the scene of the crime.
Only dopes. He'll never figure out I doubled back.
I'LL HIDE BEHIND THAT WHITE DOVE.
KR-KSSH
LET GO OF ME!

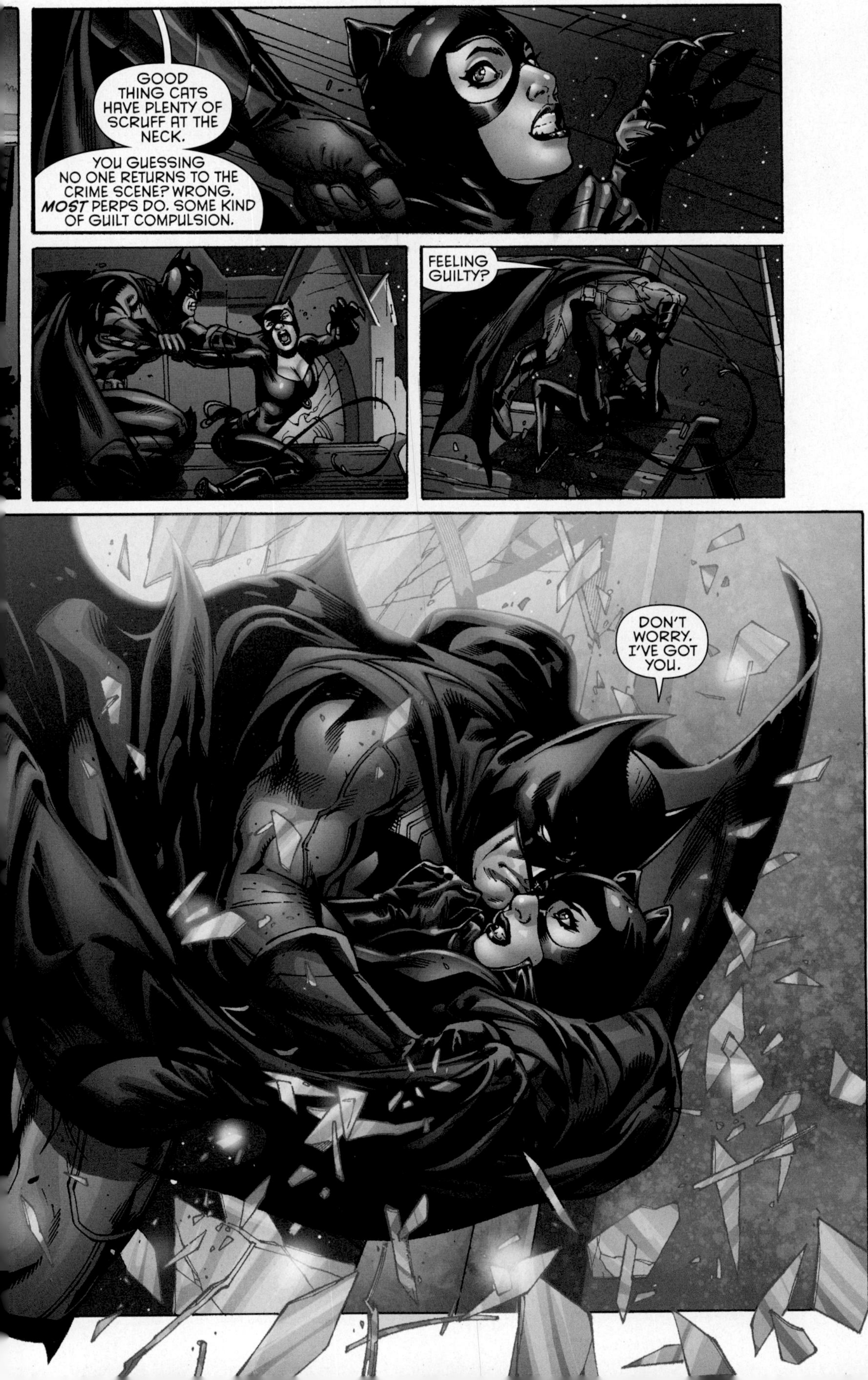
GOOD THING CATS HAVE PLENTY OF SCRUFF AT THE NECK.
YOU GUESSING NO ONE RETURNS TO THE CRIME SCENE? WRONG. *MOST* PERPS DO. SOME KIND OF GUILT COMPULSION.
FEELING GUILTY?
DON'T WORRY. I'VE GOT YOU.

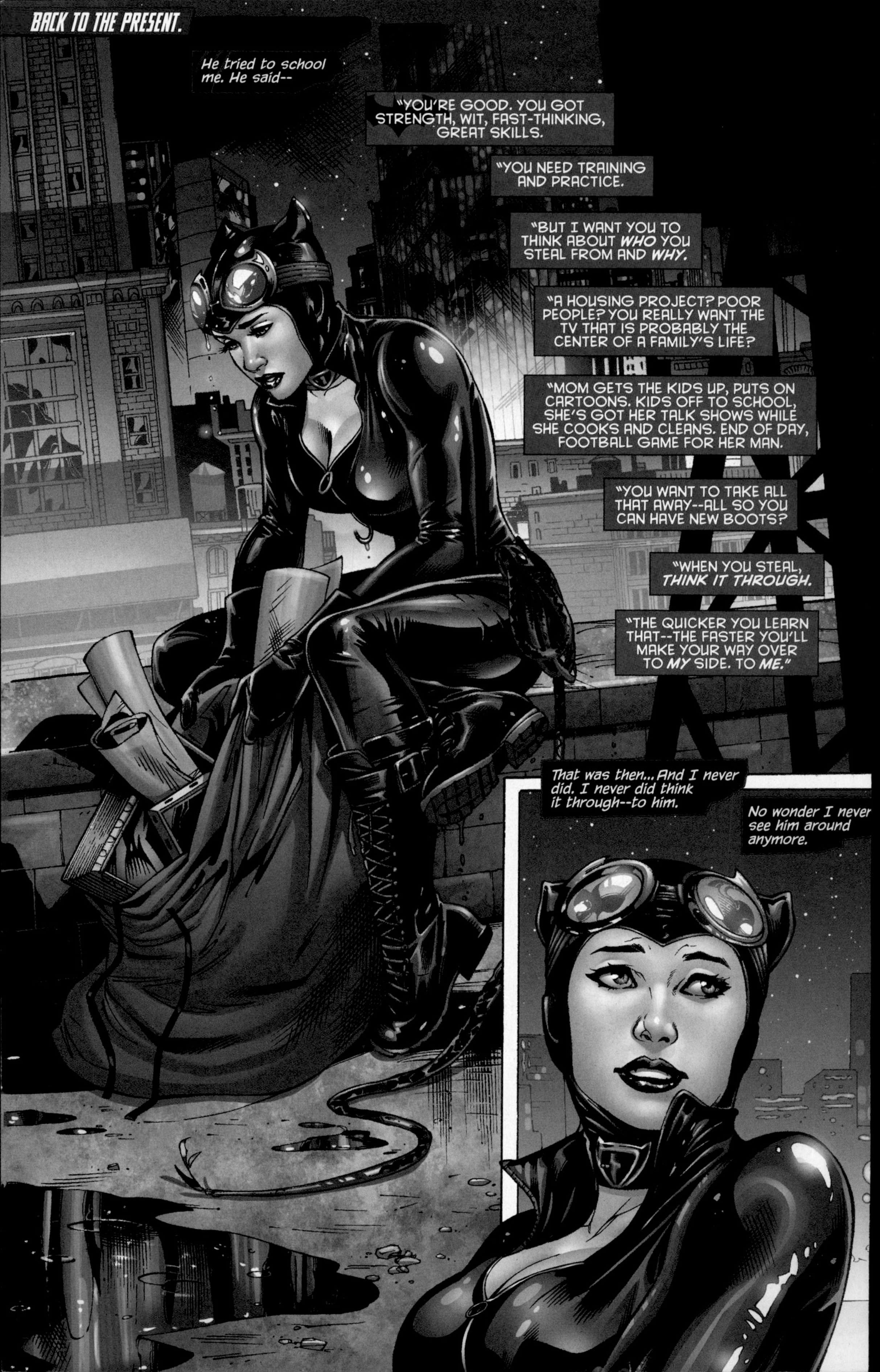
BACK TO THE PRESENT.
He tried to school me. He said--
"YOU'RE GOOD. YOU GOT STRENGTH, WIT, FAST-THINKING, GREAT SKILLS.
"YOU NEED TRAINING AND PRACTICE.
"BUT I WANT YOU TO THINK ABOUT WHO YOU STEAL FROM AND WHY.
"A HOUSING PROJECT? POOR PEOPLE? YOU REALLY WANT THE TV THAT IS PROBABLY THE CENTER OF A FAMILY'S LIFE?
"MOM GETS THE KIDS UP, PUTS ON CARTOONS. KIDS OFF TO SCHOOL, SHE'S GOT HER TALK SHOWS WHILE SHE COOKS AND CLEANS. END OF DAY, FOOTBALL GAME FOR HER MAN.
"YOU WANT TO TAKE ALL THAT AWAY--ALL SO YOU CAN HAVE NEW BOOTS?
"WHEN YOU STEAL, THINK IT THROUGH.
"THE QUICKER YOU LEARN THAT--THE FASTER YOU'LL MAKE YOUR WAY OVER TO MY SIDE. TO ME."
That was then... And I never did. I never did think it through--to him.
No wonder I never see him around anymore.

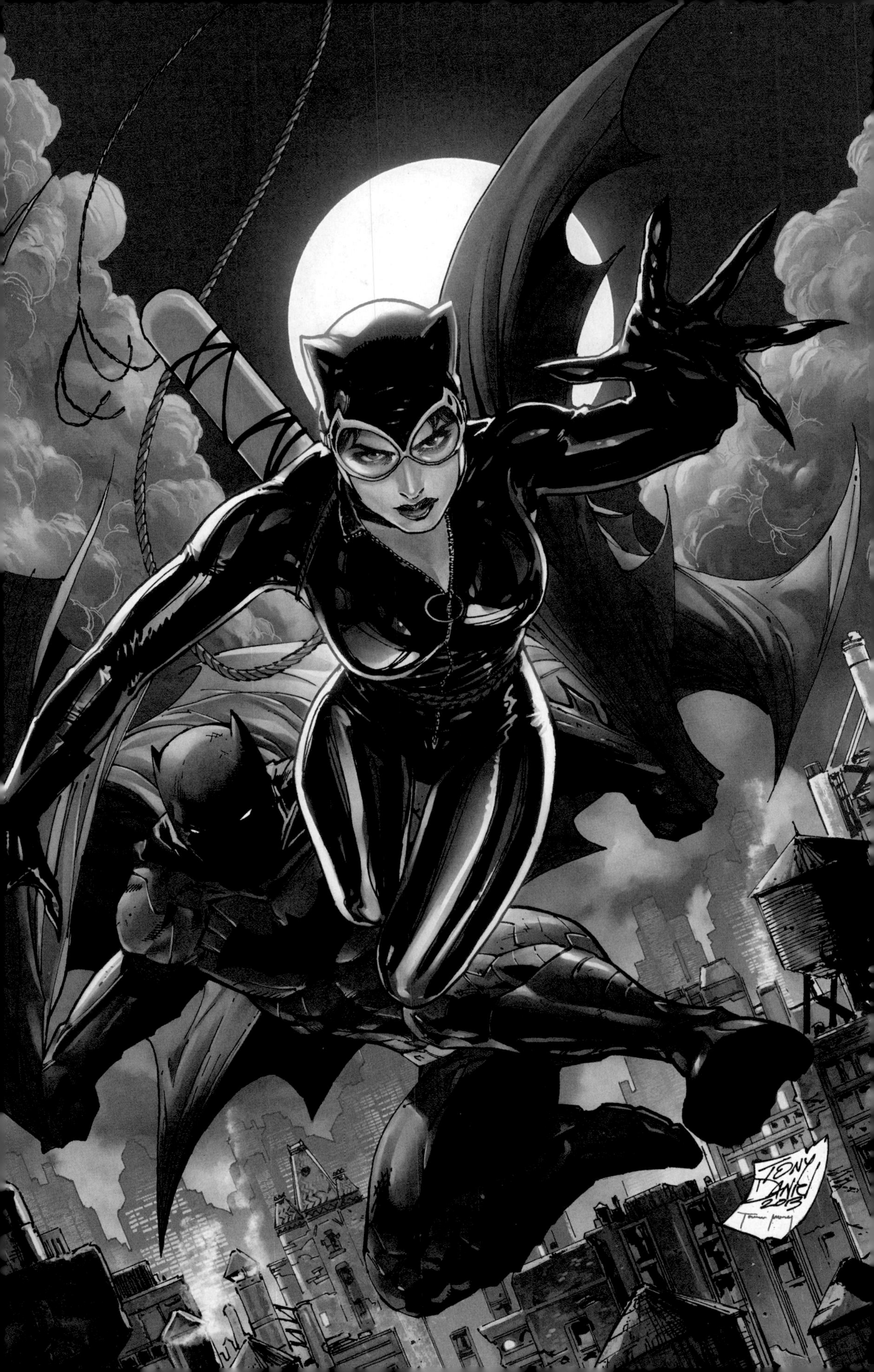

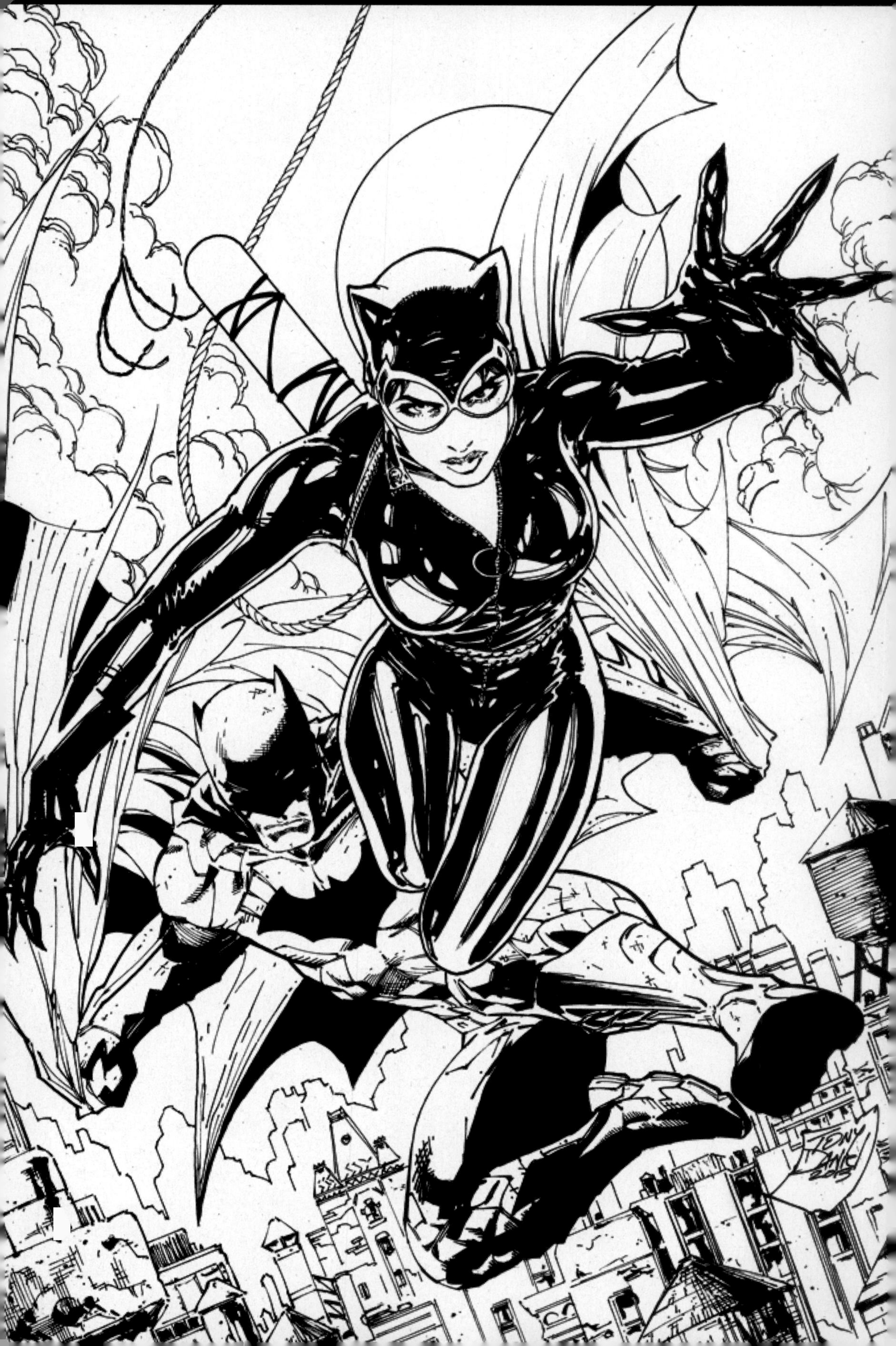

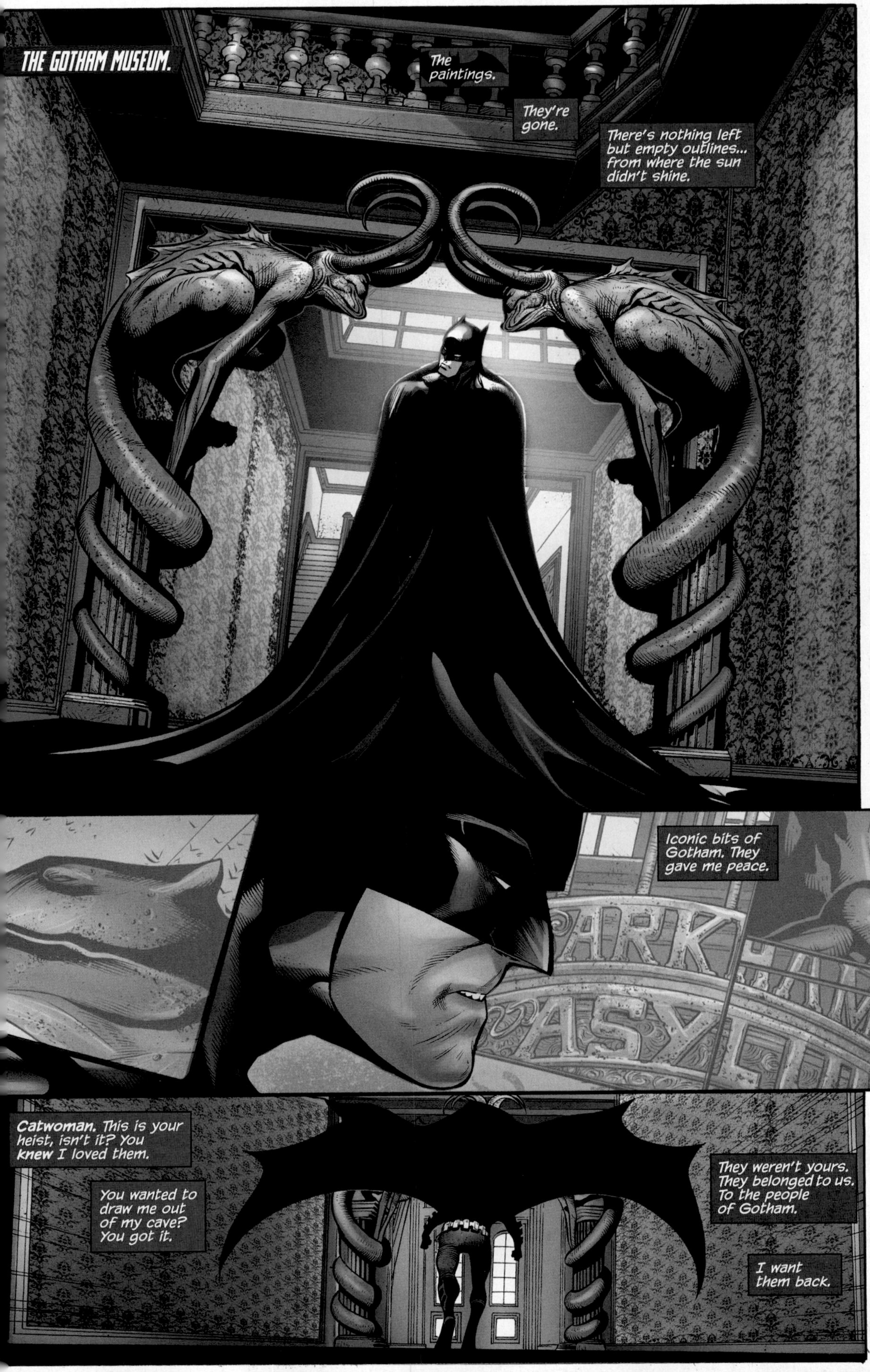
THE GOTHAM MUSEUM.
The paintings.
They're gone.
There's nothing left but empty outlines... from where the sun didn't shine.
Iconic bits of Gotham. They gave me peace.
ARK
ASY
Catwoman. This is your heist, isn't it? You knew I loved them.
You wanted to draw me out of my cave? You got it.
They weren't yours. They belonged to us. To the people of Gotham.
I want them back.

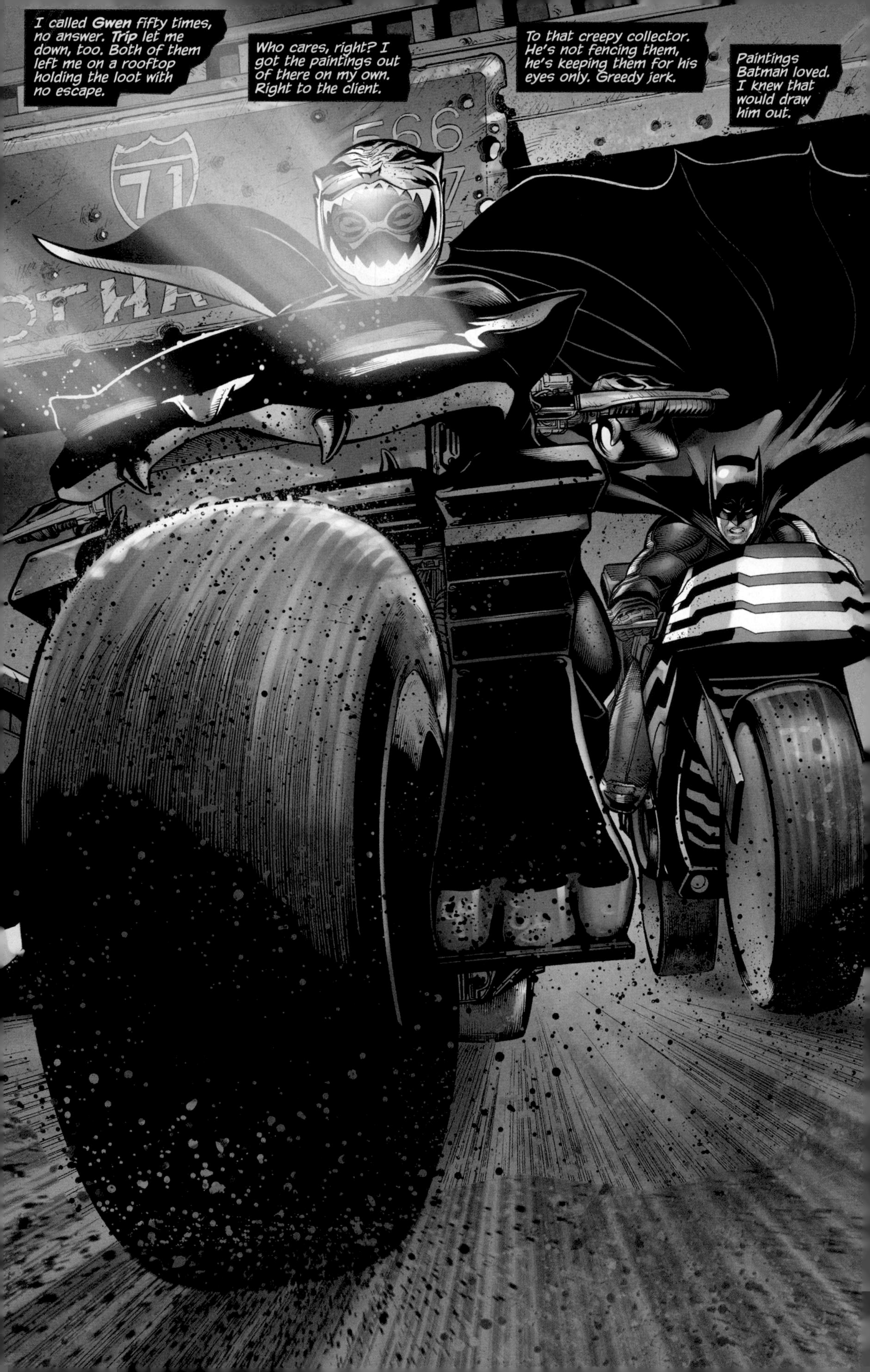

I called **Gwen** fifty times, no answer. **Trip** let me down, too. Both of them left me on a rooftop holding the loot with no escape.
Who cares, right? I got the paintings out of there on my own. Right to the client.
To that creepy collector. He's not fencing them, he's keeping them for his eyes only. Greedy jerk.
Paintings Batman loved. I knew that would draw him out.

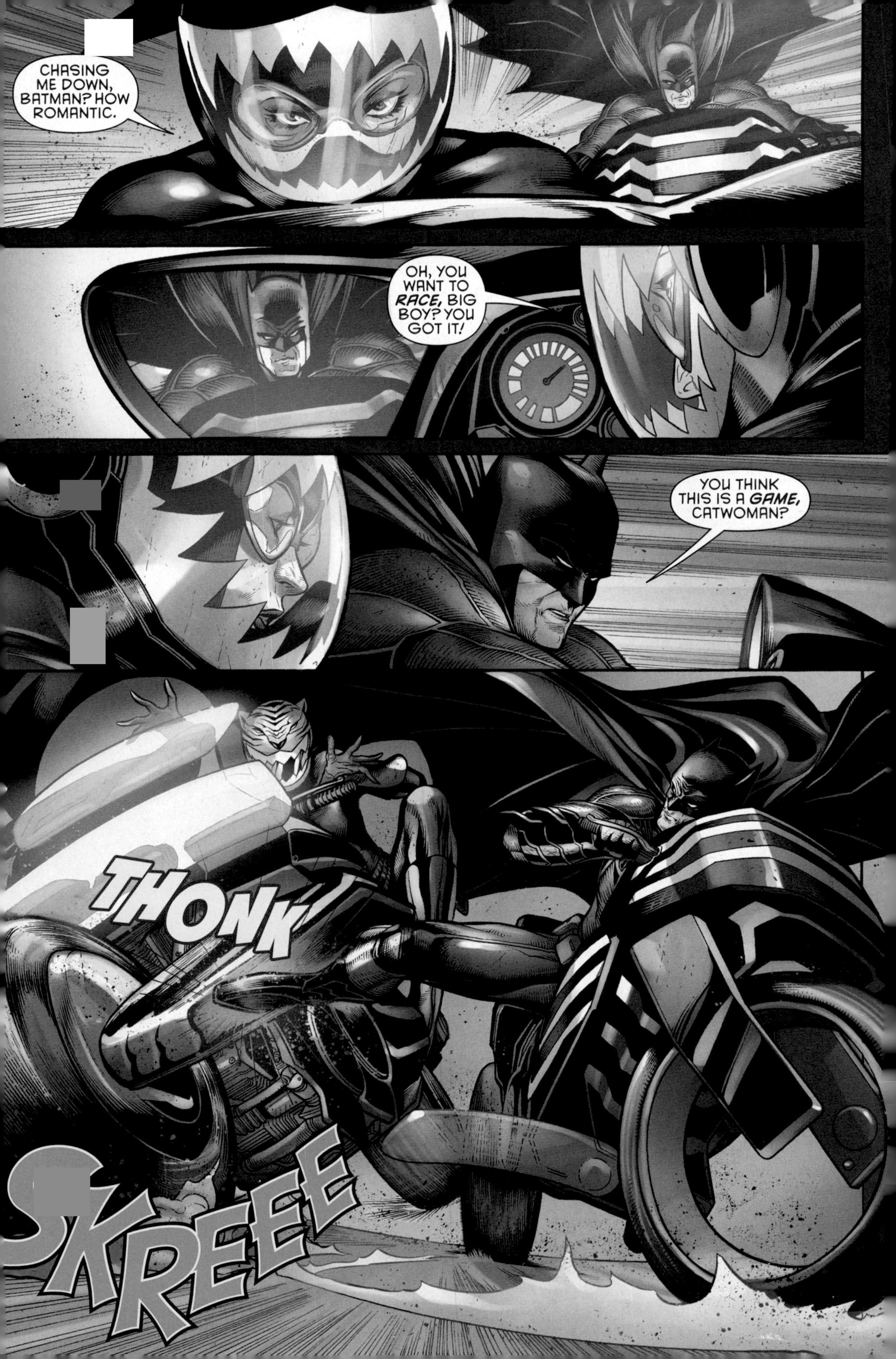
CHASING ME DOWN, BATMAN? HOW ROMANTIC.
OH, YOU WANT TO RACE, BIG BOY? YOU GOT IT!
YOU THINK THIS IS A GAME, CATWOMAN?
THONK
SKREEE

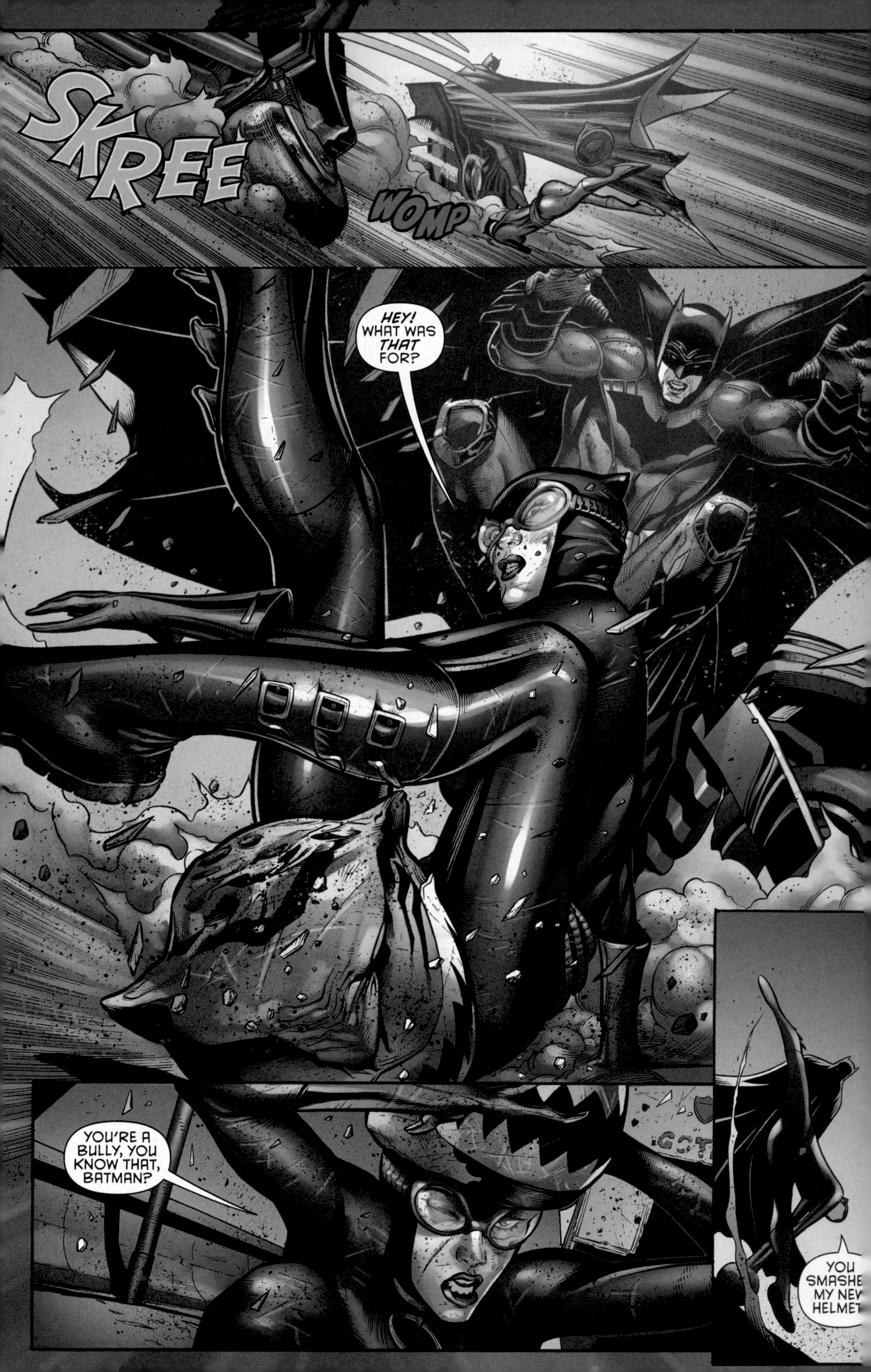
SKREE
WOMP
HEY! WHAT WAS THAT FOR?
YOU'RE A BULLY, YOU KNOW THAT, BATMAN?
YOU SMASHE MY NEW HELMET

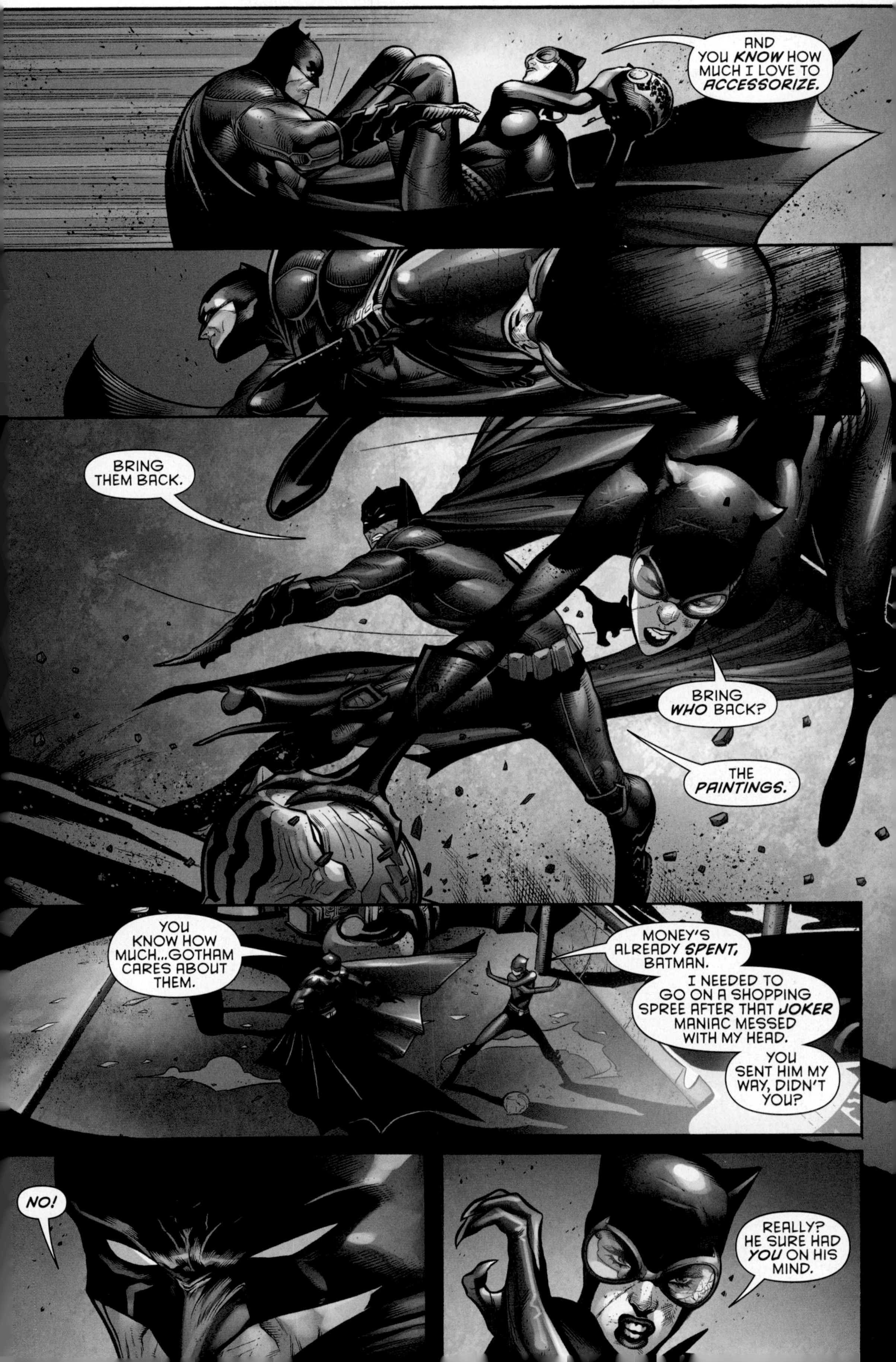
AND YOU **KNOW** HOW MUCH I LOVE TO **ACCESSORIZE.**
BRING THEM BACK.
BRING **WHO** BACK?
THE **PAINTINGS.**
YOU KNOW HOW MUCH...GOTHAM CARES ABOUT THEM.
MONEY'S ALREADY **SPENT,** BATMAN.
I NEEDED TO GO ON A SHOPPING SPREE AFTER THAT **JOKER** MANIAC MESSED WITH MY HEAD.
YOU SENT HIM MY WAY, DIDN'T YOU?
NO!
REALLY? HE SURE HAD **YOU** ON HIS MIND.

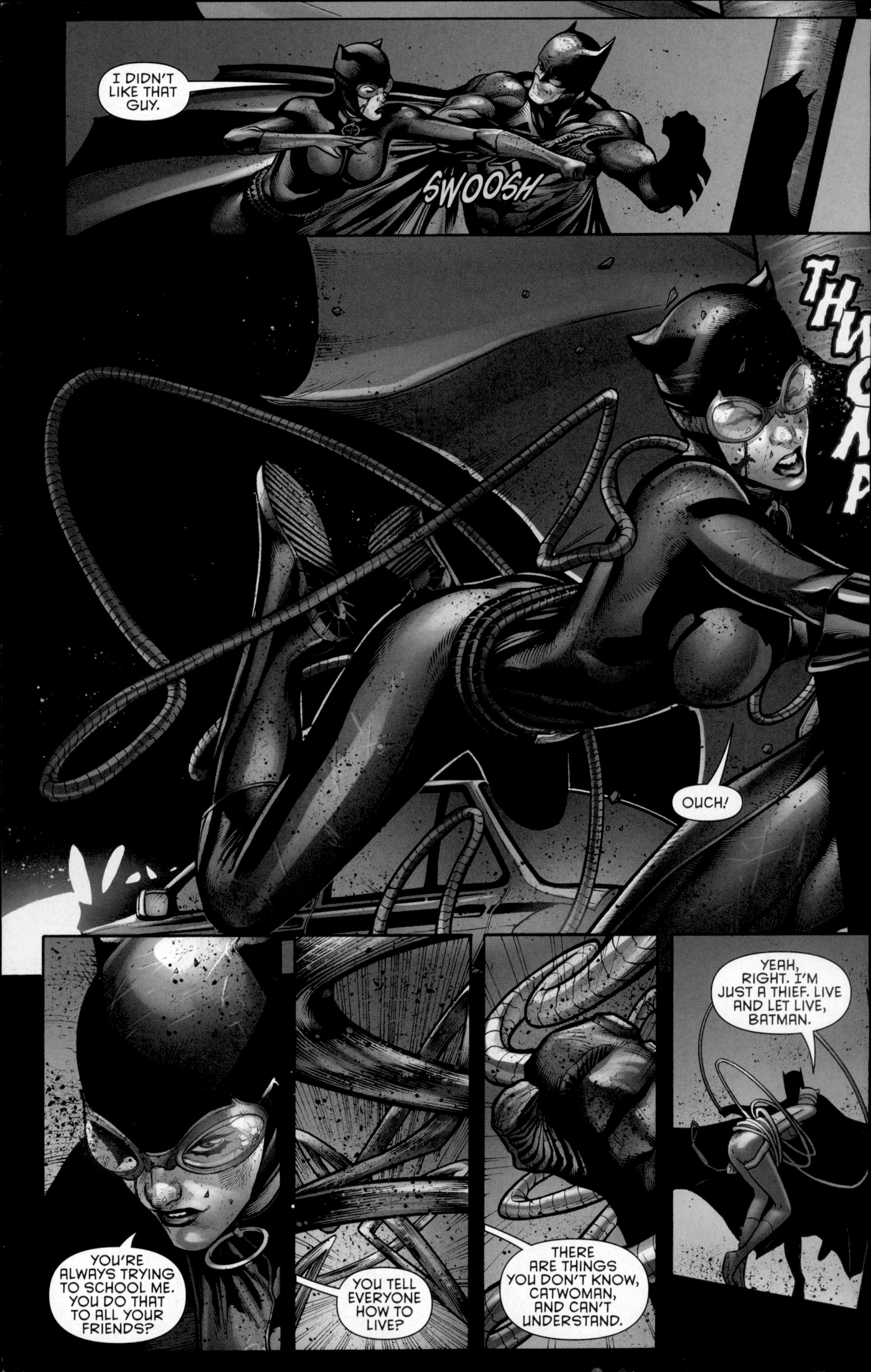
I DIDN'T LIKE THAT GUY.
SWOOSH
THWACK
OUCH!
YOU'RE ALWAYS TRYING TO SCHOOL ME. YOU DO THAT TO ALL YOUR FRIENDS?
YOU TELL EVERYONE HOW TO LIVE?
THERE ARE THINGS YOU DON'T KNOW, CATWOMAN, AND CAN'T UNDERSTAND.
YEAH, RIGHT. I'M JUST A THIEF. LIVE AND LET LIVE, BATMAN.

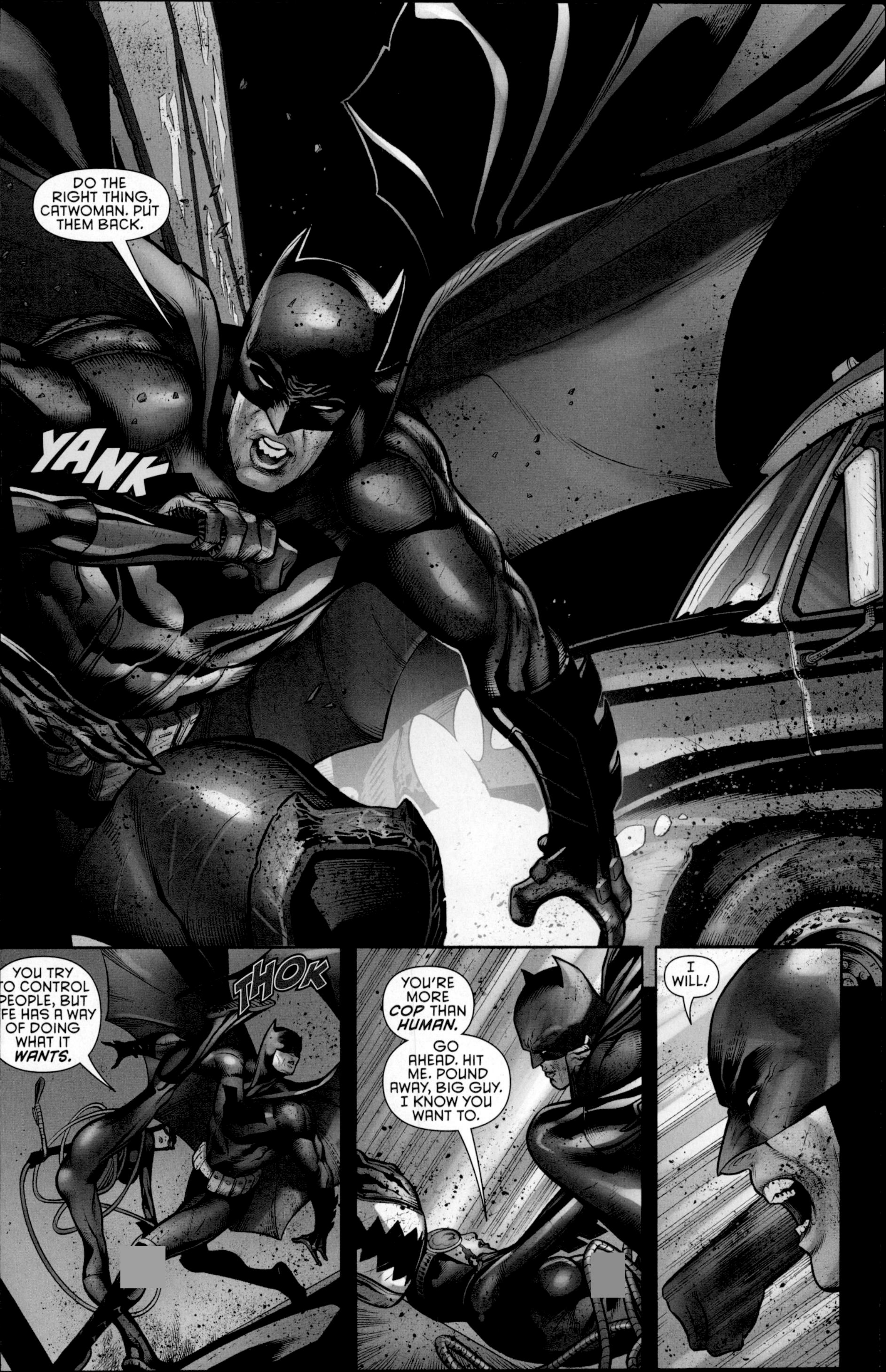
DO THE RIGHT THING, CATWOMAN. PUT THEM BACK.
YANK
YOU TRY TO CONTROL PEOPLE, BUT LIFE HAS A WAY OF DOING WHAT IT WANTS.
THOK
YOU'RE MORE COP THAN HUMAN.
GO AHEAD. HIT ME. POUND AWAY, BIG GUY. I KNOW YOU WANT TO.
I WILL!

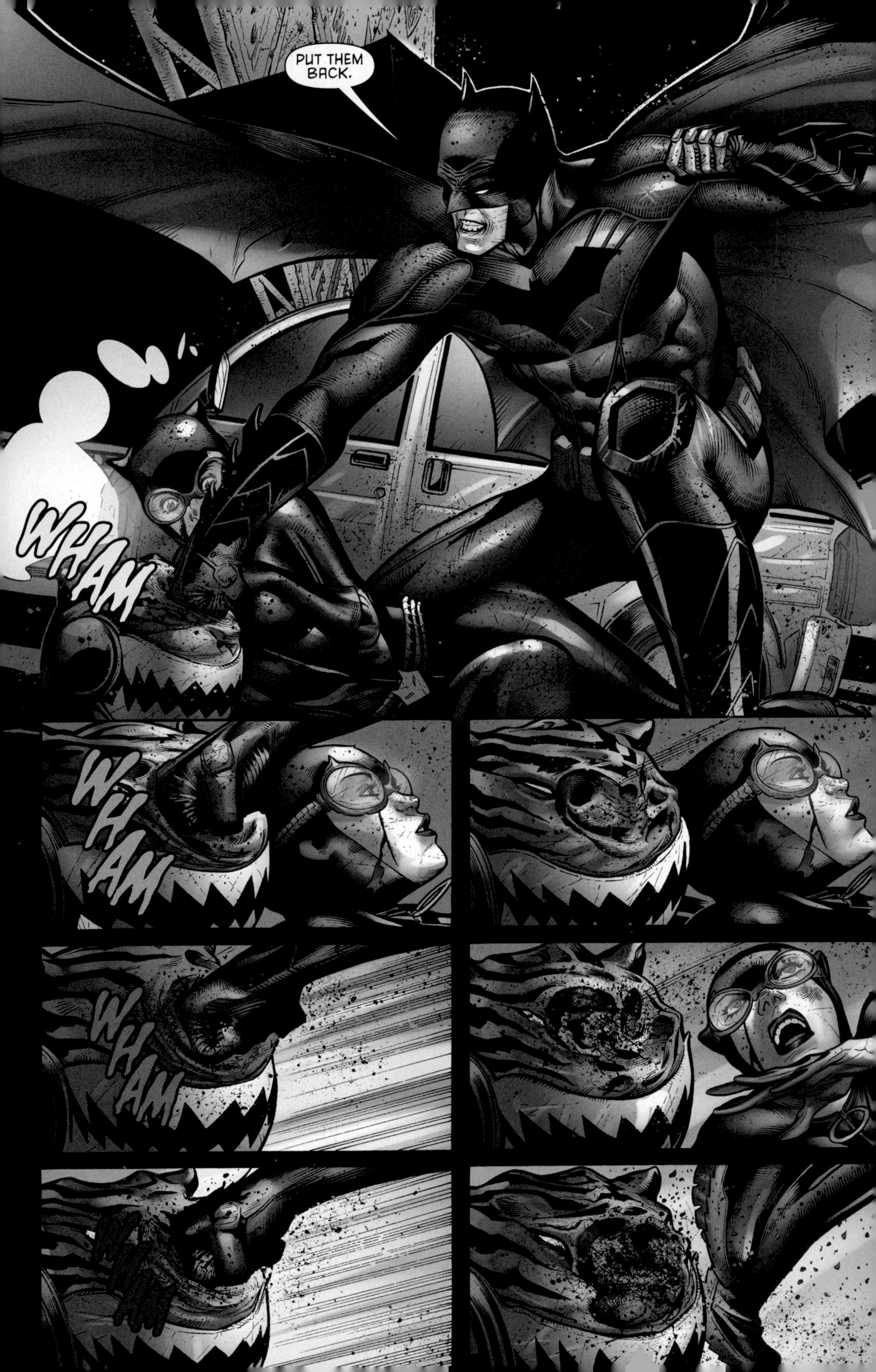
PUT THEM BACK.
WHAM
WHAM
WHAM

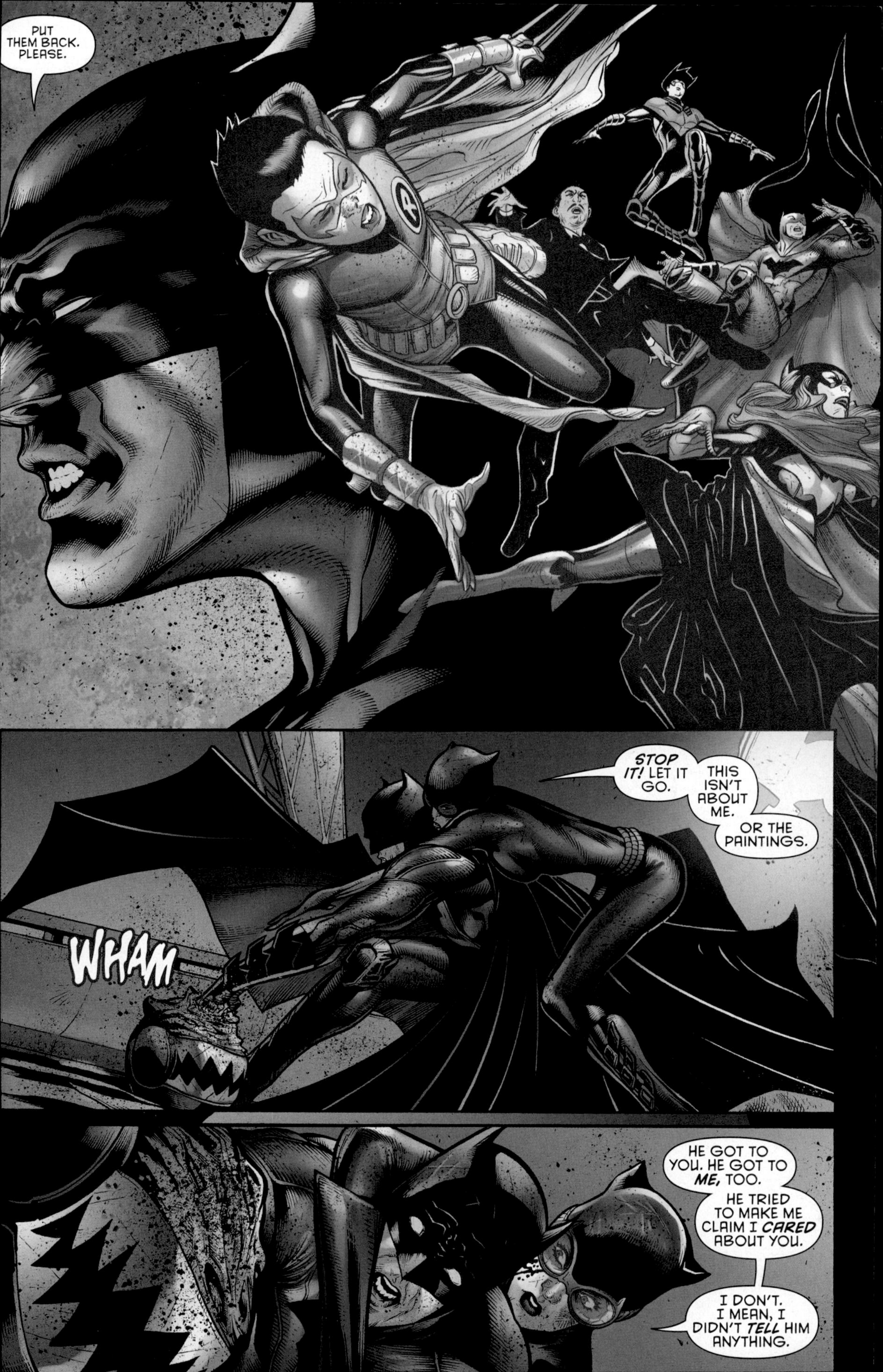
PUT THEM BACK. PLEASE.
STOP IT! LET IT GO.
THIS ISN'T ABOUT ME.
OR THE PAINTINGS.
WHAM
HE GOT TO YOU. HE GOT TO ME, TOO.
HE TRIED TO MAKE ME CLAIM I CARED ABOUT YOU.
I DON'T. I MEAN, I DIDN'T TELL HIM ANYTHING.

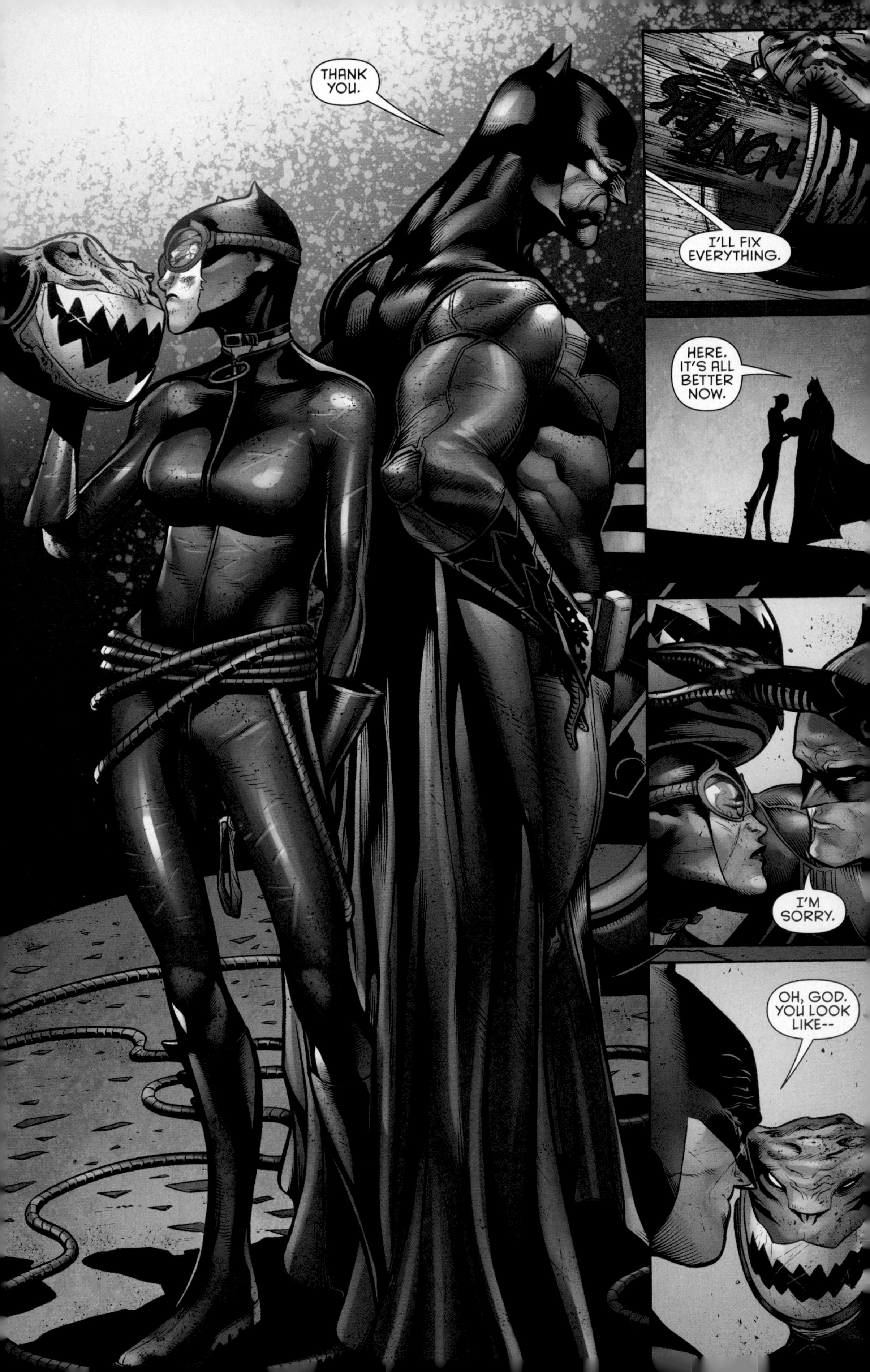

THANK YOU.
SPLUNCH
I'LL FIX EVERYTHING.
HERE. IT'S ALL BETTER NOW.
I'M SORRY.
OH, GOD. YOU LOOK LIKE--

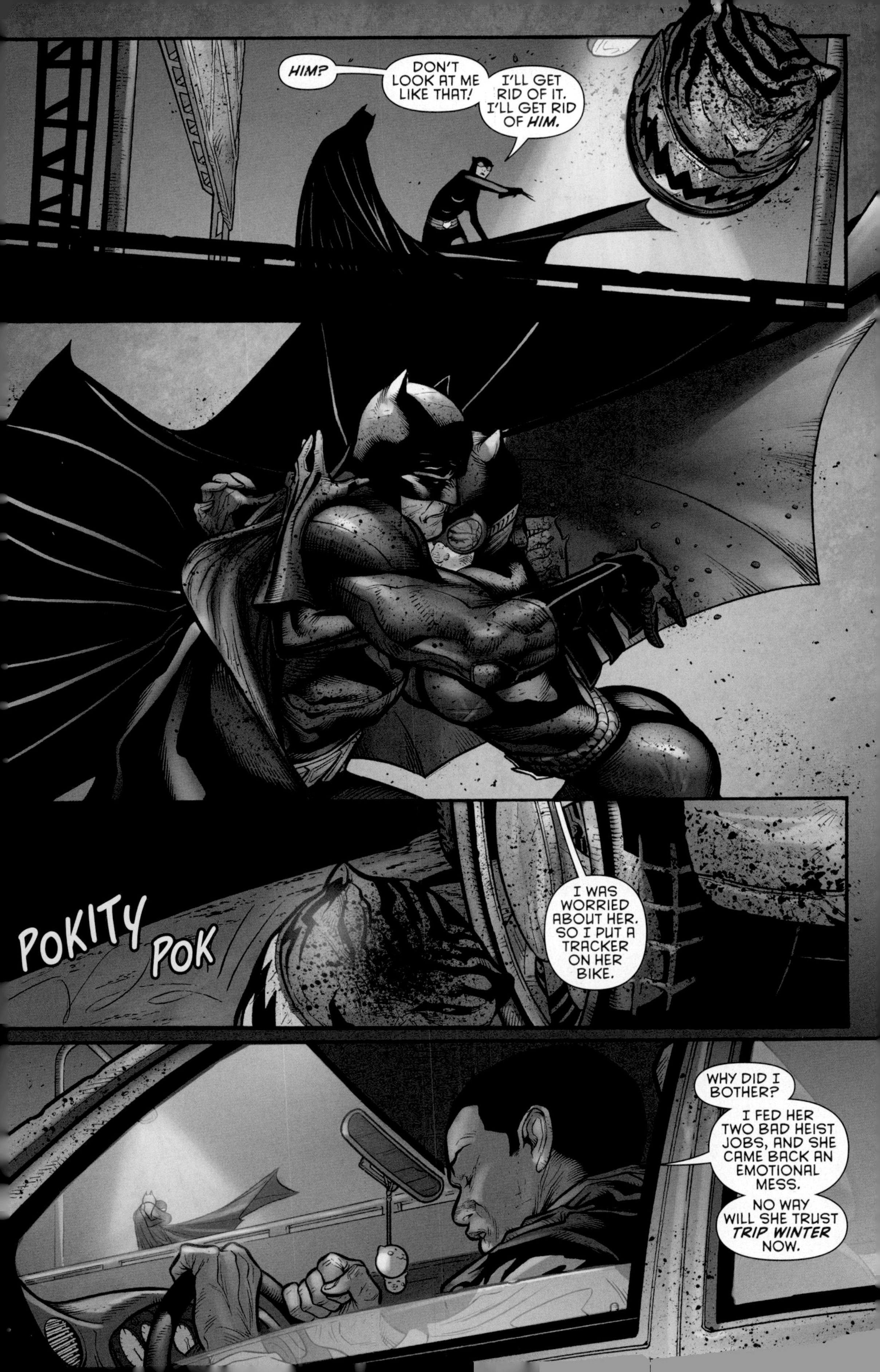
HIM?
DON'T LOOK AT ME LIKE THAT!
I'LL GET RID OF IT. I'LL GET RID OF *HIM.*
POKITY POK
I WAS WORRIED ABOUT HER. SO I PUT A TRACKER ON HER BIKE.
WHY DID I BOTHER?
I FED HER TWO BAD HEIST JOBS, AND SHE CAME BACK AN EMOTIONAL MESS.
NO WAY WILL SHE TRUST *TRIP WINTER* NOW.

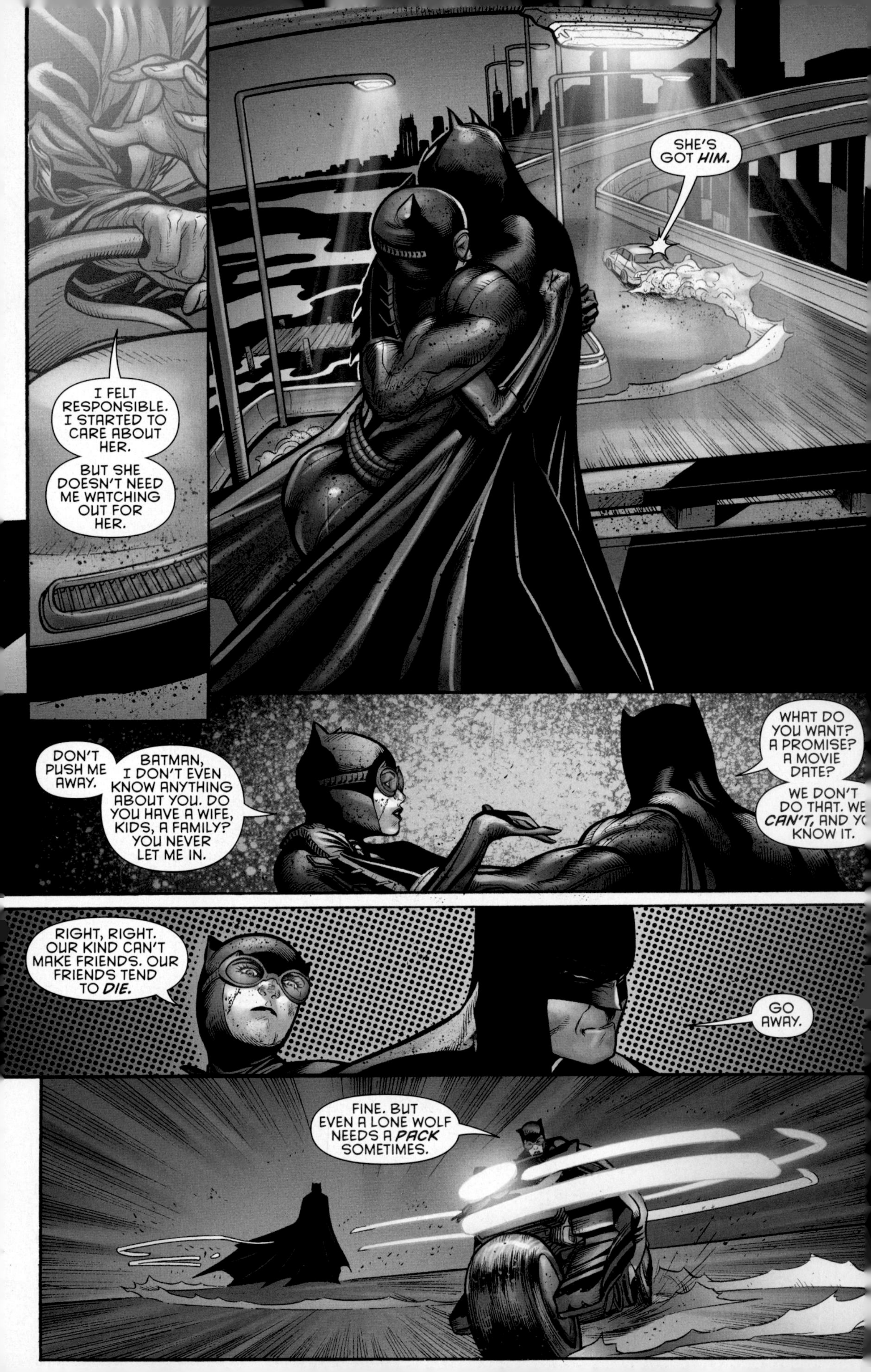
I FELT RESPONSIBLE. I STARTED TO CARE ABOUT HER.
BUT SHE DOESN'T NEED ME WATCHING OUT FOR HER.
SHE'S GOT *HIM.*
DON'T PUSH ME AWAY.
BATMAN, I DON'T EVEN KNOW ANYTHING ABOUT YOU. DO YOU HAVE A WIFE, KIDS, A FAMILY? YOU NEVER LET ME IN.
WHAT DO YOU WANT? A PROMISE? A MOVIE DATE?
WE DON'T DO THAT. WE *CAN'T,* AND YO KNOW IT.
RIGHT, RIGHT. OUR KIND CAN'T MAKE FRIENDS. OUR FRIENDS TEND TO *DIE.*
GO AWAY.
FINE. BUT EVEN A LONE WOLF NEEDS A *PACK* SOMETIMES.

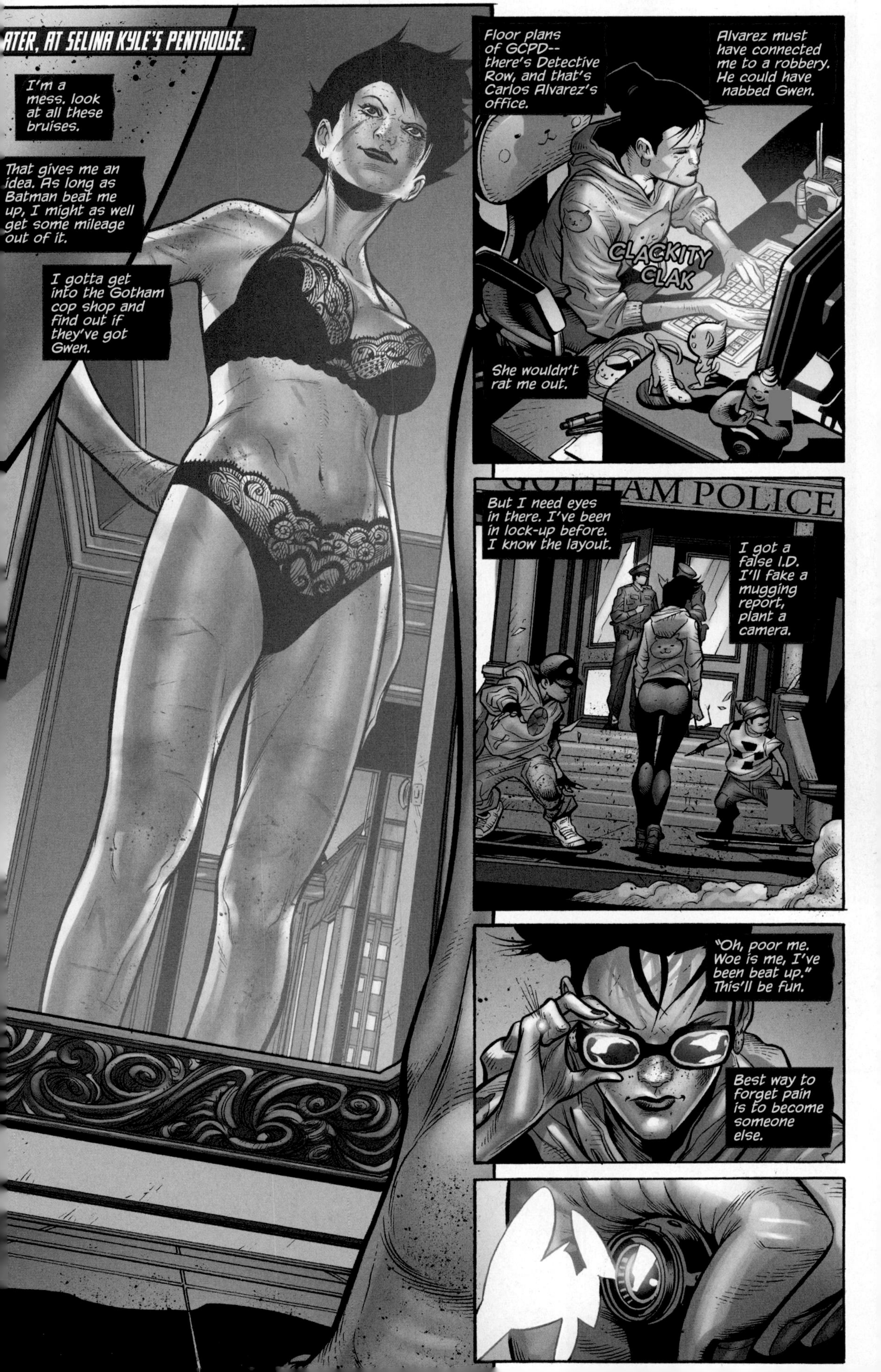
ATER, AT SELINA KYLE'S PENTHOUSE.
I'm a mess. look at all these bruises.
That gives me an idea. As long as Batman beat me up, I might as well get some mileage out of it.
I gotta get into the Gotham cop shop and find out if they've got Gwen.
Floor plans of GCPD-- there's Detective Row, and that's Carlos Alvarez's office.
Alvarez must have connected me to a robbery. He could have nabbed Gwen.
CLACKITY CLAK
She wouldn't rat me out.
AM POLICE
But I need eyes in there. I've been in lock-up before. I know the layout.
I got a false I.D. I'll fake a mugging report, plant a camera.
"Oh, poor me. Woe is me, I've been beat up." This'll be fun.
Best way to forget pain is to become someone else.

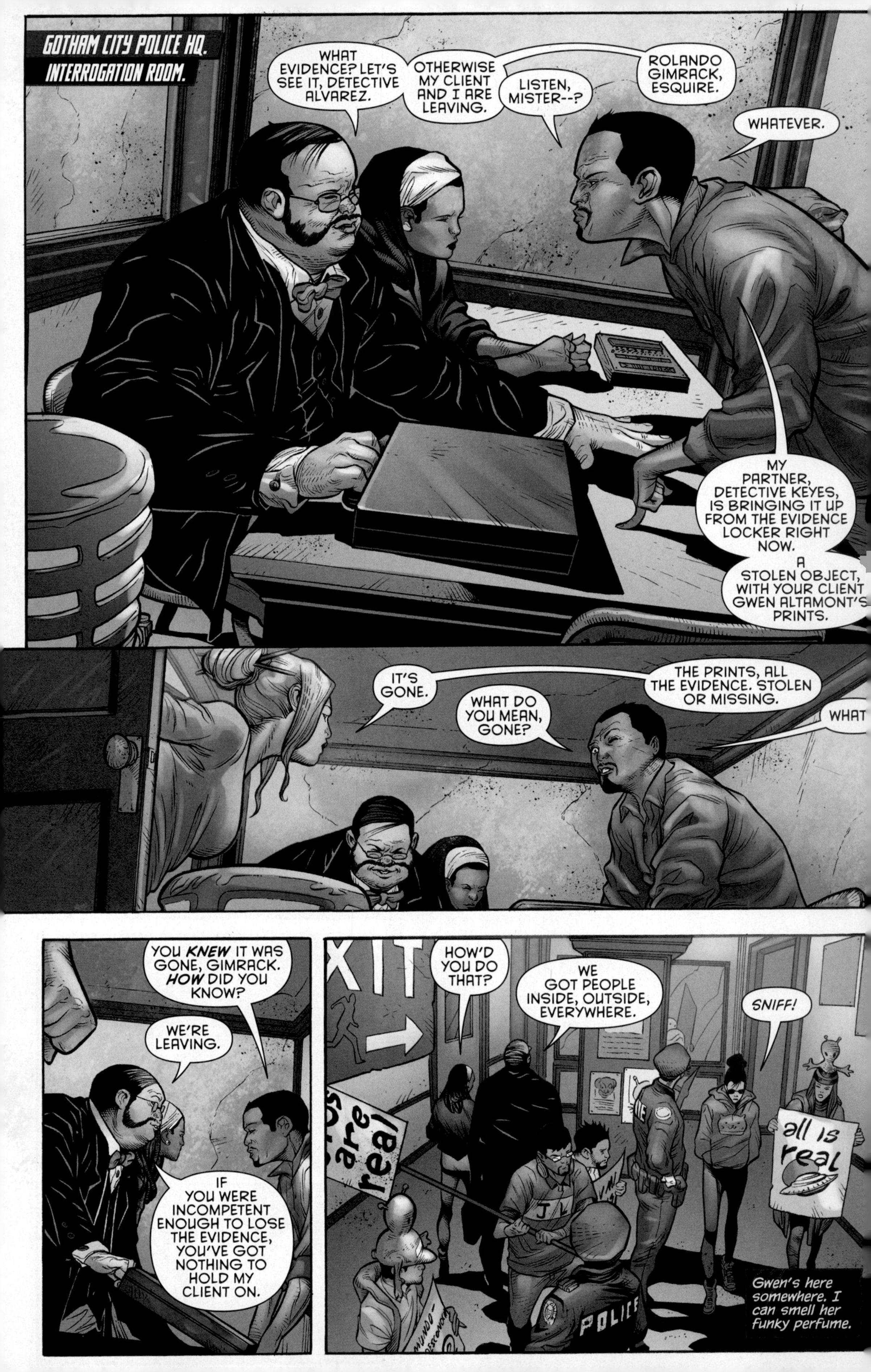
GOTHAM CITY POLICE HQ.
INTERROGATION ROOM.
WHAT EVIDENCE? LET'S SEE IT, DETECTIVE ALVAREZ.
OTHERWISE MY CLIENT AND I ARE LEAVING.
LISTEN, MISTER--?
ROLANDO GIMRACK, ESQUIRE.
WHATEVER.
MY PARTNER, DETECTIVE KEYES, IS BRINGING IT UP FROM THE EVIDENCE LOCKER RIGHT NOW.
A STOLEN OBJECT, WITH YOUR CLIENT GWEN ALTAMONT'S PRINTS.
IT'S GONE.
THE PRINTS, ALL THE EVIDENCE. STOLEN OR MISSING.
WHAT DO YOU MEAN, GONE?
WHAT
YOU KNEW IT WAS GONE, GIMRACK. HOW DID YOU KNOW?
WE'RE LEAVING.
IF YOU WERE INCOMPETENT ENOUGH TO LOSE THE EVIDENCE, YOU'VE GOT NOTHING TO HOLD MY CLIENT ON.
XIT
HOW'D YOU DO THAT?
WE GOT PEOPLE INSIDE, OUTSIDE, EVERYWHERE.
SNIFF!
are real
all is real
POLICE
Gwen's here somewhere. I can smell her funky perfume.

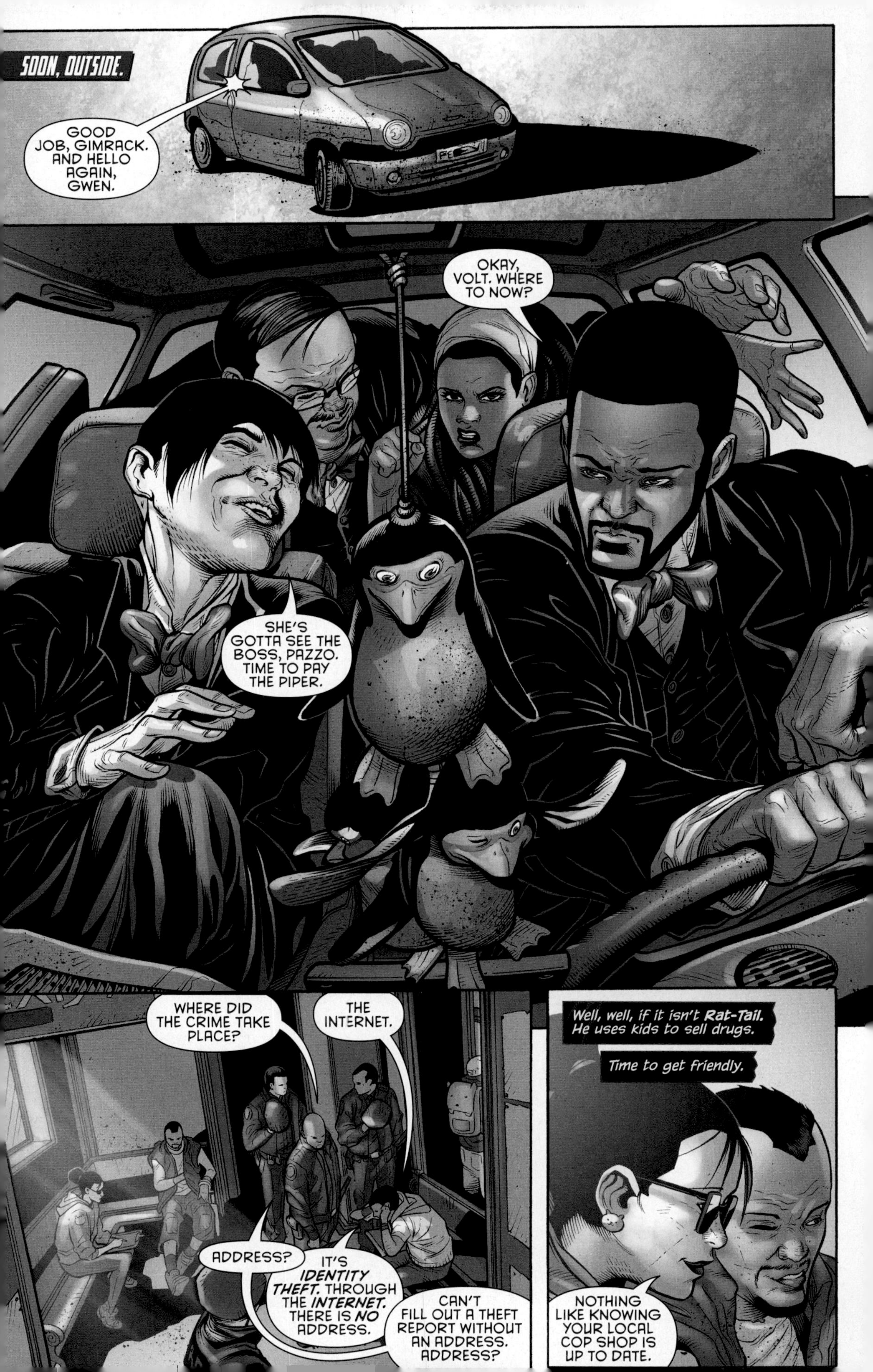
SOON, OUTSIDE.
GOOD JOB, GIMRACK. AND HELLO AGAIN, GWEN.
OKAY, VOLT. WHERE TO NOW?
SHE'S GOTTA SEE THE BOSS, PAZZO. TIME TO PAY THE PIPER.
WHERE DID THE CRIME TAKE PLACE?
THE INTERNET.
ADDRESS?
IT'S *IDENTITY THEFT*. THROUGH THE *INTERNET*. THERE IS *NO* ADDRESS.
CAN'T FILL OUT A THEFT REPORT WITHOUT AN ADDRESS. ADDRESS?
Well, well, if it isn't **Rat-Tail**. He uses kids to sell drugs.
Time to get friendly.
NOTHING LIKE KNOWING YOUR LOCAL COP SHOP IS UP TO DATE.

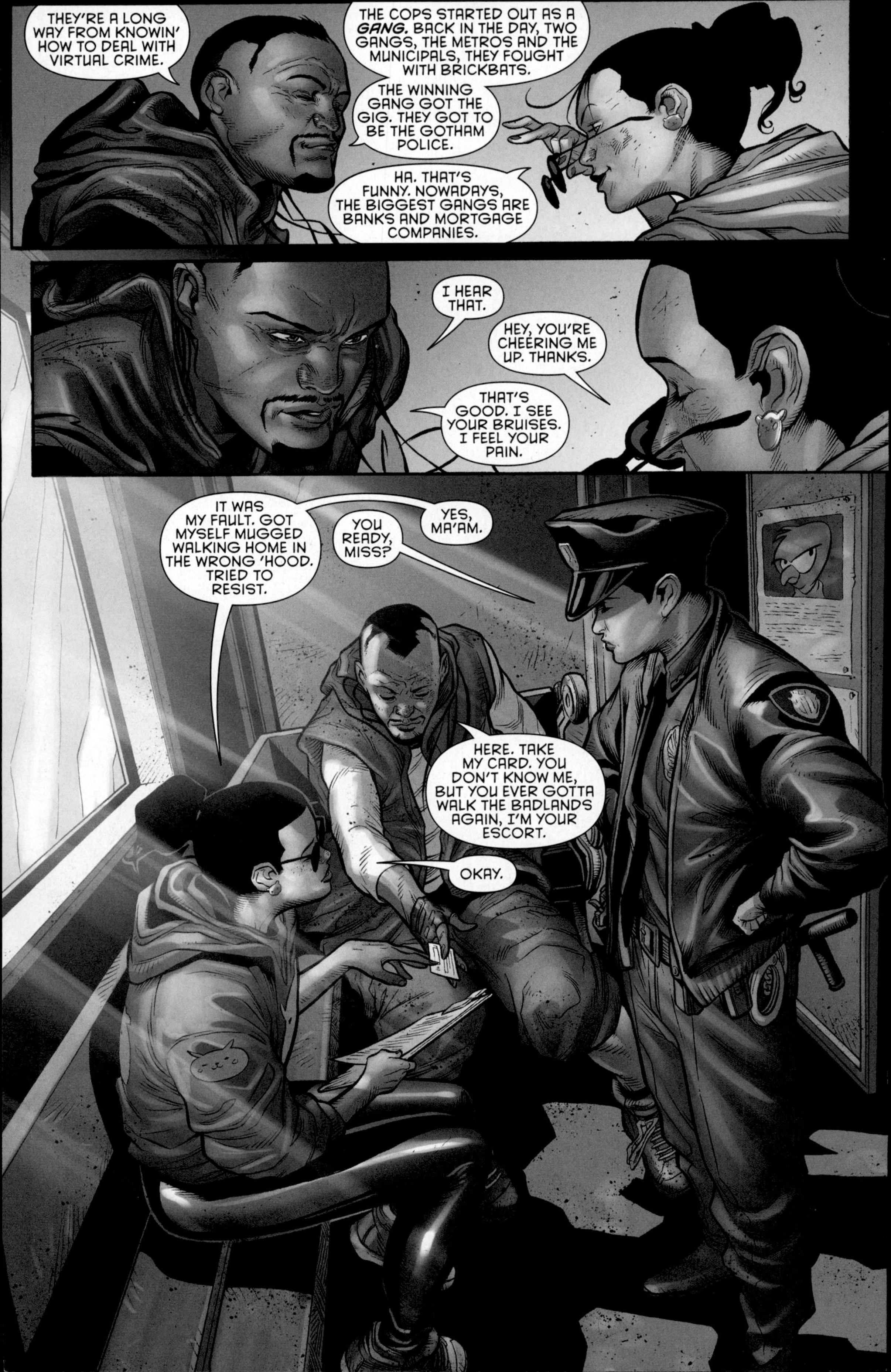
THEY'RE A LONG WAY FROM KNOWIN' HOW TO DEAL WITH VIRTUAL CRIME.
THE COPS STARTED OUT AS A *GANG.* BACK IN THE DAY, TWO GANGS, THE METROS AND THE MUNICIPALS, THEY FOUGHT WITH BRICKBATS.
THE WINNING GANG GOT THE GIG. THEY GOT TO BE THE GOTHAM POLICE.
HA. THAT'S FUNNY. NOWADAYS, THE BIGGEST GANGS ARE BANKS AND MORTGAGE COMPANIES.
I HEAR THAT.
HEY, YOU'RE CHEERING ME UP. THANKS.
THAT'S GOOD. I SEE YOUR BRUISES. I FEEL YOUR PAIN.
IT WAS MY FAULT. GOT MYSELF MUGGED WALKING HOME IN THE WRONG 'HOOD. TRIED TO RESIST.
YOU READY, MISS?
YES, MA'AM.
HERE. TAKE MY CARD. YOU DON'T KNOW ME, BUT YOU EVER GOTTA WALK THE BADLANDS AGAIN, I'M YOUR ESCORT.
OKAY.

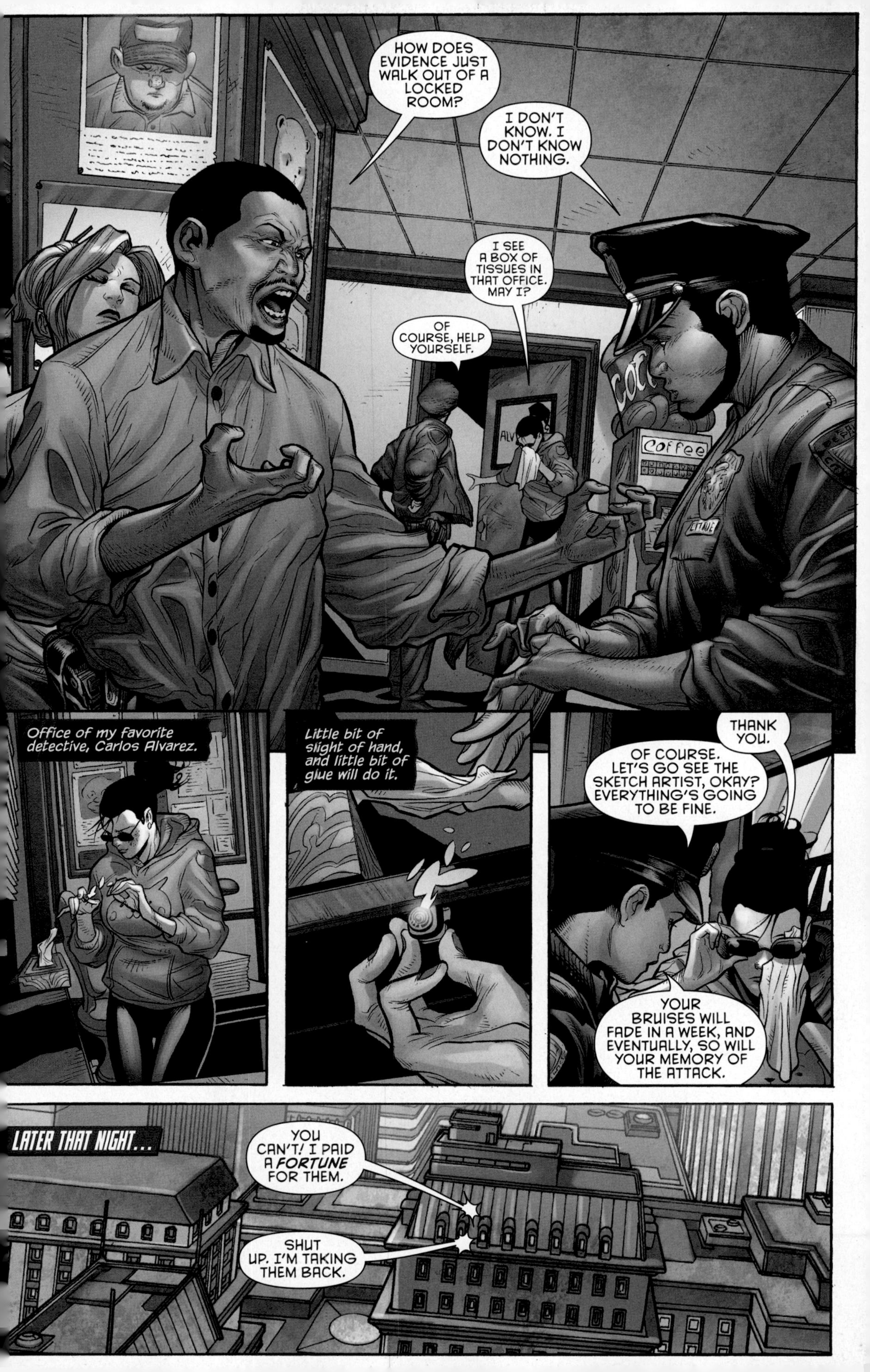
HOW DOES EVIDENCE JUST WALK OUT OF A LOCKED ROOM?
I DON'T KNOW. I DON'T KNOW NOTHING.
I SEE A BOX OF TISSUES IN THAT OFFICE. MAY I?
OF COURSE, HELP YOURSELF.
COFFEE
Office of my favorite detective, Carlos Alvarez.
Little bit of slight of hand, and little bit of glue will do it.
THANK YOU.
OF COURSE. LET'S GO SEE THE SKETCH ARTIST, OKAY? EVERYTHING'S GOING TO BE FINE.
YOUR BRUISES WILL FADE IN A WEEK, AND EVENTUALLY, SO WILL YOUR MEMORY OF THE ATTACK.
LATER THAT NIGHT...
YOU CAN'T! I PAID A FORTUNE FOR THEM.
SHUT UP. I'M TAKING THEM BACK.

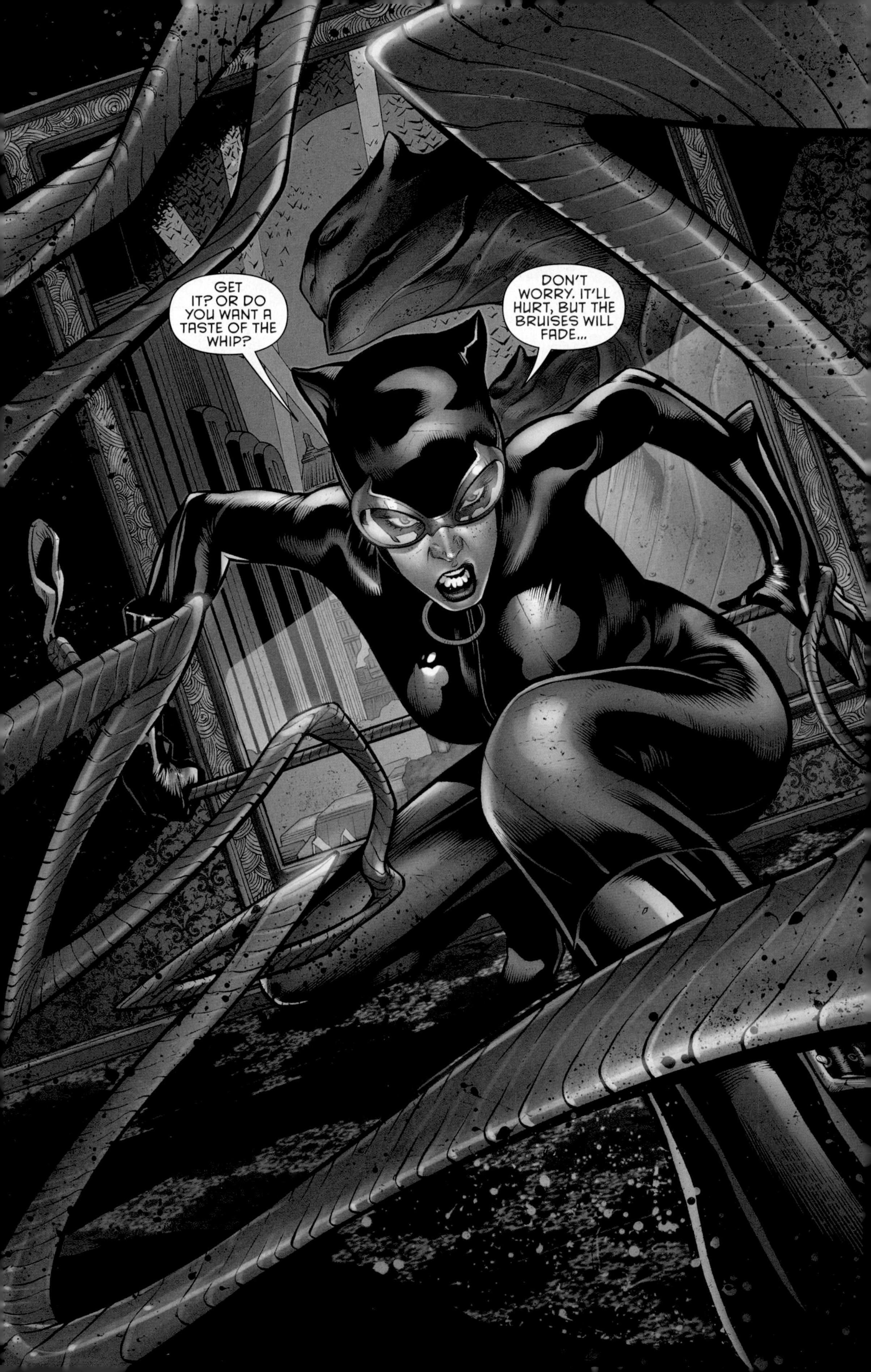
GET IT? OR DO YOU WANT A TASTE OF THE WHIP?
DON'T WORRY. IT'LL HURT, BUT THE BRUISES WILL FADE...

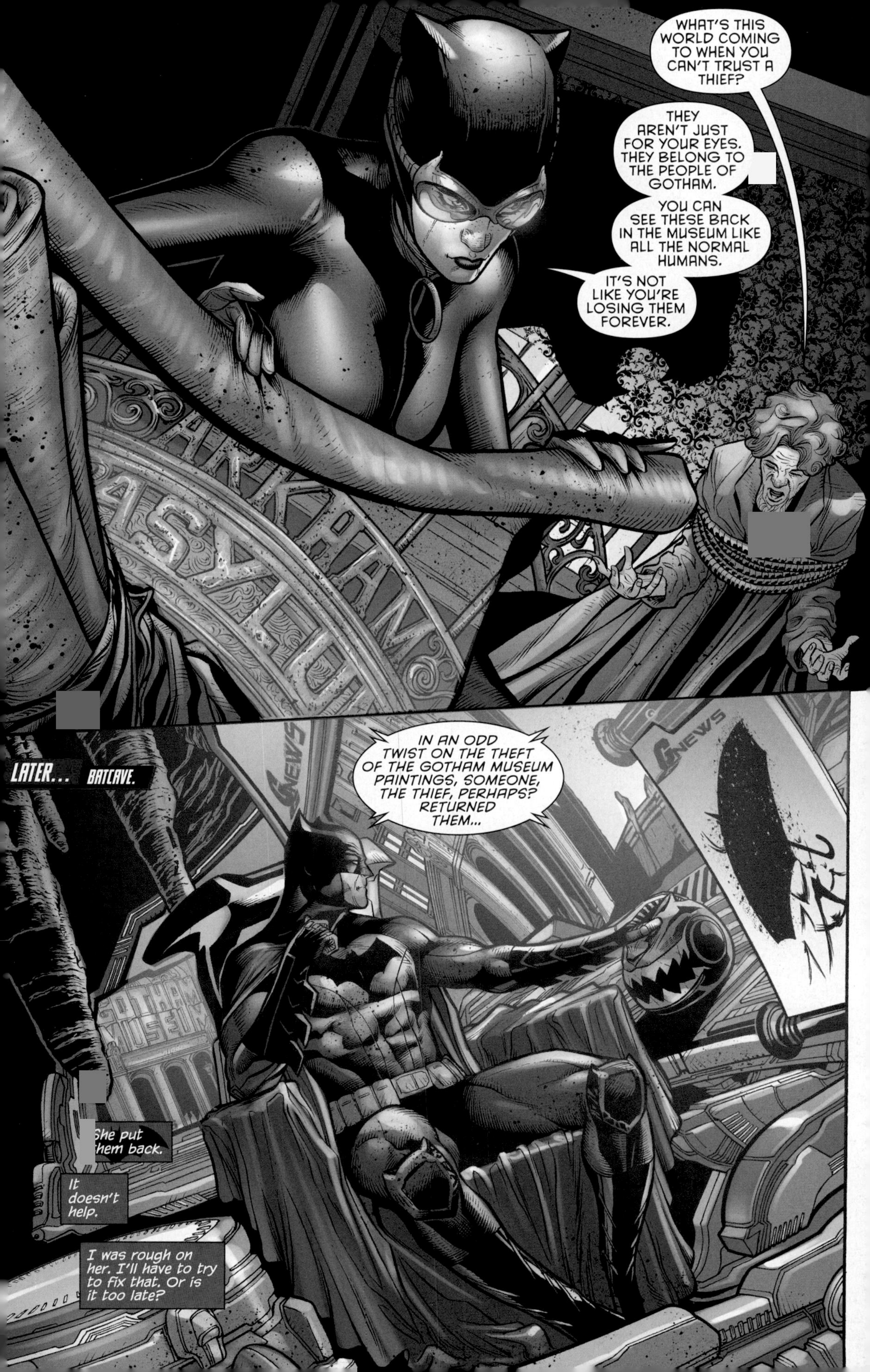
WHAT'S THIS WORLD COMING TO WHEN YOU CAN'T TRUST A THIEF?
THEY AREN'T JUST FOR YOUR EYES. THEY BELONG TO THE PEOPLE OF GOTHAM.
YOU CAN SEE THESE BACK IN THE MUSEUM LIKE ALL THE NORMAL HUMANS.
IT'S NOT LIKE YOU'RE LOSING THEM FOREVER.
ARKHAM ASYLUM
LATER... BATCAVE.
IN AN ODD TWIST ON THE THEFT OF THE GOTHAM MUSEUM PAINTINGS, SOMEONE, THE THIEF, PERHAPS? RETURNED THEM...
GOTHAM MUSEUM
She put them back.
It doesn't help.
I was rough on her. I'll have to try to fix that. Or is it too late?

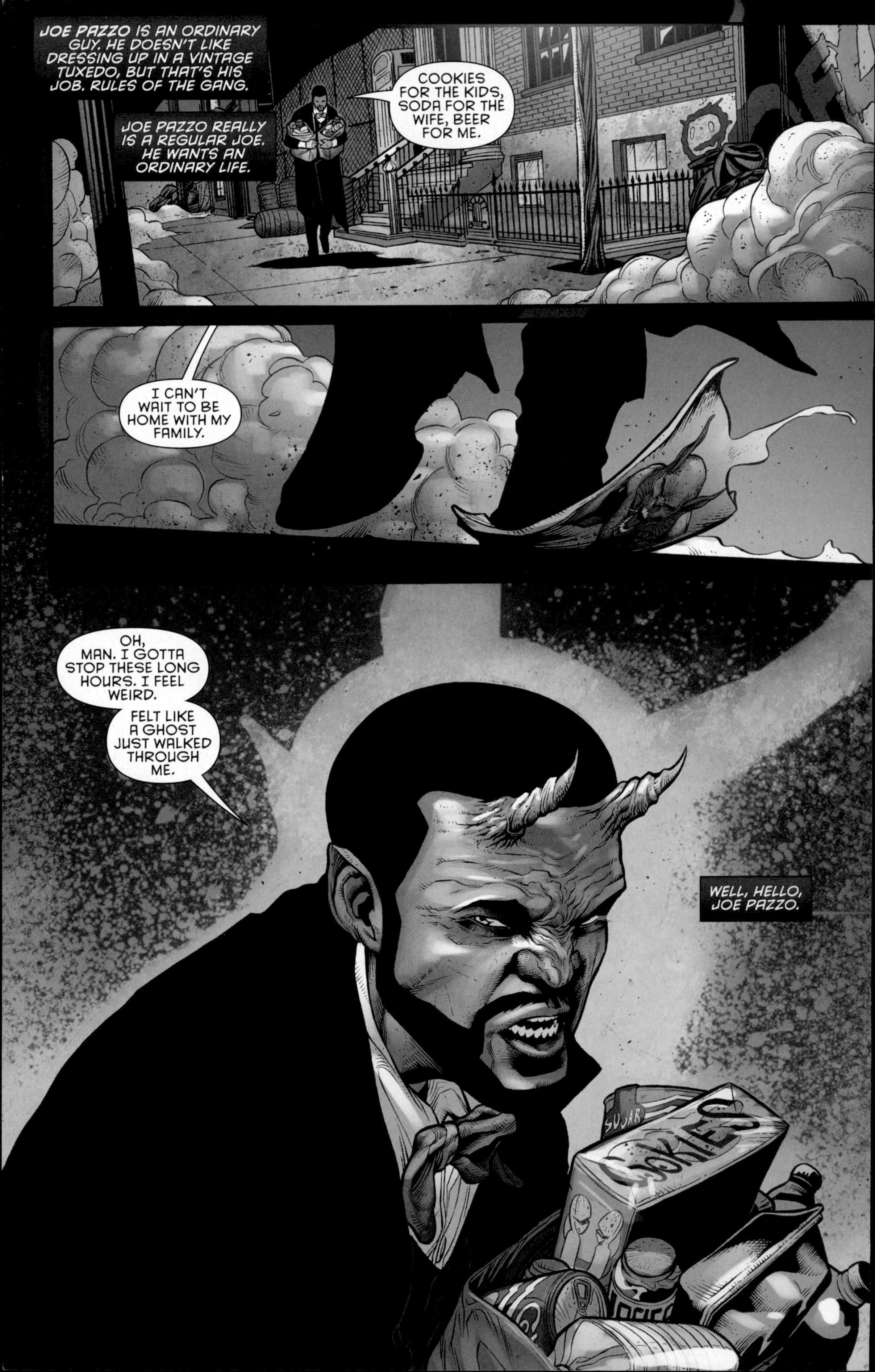

JOE PAZZO IS AN ORDINARY GUY. HE DOESN'T LIKE DRESSING UP IN A VINTAGE TUXEDO, BUT THAT'S HIS JOB. RULES OF THE GANG.
JOE PAZZO REALLY IS A REGULAR JOE. HE WANTS AN ORDINARY LIFE.
COOKIES FOR THE KIDS, SODA FOR THE WIFE, BEER FOR ME.
I CAN'T WAIT TO BE HOME WITH MY FAMILY.
OH, MAN. I GOTTA STOP THESE LONG HOURS. I FEEL WEIRD.
FELT LIKE A GHOST JUST WALKED THROUGH ME.
WELL, HELLO, JOE PAZZO.
SUGAR
COOKIES

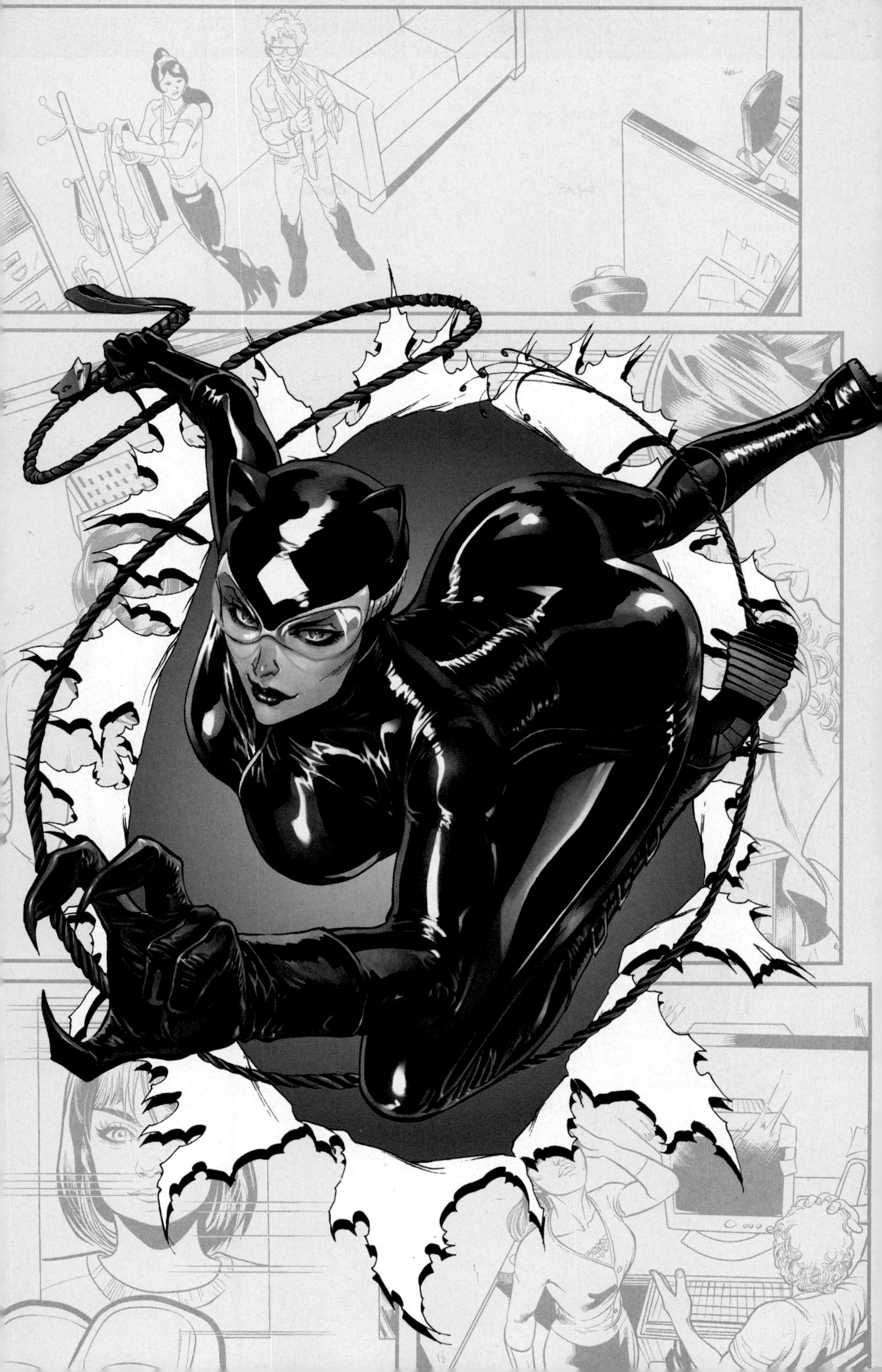

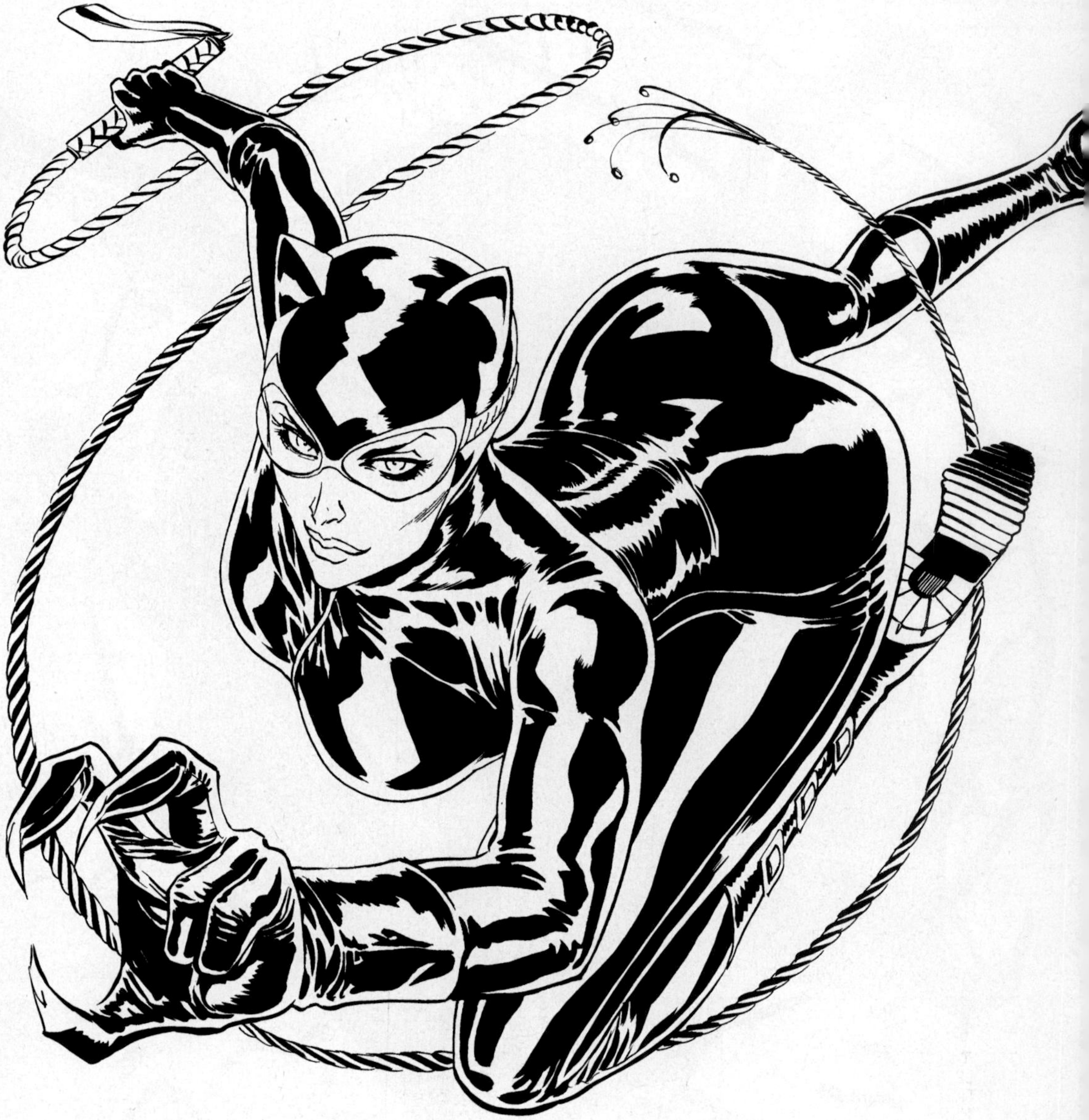

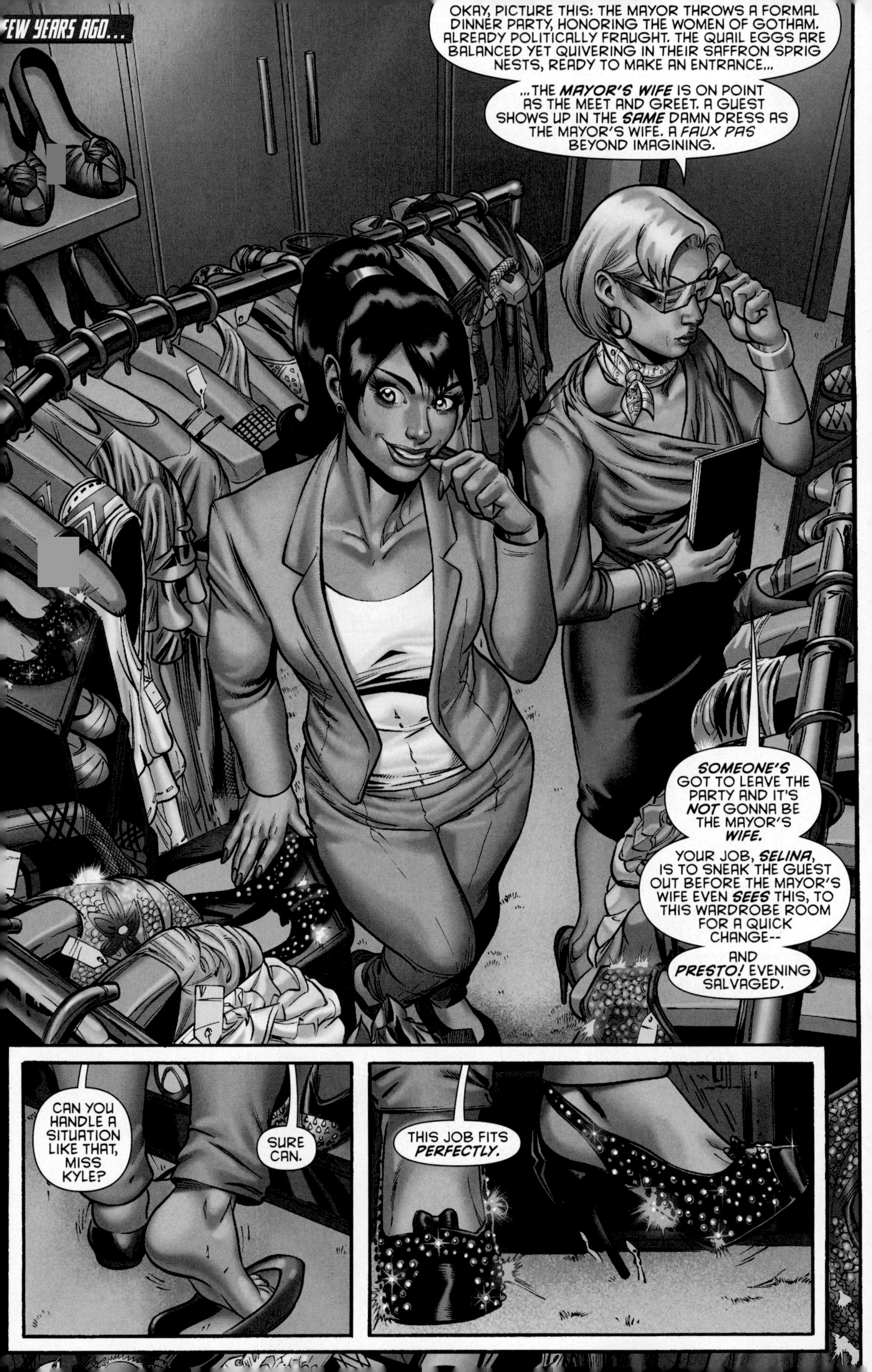
EW YEARS AGO...
OKAY, PICTURE THIS: THE MAYOR THROWS A FORMAL DINNER PARTY, HONORING THE WOMEN OF GOTHAM. ALREADY POLITICALLY FRAUGHT. THE QUAIL EGGS ARE BALANCED YET QUIVERING IN THEIR SAFFRON SPRIG NESTS, READY TO MAKE AN ENTRANCE...
...THE MAYOR'S WIFE IS ON POINT AS THE MEET AND GREET. A GUEST SHOWS UP IN THE SAME DAMN DRESS AS THE MAYOR'S WIFE. A FAUX PAS BEYOND IMAGINING.
SOMEONE'S GOT TO LEAVE THE PARTY AND IT'S NOT GONNA BE THE MAYOR'S WIFE.
YOUR JOB, SELINA, IS TO SNEAK THE GUEST OUT BEFORE THE MAYOR'S WIFE EVEN SEES THIS, TO THIS WARDROBE ROOM FOR A QUICK CHANGE--
AND PRESTO! EVENING SALVAGED.
CAN YOU HANDLE A SITUATION LIKE THAT, MISS KYLE?
SURE CAN.
THIS JOB FITS PERFECTLY.

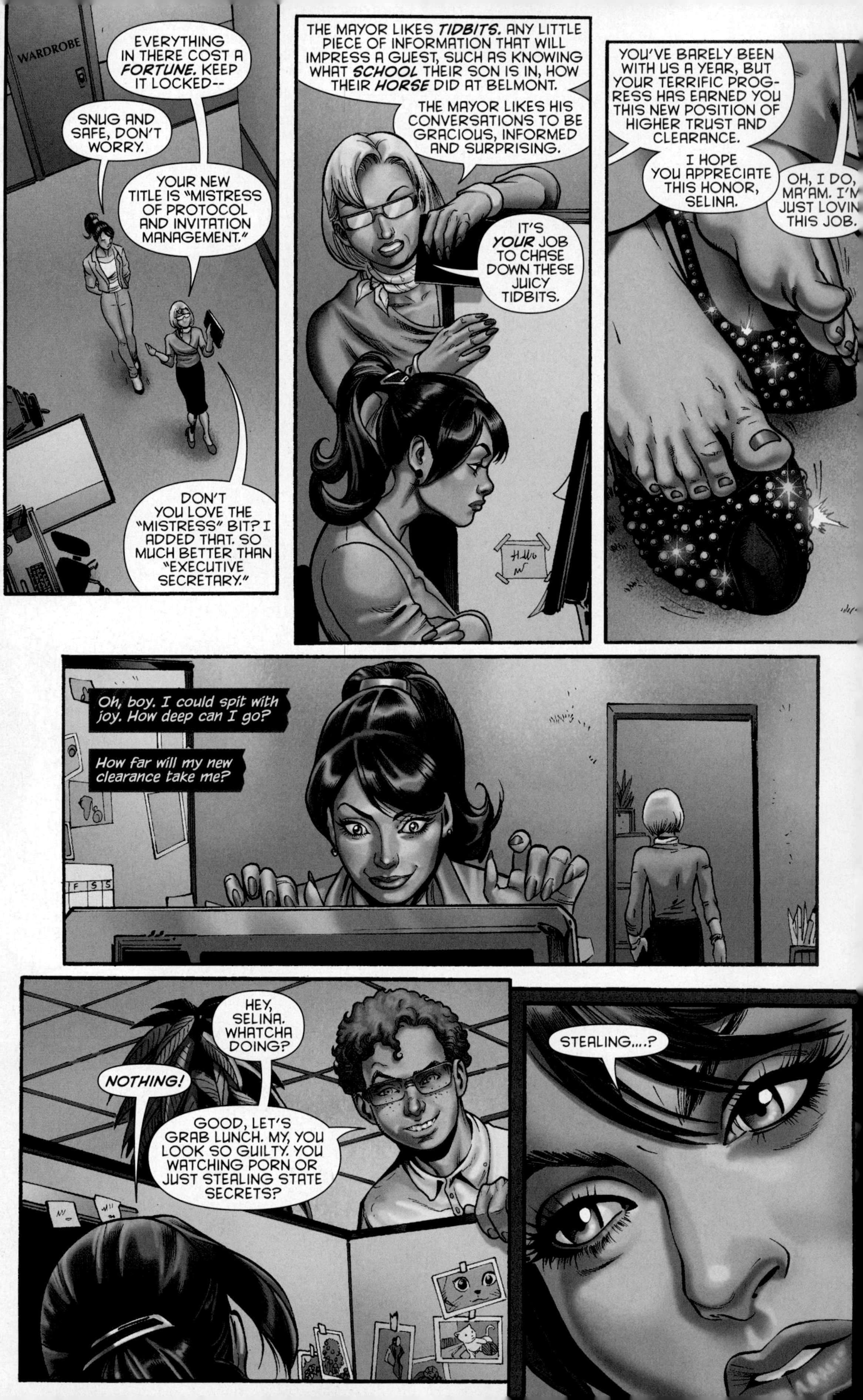
WARDROBE
EVERYTHING IN THERE COST A FORTUNE. KEEP IT LOCKED--
SNUG AND SAFE, DON'T WORRY.
YOUR NEW TITLE IS "MISTRESS OF PROTOCOL AND INVITATION MANAGEMENT."
DON'T YOU LOVE THE "MISTRESS" BIT? I ADDED THAT. SO MUCH BETTER THAN "EXECUTIVE SECRETARY."
THE MAYOR LIKES TIDBITS. ANY LITTLE PIECE OF INFORMATION THAT WILL IMPRESS A GUEST, SUCH AS KNOWING WHAT SCHOOL THEIR SON IS IN, HOW THEIR HORSE DID AT BELMONT.
THE MAYOR LIKES HIS CONVERSATIONS TO BE GRACIOUS, INFORMED AND SURPRISING.
IT'S YOUR JOB TO CHASE DOWN THESE JUICY TIDBITS.
YOU'VE BARELY BEEN WITH US A YEAR, BUT YOUR TERRIFIC PROGRESS HAS EARNED YOU THIS NEW POSITION OF HIGHER TRUST AND CLEARANCE.
I HOPE YOU APPRECIATE THIS HONOR, SELINA.
OH, I DO, MA'AM. I'M JUST LOVIN THIS JOB.
Oh, boy. I could spit with joy. How deep can I go?
How far will my new clearance take me?
HEY, SELINA. WHATCHA DOING?
NOTHING!
GOOD, LET'S GRAB LUNCH. MY, YOU LOOK SO GUILTY. YOU WATCHING PORN OR JUST STEALING STATE SECRETS?
STEALING....?

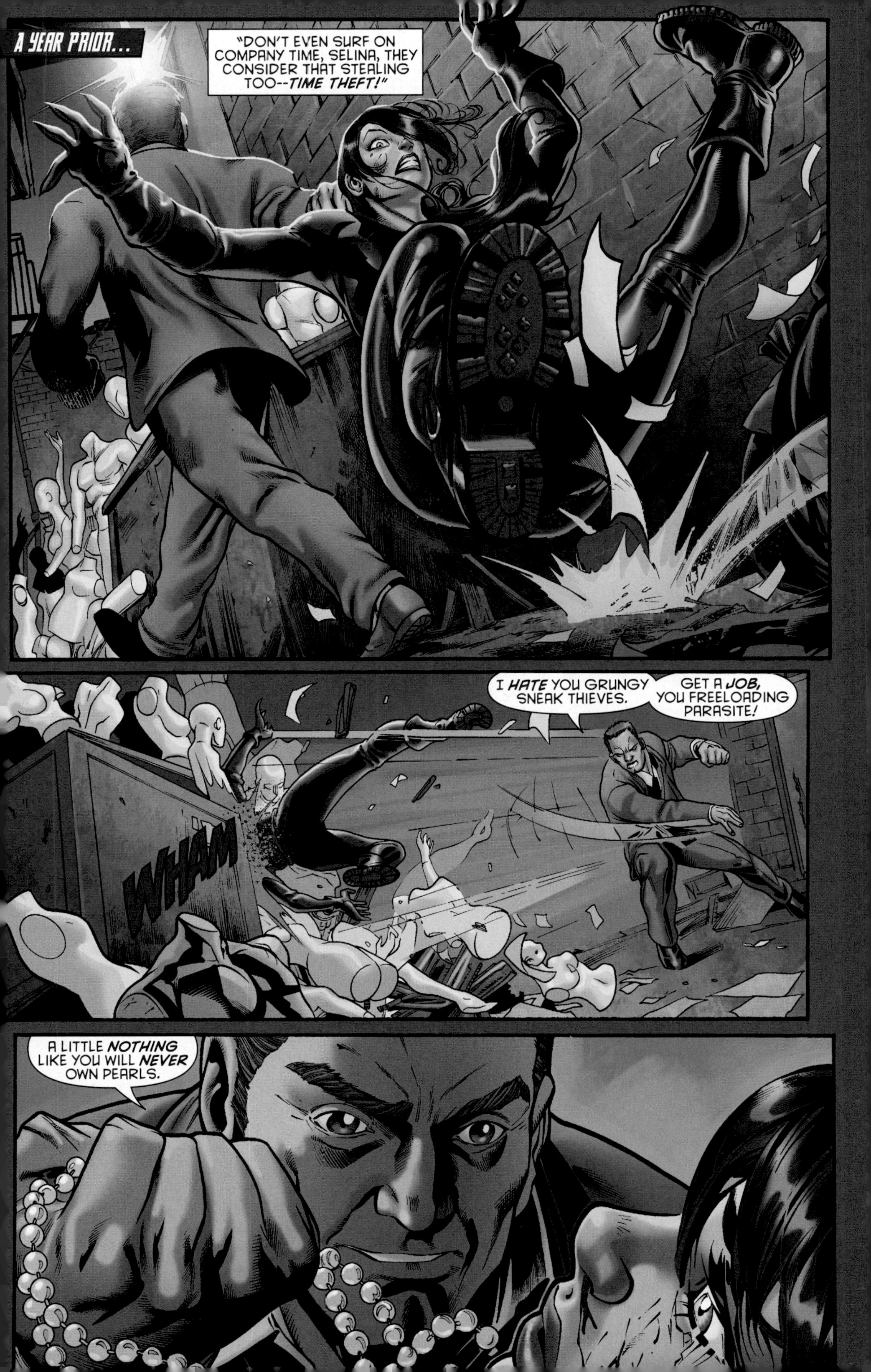
A YEAR PRIOR...
"DON'T EVEN SURF ON COMPANY TIME, SELINA, THEY CONSIDER THAT STEALING TOO--TIME THEFT!"
I HATE YOU GRUNGY SNEAK THIEVES.
GET A JOB, YOU FREELOADING PARASITE!
WHAM
A LITTLE NOTHING LIKE YOU WILL NEVER OWN PEARLS.

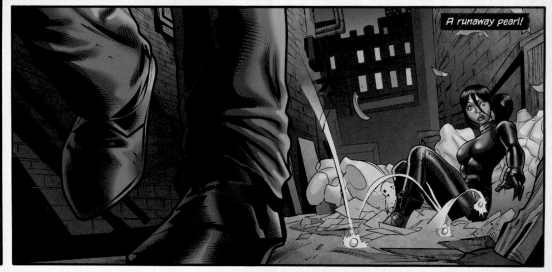

A runaway pearl!

Mine!

YOUNG LADY! ARE YOU OKAY?

DON'T BE AFRAID, I WANT TO *HELP* YOU. I RUN A PROGRAM CALLED "SECOND CHANCE" WITH THE CITY OF GOTHAM, THE MAYOR'S OFFICE...

WE WANT TO HELP ALL THE *STREET KIDS* WHO HAVE FALLEN THROUGH THE CRACKS AND BECOME *INVISIBLE* TO SOCIETY. WHERE ARE YOUR PARENTS?

NO PARENTS. I'M A BASTARD CHILD! CAN'T YOU TELL?

AND I *LIKE* BEING INVISIBLE.

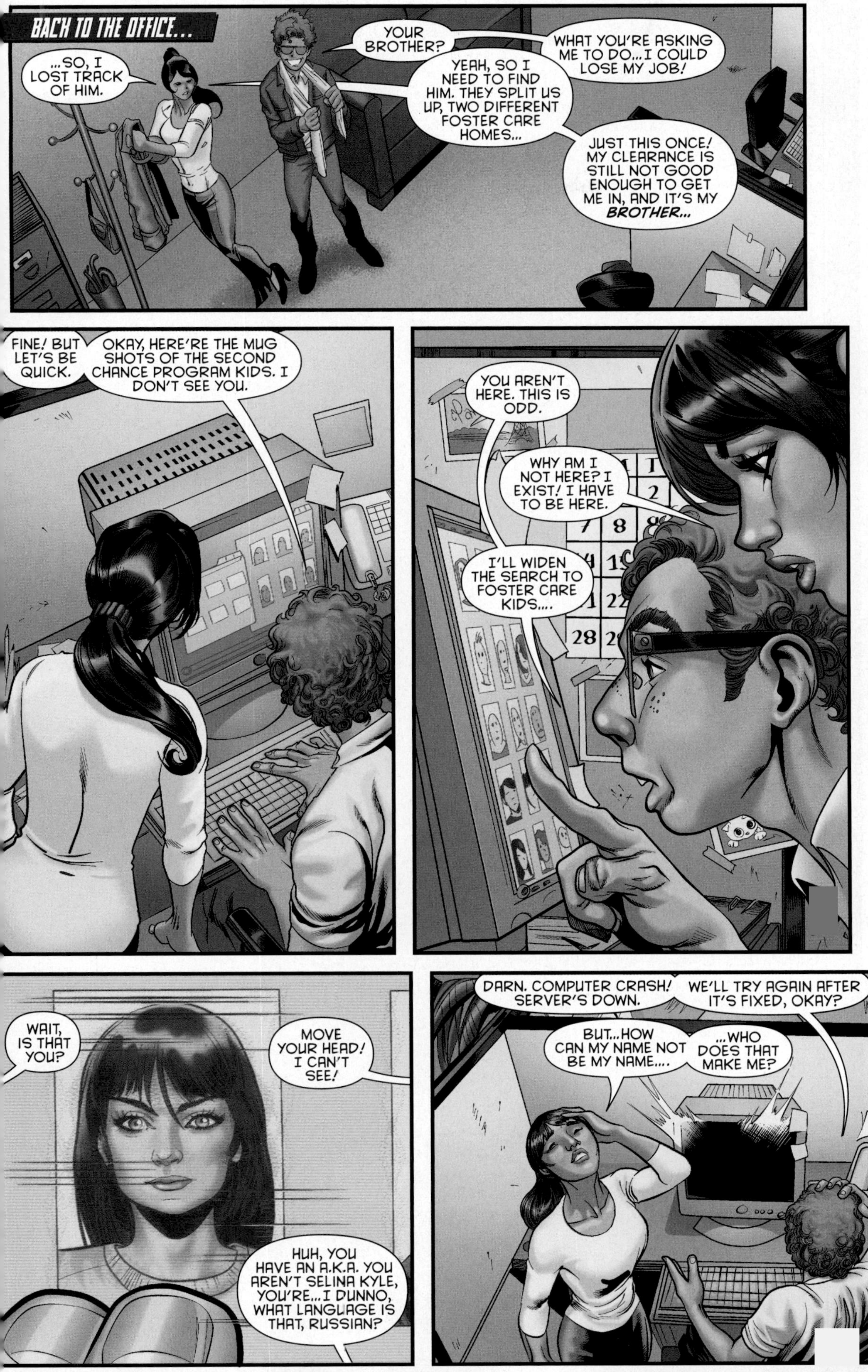
BACK TO THE OFFICE...
...SO, I LOST TRACK OF HIM.
YOUR BROTHER?
YEAH, SO I NEED TO FIND HIM. THEY SPLIT US UP, TWO DIFFERENT FOSTER CARE HOMES...
WHAT YOU'RE ASKING ME TO DO...I COULD LOSE MY JOB!
JUST THIS ONCE! MY CLEARANCE IS STILL NOT GOOD ENOUGH TO GET ME IN, AND IT'S MY BROTHER...
FINE! BUT LET'S BE QUICK.
OKAY, HERE'RE THE MUG SHOTS OF THE SECOND CHANCE PROGRAM KIDS. I DON'T SEE YOU.
YOU AREN'T HERE. THIS IS ODD.
WHY AM I NOT HERE? I EXIST! I HAVE TO BE HERE.
I'LL WIDEN THE SEARCH TO FOSTER CARE KIDS....
WAIT, IS THAT YOU?
MOVE YOUR HEAD! I CAN'T SEE!
HUH, YOU HAVE AN A.K.A. YOU AREN'T SELINA KYLE, YOU'RE...I DUNNO, WHAT LANGUAGE IS THAT, RUSSIAN?
DARN. COMPUTER CRASH! SERVER'S DOWN.
WE'LL TRY AGAIN AFTER IT'S FIXED, OKAY?
BUT...HOW CAN MY NAME NOT BE MY NAME....
...WHO DOES THAT MAKE ME?

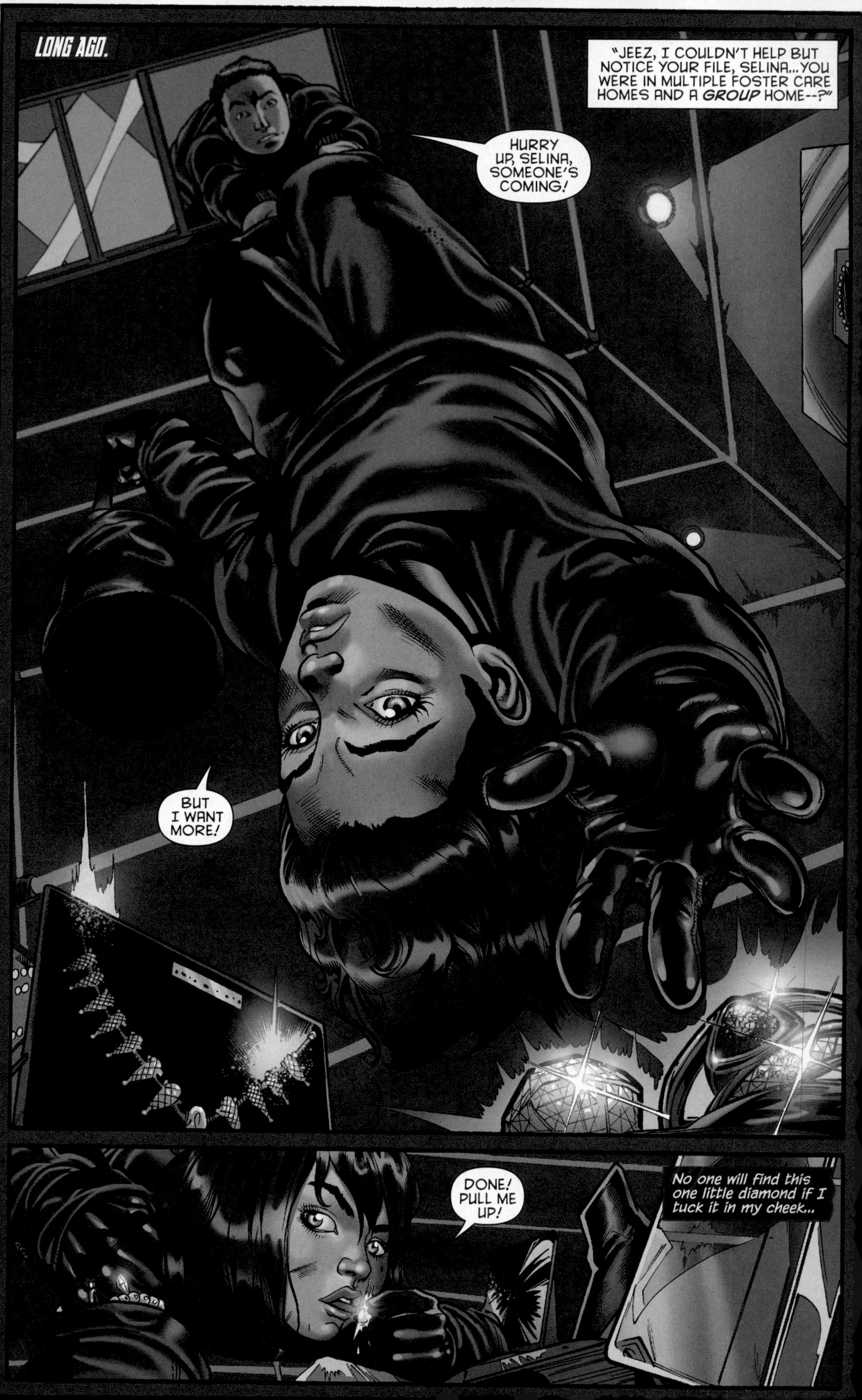
LONG AGO.
"JEEZ, I COULDN'T HELP BUT NOTICE YOUR FILE, SELINA... YOU WERE IN MULTIPLE FOSTER CARE HOMES AND A GROUP HOME--?"
HURRY UP, SELINA, SOMEONE'S COMING!
BUT I WANT MORE!
DONE! PULL ME UP!
No one will find this one little diamond if I tuck it in my cheek...

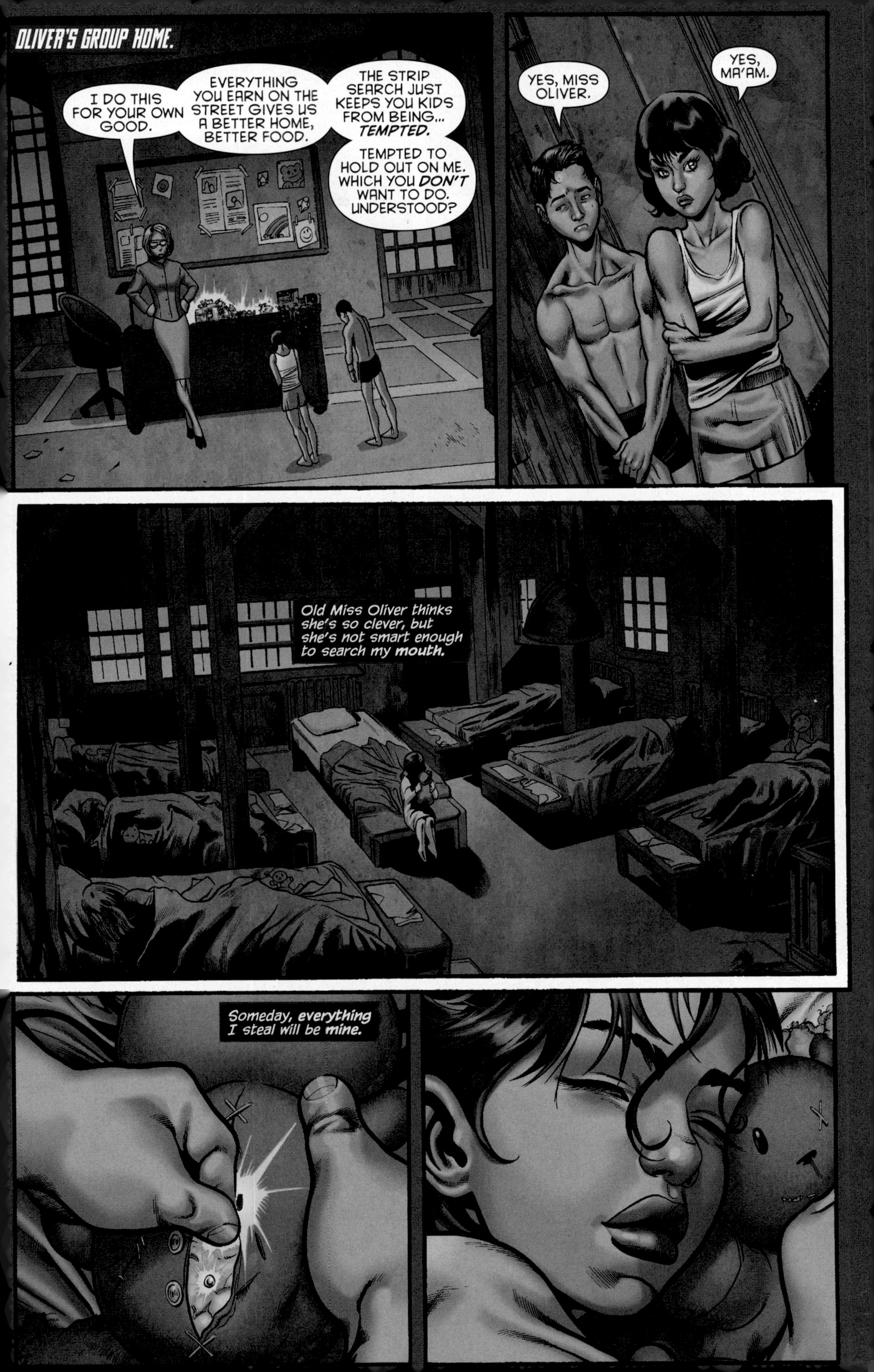
OLIVER'S GROUP HOME.
I DO THIS FOR YOUR OWN GOOD.
EVERYTHING YOU EARN ON THE STREET GIVES US A BETTER HOME, BETTER FOOD.
THE STRIP SEARCH JUST KEEPS YOU KIDS FROM BEING... *TEMPTED.*
TEMPTED TO HOLD OUT ON ME. WHICH YOU *DON'T* WANT TO DO. UNDERSTOOD?
YES, MISS OLIVER.
YES, MA'AM.
Old Miss Oliver thinks she's so clever, but she's not smart enough to search my **mouth.**
Someday, **everything** I steal will be **mine.**

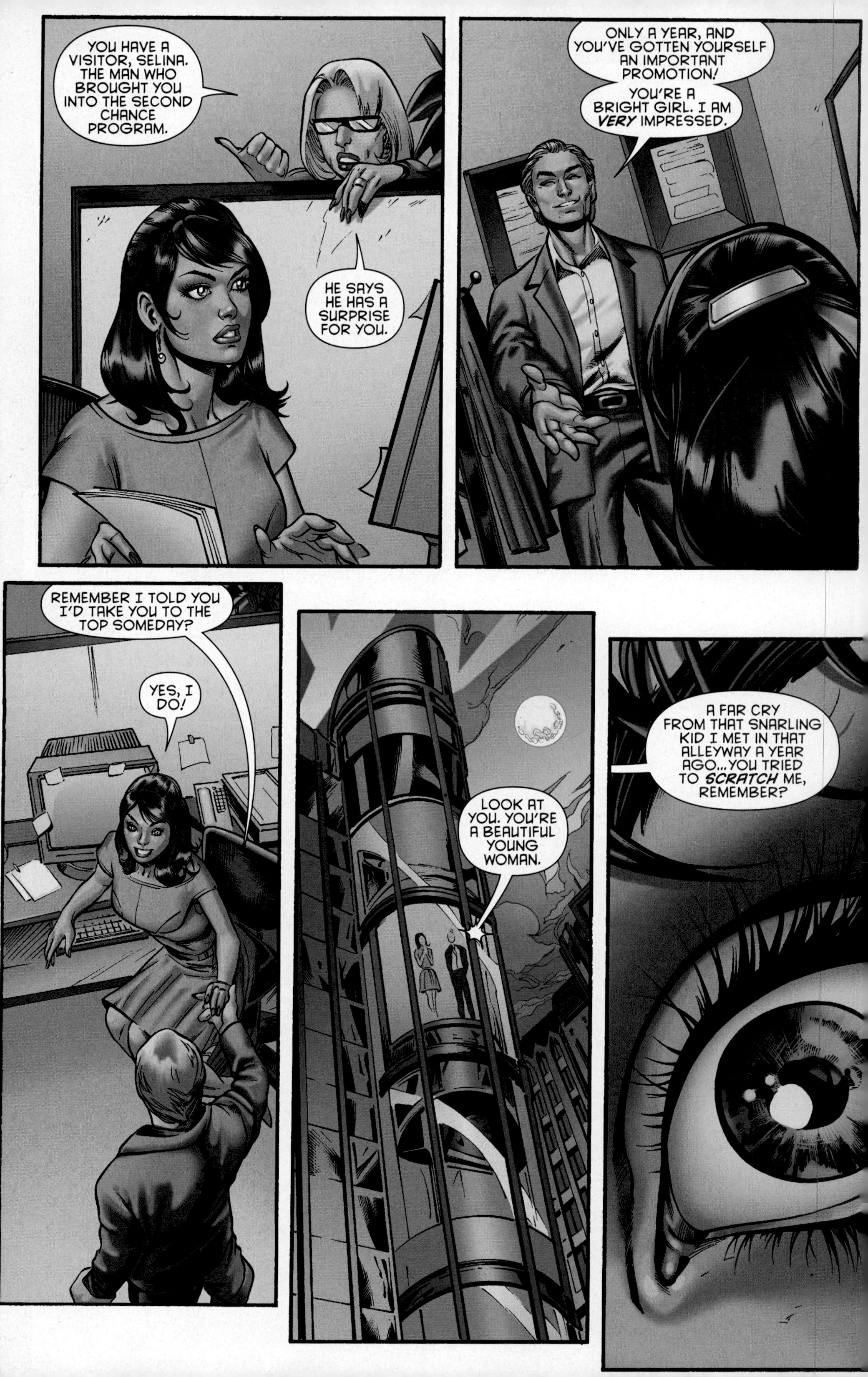
YOU HAVE A VISITOR, SELINA. THE MAN WHO BROUGHT YOU INTO THE SECOND CHANCE PROGRAM.
HE SAYS HE HAS A SURPRISE FOR YOU.
ONLY A YEAR, AND YOU'VE GOTTEN YOURSELF AN IMPORTANT PROMOTION!
YOU'RE A BRIGHT GIRL. I AM *VERY* IMPRESSED.
REMEMBER I TOLD YOU I'D TAKE YOU TO THE TOP SOMEDAY?
YES, I DO!
LOOK AT YOU. YOU'RE A BEAUTIFUL YOUNG WOMAN.
A FAR CRY FROM THAT SNARLING KID I MET IN THAT ALLEYWAY A YEAR AGO...YOU TRIED TO *SCRATCH* ME, REMEMBER?

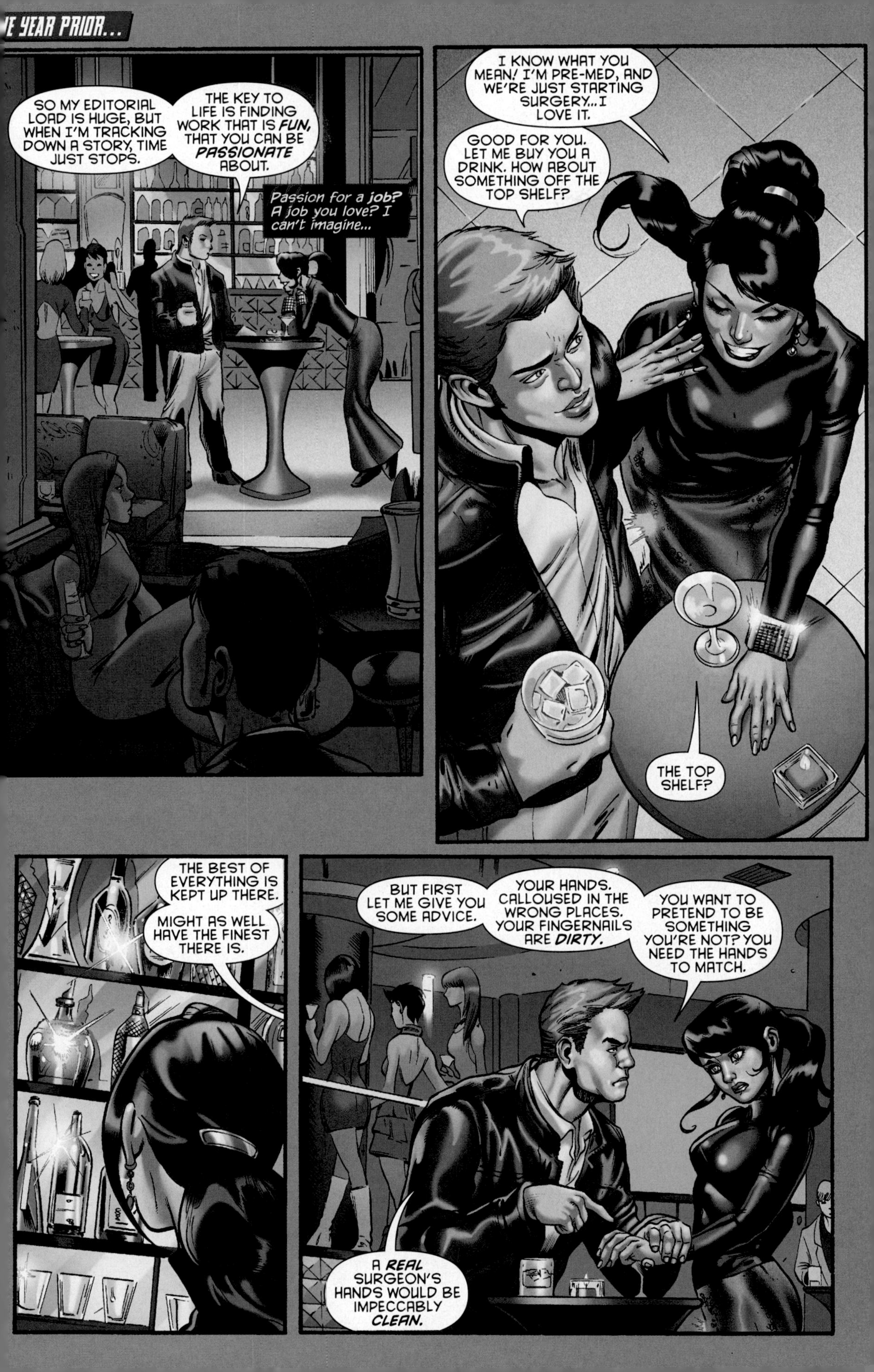
...E YEAR PRIOR...
SO MY EDITORIAL LOAD IS HUGE, BUT WHEN I'M TRACKING DOWN A STORY, TIME JUST STOPS.
THE KEY TO LIFE IS FINDING WORK THAT IS FUN, THAT YOU CAN BE PASSIONATE ABOUT.
Passion for a job? A job you love? I can't imagine...
I KNOW WHAT YOU MEAN! I'M PRE-MED, AND WE'RE JUST STARTING SURGERY...I LOVE IT.
GOOD FOR YOU. LET ME BUY YOU A DRINK. HOW ABOUT SOMETHING OFF THE TOP SHELF?
THE TOP SHELF?
THE BEST OF EVERYTHING IS KEPT UP THERE.
MIGHT AS WELL HAVE THE FINEST THERE IS.
BUT FIRST LET ME GIVE YOU SOME ADVICE.
YOUR HANDS. CALLOUSED IN THE WRONG PLACES. YOUR FINGERNAILS ARE DIRTY.
YOU WANT TO PRETEND TO BE SOMETHING YOU'RE NOT? YOU NEED THE HANDS TO MATCH.
A REAL SURGEON'S HANDS WOULD BE IMPECCABLY CLEAN.

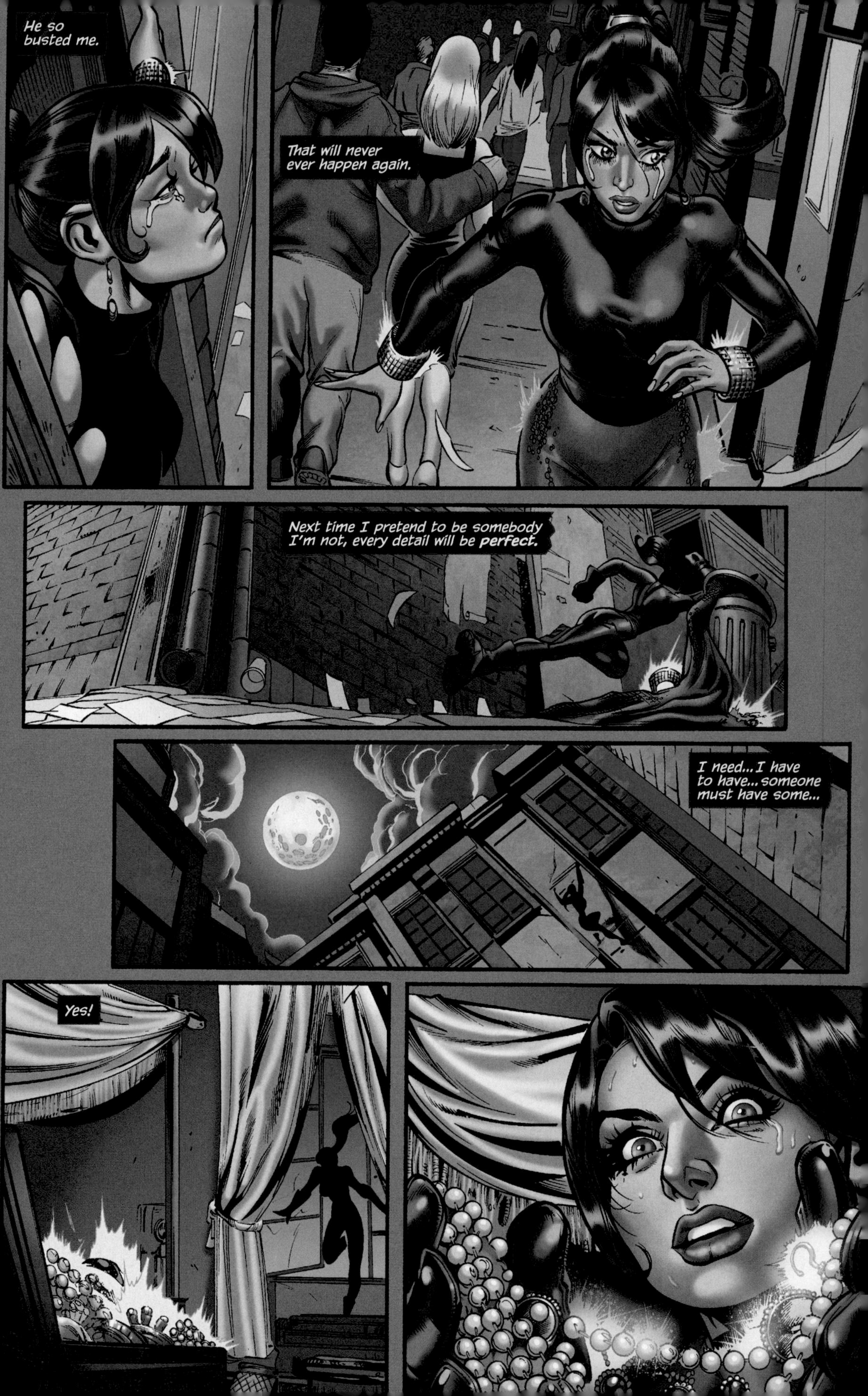
He so busted me.
That will never ever happen again.
Next time I pretend to be somebody I'm not, every detail will be **perfect.**
I need... I have to have... someone must have some...
Yes!

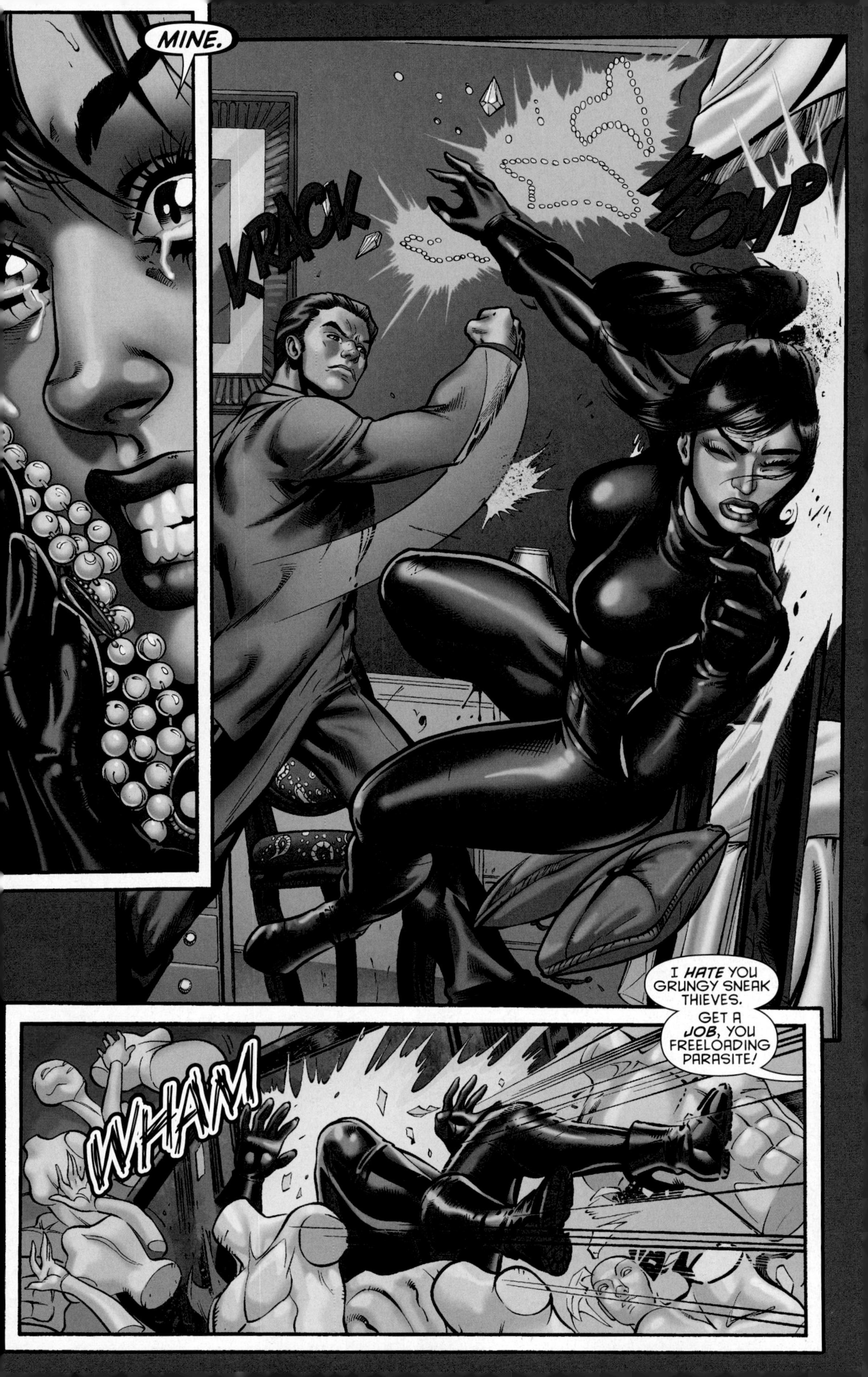
MINE.
KRACK
WHOMP
I HATE YOU GRUNGY SNEAK THIEVES.
GET A JOB, YOU FREELOADING PARASITE!
WHAM

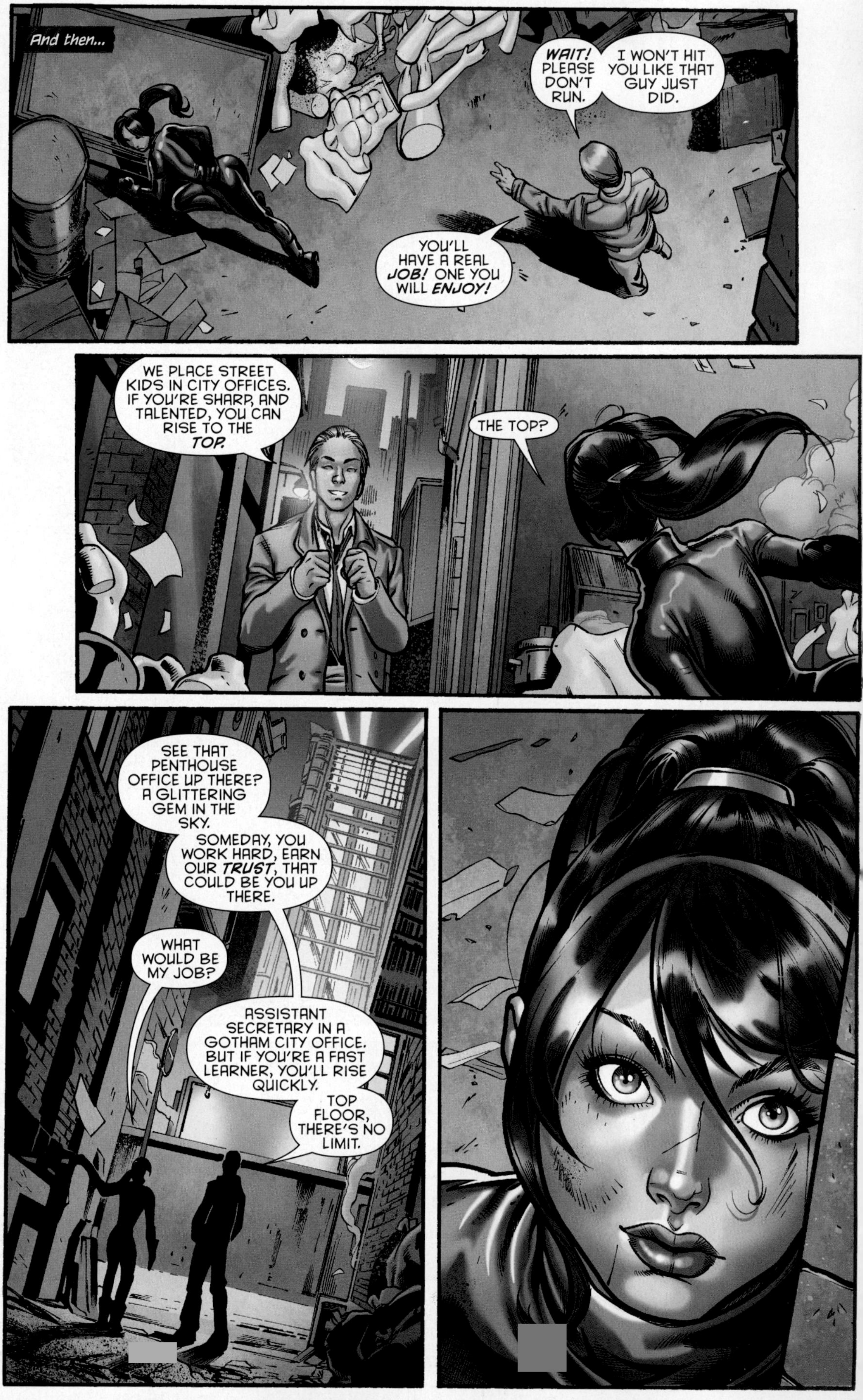
And then...
WAIT! PLEASE DON'T RUN.
I WON'T HIT YOU LIKE THAT GUY JUST DID.
YOU'LL HAVE A REAL JOB! ONE YOU WILL ENJOY!
WE PLACE STREET KIDS IN CITY OFFICES. IF YOU'RE SHARP, AND TALENTED, YOU CAN RISE TO THE TOP.
THE TOP?
SEE THAT PENTHOUSE OFFICE UP THERE? A GLITTERING GEM IN THE SKY.
SOMEDAY, YOU WORK HARD, EARN OUR TRUST, THAT COULD BE YOU UP THERE.
WHAT WOULD BE MY JOB?
ASSISTANT SECRETARY IN A GOTHAM CITY OFFICE. BUT IF YOU'RE A FAST LEARNER, YOU'LL RISE QUICKLY.
TOP FLOOR, THERE'S NO LIMIT.

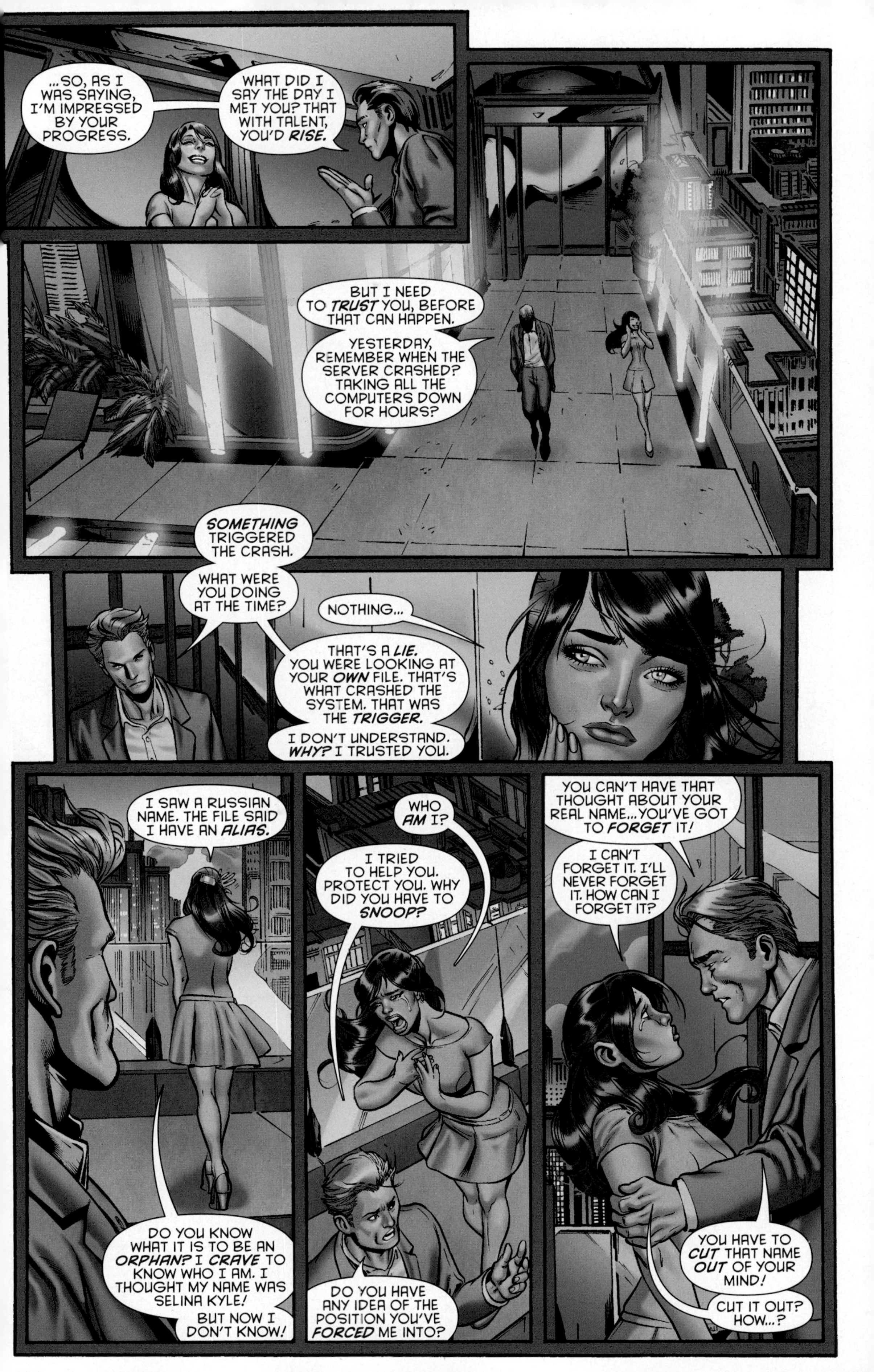
...SO, AS I WAS SAYING, I'M IMPRESSED BY YOUR PROGRESS.
WHAT DID I SAY THE DAY I MET YOU? THAT WITH TALENT, YOU'D *RISE.*
BUT I NEED TO *TRUST* YOU, BEFORE THAT CAN HAPPEN.
YESTERDAY, REMEMBER WHEN THE SERVER CRASHED? TAKING ALL THE COMPUTERS DOWN FOR HOURS?
SOMETHING TRIGGERED THE CRASH.
WHAT WERE YOU DOING AT THE TIME?
NOTHING...
THAT'S A *LIE.* YOU WERE LOOKING AT YOUR *OWN* FILE. THAT'S WHAT CRASHED THE SYSTEM. THAT WAS THE *TRIGGER.*
I DON'T UNDERSTAND. *WHY?* I TRUSTED YOU.
I SAW A RUSSIAN NAME. THE FILE SAID I HAVE AN *ALIAS.*
DO YOU KNOW WHAT IT IS TO BE AN *ORPHAN?* I *CRAVE* TO KNOW WHO I AM. I THOUGHT MY NAME WAS SELINA KYLE!
BUT NOW I DON'T KNOW!
WHO *AM* I?
I TRIED TO HELP YOU. PROTECT YOU. WHY DID YOU HAVE TO *SNOOP?*
DO YOU HAVE ANY IDEA OF THE POSITION YOU'VE *FORCED* ME INTO?
YOU CAN'T HAVE THAT THOUGHT ABOUT YOUR REAL NAME...YOU'VE GOT TO *FORGET* IT!
I CAN'T FORGET IT. I'LL NEVER FORGET IT. HOW CAN I FORGET IT?
YOU HAVE TO *CUT* THAT NAME *OUT* OF YOUR MIND!
CUT IT OUT? HOW...?

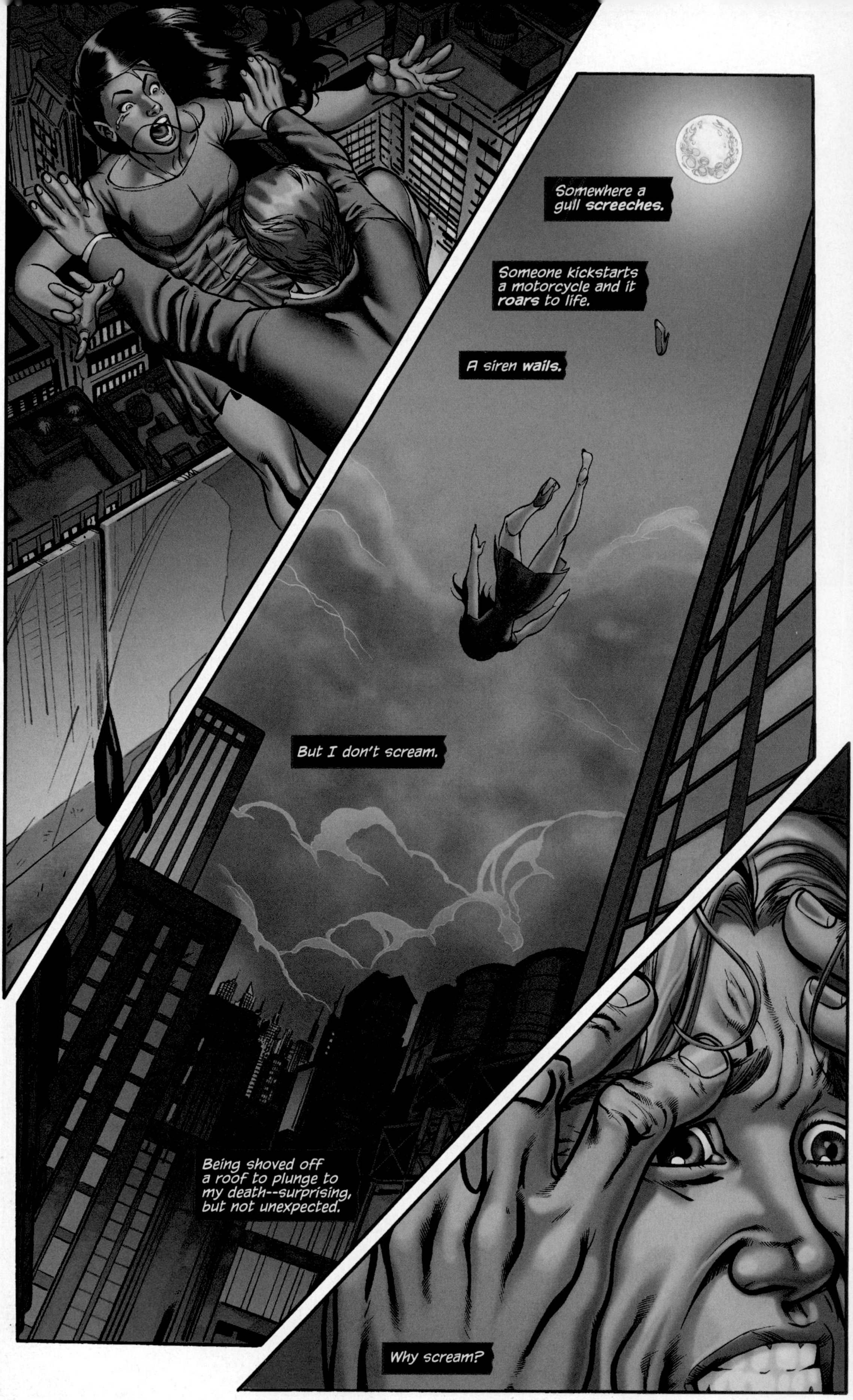
Somewhere a gull screeches.
Someone kickstarts a motorcycle and it roars to life.
A siren wails.
But I don't scream.
Being shoved off a roof to plunge to my death--surprising, but not unexpected.
Why scream?

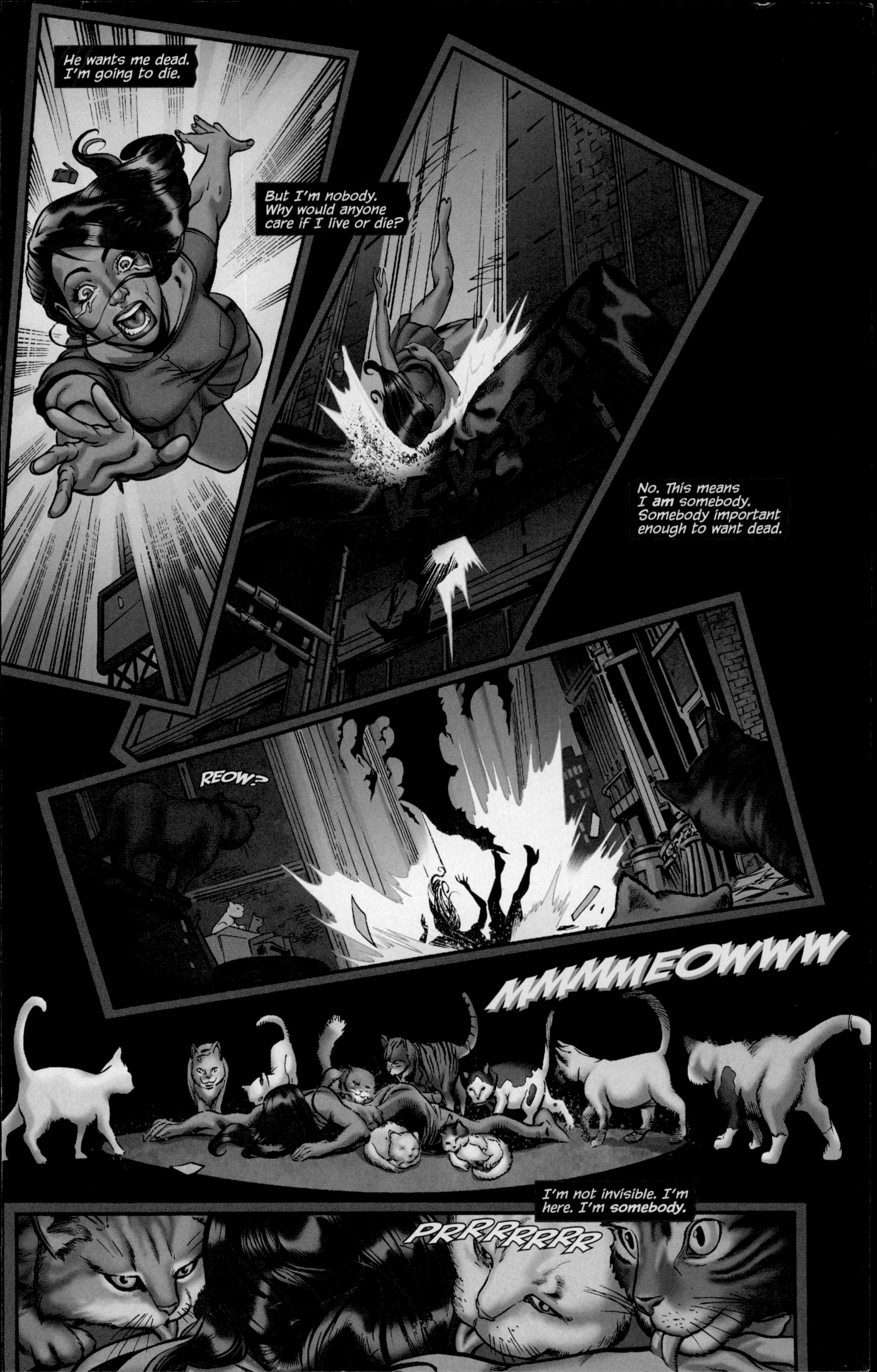
He wants me dead. I'm going to die.
But I'm nobody. Why would anyone care if I live or die?
No. This means I **am** somebody. Somebody important enough to want dead.
REOW?
MMMMEOWWW
I'm not invisible. I'm here. I'm **somebody.**
PRRRRRRR

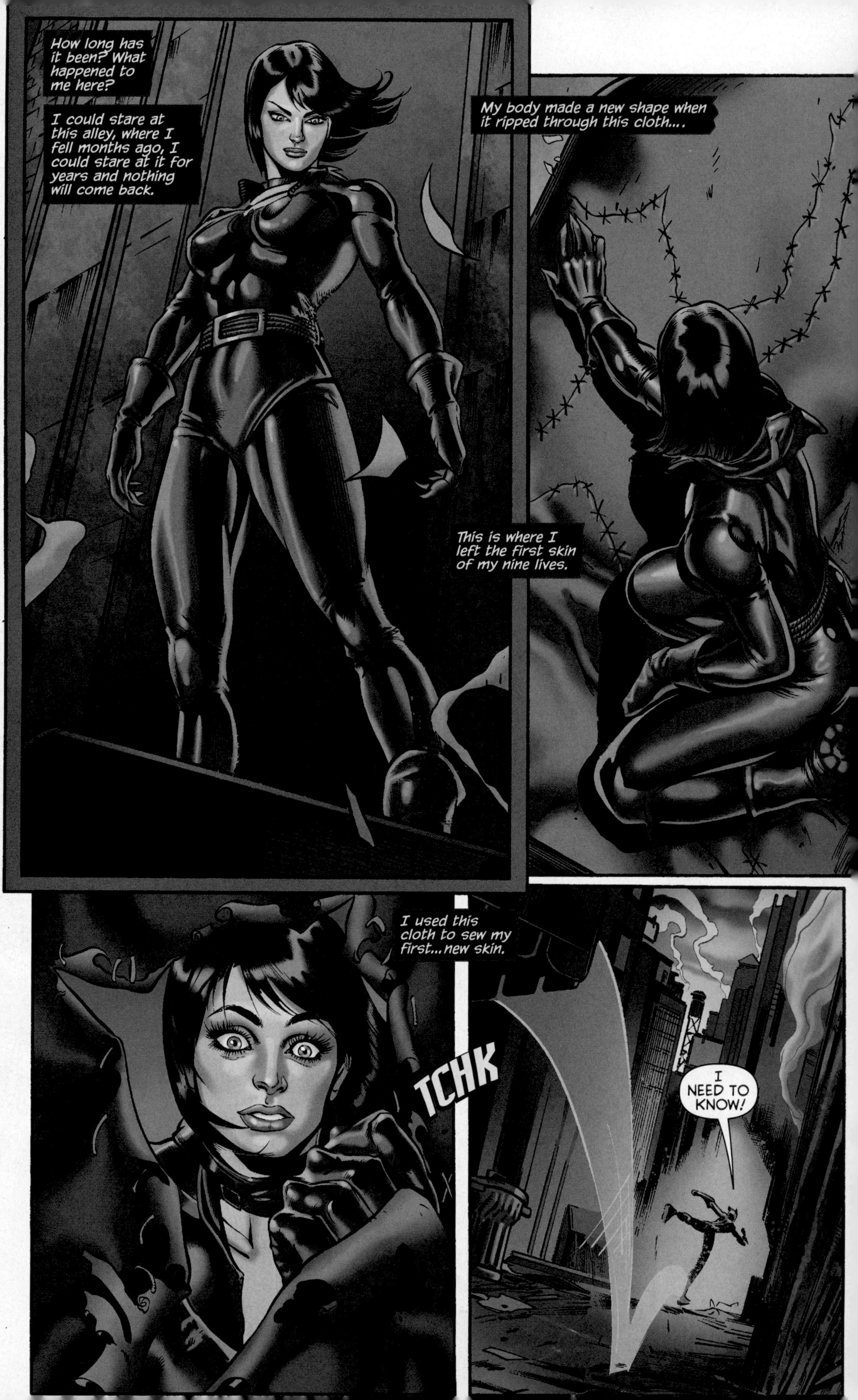
How long has it been? What happened to me here?
I could stare at this alley, where I fell months ago, I could stare at it for years and nothing will come back.
My body made a new shape when it ripped through this cloth....
This is where I left the first skin of my nine lives.
I used this cloth to sew my first...new skin.
TCHK
I NEED TO KNOW!

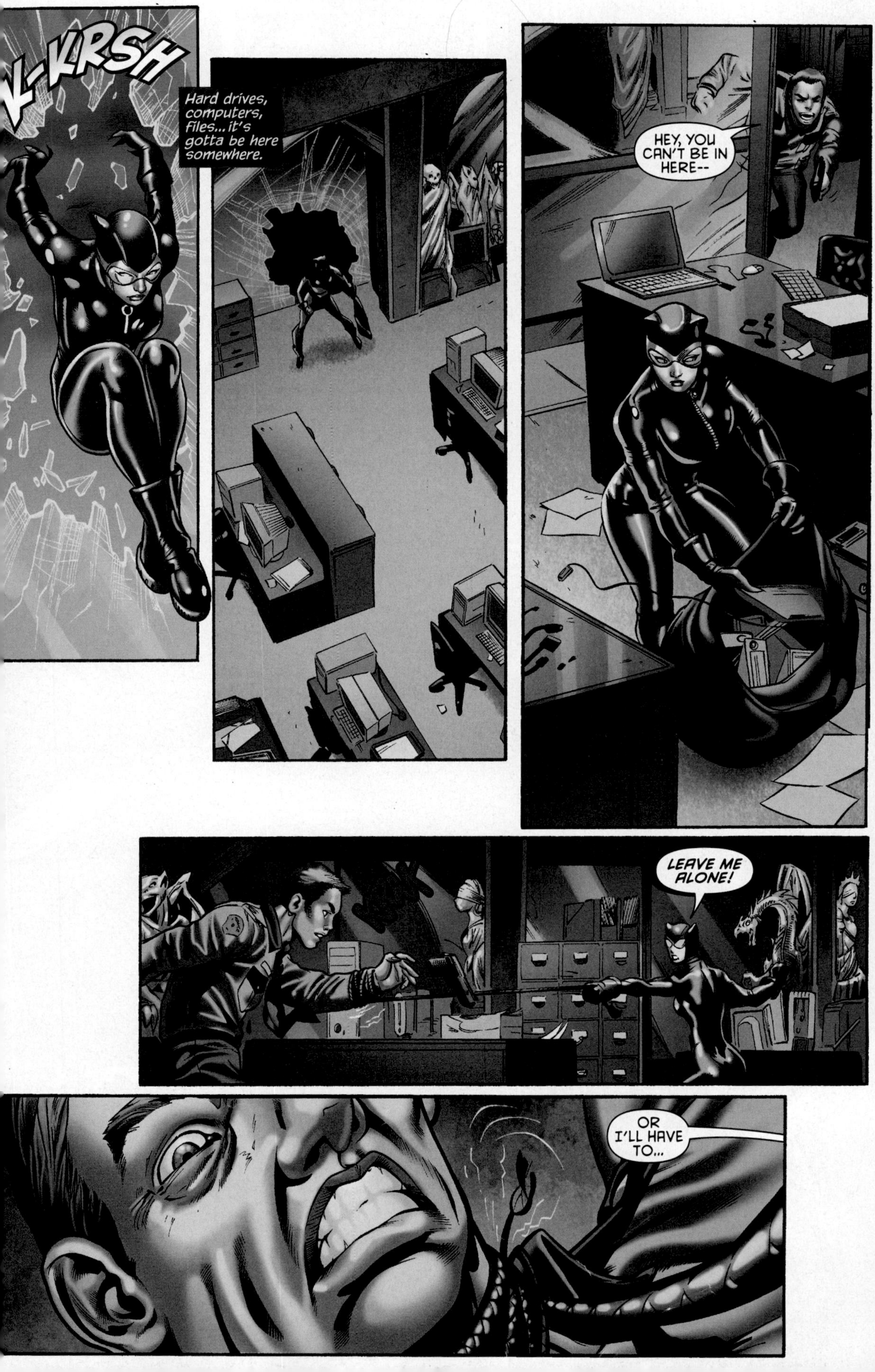
K-KRSH
Hard drives, computers, files...it's gotta be here somewhere.
HEY, YOU CAN'T BE IN HERE--
LEAVE ME ALONE!
OR I'LL HAVE TO...

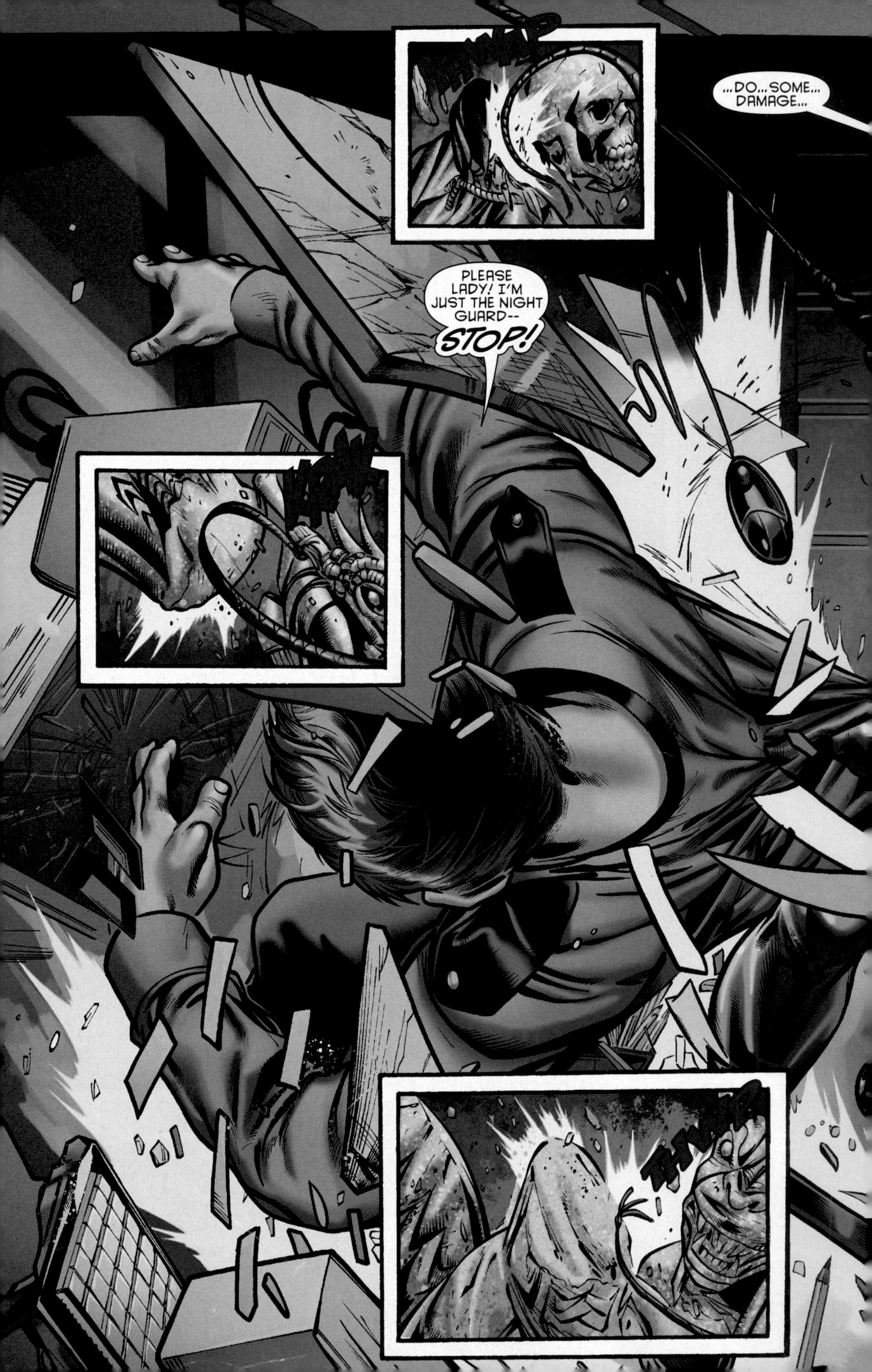
...DO... SOME... DAMAGE...
PLEASE LADY! I'M JUST THE NIGHT GUARD-- STOP!

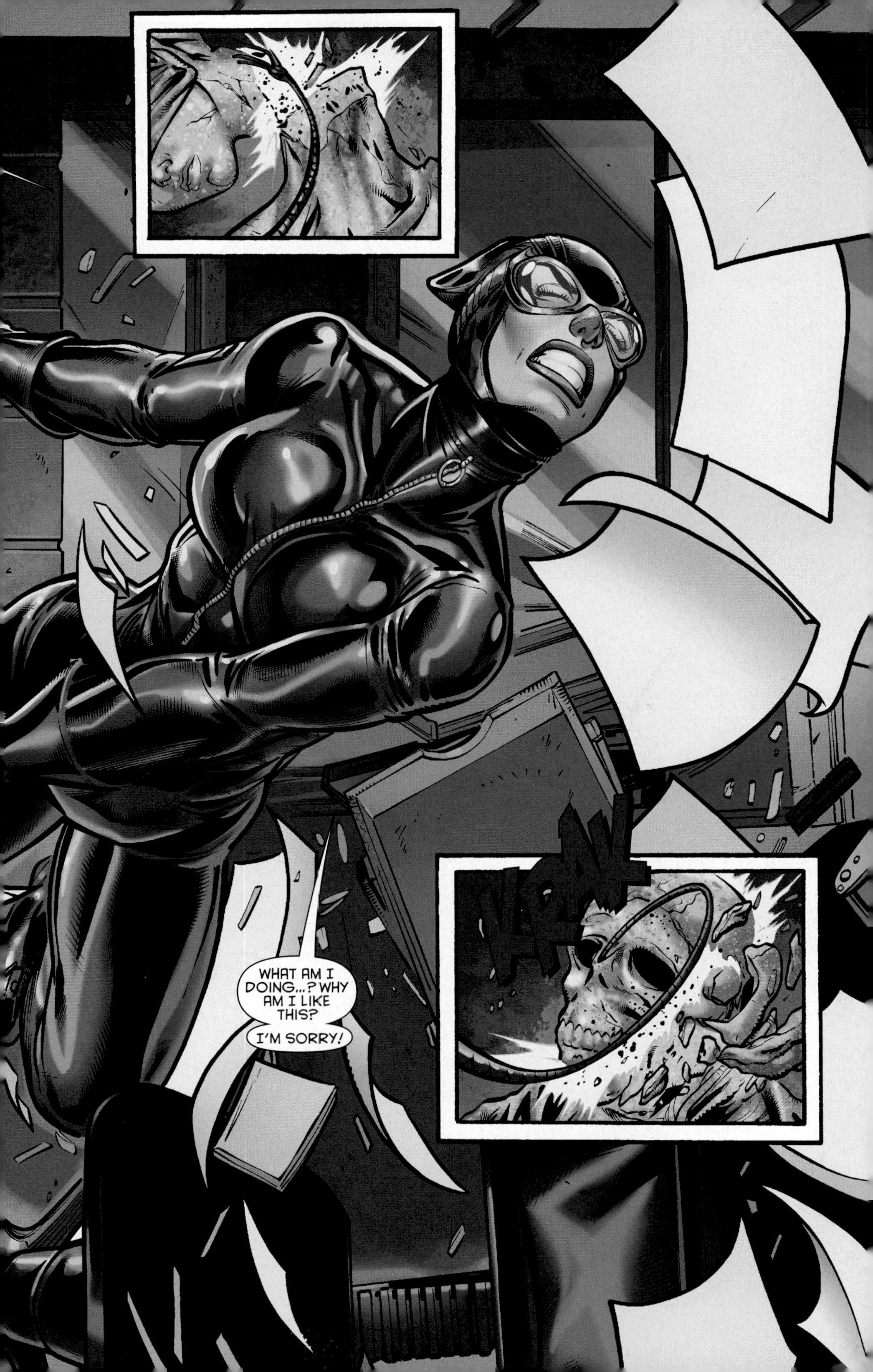
WHAT AM I DOING...? WHY AM I LIKE THIS?
I'M SORRY!

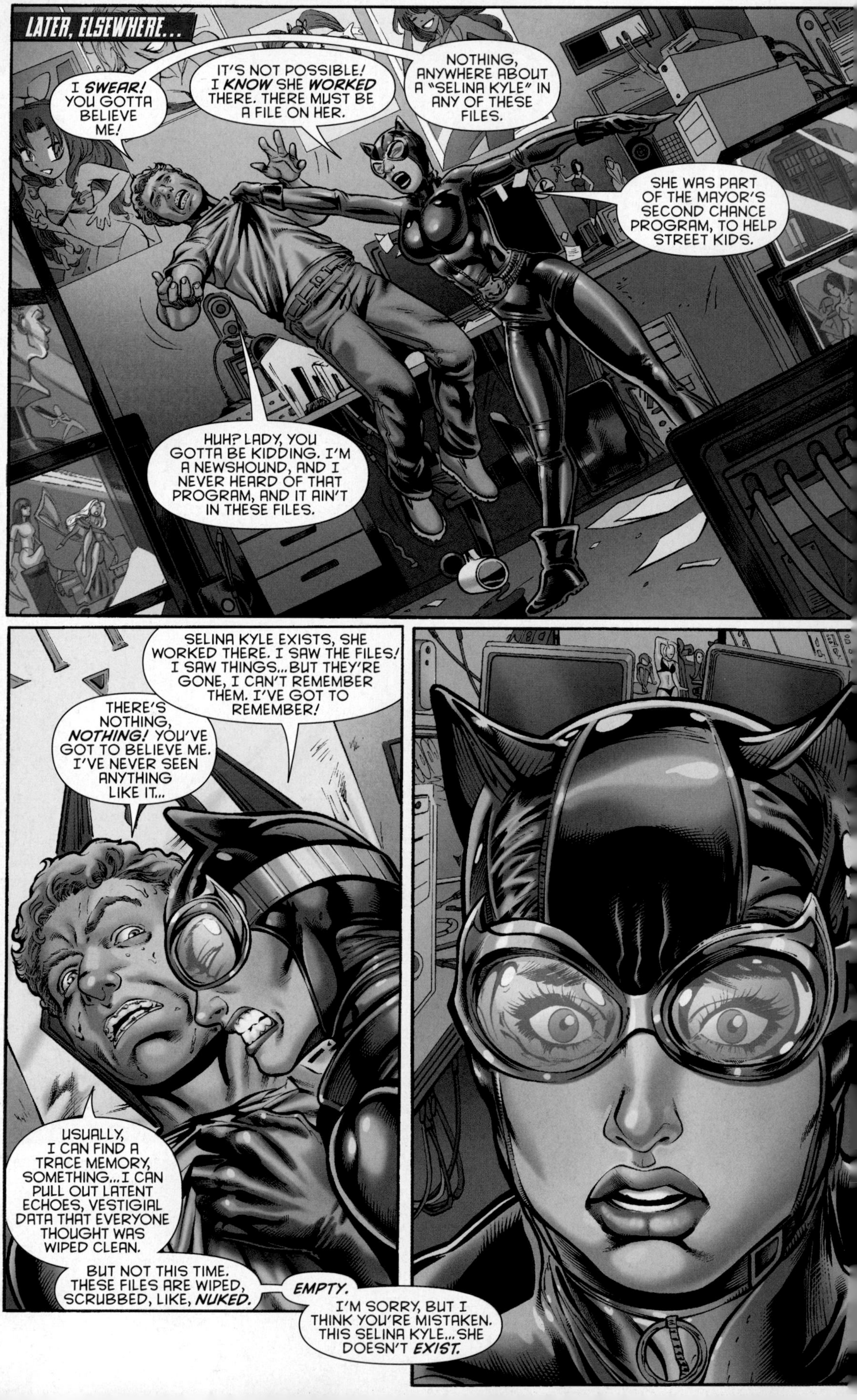
LATER, ELSEWHERE...
NOTHING, ANYWHERE ABOUT A "SELINA KYLE" IN ANY OF THESE FILES.
IT'S NOT POSSIBLE! I KNOW SHE WORKED THERE. THERE MUST BE A FILE ON HER.
I SWEAR! YOU GOTTA BELIEVE ME!
SHE WAS PART OF THE MAYOR'S SECOND CHANCE PROGRAM, TO HELP STREET KIDS.
HUH? LADY, YOU GOTTA BE KIDDING. I'M A NEWSHOUND, AND I NEVER HEARD OF THAT PROGRAM, AND IT AIN'T IN THESE FILES.
SELINA KYLE EXISTS, SHE WORKED THERE. I SAW THE FILES! I SAW THINGS...BUT THEY'RE GONE, I CAN'T REMEMBER THEM. I'VE GOT TO REMEMBER!
THERE'S NOTHING, NOTHING! YOU'VE GOT TO BELIEVE ME. I'VE NEVER SEEN ANYTHING LIKE IT...
USUALLY, I CAN FIND A TRACE MEMORY, SOMETHING...I CAN PULL OUT LATENT ECHOES, VESTIGIAL DATA THAT EVERYONE THOUGHT WAS WIPED CLEAN.
BUT NOT THIS TIME. THESE FILES ARE WIPED, SCRUBBED, LIKE, NUKED.
EMPTY.
I'M SORRY, BUT I THINK YOU'RE MISTAKEN. THIS SELINA KYLE...SHE DOESN'T EXIST.

CATWOMAN #13
Variant cover by ANDY CLARKE

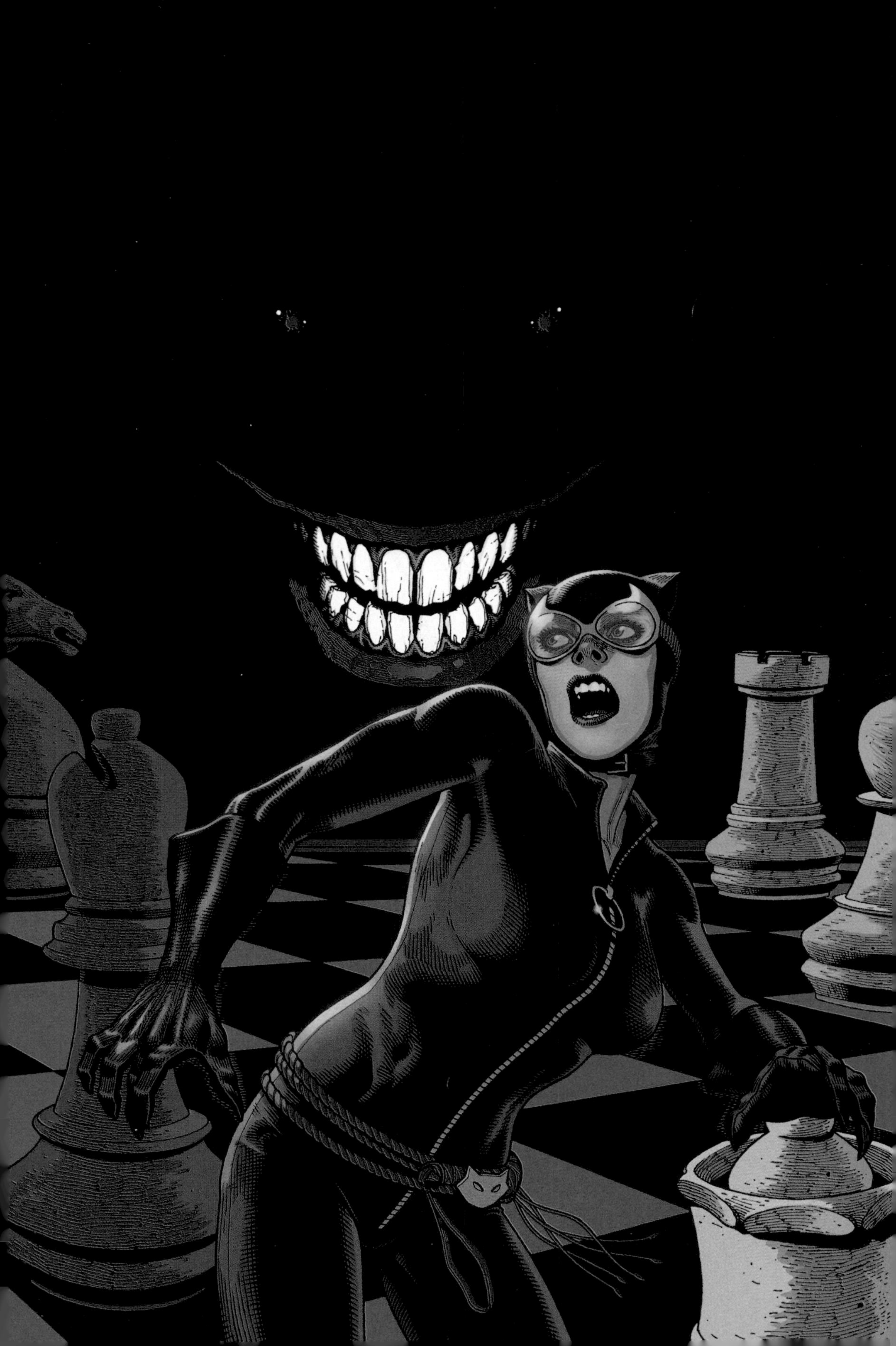

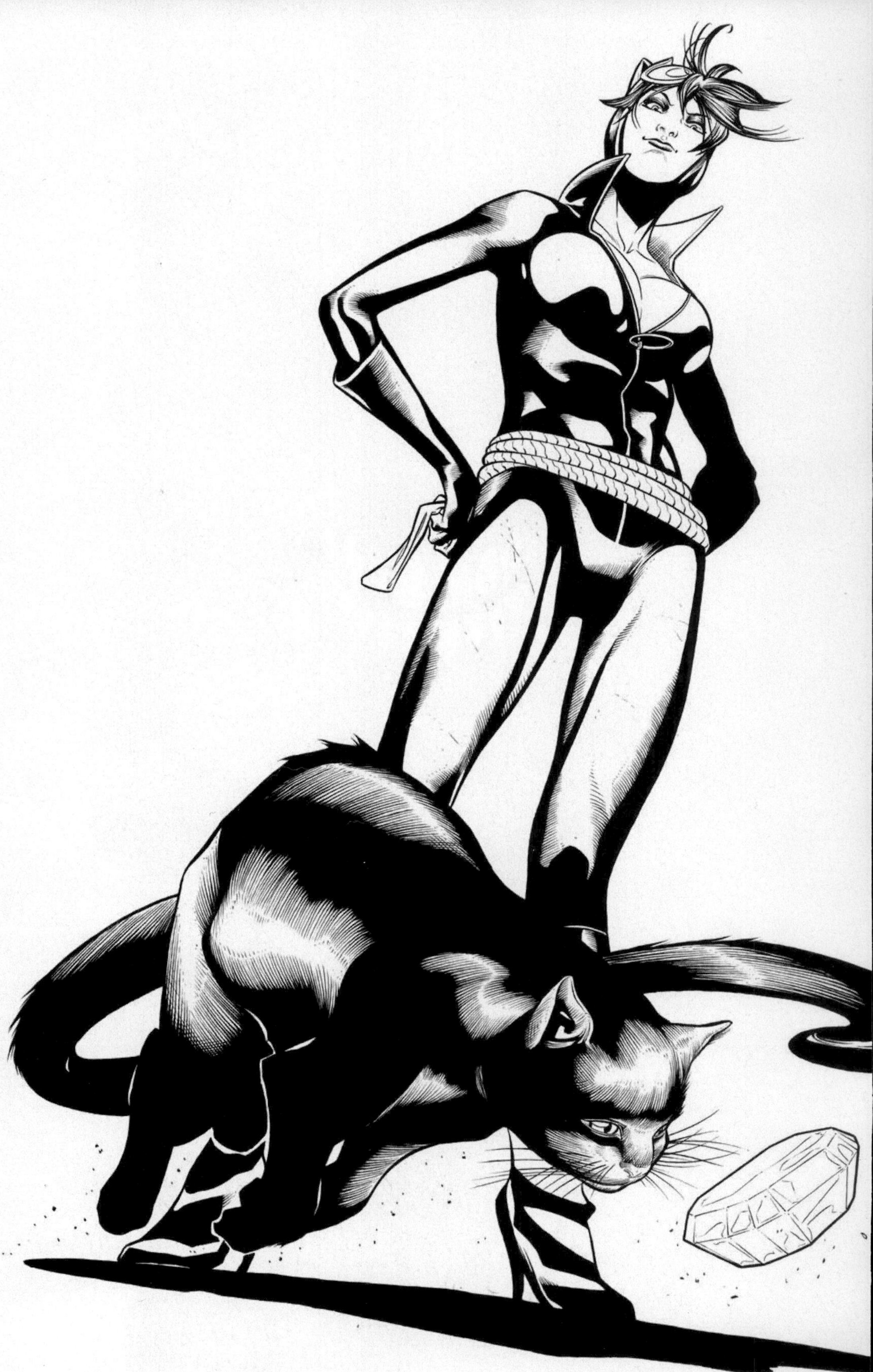

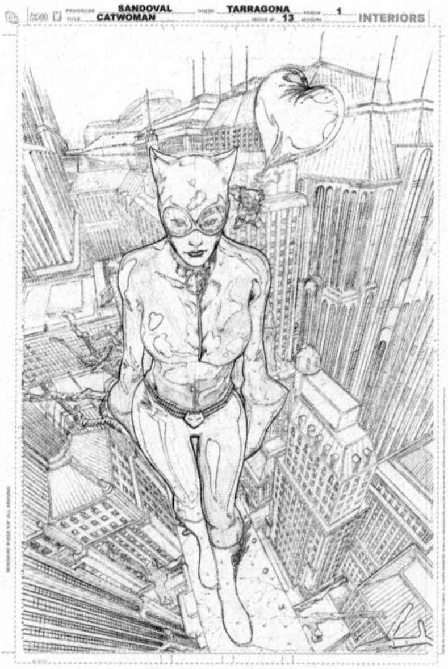
SANDOVAL
TARRAGONA
1
CATWOMAN
13
INTERIORS

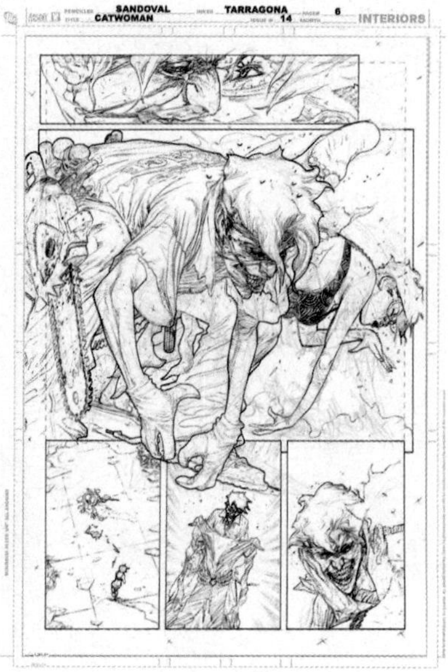
SANDOVAL
TARRAGONA
6
CATWOMAN
14
INTERIORS

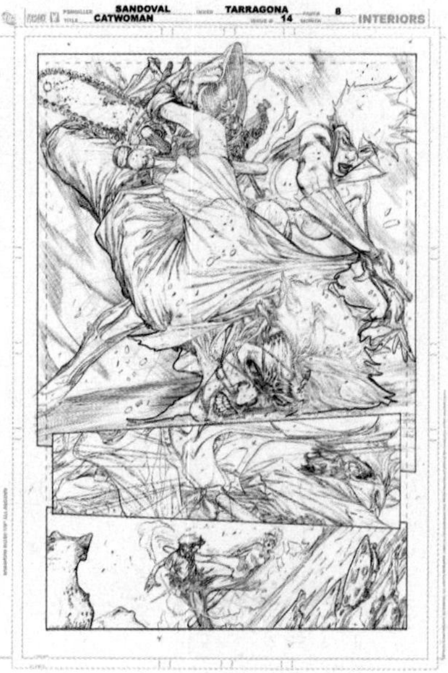
SANDOVAL
TARRAGONA
8
CATWOMAN
14
INTERIORS

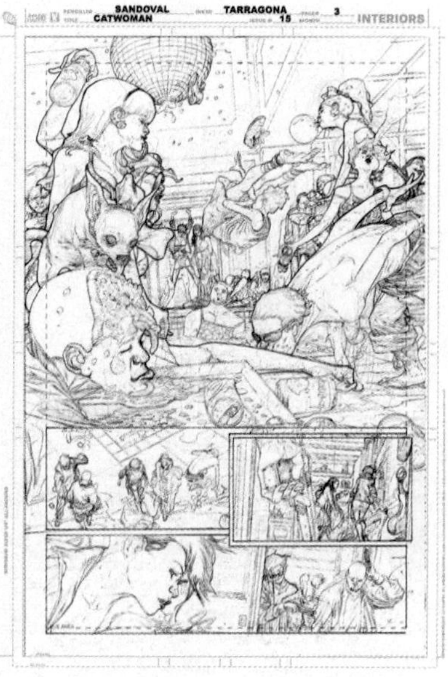
SANDOVAL
TARRAGONA
3
CATWOMAN
15
INTERIORS

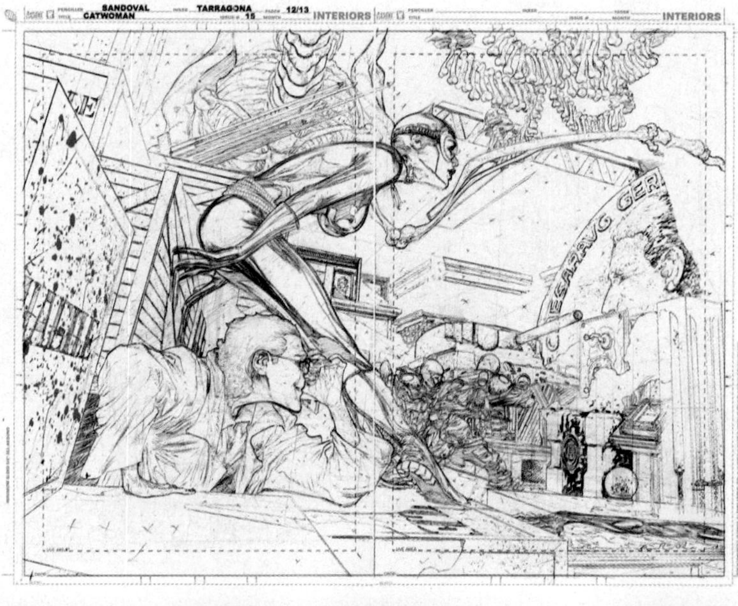
SANDOVAL
TARRAGONA
12/13
CATWOMAN
15
INTERIORS
INTERIORS

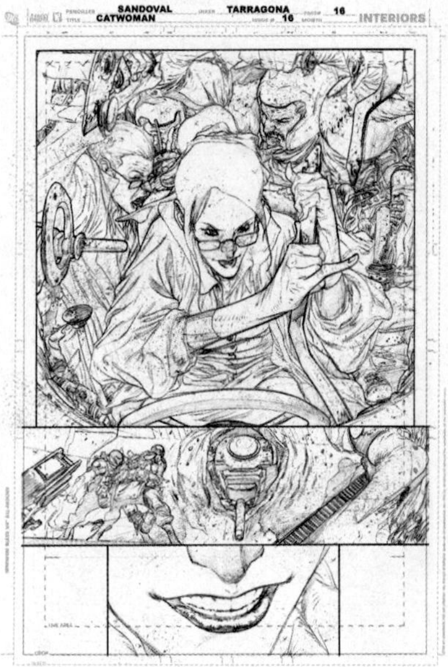
SANDOVAL
TARRAGONA
16
CATWOMAN
16
INTERIORS

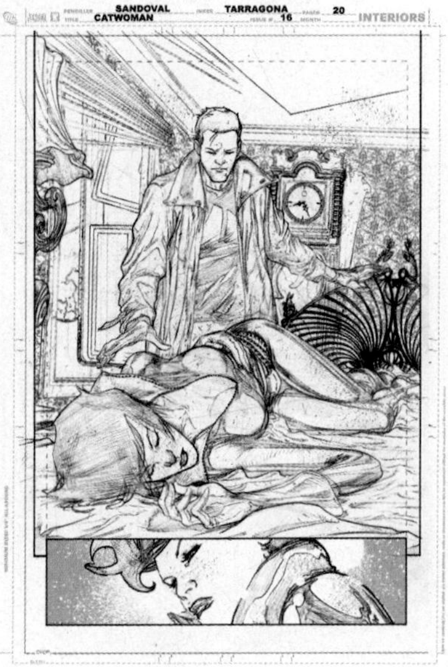
SANDOVAL
TARRAGONA
20
CATWOMAN
16
INTERIORS

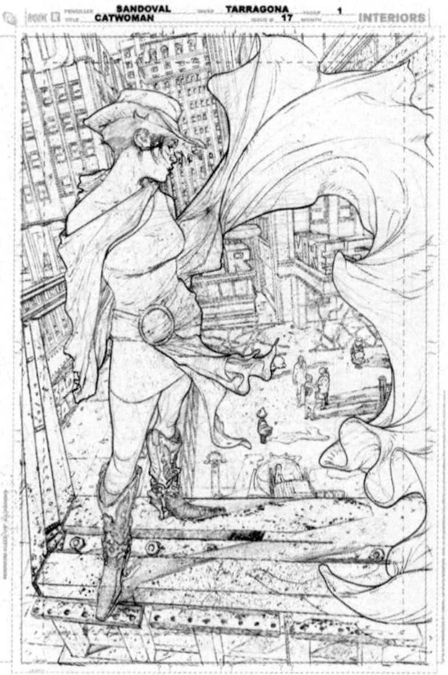
SANDOVAL
TARRAGONA
1
CATWOMAN
17
INTERIORS

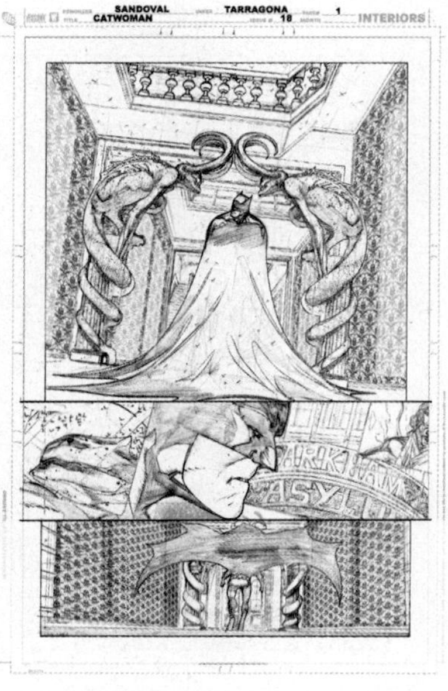
SANDOVAL
TARRAGONA
1
CATWOMAN
18
INTERIORS

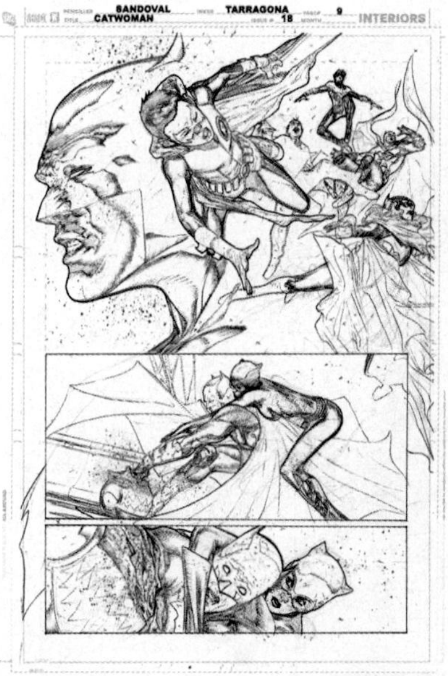
SANDOVAL
TARRAGONA
9
CATWOMAN
18
INTERIORS

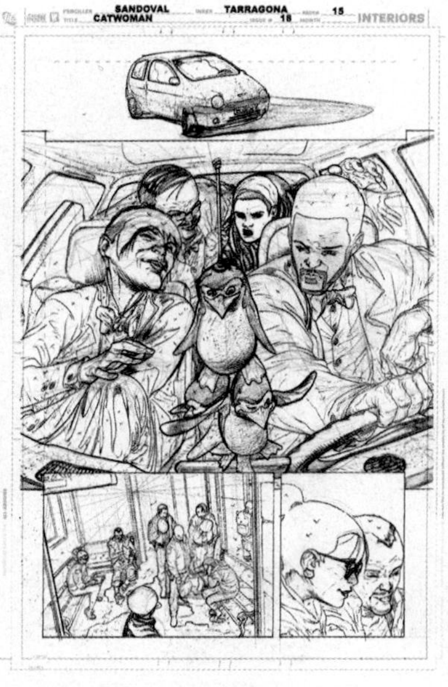
SANDOVAL
TARRAGONA
15
CATWOMAN
18
INTERIORS

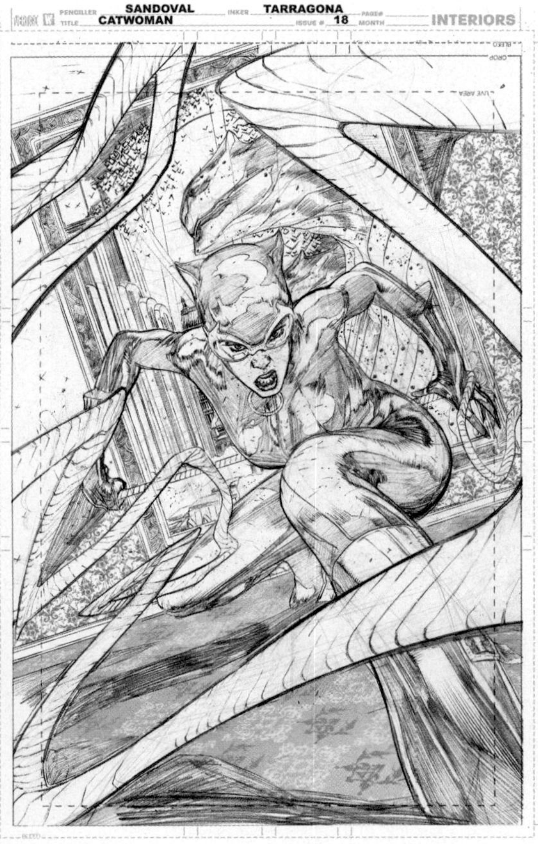
PENCILLER SANDOVAL INKER TARRAGONA PAGE#
TITLE CATWOMAN ISSUE # 18 MONTH
INTERIORS

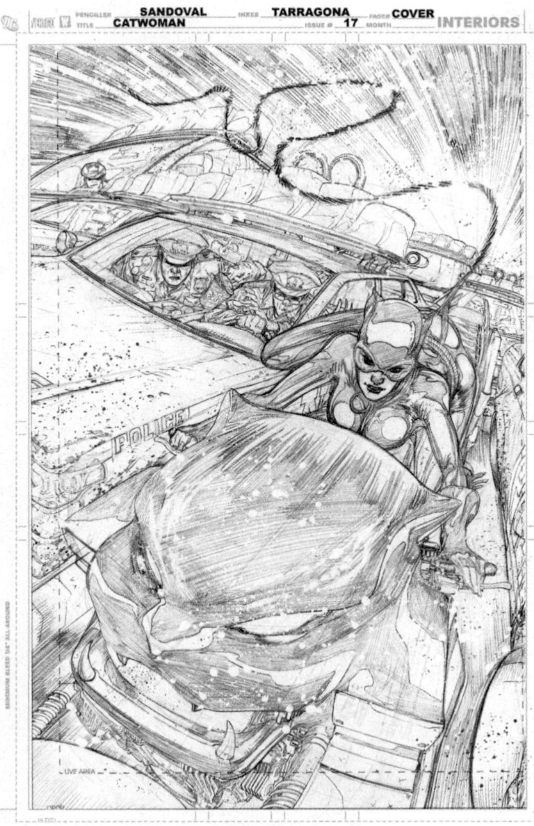
PENCILLER SANDOVAL INKER TARRAGONA PAGE# COVER
TITLE CATWOMAN ISSUE # 17 MONTH
INTERIORS
POLICE

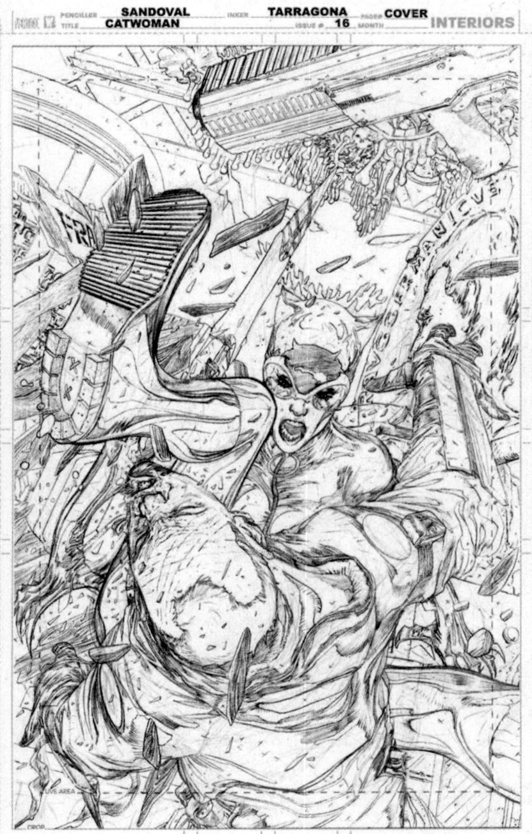
PENCILLER SANDOVAL INKER TARRAGONA PAGE# COVER
TITLE CATWOMAN ISSUE # 16 MONTH
INTERIORS

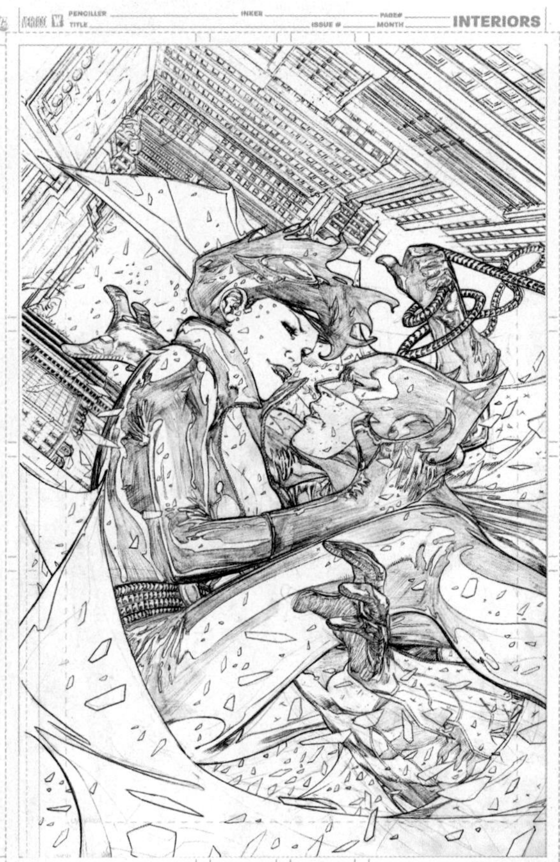
PENCILLER INKER PAGE#
TITLE ISSUE # MONTH
INTERIORS

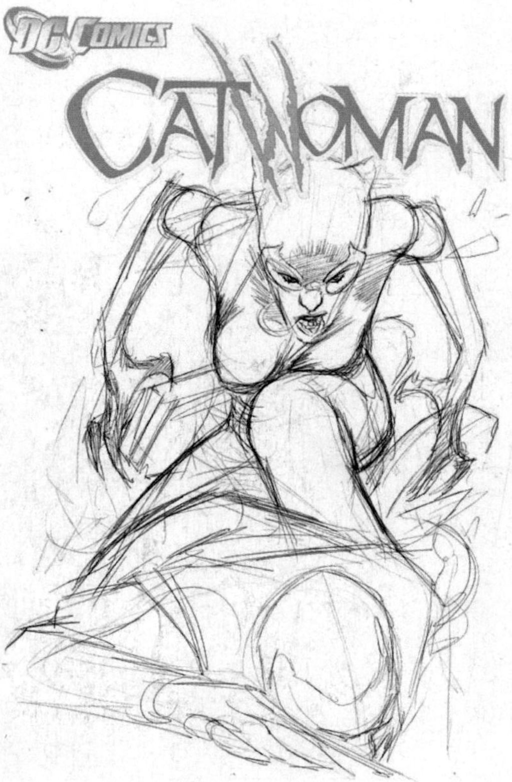
DC COMICS
CATWOMAN

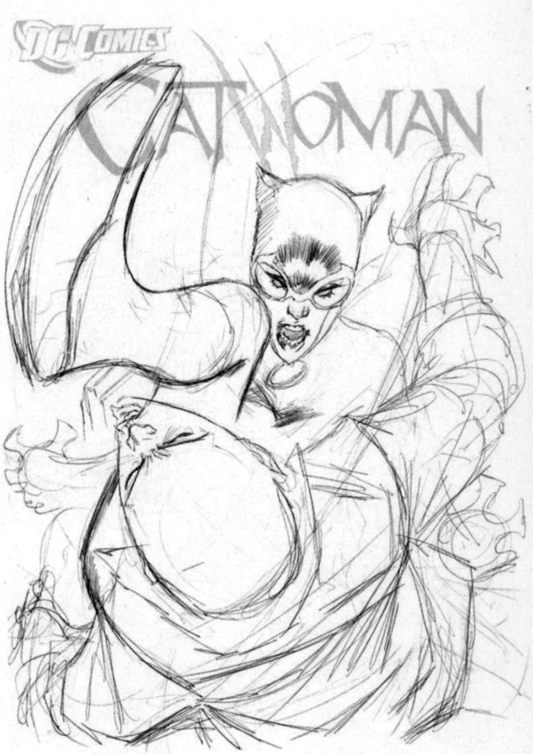
DC COMICS
CATWOMAN

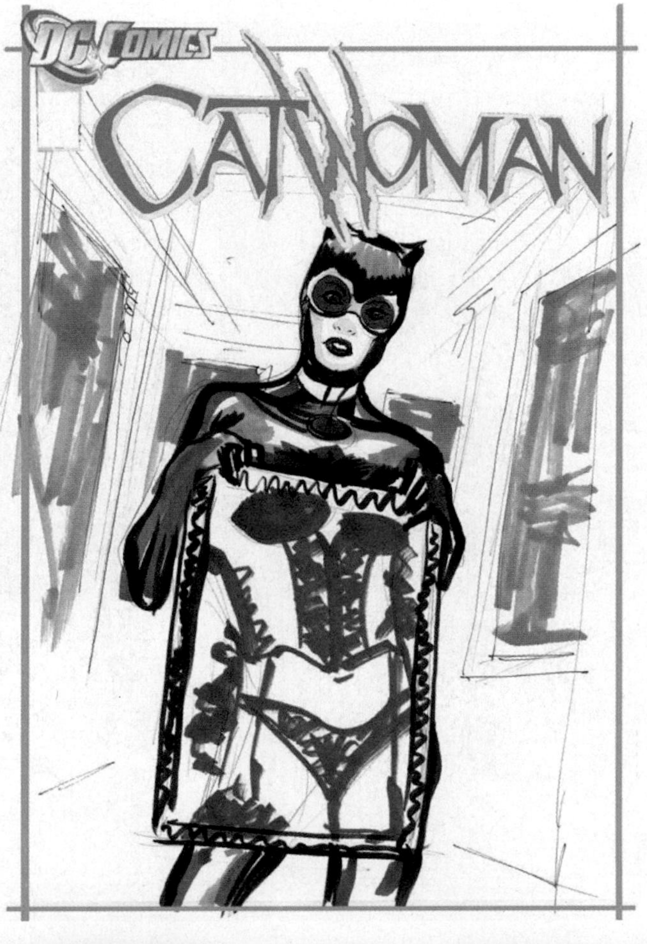
DC COMICS
CATWOMAN

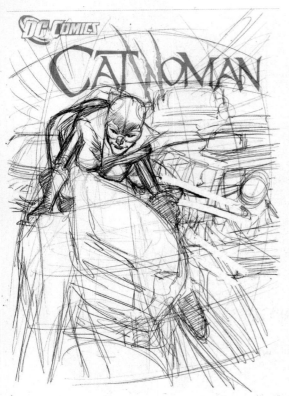

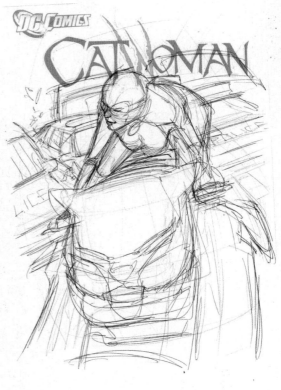

JOKER